Business objects

Recent Titles in the IBM McGraw-Hill Series

Open Systems and IBM Integration and Convergence	Pamela Gray
Risk Management for Software Projects	Alex Down Michael Coleman Peter Absolon
The New Organization Growing the Culture of Organizational Networking	Colin Hastings
Investing in Information Technology Managing the Decision-making Process	Geoff Hogbin David Thomas
Commonsense Computer Security 2nd Edition Your Practical Guide to Information Protection	Martin Smith
The Advanced Programmer's Guide to AIX 3.x	Phil Colledge
The CICS Programmer's Guide to FEPI	Robert Harris
Business Objects Delivering Cooperative Objects for Client-Server	Oliver Sims
Reshaping I.T. for Business Flexibility The I.T. Architecture as a Common Language for Dealing with Change	Mark Behrsin Geoff Mason Trevor Sharpe
Writing OS/2 REXX Programs	Ronny Richardson
Practical Queueing Analysis	Mike Tanner
MVS Capacity Planning for a Balanced System	Brian MacFarlane
Supercharging the AS/400 A Guide to Performance Management	Ron Fielder Carolyn Machell

Details of these titles in the series are available from:

The Product Manager, Professional Books
McGraw-Hill Book Company Europe
Shoppenhangers Road, Maidenhead, Berkshire SL6 2QL
Telephone: 01628 23432 Fax: 01628 770224

Oliver Sims

Business objects
Delivering cooperative objects for client-server

McGRAW-HILL BOOK COMPANY

London · New York · St Louis · San Francisco · Auckland
Bogotá · Caracas · Lisbon · Madrid · Mexico · Milan
Montreal · New Delhi · Panama · Paris · San Juan · São Paulo
Singapore · Sydney · Tokyo · Toronto

Published by
McGRAW-HILL Book Company Europe
Shoppenhangers Road, Maidenhead, Berkshire SL6 2QL, England
Telephone 01628 23432
Fax 01628 770224

British Library Cataloguing in Publication Data

Sims, Oliver
  Business Objects: Delivering Cooperative
  Objects for Client-Server.—(IBM
  McGraw-Hill Series)
  I. Title II. Series
  004.65

  ISBN 0-07-707957-4

Library of Congress Cataloging-in-Publication Data

Sims, Oliver.
    Business objects: delivering cooperative objects for client
  -server / Oliver Sims.
      p. cm.—(IBM McGraw-Hill series)
    Includes bibliographical references and index.
    ISBN 0-07-707957-4
    1. Client/server computing. I. Title. II. Series.
  QA76.9. C55S55 1994
  005.2—dc20   94-7289
                                                                            CIP

Copyright © 1994 McGraw-Hill International (UK) Limited. All rights reserved. No part of
this publication may be reproduced, stored in a retrieval system, or transmitted, in any form
or by any means, electronic, mechanical, photocopying, recording, or otherwise, without the
prior permission of McGraw-Hill International (UK) Limited, with the exception of material
entered and executed on a computer system for the reader's own use.

.3 4 CUP 9 7 6 5

Typeset by Paston Press Ltd, Loddon, Norfolk
and printed and bound in Great Britain at the University Press, Cambridge

Printed on permanent paper in compliance with ISO Standard 9706

Contents

IBM Series Foreword		ix
Preface		xi
Trademarks		xvi
Introduction: Management summary		xvii

Part One The user—exploiting the PC — 1

1 Usability—the new system bottleneck — 3
- 1.1 The usability challenge — 3
- 1.2 A vital business need — 4
- 1.3 The application problem — 5
- 1.4 Usability — 7
- 1.5 New user interfaces — 9

2 Making computers familiar: object-based user interfaces — 11
- 2.1 The character-based terminal approach — 11
- 2.2 A PC-based approach — 12
- 2.3 Presenting objects on the screen — 15
- 2.4 The 'workbench problem' — 21
- 2.5 The object-based user interface — 24

3 Cooperative business objects — 27
- 3.1 The 'integration' problem — 27
- 3.2 Objects and messages — 31
- 3.3 A restatement — 34
- 3.4 Summary — 38

Part Two The programmer—application structures — 41

4 Structural overview — 45
- 4.1 Base requirements — 45
- 4.2 Application code structure — 50
- 4.3 The user vs the data — 69
- 4.4 Summary — 72

5 The user interface domain — 74
- 5.1 User logic — 76
- 5.2 'Models' and 'views' — 78
- 5.3 The view 'layout' — 83
- 5.4 Connecting to the server — 85
- 5.5 Summary — 88

6 The shared resource domain — 89
- 6.1 The nature of the SRD — 90
- 6.2 SRD design points — 93
- 6.3 Overview of SRD structure — 94
- 6.4 SRD components — 96
- 6.5 SRD CBOs — 99
- 6.6 Summary — 108

7 End-to-end summary — 110
- 7.1 Domain interaction — 110
- 7.2 Components of the end-to-end model — 110
- 7.3 Component behaviour — 111
- 7.4 Model subsets — 112

8 The CBO infrastructure — 114
- 8.1 Why an infrastructure? — 114
- 8.2 Common components — 117
- 8.3 CBO aspects — 123
- 8.4 Binding — 138
- 8.5 Code page and data conversion — 144
- 8.6 'Alien' objects — 147
- 8.7 Operating system implications — 147

Part Three Design issues — 151

9 Data placement — 155
- 9.1 Scope of data — 155
- 9.2 Kinds of data — 157
- 9.3 Local data and availability — 161

10 Data integrity — 166
- 10.1 Data on the PC — 167
- 10.2 Units of work — 168
- 10.3 To lock or not to lock — 173
- 10.4 Commit scope start and end — 176
- 10.5 Update control (multiple SRDs) — 177

11 The 'megadata' problem — 180
- 11.1 The problem — 180
- 11.2 Approaches to solutions — 183

12	**Business processes**	**189**
	12.1 Objects and business rules	189
	12.2 Processes and units of work	193
	12.3 Workflow management	195
	12.4 Aspects of objects	197
	12.5 Location of business logic	200
13	**Common design concerns**	**202**
	13.1 Introduction	202
	13.2 UID vs SRD	202
	13.3 Design in the SRD	203
	13.4 Design in the UID	206
	13.5 Methodologies and techniques	216
Part Four	**Management implications**	**221**
14	**Technical implications**	**223**
	14.1 Client/server infrastructure	223
	14.2 Network considerations	224
	14.3 Systems management	228
15	**People implications**	**233**
	15.1 Myths, dreams and panaceas	233
	15.2 The 'end-to-end view'	236
	15.3 Object orientation skills	238
	15.4 Impact on organizational structure	239
16	**Getting started**	**241**
	16.1 The 'kick-off' process	241
	16.2 The project	243
	16.3 The client/server spectrum	245
Part Five	**The future of CBOs**	**251**
17	**CBOs today**	**253**
	17.1 Customization	253
	17.2 Portability	253
	17.3 IT advantages	254
18	**CBOs tomorrow**	**256**
	18.1 IT as the facilitator of change	256
	18.2 User-written function	256
	18.3 'Out-of-the-box' integration	258
	18.4 A market in objects	259
	18.5 Looking forward	260
Appendix 1	**Object orientation**	**261**
	A1.1 Introduction	261

A1.2	What is an object?	262
A1.3	Classes	266
A1.4	Polymorphism	268
A1.5	Inheritance	270
A1.6	An example	272
A1.7	Objects, and data on disk	273
A1.8	Summary	275

Appendix 2 A technical description of CBOs — 277
    A2.1 Introduction — 277
    A2.2 The definition of 'CBO' — 278

Appendix 3 Messaging—'send' vs 'send/post' — 293
    A3.1 Single API — 294
    A3.2 Two APIs — 295

Appendix 4 Model vs local model — 297
    A4.1 A single model object? — 297
    A4.2 The need for a local model — 302
    A4.3 Conclusion — 302
    A4.4 Advantages — 303

Appendix 5 A UID prototyping technique — 304
    A5.1 Some initial considerations — 304
    A5.2 Overview — 306
    A5.3 The design process — 307

Appendix 6 Sample project proposals — 318
    A6.1 The 'pathfinder' project — 318
    A6.2 The 'vision prototype' project — 327

References and bibliography — 331
Glossary — 333
Index — 343

Foreword

The IBM McGraw-Hill Series

IBM UK and McGraw-Hill Europe have worked together to publish this series of books about information technology and its use in business, industry and the public sector.

The series provides an up-to-date and authoritative insight into the wide range of products and services available, and offers strategic business advice. Some of the books have a technical bias, others are written from a broader business perspective. What they have in common is that their authors—some from IBM, some independent consultants—are experts in their field.

Apart from assisting where possible with the accuracy of the writing, IBM UK has not sought to inhibit the editorial freedom of the series, and therefore the views expressed in the books are those of the authors, and not necessarily those of IBM.

Where IBM has lent its expertise is in assisting McGraw-Hill to identify potential titles whose publication would help advance knowledge and increase awareness of computing topics. Hopefully these titles will also serve to widen the debate about the important information technology issues of today and of the future—such as open systems, networking and the use of technology to give companies a competitive edge in their market.

IBM UK is pleased to be associated with McGraw-Hill in this series.

Sir Anthony Cleaver
Chairman
IBM United Kingdom Limited

Preface

Client/server systems promise major benefits for businesses, organizations and people. Promises include exceptional ease of use, application integration and taking IT off the critical path of business change. The question is, how do we realize these benefits?

This book describes an approach to developing application systems that can play a significant part in turning these promises into reality. It is a book about realizing the dramatic advantages to be gained from the application of object orientation to client/server systems. It describes a new approach to structuring application software. By applying object orientation to the *end-product* of the application development process (rather than to components used *within* the process), we provide both ease of programming for distributed systems and a foundation for application integration and rapid development.

Based on experience with industrial-strength systems, this book describes how delivering business-sized objects *instead of* applications best addresses the application design and coding problems otherwise found in distributed and client/server systems. Such business-sized objects are independently developed using either procedural or object-oriented programming languages. They cooperate with each other in providing business function, and hence we call them 'cooperative business objects', or CBOs. The term 'CBO' is used to distinguish between a business-sized object as an *end-product*, and an object used by a developer as a *component* of an object-oriented application. Such an application is not itself an object. A CBO is.

Just as transaction programs rather than batch suites were the best 'shape' for the on-line systems of the seventies, so CBOs are the best shape for the distributed systems of the nineties. Providing this new shape of deliverable is, arguably, the real business of objects.

The book is also about ease of programming. CBOs make client/server systems with advanced object-based graphical user interfaces easy for the average application programmer, and, indeed, for the casual programmer.

This book is written for IT managers, AD managers and technical professionals interested in implementing effective client/server systems. Although the concepts developed are widely applicable, the context for the book is medium-to-large IS systems, typically using at least one mainframe or mini computer (or large PC server), running core business systems. In particular, it is assumed that the term 'client/server systems' means systems where powerful desk-top PCs are connected to one or more larger systems, which manage a company's shared computer-based resources (typically data).

This is not a book about application design methods; nor does it address in any detail the various aspects of connectivity (line protocols, connection APIs, etc.). It is not a book about systems management, or the selection of hardware and operating system components; neither does it review existing client/server software, or OOPLs. It *is* a book that addresses these three questions:

- What does it mean to 'exploit fully' the client/server system structure—from the point of view of the users of such a system?
- What 'shape' of application-level code should we be aiming at, and what design approaches should we be adopting if we are to meet our ease-of-programming objectives?
- What additional system-level code (or 'middleware'[1]) is required to enable application programmers easily to produce code that meets user requirements of these new systems?

Lack of good answers to these three questions has been a prime cause of the difficulties faced over the past several years in exploiting fully the new system structures available to us.

This book describes the development of thinking, and the conclusions reached to date, in addressing all of these problems as a whole. From several directions, the concept of the CBO has evolved as a solution. This concept has been proved through the development of production-strength software. The detail of this software is not within the scope of this book; the concepts which that software implements are.

'Business objects' as a topic of interest in the industry is growing. Recently, the Object Management Group started a special interest group in business objects. Just as this book was completed, I received a draft of Rob Prins' book, *You Can Bank on Objects* (as yet unpublished). This presented a particularly exciting application of the business object concept for very large-scale distributed systems (and for smaller scale systems!). Rob works for IBM in the Netherlands, and is seconded as principal technical consultant to a wholly-owned IBM Netherlands subsidiary, Cyclade Consultants, in Utrecht.

---

[1] Middleware is run-time code that is not provided by the base operating system, but which should not be in the realm of the application programmer. Early examples of middleware would have included transaction processing systems, and database management systems. Current examples include distributed print capabilities, some of the remote procedure call implementations, some client/server platforms and cryptography systems. Middleware generally provides an API of some sort to the application programmer.

History

At the end of 1986, I took on the technical support role for IBM's Systems Application Architecture (SAA) (announced on 17 March 1987) within IBM United Kingdom. Towards the end of the following year, IBM introduced the concept of 'cooperative processing' into SAA.

In essence, this concept pointed towards a vision of systems that blended the best of the PC with the best of the mainframe. The PC brought user interface capabilities that far surpassed the non-programmable video display terminals typically attached to mainframes; the mainframe brought shared resource management capabilities (large shared databases, for example) that could not be matched on the PC.

Early in 1988, a small group of colleagues and I started to build a demonstration application that would illustrate the benefits of cooperative processing. Using a pre-release version of the IBM OS/2 operating system, we set to work. However, it soon became apparent that most of what we knew about structuring applications (learned through experience with batch, interactive and transaction processing applications) had to be thrown away.

We started saying to each other, 'Hey, this is a new world . . .'. And although some of what we had learned with early IBM distributed systems (e.g. the IBM 3790 and 8100 systems) remained applicable, to a large extent we found ourselves in an unexplored and uncharted land. Early in 1989, I wrote an internal IBM discussion paper entitled 'The New World'. As a result of this and other related papers, the phrase 'new world' came to have some small currency among IBM people in the UK and in a few other countries.

One thing about this new world that became very apparent is that we could not treat the PC merely as a kind of souped-up terminal. The PC is a complex and powerful computer system in its own right. What we have is not a simple hierarchical network with intelligence in the centre controlling a large number of simple devices; we have a peer-to-peer network of large numbers of powerful computers.

For the last five years (among other things), I have worked towards understanding how best to exploit this new system structure, focusing on the following goals:

- Ease of application programming (for both the professional and the casual programmer)
- Full exploitation of the PC graphical user interface
- Cooperative application code (cross-system)
- Application integration

Today, we can say that we have had a considerable measure of success in achieving these goals. At the time of writing, achieving *all* of the goals is within sight. There is a great sense that, although the new technology of CBOs is in its early form, it is fundamentally moving in the right direction.

This book is a summary of the concepts proved and lessons learned in addressing these goals through a series of industrial-strength software developments. Throughout, a central theme has been to build an understanding of the appropriate 'shape' of application software (CBOs), and to construct a software infrastructure that enables that shape. The infrastructure developed has been used successfully by a smaller number of UK companies in some major projects.

In August 1993, IBM and Softwright (a UK-based software house) launched a joint venture company called *Integrated Object Systems Limited*. In May 1994, Integrated Objects announced and shipped a product called *Newi* (New World Infrastructure). Newi is a CBO-enabling software infrastructure which implements, among other things, the concepts described in this book.

Acknowledgements

Writing this book has been largely a spare-time effort. I could not have done it without the unfailing support of my wife, Heather, who gave me the encouragement I needed to develop some of the initial concepts, and to pursue their development.

Concepts, however, are only proven through excellent software design and industrial-strength code. Here I owe a great debt to Martin Anderson, Chairman of Softwright Systems Limited (and now Managing Director of Integrated Objects), and Alan Boother, chief software designer at Softwright. Both Martin and Alan shared in the vision. Martin caused it to be realized; Alan, through his technical expertise, transformed it into reality.

Late in 1991, Charles Brett of Spectrum Reports encouraged me to put some of the concepts into writing. His support, and editorial assistance, helped me hone my ideas to a considerable extent. Several sections in this book include extracts from articles written for the February 1992, May 1992 and August 1992 edition of *SAA and Open Software Spectrum*, and for the November 1992 edition of *Open Transaction Management Reports*. These extracts are reproduced by kind permission of the publisher.

In May 1992, IBM in Sweden announced a product called 'Object-Oriented Infrastructure/2'. This was developed by Softwright under a contract for which I was the technical architect. This development helped immeasurably in moving the concepts of CBOs and the required CBO infrastructure forward. It could not have been done without the enthusiastic support and dedication of Johan Emilsson, Lars Magnusson and Thomas Jonsson, all of IBM Sweden.

I must also thank Martin Anderson (Integrated Objects), Rob Prins, David Hutton-Squire, Dave Schofield, Ray Warburton and Chris Winter (IBM), who read drafts of the book, and whose comments and feedback were always relevant and helpful. In particular, I would like to thank Hugh Varilly of IBM, whose detailed reading and checking of the final draft was especially beneficial—in both technical and non-technical areas.

Section 1.4 derives largely from an internal IBM paper written by Ray Warburton, and secs 9.2 and 10.3 benefited greatly from discussions with Dave Schofield and from an internal IBM paper written by him. Any errors or omissions, however, I claim as my own.

Finally, I am grateful to the many professional colleagues in IBM, both in the UK and in other countries, who have provided encouragement, constructive comments and support. My thanks to them all.

Structure of the book

The Introduction gives an overview of the major arguments presented in the book.

Part One discusses how the *user* should perceive the system: how to get the best for the business out of these expensive GUIs. Exploiting the GUI leads to object-based user interfaces, and from there to the concept of cooperative business objects as the thing the programmer should build.

In Part Two we examine what the *programmer* should see in dealing with distributed systems. Here we define the general 'shape' of the application code that we would *like* application programmers to write. We discover that cooperative business objects are the right shape for distributed application code as well as for object-based GUIs. Given this shape, we then discuss the kind of enabling 'middleware'—or infrastructure—needed to implement it.

However, no matter how easy we make it to *build* application code, there is always the question of how you *design* application systems for the distributed processing and data inherent in client/server systems. Part Three presents some solutions to the design issues and concerns commonly met by, it seems, everyone who is starting out with client/server.

All of this has implications for IS management, and in Part Four we look briefly at two areas—technical implications and people implications. How to handle these, and how to make a start, are different questions, of course, and at the end of this part we discuss getting started.

In Part Five we peer into the future a little, to outline some of the areas that initial experience suggests the new technology of CBOs may take us.

Finally, there are a number of appendices that delve into greater technical detail about some of the areas covered in the body of the book. These are:

- A high-level introduction to object orientation (Appendix 1)
- A technical description of 'cooperative business objects' (Appendix 2)
- A short discussion on approaches to handling both synchronous and asynchronous messages (Appendix 3)
- A rationale for having a 'model' object held locally in the PC as well as in the server (Appendix 4)
- A process I have found useful for rapid development of GUI prototypes (Appendix 5)
- Two sample project proposals for getting started (Appendix 6)

Trademarks

C++ is a trademark of AT&T.

CICS is a trademark of IBM Corporation.

CUA is a trademark of IBM Corporation.

ENFIN/3 is a trademark of Easel Corporation.

Motif is a trademark of Open Software Foundation Inc.

OS/2 is a trademark of IBM Corporation.

REXX is a trademark of IBM Corporation.

SAA is a trademark of IBM Corporation.

Smalltalk/V PM is a trademark of Digitalk Inc.

Windows is a trademark of Microsoft Corporation Inc.

Some of the artwork in this book is from Lotus Freelance Graphics for Windows, © 1993 Lotus Development Corporation. Lotus and Freelance Graphics are registered trademarks of Lotus Development Corporation.

Introduction: Management summary

This book is about a new development in application structuring. It describes a new kind of deliverable from the application development process—the 'cooperative business object' or CBO. (A brief introduction to object orientation is provided in Appendix 1.)

It seems that, whenever we in information technology (IT) get comfortable with a technology, and consider it mastered in terms of operation, management, methodologies, software and hardware, then along comes a whole parcel of new things to be handled. The kind of new things that are most difficult are not those which are bigger, or smaller, or faster; but those which are *different*. Distributed and client/server systems are different, and have proved difficult. CBOs, however, bring ease of programming to the new environment. A major theme that we develop in this book is that CBOs, rather than more traditional structures, best fit the application programming needs of the nineties.

But what is driving this change? Well, IT change is often driven by changes in business needs, and the move to client/server is no different.

New business needs

Perhaps the most significant of current business needs is the imperative many companies face to enable *people* to become more *effective*.

This need is expressed in many forms, and comes not only from competitive pressures (e.g. a need to provide much better customer service) but also from cost pressures that force a reduction in depth of organizational hierarchies. This can lead to a significant enhancement of people's jobs—to empowerment. But empowerment means people addressing more aspects of the business, or addressing the same aspects in greater depth, or both.

Being more effective also means being more flexible as businesses increase the rate at which they change. People need to handle new organizations, new products, new policies, new processes, new customers, new suppliers and new business environments. At the same time, there is a need to reduce training times for new staff.

All of this means that people need much better computer support. In particular, they need to be able to handle many more application areas than hitherto.

Very often, businesses turn to their IT organizations for the support people need to deliver the greater effectiveness being sought. One of the main IT responses to these demands is to find new ways for users to *exploit* the investment in data and function present in their computer systems.

Specifically, the search is for approaches that will provide greater ease of use, reduced training times, application integration for the user, and the ability to react to new requirements fast—ideally faster than other areas of the organization, so that IT can become a facilitator of change. Client/server systems are seen by many to be part of the solution.

New challenges for application development

The whole point of building client/server systems is to combine the usability of graphical user interfaces (GUIs) with the strengths of traditional IT systems—access to and management of shared resources such as data. The promise of such systems is great, boasting exceptional ease of use, application integration and taking IT off the critical path of business change. However, if we are really to benefit from these new systems, we must understand not only how best to exploit the GUI, but also how to do so in a distributed systems environment. One without the other is not particularly useful.

In addition, we need to effect such exploitation using the skills of the average application programmer; and eventually we must harness the capabilities of those many end-users who have programming aptitude and are willing and able to apply it. A vital requirement for this new environment is, therefore, ease of programming.

However, the acquisition of many more applications by itself is not enough. These new applications must integrate successfully with others. One of the main promises of the GUI is to allow users to have applications interact effectively with each other on the screen; but there is a problem. Even with a GUI, traditionally-designed applications do not deliver the desired levels of integration, no matter how many icons there might be. Object-based GUIs, together with new application programming constructs, offer a way ahead.

In the nineties, then, we can see four major challenges for application development:

- Enabling advanced object-based graphical user interfaces
- Building cooperatively processing application function across client/server and distributed systems
- Providing for application functions to be easily integrated with others
- Enabling ease of programming for all of the above

Perhaps the most important thing to appreciate is that we are facing a radical new technology curve that demands new ways of thinking, and new approaches to design. (A 'technology curve' is a (generally) S-shaped graph describing the life cycle of a given technology. See Glossary for further information.)

A new-technology curve

In the fifties and sixties, most systems were batch. We can say that such systems formed a specific technology curve as shown in Fig. I1.1. The seventies and eighties saw the evolution of a second technology curve, based on video display terminals such as the IBM 3270 family. This evolution generated a huge change in the way people used systems, in the way we built applications and in the structure of systems.

Such change does not come easily. Initially, we tend to treat the new technology curve as if it is an extension to what we already know. In the early seventies, I remember working with an IT department who were installing their first video terminals. These were intended to replace a number of card punches. Data would be entered directly into the system through terminals, so saving a lot of money on punch cards. The existing batch applications would be unchanged.

The first application placed card images on the screen. Later, a purpose-built data-entry system was introduced, which made the screen formats much friendlier; but the core business systems were still batch; there was no on-line access or update.

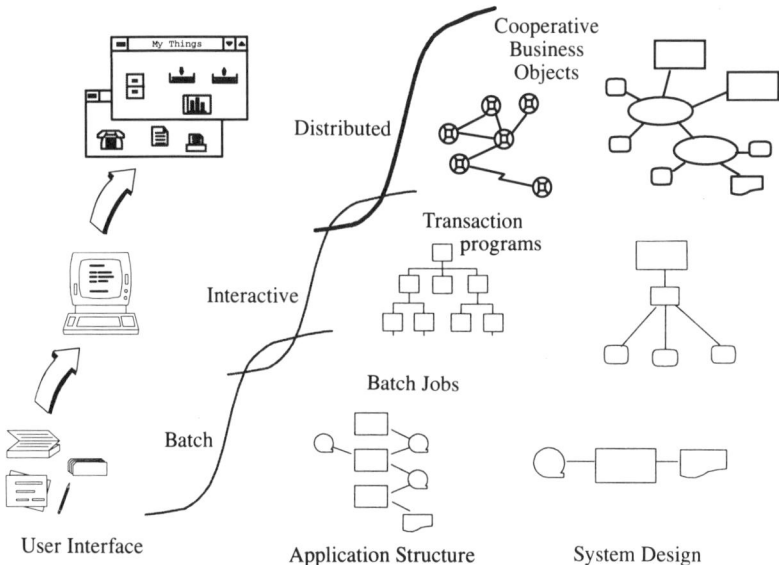

Figure I1.1. A new-technology curve.

Looking back, we can see that front-ending the existing batch systems with data-entry screens was not the best way to exploit the new technology (video terminals, teleprocessing and database). To a casual onlooker observing the screens, there would appear to be little difference between data entry and full on-line update with data integrity. However, the user, and the application developer, would certainly know the difference.

Only when on-line access and update via effective transaction processing systems was introduced did the technology start to be fully exploited. The idea of transaction processing introduced a new 'shape' of application code—the transaction program—and to enable programmers to build transaction programs easily, a new form of middleware was developed—the transaction processor. Until then, one might say that using the technology for data entry only was little more than just putting punch-card images on screens.

Such under-utilization of a new technology is typical of how a new computer technology curve is often approached. We apply tried and tested methods to the new technology, even though they may not fit. If we really want to exploit the technology fully, we have to understand the software structures best suited to it. Then we can build the middleware and tools required to make it easy. By definition, a new technology does not come equipped with these things.

Today, we are in the same position. Many of the tools being used to address the new client/server environment do little more than the equivalent of putting punch cards on the screen. Some products make GUI-based applications easy to develop; others make it easy to connect a personal computer (PC) to a server. Few products today enable you to build advanced object-based user interfaces *and* to connect application code across systems *and* to address directly the challenge of application integration *and* to do all of this easily, in the language of your choice. Yet these are the major areas we must conquer if the full promise of client/server technology is to be realized.[1]

Just as, 20 years ago, the casual observer saw little difference between data entry and full on-line transaction processing, so today the casual observer often sees icons and windows on a graphical user interface as being the full extent of the new technology. However, putting icons on a screen does not by itself mean that the client/server system behind it is being fully exploited.

So, we are currently at the beginning of the next evolutionary step—moving user interface and application function out from mainframe systems to the PC, and linking system components in cooperative client/server structures across local area networks (LANs) and wide area networks (WANs).

---

[1] There are, of course, other things that have to be done: effective end-to-end systems management, data distribution, design methods for complex computer networks with thousands of PCs and hundreds of servers, connection technologies, development of new analysis and design methods, etc. Today, although we see a world where great strides have been made in establishing this essential technical infrastructure for distributed systems, very little has been done to bring ease of programming to this new world.

Driven by the business pressures for user flexibility and change, the full exploitation of these systems is taking us into new user interface capabilities, new approaches to application connectivity across distributed systems, new ways to structure application software (the cooperative business objects shown in Fig. I1.1) and new software design techniques.

New user interface technology

By providing an increasing range of system resources (function and data) to users, IT delivers an increasing potential benefit. But this by itself is not enough. A user interface is needed that enables users to turn this *potential* benefit into *delivered* benefit.

The PC gives us a new level of user interface function—an incredibly high level compared to character-based terminals. Furthermore, this level of function is *standard* on most if not all PCs today. This point is worth emphasizing. Although it is true that this level of function has been around for some time (starting perhaps with the Xerox Star in the late seventies), only recently has it become *generally* available as a *base* function on *all* PCs.

However, as users are required to handle an ever-widening range of applications, the very fact of handling more applications makes the additional applications increasingly difficult to use. From a system point of view, this can be seen as a bandwidth constraint—except that the bandwidth in question is a person's ability to handle an increasing number of things. Since we cannot change the human brain, the only way to increase the effective bandwidth is to change the way in which computer systems are *perceived* by their users.

With the technology of character-based terminals, we presented the user with lists of functions that could be used, and constrained business processes to those defined, not by the business, but by the application designer's idea of what the business required of a user.

With PC technology, on the other hand, we can provide the impression that the computer handles 'things', such as invoices, insurance policies, bank accounts, notepads, etc.—thus matching the user's perception of the world outside IT systems. Instead of the computer appearing to the user as a separate and different universe, we can present computer systems as an *extension* of the user's world. Indeed, in this extension, we can *improve* on real life (for example, we can have an order form that will tell the user if a mistake has been made—or a shredder that can de-shred). We are talking here of a 'thing-based' user interface rather than a function-based one. It is what is called an 'object-based' user interface.

This approach can free the user from previous technology-based constraints, hide completely the underlying system complexities, and allow for much greater application integration—all of this while ensuring that the required business rules are enforced.

Object-based user interfaces are a new universe of user interface design. But when you exploit the new PC technology in this way, you find that you need an application software structure that is significantly different from the familiar menu/panel hierarchy structures we use to drive character-based terminals.

It turns out that the easiest way (by far!) to implement the new object-based user interface is to build and deliver CBOs (independent software objects) *instead of* applications. Each CBO maps to one of the objects that the user deals with on the screen.

However, new user interface technology by itself is not enough. It is the use of this technology in distributed client/server systems that really makes the difference.

New application connectivity

Since corporate data is generally held on a mainframe or minicomputer—a 'server'—the PC application code must be able to cooperate with server application code in order to handle corporate shared data.

The PC handles the graphical user interface and user interaction, and, since much of this is user-driven, we find that the best way to access shared resources (such as corporate shared data) is to build the PC as a client, making requests of separate drivers. By 'servers' we mean application code that handles independent requests from clients anywhere.

This is a significant change from the more traditional approach; it means that mainframe applications stop driving the business (by driving the user) and become servers, which provide both controlled access to shared resources, and secure enforcement of the business rules.

But, more than just connecting a PC to a server, we are looking at a world where computers of all sizes, whether clients or servers, are being linked together in peer-to-peer networks.

However, connecting one piece of application code to another is not easy—especially when (as in the case of the PC and a server) asynchronous connection is required. The solution to this problem is to use event-loop and message-driven application structures, where some middleware handles the event loop, the messaging and the initiation of the application code.

This is the shape of CBOs, which were so useful for the user interface. So we find that the same new software structure is the right shape for client/server and peer-to-peer systems as well as for the user interface.

New software structures—CBOs

Most OO (object orientation) tools today enable a developer to use objects in the process of building some software deliverable that will be handed to a user to run. But that deliverable is not itself an object. The benefits of OO are seen by the developer at build time, but not by the user at run-time. A cooperative business object (CBO) is a deliverable that is handed to users to run, but which is itself an object. Thus it provides all of the benefits of object orientation to the run-time environment. Since a CBO is a deliverable, it is 'language-neutral'; that is, you can use any one of a number of languages to build it. You could use COBOL—or an OO language.

The cooperative business objects add a new answer to the question posed of application designers, 'In implementing the business process, what is the thing that you are building—what is the end-product?' Previously, the answer was typically one of:

- A batch program (or suite of batch programs)
- A transaction program (or set of transaction programs)
- An interactive application (such as a PC application)

Now we add the answer 'a CBO'. The discovery of this as a desired *shape* of software—as a desired end-product of a development process—is a major new element in client/server systems, and we examine this new phenomenon in depth in this book.

With CBOs, we can see new horizons of potential software re-use—even a market in such software projects (we might read in a few years advertisements such as 'Buy XYZ's Invoice CBO—first in Pan-European VAT support . . .').

New middleware

To run CBOs, a new form of middleware is required. Why? Well, here is an analogy:

At the end of the sixties and the beginning of the seventies, we found that to exploit fully the then new system potential of terminals connected to computers via telephone wires, several essential system infrastructure components were required:

- Teleprocessing software
- Teleprocessing hardware at the mainframe
- Database management software

However, even with this infrastructure in place, it was soon discovered that the 'shape' of the application software—'transactions'—required a further underlying piece of software infrastructure—a transaction processor—if programming was to be made easy.

Systems of the nineties comprise PCs with powerful GUI capabilities providing secure access to extensive, distributed and high-value corporate resources. These systems also need a new 'shape' of application software—the CBO—and a new layer of software 'middleware'—a CBO enabling layer—upon which to run.

Know-how

New system and application structures raise many questions. For example, how do we manage the multiple update problem? Do we need to design and build this 'middleware' code to support the new client/server structure? How are business rules enforced with an object-based user interface? What design methods will deliver the new software structures required?

Although, today, the understanding of how to answer these and other related questions is not yet widespread, the answers do exist, and the know-how is available.

Clearly, many new skills will be required. There is an old adage that says, 'Hear and forget; see and remember; do and understand.' In this area, as in others, experience shows that these new skills come only from *doing*—from actually building systems.

Does this all mean a revolution in application development? Do we have to retrain everyone in some 'big-bang' conversion to the new-technology curve? The answer to this is no. Techniques have been developed that provide an evolutionary path to the new system structures. The necessary know-how and skills can be developed by a small core of people, and then spread more widely in a controlled way. New client/server systems can be grown alongside more traditional systems in such a way that they coexist.

Summary

Today we face a *major* challenge—understanding how to climb the new-technology curve, building systems that exploit:

- Cooperative processing in a client/server environment
- Object-based graphical user interfaces on the PC
- Application integration

and that are:

- Easy for the average application programmer to build

A major theme of this book is that the CBO is the right 'shape' of application-level to meet these challenges. The CBO structure, together with its enabling middleware, provides us with a way forward into this new world.

Part One
The user—exploiting the PC

The driving force behind the adoption of graphical user interfaces (GUIs) is usability—enabling users to address a much wider range of functions than hitherto. This is driven in turn by changes in the business environment, such as an organization's move away from deep hierarchies of task-oriented departments towards flatter organizations, employee empowerment and emphasis on customer service.

Thus an important question for information technology (IT) departments is not merely how to implement a GUI (although this by itself may be useful and may add benefit), but how to exploit *fully* the capabilities of the GUI, and how to bring ease of application programming to distributed client/server systems that place advanced GUIs on users' desks.

It seems trite to say that, before we design and build code, we should know what we are trying to produce. But it is worth repeating. In the seventies and eighties, many people used video terminals to do data entry into a batch transaction file. But this was merely a step on the way to the goal—on-line update against industrial-strength databases—for which they would need to build, not batch suites, but transaction programs. What we see in the nineties is many people implementing GUIs in a way that is really little more than the nineties' equivalent of batch data entry. This is a step on the way to the nineties' goal of object-based user interfaces.

In this part we present and justify a goal for the GUI: object-based user interfaces (OBUIs).

We also develop the rationale for a new kind of software structure that is ideal for implementing object-based user interfaces. Just as there is a world of difference in the software implementation between batch data entry and on-line update of shared data, so there are major differences in software structure—and in inherent benefit—between application-oriented and object-based GUIs.

Our use of the word 'object' should not lead you to assume that we are talking about object-oriented programming versus procedural application code; we are not. Rather, we introduce the concept of a software object as a *deliverable*, rather than as something used by a developer to build a deliverable that is not itself an object.

These objects are a better alternative to functionally oriented applications. They have a structure that solves many of the technical problems of object-based user interfaces. We give them the name 'cooperative business objects' in order to distinguish them from the objects used to create object-oriented applications that are not themselves objects.

In this part, then, we do three things:

- In Chapter 1 we discuss why there is a problem with application-oriented user interfaces, and show how object-based user interfaces solve the problem.
- Then in Chapter 2 we work through an example, starting with a traditional menu/panel application, and ending by showing what we mean by an object-based user interface. In the process, we point out some 'under-the-surface' problems that are user interface problems, but have little to do with look and feel.
- Chapter 3 introduces cooperative business objects—a new kind of structure for application-level code that solves the 'under-the-surface' problems inherent in trying to build object-based GUIs using more traditional application-oriented approaches.

1
Usability—the new system bottleneck

As people are required to handle an ever-widening range of applications, so they are finding systems increasingly difficult to use. From a system point of view, this can be seen as a bandwidth constraint—except that the constraint in question is an inherent human limitation. Since we cannot change the physiology of the human brain, the only way to increase the effective bandwidth is to change the way in which computer systems are perceived by their users. This chapter discusses the nature of that change.

1.1 The usability challenge

Many companies have invested huge amounts over the past 20 years in data, systems infrastructure and systems management—managed and controlled on behalf of the business by the IT organization. As pressures on businesses increase to re-organize, restructure, diversify, consolidate and slim down, they look to their information systems (IS) functions to provide flexible and changing access to that investment.

Thus there is increasing pressure on IS departments to provide computing services that will exploit existing investments for both of the following:

- A wider range of users and processes
- New processes in new business areas

Often the response by the IS department is to embark on large projects aimed at integrating applications, often in conjunction with a change to a more distributed (client/server) system structure.

Yet there is little point in spending huge sums on integrating applications, and data, if this investment fails to deliver benefit because the new systems prove too difficult to use. As someone said (in the context of on-line systems):

> Computer systems themselves deliver no business benefit. All they deliver is *potential* benefit to the screen. It is *users* who realize that potential, and so deliver benefit to the organization.

This seems self-evident; but it does mean that the benefit that can be realized from computer systems is dependent to a large extent on the user interface.

But is there a problem? The answer is yes—because the demands on users, and on user interfaces, are changing and increasing. To explore this problem, and to identify the solution, we must first understand the business need that is behind those demands.

1.2   A vital business need

Among the several imperatives that many companies face today is the need to make much better use of the inherent abilities of their people. This derives from various pressures, such as slimming down staffing and bureaucracies, restructuring towards flatter organizations and winning competitive edge through significantly improved customer service.

Typical comments heard from executives across a variety of enterprises in recent years have one common thread—the need to obtain greater staff effectiveness—and such comments include:

- 'We need "whole job" people. . . .'
- '. . . move them out to the front office.'
- 'Competitive edge through better service. . . .'
- 'If we could integrate our applications, our people could. . . .'
- 'People need to be (made) more effective. . . .'
- 'We need to cut learning time. . . .'
- 'We must *enable* people to do more. . . .'

Effectiveness does not mean only productivity. It means people addressing a wider range of activities than previously:

- Bank tellers moving from behind the counter to become customer service and sales people.
- Insurance claims clerks handling agents' commissions and customer queries as well as processing claims.
- Order entry clerks becoming 'account administrators', so enabling business transformation by providing full single-call customer service, with an eye to additional marketing opportunities as well.

It also means providing for depth—extending jobs so that a person can do the *next* step in a process. For example, an insurance clerk may be enabled to handle some of the more complex queries, instead of having to pass them all along to the specialist support.

IT implications

In IT terms, this demand for increased effectiveness also has a common thread: the need to enable people to access a much wider range of business processes than they did before. Clearly, one way to address this need is through the use of IT systems. Other options—such as increased training time or more staff—are today no longer viable. If supported by appropriate systems, the normal human capabilities of most people should be adequate for this extended role. The 64 000 dollar question is, can we build these 'appropriate systems'?

Today, PCs and client/server systems can give the user multiple applications concurrently. This means that the technical constraints imposed by character-based terminals on dialogues (including limited or no dialogue concurrency) can be overcome. Will this provide an answer? Initial experience suggests that the longer-term answer is no. Why not?

1.3 The application problem

Consider an order processing system user. The column towards the left-hand side of Fig. 1.1 shows how the application development (AD) department might traditionally deliver this function. It would:

- Analyse the process (the leftmost of the three 'clouds' at the top of the figure).
- Identify that this process involved key corporate data entities—such as the customer.

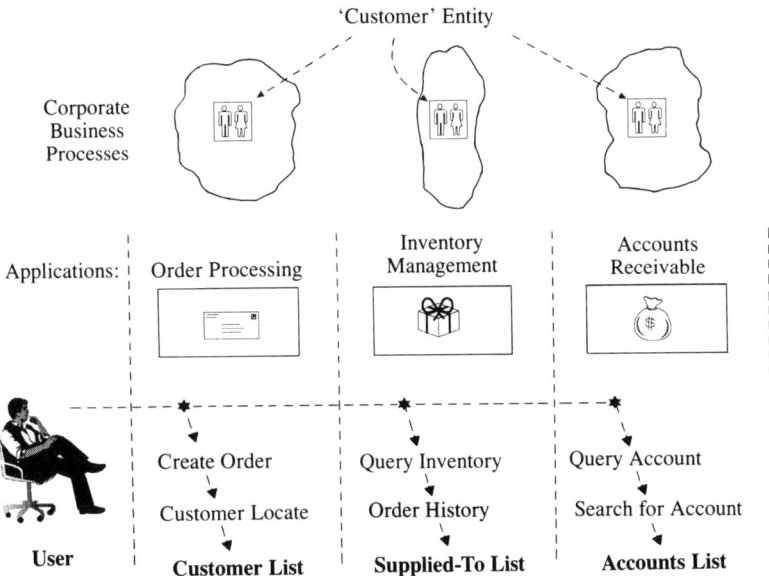

Figure 1.1. Application orientation

- Design and build an application, to appear as one of several windows on the user's PC.

Such an application encapsulates the function required to perform the process. Conventionally that is what is meant by the word 'application'. Probably, within the application, the code accesses the common corporate customer database.

Suppose, however, that the users, in addition to taking and entering customer orders, are now required to handle:

- General customer enquiries
- Product returns from customers
- Journal entries for customer account adjustments

In principle, this is no problem—two additional applications that may even already exist are provided (see Fig. 1.1). But consider the consequences.

We find that, although all three applications may use the common customer database to access customer details, each application presents a list of customers (the same customers) in a different way. So what? Well, assume that, in responding to a customer on the phone, the user needs to look at the customer's balance outstanding, and at the date of the last order. Such data may well be in two different customer lists. The user therefore has to choose the correct two customer lists—by accessing the appropriate two applications—to get at the needed information.

The practical consequence is that the application developers have unwittingly given users a new problem—by expecting them to be experts in:

- Understanding situations where one list rather than another must be used.
- Knowing which application provides the relevant list.
- Knowing how to start (get into) that application.
- Understanding how to navigate through the application in order to produce the required list.
- Understanding that in some situations two lists will be required concurrently on the screen, and knowing how to produce that effect.

Indeed, where a specific 'customer query' application (yet another application!) has not been provided, the user may well have to create a fictitious order, use the order processing application to do a search for the customer, then delete the order—merely to look at a list of customers (the result of the search)!

Exporting problems to users

Now the IS department did not plan to give the user a problem. It is just that the very design technology we have used so successfully over the past 30 years—choosing 'applications' as the vehicle for delivering business function—is now becoming a serious constraint: on IS's ability to deliver the level of integration and ease of use required, on users' ability to get the most out of the IT investment, and hence on the ability of the company to realize the return on investment expected.

In fact, the problem may be worse than this. Many companies today are planning staff empowerment that envisages users accessing (not all at once!) up to 30 applications. Yet one such company already estimates that after around 12 applications there is a diminishing return, at an increasing rate, for every application added. The increasing user load makes each additional application effectively less usable than the last. This applies despite improved ease of use of any given application—including those with a GUI.

Thus we face a major problem: Although our technology now allows the user to access many applications concurrently, their very nature makes them *difficult to use together*. But use them together is precisely what the user expects when he or she sees them on the screen concurrently! Furthermore, the problem exists *even when* a set of consistent 'look-and-feel' user interface standards are applied across applications.

This problem derives from the very nature of today's typical application, which is:

- A software encapsulation of a single business process.
- Essentially stand-alone with respect to other applications.

Consider: the one thing that a typical application is seldom if ever designed to do is to talk openly as a matter of course with other as yet undefined applications.

Encapsulation on conventional process boundaries makes it infeasible for users to use something from one application in another application (other than trivially through a cut-and-paste function)—even though they may be viewing them side by side, each with an attractive graphical user interface, on the same screen. Clearly, since our systems can deliver the required business function to the screen of a user's PC, then there must be something wrong with the *way* it is delivered at the screen.

So how do we overcome this? To answer this, we first consider briefly the nature of the general problem of usability.

1.4 Usability

The conventional way to address usability is through intensive training. But the time required is prohibitive. Already, reducing training time is a key business need.

There is another way: Instead of trying to teach the user about *how* the computer system works, we can exploit knowledge *already in the user's head*. But how do we do that? Let us start by considering how people deal with technology in general, and then apply it to computers.

In discussing how people use technology (such as a video player, a swing door, a cooker, or a computer), Donald Norman identifies three conceptual, or mental, models that are important in the operation of such devices (Norman, 1990). These are:

- The *user's model* (the user's concept of how the device works).
- The *designer's model* (how the device actually works).
- The *system image* (what the user sees).

In practical terms, the system image is the user's *only* access to the designer's model of the system. Thus, for a person to formulate a good user's model, the designer must make the (designer's) model obvious through the system image.

The difficulty is understanding how the user builds a conceptual model. Norman describes the psychology of the user's conceptual model as being built from everyday experience. The user will attempt to transfer existing knowledge to new systems:

- If the new system fails to match the conceptual model, the user will find it difficult to learn (leading potentially to frustration and rejection).
- If it *does* match, the user will rapidly gain confidence in its relevance and applicability.

The 'usability iceberg'

Mapping this to computer user interfaces indicates that users' conceptual models are of crucial importance to computer usability. This is illustrated by the 'iceberg' concept,[1] which shows (see Fig. 1.2) system usability as being dependent on three factors:

1 Usability is dependent on the presentation of the system to the user. This includes factors such as layout, colour and the aesthetic appearance of the system. However, these factors account for only 10 per cent of the usability of the system. For example, in a car the layout of the instruments does not significantly affect driving the car.
2 We derive usability from the effectiveness of user interaction with the system—how the user makes it do things. This includes editing techniques, scrolling, mouse use, pop-up panels, keyboard use, etc. Consistency of interaction is a very important factor in achieving usability; but the contribution of these factors is only 30 per cent of the total.
3 The remaining 60 per cent of the look-and-feel iceberg—the bit under the water—comes from how well the system maps to the user's view of the world. In other words, how easily can the user build a mental picture (a conceptual model) of the way the system works, so that he or she can accurately predict how the system will behave?

---

[1] This concept is based on research work done at Xerox PARC (unfortunately unpublished). The 'iceberg' representation of the research findings was introduced by David F. Liddle, Chairman of Metaphor Computer Systems (Liddle, undated). In addition, the 'iceberg' concept is discussed in the *IBM CUA-91 Manual* (IBM, 1991a), which also describes the designer's and user's models in relation to graphical user interfaces, and stresses the importance of matching the two.

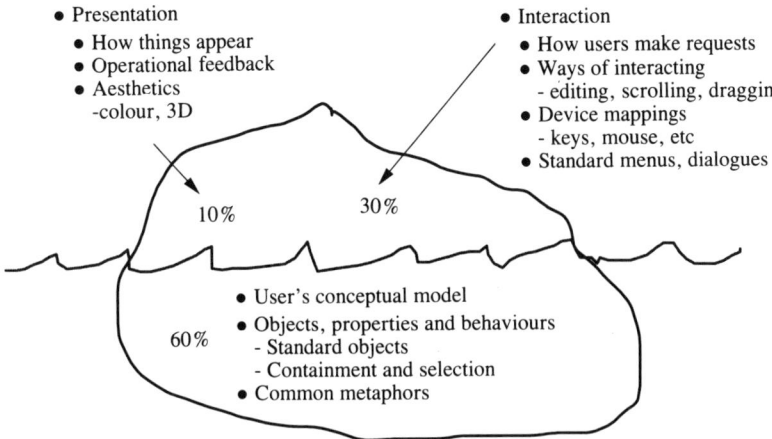

Figure 1.2. The usability iceberg (*source*: D. F. Liddle, Metaphor Computer Systems).

This last point suggests that IS should put onto the *user* the responsibility for building the correct conceptual model. However, a better way must surely be for IS to provide a system image that naturally maps to the user's model of the world.

What is the user's world?

But what is the user's world? Looking at a typical office, it is a world of things, of tools (used to perform tasks), such as:

- Forms
- Ledgers
- Files
- Notepads
- Manuals
- Phones

In fact, on looking round an office, you will never see an 'application'. Of course, there are procedure manuals, and instructions on forms that represent the actions required, etc. But what you *see* are manuals, forms, etc., not the 'procedures' themselves.

Considered in this way, it becomes apparent that the notion of an 'application' is an artifice of the IS world. Until recently, the only way to deliver business function through IT systems was by building code around this artifice.

1.5 New user interfaces

To explore how these considerations can help us to find a solution, let us return to our example of the users of an order processing system. Their 'extended job' would be made much easier if the customer list could be presented:

- As a single thing (a list of customers)
- As being usable in whatever business process it is required

This would mean not only that experienced users could do their job more efficiently, but also that new users would benefit. A manual order entry clerk would be familiar with a 'customer list' to which he or she could refer whenever necessary. Thus the system would work in the way he or she would expect.

This, of course, is the prime consideration. For users will find a system much easier to use if, as we indicated above, it maps well to their own view of the world. Remember that 60 per cent of the usability of a system depends on how easily a user can build a conceptual model of how the system works; and a user can do this most easily if IS provides a system that naturally maps to that user's world of everyday things.

With these concepts understood, it should be possible to build a user interface that keys into the well evolved world of the office or workplace. What is needed is provision of a 'thing-based' rather than a 'function-based' user interface.

This is quite possible, but only via the local power of the PC. The PC can present on the screen sets of 'things' or 'objects'—reference material, ledgers, forms, files, notepads, etc. Instead of the computer presenting to the user some list of *functions* that can be done, it should present the set of *things* the users need to do their job.

For example, referring back to the multiple application problem, a user will probably find it difficult to build a mental model of the behaviour of a 'customer list' when:

- It appears in several different forms.
- It shows different underlying behaviour.
- It is accessible in different ways.

But if the customer list is presented as a single thing, usable wherever needed (following our previous discussion), then it should be *much* easier to use. (For data analysts, such commonality of data is not something new. But for application developers, and for end-users, common presentation of such data entities across business processes—or 'applications'—*is* new.)

With this approach, separate education for each application should not *have* to be given. 'Thing-based' (or 'object-based') user interfaces make use of knowledge that *already exists* in the user's head—knowledge about 'how the world is'. Providing user interfaces that exploit this knowledge is the key.

Suppose we adopt such an approach—what would it look like to the user? To examine this question, the next chapter shows the train of design thinking, starting from a typical character-based terminal application, and ending with an 'object-based' user interface of the kind described.

2
Making computers familiar: object-based user interfaces

Starting with an old-style menu/panel character-based terminal application, this chapter traces the development towards an object-based user interface. In particular, two underlying principles of object-based user interfaces are introduced:

- The user should be able to use a given object in all processes ('applications') where that object is required.
- The user should be able to regroup objects in folders or containers (themselves other 'container' objects) to suit their way of working.

It is in the implementation of these two principles that we will see the necessity for the new software structures.

To illustrate the solution, and why the underlying technical implications are non-trivial, we use a sample application—order entry.

First, we look at how this application might be done with character-based terminals, and then examine some of the ways we can exploit PC technology. Then we assess this PC solution in the light of the key usability factors discussed in the previous chapter. Finally, we show how our example application develops beyond application boundaries into a true object-based user interface.

2.1 The character-based terminal approach

Figure 2.1 shows a sample initial panel of an order entry application, running on a non-programmable character-based terminal such as an IBM 3192 or 3278.

The *implications* of this technology are as follows (and we take this list from what we *observe* about real applications):

- The user selects what to do from a list (a 'menu'), which has been defined by IS.
- The user can do only one thing at a time.
- The interface is typically 'modal'—that is, once the user has chosen one function, then in order to go to another function he or she has first to complete the current function. A good example of this is where the user has to handle an

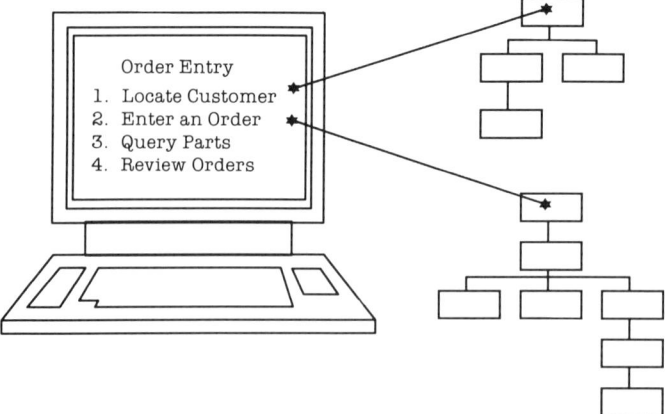

Figure 2.1. Character-based terminal—menu/panel user interface.

enquiry in the middle of an entry transaction (such as entering a customer order). Before answering the enquiry, the user first either has to cancel out of the order, or complete it. In other words, the user is bound by the 'mode' (in our example, he or she is in 'order entry mode').
- Two or more functions typically cannot be handled concurrently. For example, we are not able to allow the user to process both a customer enquiry and an order panel concurrently.[1]

In summary, we might say that the current character-based terminal interface is *single-function modal*. By 'modal' we mean that the dialogue with the user is placed in a certain mode, and while in that mode, the user cannot do other things.

However, the menu/panel hierarchy design approach for character-based terminals has two great advantages:

- The design technique maps well to the technology (where each box in the function hierarchy typically maps to a menu or panel).
- It enforces business rules by encapsulating them in one or more 'transactions', and so guides the user through the required business process.

With PC technology, we can throw away the first of these; but we *must* retain enforcement of required business rules.

2.2 A PC-based approach

Here we see how we might start to exploit the PC technology.

---

[1] Note that, although we describe here various limitations of character-based terminal systems, we do not mean that these are necessarily *technical* limitations. We mean, rather, that people in practice are observed to build systems like this—because removing these limitations, while not technically impossible, is impracticable.

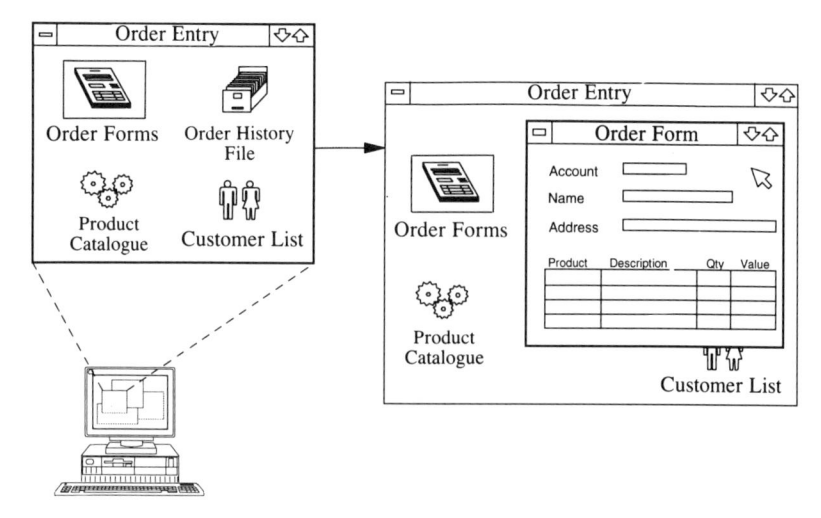

Figure 2.2. PC—graphical user interface.

Figure 2.2 shows a PC (bottom left) with four application windows. (The PC screens illustrated in this book are stylized for presentation purposes—they do not accurately show all the detail.) The Order Entry window is shown enlarged (top left), and this shows a PC alternative to the initial menu/panel on a character-based terminal. Instead of a list, the user sees four icons:

- The Customer List (bottom right)
- The Product Catalogue (bottom left—this company specializes in gear wheels and sprockets)
- A pad of Order Forms (top left)
- The Order History File (top right)

To enter an order, the user would 'tear off' a new order form by dragging one (with a mouse) from the Order Forms icon. The result might look like the window on the right of Fig. 2.2, where the new Order Form is shown.

Note that the Order History File is now hidden (under the Order Form). This is not a problem, as the user (not the application) controls the positioning of windows, and so can easily slide the Order Form to one side to reveal the Order History File icon if that is what is wanted. (The application can, if desired, take over control of window positioning; however, except in very special circumstances, experience has shown this to be user-hostile behaviour for this style of user interface.)

GUI principles

With this application, we can now go on to illustrate four important principles of a GUI. Without all of these principles, the user productivity potential is severely

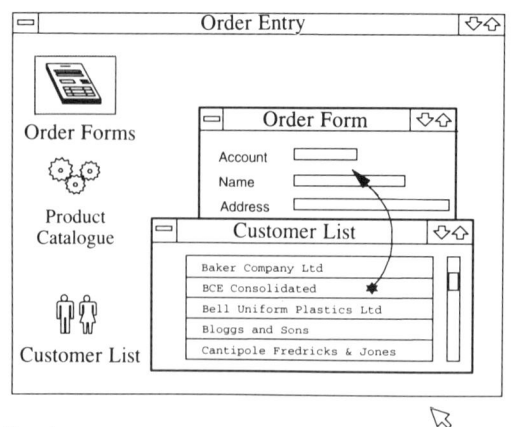

Figure 2.3. Application concurrency.

constrained. Note also that, while these principles are relatively easy to implement on a PC, they are difficult or impossible with the typical character-based terminal.

1. *Multiplicity* What if the user wanted to work on two orders concurrently? With a PC, this is very easy—you can have as many order forms up as you like. This ability to display multiple instances of the same class of thing we call *multiplicity*.
2. *Concurrency* How does the user fill in the order? Well, the Customer List icon is clicked to bring up a list of customers (see Fig. 2.3). The user would search through this list until the customer record is found.[2] Note that the user now has two things up on the screen. Showing several different things on the screen concurrently we call *concurrency*.
3. *Amodality* Further, the user should be able to switch between the two things at will. If he or she had to complete work with the Customer List before continuing with completing the order, then that would be a 'modal' way of operating. In general, modal operation is undesirable, and a non-modal or *amodal* interface is almost always highly preferable.
4. *Direct manipulation* To fill in the details on the Order Form, the user just clicks on the customer record, holds the mouse button down, moves the mouse over to the Order Form, and releases the button. The system then fills in customer number, name and address details. Note that this is more than cut and paste. The name for this type of operation is *direct manipulation*.

In this example we have seen how the user is 'in control'—even in a structured clerical process like an order entry application. We have also seen how the four GUI principles greatly help with achieving the usability aims set out in the last

---

[2] This is, of course, not the only way to identify the correct customer. There are many ways. The objective is to combine the best of PC-style interfaces on the one hand with record location in say a five-million-row host database on the other. We call this the 'megadata problem'—and there are several satisfactory solutions to it, described in Chapter 11.

chapter—of enabling the user to deal with 'things', just as in the real world, rather than with functions.

However, we are still dealing with an application—the order entry application in our example—and we have not yet dealt with the 'application problem' (discussed in Sec. 1.3). To recap, the application problem is the inability of a user to use effectively information from one application in another. This is fundamental, and we now go on to address it.

2.3 Presenting objects on the screen

Our problem really lies in our overall mind-set. For all we have done is to look at how the new technology could be used for a standard application such as order entry. What we have effectively done so far has been little more than to transfer our unconscious knowledge of what an application *is*, to the new technology.

In the early days of the character-based terminal, some IS departments saw it as a kind of superior card punch, which would save money on cardboard (punch cards). They actually put card images on the screen. What we have done in our examples is the nineties' equivalent of putting card images on a screen.

What we have *not* done has been really to ask, 'How can we use this new technology to further our business objectives? We did not ask this because we know that the answer has always been 'through building applications . . .', and we assumed unconsciously that this is still the right answer. And of course, in the sense that we still need to address business processes, it still is. However, in answering the question, we have also dragged along all our notions about what an application *is*. This is a fundamental design error.

2.3.1 A 'workbench'

Now let us come back to our question (which was, 'How can we use this new technology to further our business objectives?'), and at the same time look at an alternative to our traditional notions of application structure and presentation. We build on the concepts introduced in Sec. 1.5. (These concepts are reflected in such modern user interface guidelines as the *IBM CUA-91 Manual* (IBM, 1991a,b).) Thus we present an interface where the user manipulates and uses everyday real things (or objects) directly on the screen. Let us develop this idea.

Figure 2.4 shows what one might call a 'workbench'—a window containing the *things* or objects required by the user to do sales support tasks. Objects are shown by the small pictures—or 'icons'. The user manipulates these with a pointing device. For example, an object can be looked at by 'opening' it (through a double click with mouse button 1). Again, an object such as Product X567 may be printed by dragging it to the printer icon and dropping it (mouse pointer over the Product X567 icon, press and hold button 2, drag pointer over to the Printer icon, release button 2).

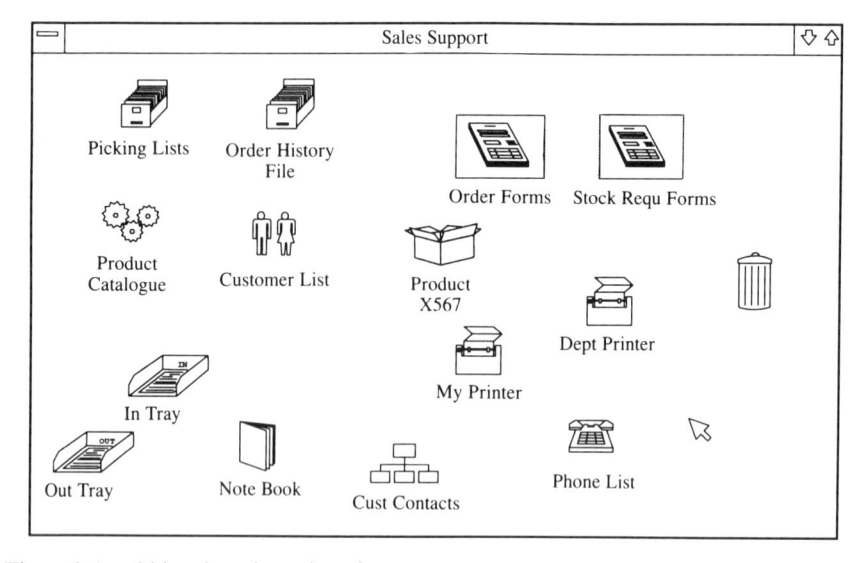

Figure 2.4. Object-based user interface.

Some things remain the same as our previous design—we still see the pad of order forms, the customer list, etc. However, we have added some of the other things a user might use from day to day, such as an in and out tray, a bin, a notebook, etc. Two questions arise:

- Figure 2.4 shows only a fraction of the objects a real end-user would normally deal with, and the screen still looks messy. We need a way to let the user tidy it up.
- Much more importantly, *where have the business processes gone*? For example, how does the user enter a customer order? Or query the status of a part? Or update a customer record? We need to ensure that such business processes are retained in our move to an object-based user interface.

Tidying the messy desk

First let us look at the problem of keeping things tidy. The major solution to this is to put things in 'containers' (The *IBM CUA-91 Manuals* describe in detail this approach, and identify it as a key user model concept. They also introduce other useful techniques for keeping things tidy.) In Fig. 2.5 we see two container objects called 'Store Room' (the icon is meant to represent a cupboard) and 'Stationery'. The user has tidied most of the objects into one of these two. Figure 2.5 shows how the user has double clicked on the Store Room icon (bottom left), and has 'opened' it, resulting in a window showing the contents of the Store Room.

Making computers familiar: object-based user interfaces

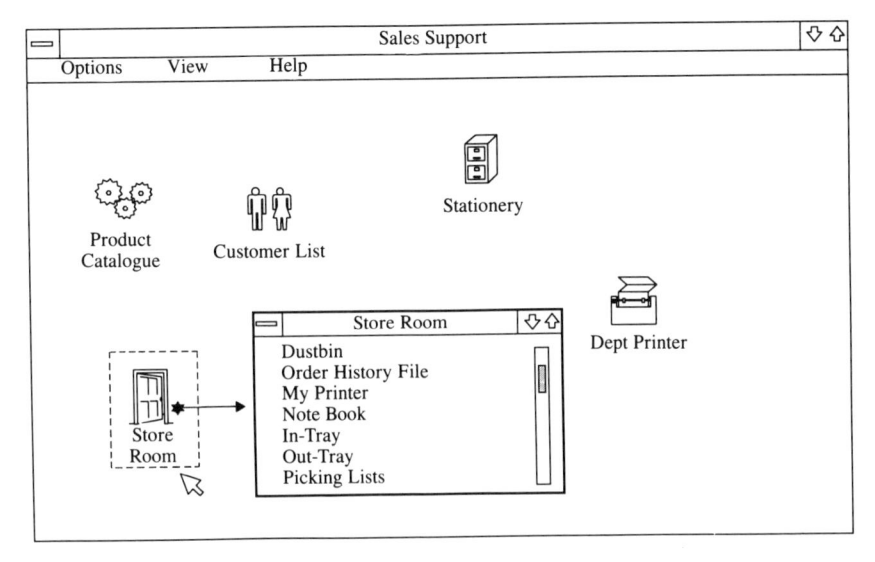

Figure 2.5. 'Container' objects.

The user has pulled out (by direct manipulation) several objects (Customer List, Product Catalogue, the Stationery container, and the Department Printer) from the Store Room. Note that the 'Stationery' object is also a container object, and will contain the various pads of forms required.

The business process

The second question—how to tell the users about the clerical or administrative procedures the company requires them to follow—is not as difficult as it might first appear. Two approaches to this are:

- First, we might make use of the 'procedures' manual that exists in most companies, even though it sometimes gathers dust in a forgotten cupboard. This manual defines clerical and administrative procedures. The idea is to put this manual on-line as another object on the screen. This is shown in Fig. 2.6, which shows the workbench as it might look half-way through the day, while the user is in the midst of taking a customer order.[3] The procedures manual is open at the 'Take Order' page (top right in Fig. 2.6). The individual 'Take Order' procedure is itself an object, and the procedures manual (not shown in Fig. 2.6) is a 'container' object containing many different administrative clerical procedures.

---

[3] In this book, we cannot do justice to this user interface. It is essentially a dynamic thing, and is best explained through use. All we can do here is to show a snapshot, which leaves out the most important part—the 'feel' of the interface. As an aside to the current discussion, it is worth noting that object-based GUIs are probably better run on a high-resolution screen (1024 × 768, 14 or 15 inch) than on the more traditional VGA (640 × 480, 12 or 14 inch) screen.

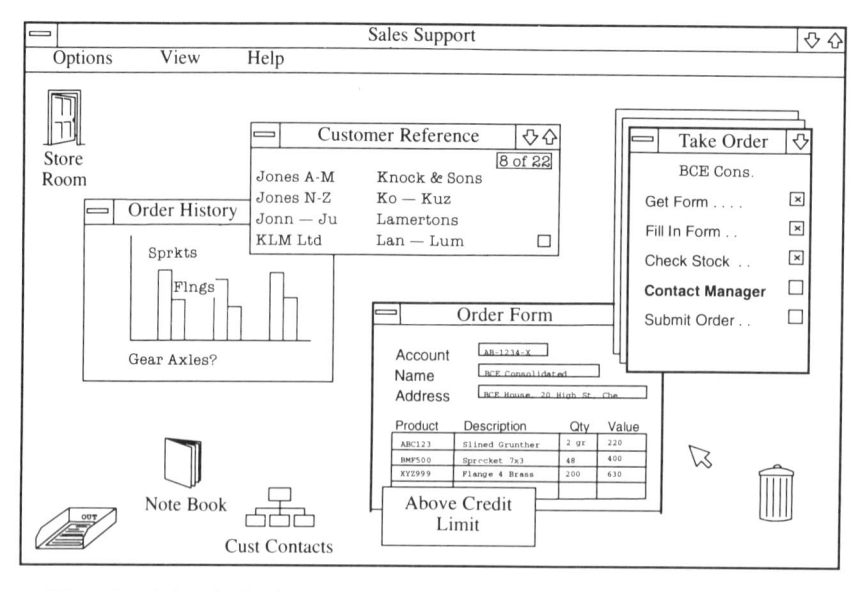

Figure 2.6. Retaining the business process.

As the user completes the order, appropriate boxes in the procedure are automatically checked off by the system. If a job is incomplete (say at end of day) then it can be filed away to be opened and worked on the next day.

Notice also that in the example shown in Fig. 2.6, there were initially four steps in the procedure. In the course of filling the order, an exception condition was met (above credit limit). The system can automatically insert an additional step into the procedure (in this case, 'contact manager'). Indeed, a major application of expert systems to business processes will probably be in the area of guiding people through complex administrative and clerical procedures.

- Secondly, we could use the Help function, along with an 'intelligent' form. The user would first look up Order Entry (for example) in Help. This would tell him or her to open an Order Form (and give guidance on how to do it). The Order Form in turn would have behind it the business logic to guide the user through the form, warn of errors and insist on business-determined sequences and completion criteria.

In general, the second approach is to be preferred. Although on first sight the first approach might *look* better, experience has shown that, for single-form processes, the user can easily see the state of the process merely by looking at the form. Showing a 'procedures' page merely uses up the screen unnecessarily.

Where a process uses more than one form, or where it goes past more than one user (or both), then we can encapsulate that process in a 'folder'. This folder will hold all the objects (things) required for the various users to do their part of the process. An essential attribute of this folder would be a list of the steps to be taken. This list would be 'intelligent', and would behave rather like the 'procedures object' in the example above. It might be implemented as a separate object within the folder, or as data 'belonging' to the folder.

'Tool' objects

This approach can provide an extremely effective environment for 'tools', which, although individually trivial, can add substantially to user effectiveness. Figure 2.6 shows two such tools:

- A notebook (bottom left, next to the out tray). The idea here is that the user can make free-form notes on anything relevant (such as the information that a customer buys a product from another company) and then mail that note through the electronic mail system simply by picking up the note with the mouse and dropping it on the out-tray.
- A 'customer contacts' tool (shown by a little organization chart). The user can keep here specific contact details by customer. For example, he or she might record that for company X, the normal contact is Joe, Joe's manager is Mary, and Fred stands in for Joe when Joe is away. If our user belongs to a company that sends Christmas presents to customers, then Joe and Mary's gift preferences might be kept. Then, when our user takes a vacation, this object can be mailed to the stand-in, so that small personal contact details are not lost.

Other objects

Finally, at the top left are two windows that the user might have been using before starting the order entry procedure. The first is some simple analysis (prompted by another administrative procedure) of a customer's order history; the second shows a high-level index to the customer file, illustrating one possible approach to handling large amounts of data at the user interface.

Advantages

This sort of approach—the building of what we might call a 'sales support environment' for clerical staff—is clearly achievable with PC and cooperative processing technology. It is not particularly obvious that we could do it with character-based terminal technology.

So, it appears that the advantages, and design implications, with PC technology are:

- The user has a choice of several things that can be done.
- Once the user has chosen to do one thing, then he or she can at any time switch to another—as easily as taking out a new file from a desk drawer and laying it on top of the old one—in fact, probably even more easily than that. Things that are suspended are not in a different state than when they are active; it is just that

mouse and keyboard input do not go to the 'suspended' things, they go to the 'active' thing.
- The user can have multiple objects concurrently on the screen, such as an administrative procedure, an order form, a customer list, a mailbox or out tray, etc. Users quickly adjust to their own comfort level of concurrency and multiplicity. Indeed, this is a major advantage of PC technology—if properly exploited, it can (as it were) automatically adjust to an individual's needs.
- We do not really have 'applications'; rather a business process is built from a set of 'application objects', where a single given object may be used by more than one business process. For example, a 'customer object' could be used in the following processes:
  —Customer enquiry
  —Order entry
  —Billing
  —Customer locate
  —Customer record maintenance

Now compare Fig. 2.6 with where we started—Fig. 2.2. To the extent that business benefit is delivered at the glass (at the user interface), it is arguable that the sort of capability illustrated through Fig. 2.6 can potentially deliver a far greater and more effective range of business function and hence benefit than that shown by Fig. 2.2.

2.3.2 Summary

To summarize, we can say that—in addition to graphics and image—a PC can exploit the following functions, which are typically not available on character-based terminals:

- Multiplicity
- Concurrency
- Amodality
- Direct manipulation
- Presentation of objects
- Presentation of container objects (which hold other objects)

These functions allow us to build a workbench within which application objects reside. With such capability, we can design imaginative and innovative application solutions that can contribute substantially to the effectiveness of the enterprise, and hence to the business case for high-function PCs.

However, the design we have built up so far has one important flaw. We have presented everything in a single window. This approach, when implemented, allows one all too easily to slip back into the old application-oriented way of thinking. If this happens, then we can be in danger of throwing away much of what we have built.

2.4 The 'workbench problem'

The approach required in designing an object-based user interface is to ask not what *function* does the user need, but rather, 'What are the *things* the user needs to perform the required tasks?' Given this, the trap one can fall into is to deliver this set of objects wrapped up in an application—which appears to the user as a 'workbench'.

What can happen is that different development groups, each addressing a different business process, each build their own 'workbench'. The problem arises when the designer's model of this workbench is that of an application that contains all the things required *for the given set of business processes*.

This is the flip-side—the developer's side—of the 'application problem', and in this section we further explore the problem. As a vehicle for discussion, we shall look at what actually happened in one company that took this approach (although the details have been changed to fit our example—and to protect the innocent!).

The company decided that new developments would have an object-based user interface on PCs (and that data would be held on a mainframe). Shortly after this decision was made, the AD department was asked to implement two different business processes—order entry and contracting. Thus they initiated two projects, each with its own development team.

The first project started work on an 'order processing workbench' for a set of people in the marketing division. The project team's initial analysis suggested that this type of end-user needed seven objects:

- Customer list
- Customer
- Order history file
- Pad of order forms
- Order form
- Parts catalogue (a list of products)
- Part (a product object)

Figure 2.7 shows the Order Processing workbench as the top left window, with an Order Form opened to the right (the icon for this is not shown).

A few weeks later, the second project began development of a 'contracting workbench' (all the things needed to handle contracts with customers) for people in both the manufacturing and marketing divisions. Analysis suggested that users needed seven objects with which to handle this business area:

- Customer list
- Customer

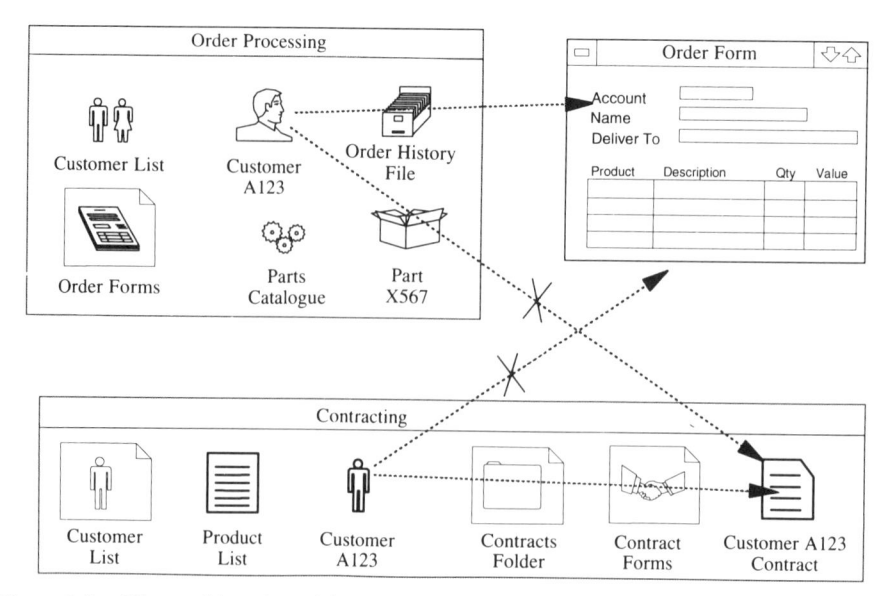

Figure 2.7. The workbench problem.

- Product list (a catalogue of parts)
- Product (a part object) (not shown in Fig. 2.7)
- Contracts folder
- Pad of contract forms
- Contract

This workbench is shown at the bottom of Fig. 2.7.

As it happened, many of the users in marketing needed to handle both customer orders *and* contracts. When (luckily at a prototype stage) these two workbenches were put together on a single user's PC, it immediately became apparent that the system—as a whole—would be very difficult to use, because:

- There were two customer lists (each with the same name—suggesting that they were the same—but each with a different icon—suggesting that they were different).
- There were two different 'customer' objects, each containing much the same information. But worse than that, the users found that they could use the customer object from the Order Processing workbench *only* with the Order Form, not with the Contract Form. In addition, the contracting customer object could only be used with the Contract Form object. These limitations are shown by the 'X's in Fig. 2.7.
- There were two different product lists—one of them being called a 'parts catalogue'. At least both the names and icons were different. The only problem was that they both contained the same information.

- There were two different 'product' objects, with the same difficulties as the product/parts lists.

Instead of an easy-to-use natural real-world user interface, the user found confusion and inconsistency. In fact, by presenting objects within application boundaries, the AD department had inadvertently given the user the worst of both worlds:

- An interface that suggested the user was using *things* rather than functions, without showing the user the boundaries of where those things could be used.
- Application boundaries that relied on the user recognizing 'modes' of use—without giving the user any indication at all about where those boundaries were, or how to switch into one of the modes.

In essence, the AD department was producing what I call 'iconic applications'. In the two workbenches, there are 14 objects (12 shown in Fig. 2.7, two not shown)—which, by all the conventions of object-based user interfaces, states quite categorically to the user that there are 14 objects (things) needed for order processing and contracting. However, the user knows quite well that only ten are needed (customer, customer list, product, product list, order history file, pad of order forms, order form, pad of contract forms, contract form, contracts folder).

To summarize, the essence of the workbench problem is this:

- In building code, we duplicate items across our applications. Over the past 20 years, we have learned not to do this when it comes to data; we try to design databases so that data is not duplicated. Yet we still duplicate the application function that accesses that data. If we adopt object-oriented programming techniques, we may avoid actually rewriting the various duplicated items. But that is typically at the source code level; when the applications are delivered, we still have the situation where the executable code consists of much duplicated function—which leads to a greater maintenance load.
- Great difficulty in 'integrating' applications. This does not mean running them concurrently; on today's PCs that is trivial. What it means is enabling both the developers and the users to re-use parts of one application in another business process.
- If each application presents an object-based user interface, then the user may see several of the same object—each of which behaves differently, and none of which can be used outside their own 'application' environment. Experience has shown this to have very poor usability.

A good principle for object-based user interface design is the principle of 'least astonishment', which goes something like this, and where 'correct' means correct in human factors terms: For any given user action, the *result that least astonishes* the user is most likely to be the correct result.

In our example, four business objects were represented to the user as eight objects. Each of these looked different, behaved differently and interacted with other things in different ways than their duplicates. That astonished the users. The result was an unusable interface. The company in question had to go back and do a fundamental rethink, and redesign.

The lesson here is simple: An iconic user interface that does not present objects as the user understands them is not an object-based user interface.

Thus in spite of consciously setting out to do so, the AD department *failed* to provide an object-based user interface for the users; what they provided was an *application-oriented* interface that used icons to represent application objects. Instead of an object-based interface, AD actually produced two *iconic applications*. If the objective is to produce an object-based user interface, then building iconic applications is a fundamental error.

Let us now complete the picture of the solution to the business need by deriving some important lessons from the 'workbench' problem.

2.5 The object-based user interface

Given that there is a consistent standard for presentation and interaction (the 'usability iceberg' above the water), then two principles of an object-based user interface from 'below the waterline' are of crucial importance—for both usability *and* implementation. These two principles are:

- *Object re-use* Any given object must be re-usable across business processes where appropriate.
- *User-defined grouping* A user can put any object in any container he or she chooses (subject to business rules). A container is an object.

Object re-use

The principle here is that a single given object can be used across multiple business processes. Figure 2.8 shows a simple example of this, where the customer object is used both in order processing (the user can 'drop' it on to the order form to enter the customer details) and in the contracting process (where the user can similarly use the customer object to complete a contract form). Again, this same customer object can, of course, be used for customer enquiries, and to update the customer record. To look at (and perhaps update) the customer details, the user merely has to get a 'view' of the object. (The CUA practice for this is to do a double click on the Customer icon with button 1 of the mouse.)

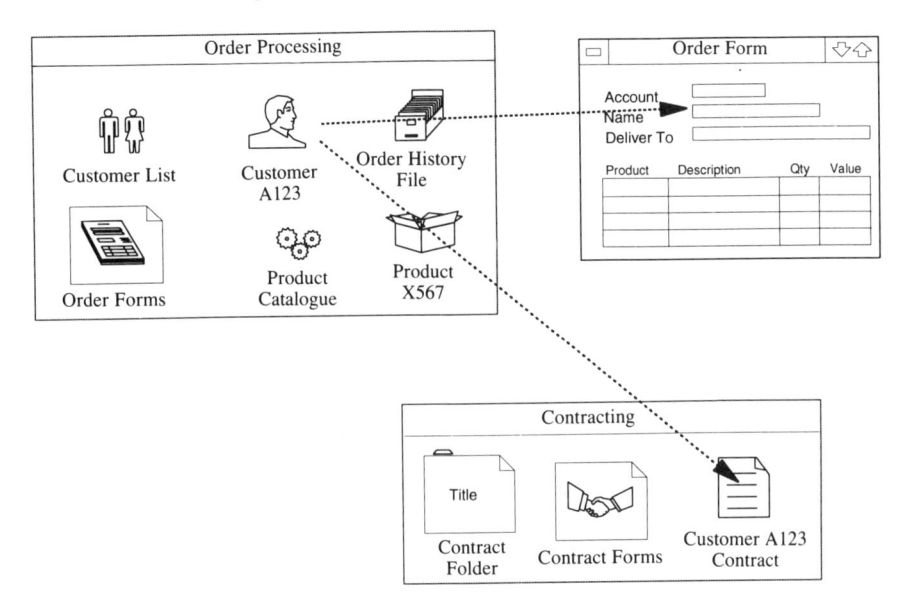

Figure 2.8. Object re-use by the user.

User-defined object 'grouping'

The second principle is that users can 'group' or locate objects to suit their own needs. Suppose, as shown in Fig. 2.9, that AD delivered to the user an 'order processing' object (a container or 'work area' containing the things needed to process customer orders). What the 'user grouping' principle means is that the user can, if

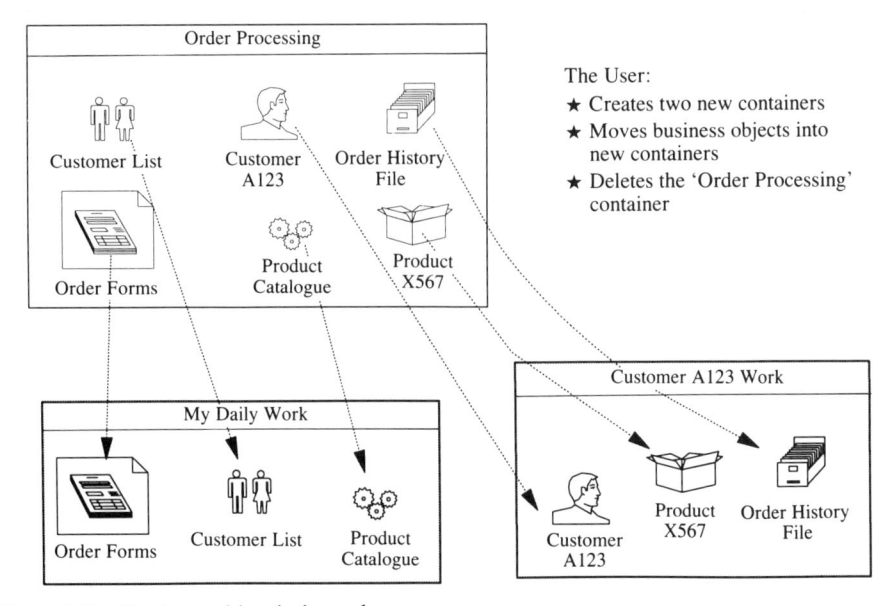

Figure 2.9. Business object independence.

he or she wishes (and assuming the business rules allow it), regroup the contained objects in other container objects. Figure 2.9 shows an example of this, where the user:

- Creates two new containers—'Customer A123 Work' (perhaps because there is some significant piece of work to be done with this customer) and 'My Daily Work' (to hold the things needed for the user's normal daily tasks).
- Moves objects from the 'Order Processing' container to the two newly created containers.
- Then deletes the original 'Order Processing' container, since he or she does not intend to use it. (Deleting this container does not necessarily mean removing it from the system—it generally means removing it from the user's PC only.)
- Finally, gets the 'Customer A123' object out of the Customer List object—which is also a container—and moves it to the 'Customer A123 Work' container.

The regrouping would be permanent as far as that particular user is concerned—positions of objects on the screen are normally only changed by the user, and are maintained by the system over power-off.

Now let us consider these two principles from the point of view of the developer. The key question here is, if this behaviour is available to the user, then what was it that development developed?

If 'applications' were developed, then how did the user regroup them? What sort of application is it when the users can interactively—and extremely easily—tear it into pieces and reassemble the pieces to suit themselves?

We answer this question in the next chapter, in which we find that implementing this behaviour has enormous implications on the software structures required.

3
Cooperative business objects

In the previous chapters, we have seen how an object-based user interface can let people use IT resources without stumbling across artificial 'application' barriers. Building this style of user interface, however, is not easy. In particular, implementing the two important principles of object-based GUIs—object re-use and object regrouping—has proven elusive when attacked with commonly available programming tools.

This problem we call the 'integration problem', as it revolves around how to build independent and (possibly) separately developed units of software that map to the objects on the user interface in such a way that integrating them—at runtime—is easy to program. It is the flip-side of the workbench problem (see Sec. 2.4), which was how to *avoid* building 'workbenches' that are really applications, with application boundaries). From now on, we refer to this problem under the single name, 'integration problem'.

The problem can be overcome by adopting a new kind of software structure that has proved to have great ease-of-programming attributes for object-based GUIs. We call this new structure a 'cooperative business object' (CBO) because:

- What we deliver as the end-product of the development process is an *object* in the true object orientation sense of the word.
- The size of the object maps to 'business' things (such as a customer, an invoice, a claims form, etc.)—so it is a *business* object.
- It cooperates with other business objects to perform some desired task—hence it is a *cooperative* business object—or 'CBO'.

This chapter introduces the concept of CBOs as applied to the GUI. Later on, we will see how the same structure also brings ease of programming to cross-system communication.

3.1 The 'integration' problem

The traditional approach to structuring business function for delivery through computer systems is to build 'applications'. Figure 3.1 shows how each overall

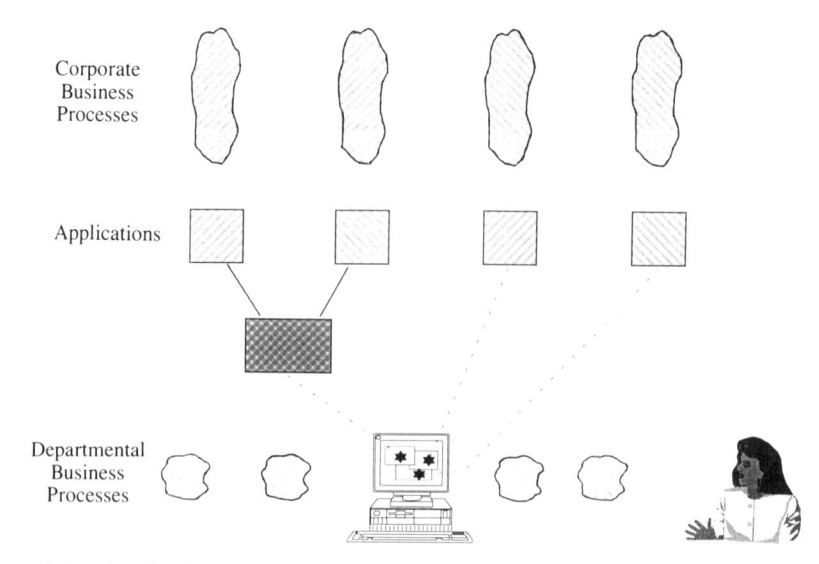

Figure 3.1. Application orientation.

business process (the 'clouds' at the top of the figure) is encapsulated into a software structure called an 'application'. On the left of the figure, we show two old character-based terminal applications being front-ended on the PC to form a single GUI application. (While this approach can bring major benefits in specific circumstances, it is not generally seen as a viable long-term structure for the majority of mission-critical systems.) We also show several *departmental* processes that people create for themselves in order to help them fulfil their corporate mission. Our traditional application approach does little or nothing for these.

Now, the problem with application-oriented software structures is that they cannot avoid the integration problem. Although they may enable us to deliver iconic applications, they cannot deliver object-based user interfaces. Let us look at two ways that have been tried in the past to address the problem using application-oriented software structures:

- Build one large application, within which the various components can communicate. All objects appearing on the user interface will be controlled by this one application.
- Build a number of small applications where each application can talk to the other applications.

The problem with the first approach is that it takes us right back to building large monolithic lumps of code, which become a nightmare to maintain—especially if different parts are produced by different development teams. While acceptable for trivial developments, this approach of putting all functions in one application just does not scale up.

The second approach runs straight into the ease-of-programming problem. It is certainly the case that expert programmers, using languages such as C or C++, can write system-level code to access the various low-level system mechanisms for inter-application communication (such low-level mechanisms include DDE, OLE, Pipes, Shared Memory, etc.). However, it is not obvious how the average application programmer using (say) COBOL—or the 'ambitious end-user' using (say) Visual Basic or REXX—can do so. Even the expert programmers must first agree on the mechanism, then the data formats to be used, not to mention agreeing the general architecture of their necessarily single solution.

As Fig. 3.2 shows, the developer of an application can use either procedural languages or object-oriented languages to build the thing that is delivered. That is not the point. The point is that what is *delivered* is an application; and the heart of the integration problem is how to make those applications interact—as interact they must do. This problem is shown in Fig. 3.3.

Not only must applications interact with each other, they must also interact with the GUI, and with other applications across the network. They must also interact with future applications if application integration is to be achieved (more on this later). The question marks in Fig. 3.3 indicate that, in creating an application that will interact effectively with other applications (both local and remote), the average programmer—or someone in the organization—has to contend with much more than just the application code. He or she has a major integration problem at the system level. In general, one or more (sometimes all) of the following problems need to be resolved:

1 *GUI APIs* The need to understand and code the system-level application programming interfaces (APIs) needed for modern GUIs. Examples are OS/2

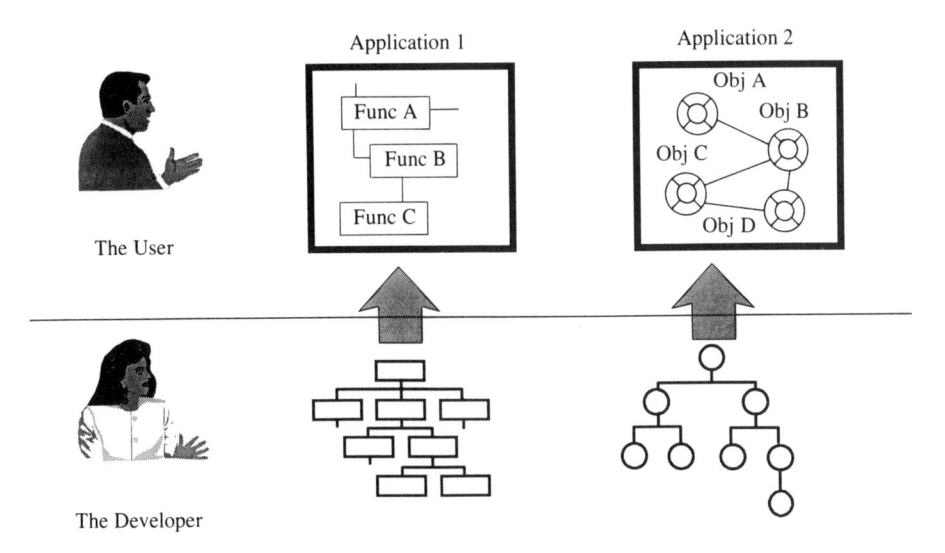

Figure 3.2. 'Application' isolation.

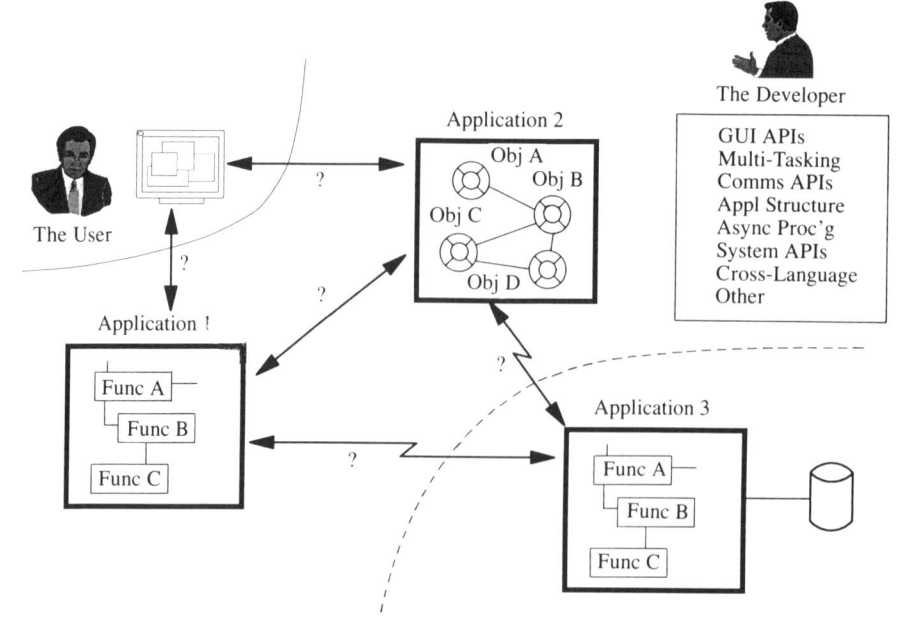

Figure 3.3. The 'integration' problem.

Presentation Manager, Windows, X-Windows. All of these require a high skill level on the part of the programmer. It can take up to six months for a good C programmer to become proficient. This explains the popularity of GUI tools, which allow one to 'paint' the window, and which hide the underlying complexities.

2 *Multi-tasking* Not required for stand-alone applications, multi-tasking is often required when the PC communicates with other systems. Otherwise window(s) can 'freeze' while interaction with a remote system is going on. This is sometimes called the 'hourglass problem' (owing to the appearance on the screen of the hourglass symbol, telling the user to wait). Handling this assumes, of course, that the programming language supports multi-tasking, which some high-level languages do not do. But there is more to multi-tasking than just starting the task. The programmer also has to handle task synchronization, inter-task communication, ending the task tidily, memory allocation for cross-task data, etc.

3 *Communications APIs* In connecting to another system, the application programmer often has to deal with system-level API calls to the communication subsystem. The programmer's real problem here is not the complexity of the APIs, but understanding what is going on.

4 *Application structuring* The application programmer has to determine how the application should be structured so that it copes with all the various external influences on the program.

5 *Asynchronous processing* If multiple threads are used to handle long-running events, the programmer has to understand how to handle asynchronous events within his or her own code.
6 *System APIs* If one program has to talk with another, there are mechanisms provided by the operating system that can be used. However, the APIs to these are often extremely complex. In addition, someone has to ensure that the writers of the other programs use the same mechanisms.
7 *Cross-language* If a program talks to another program, then not only does some inter-application communication mechanism have to be built from generally low-level system functions, but if the languages used to write the applications are different, then some form of software 'esperanto' must be built, since many languages do not talk easily to others. One form of cross-language and cross-program communication is an intermediate file. This will often not perform nearly well enough—aside from the problem of managing the file, synchronizing writes with reads, etc.
8 *Other* This includes things like how code is initiated, and how data is understood when exported from one program to another.

Although various software tools address some number of these, there are very few (if any) that address them all. This makes any effective solution to the 'workbench problem' (discussed in the previous chapter) very difficult for the average programmer building applications.

3.2 Objects and messages

It appears, then, that applications, whether large or small, will not provide us with the interaction we need without involving the programmer in layers of complexity. So we need to look at the question from another angle.

Now, real life is a continuous spectrum of complexity. In capturing some aspect of that complexity in software, the designer *must* focus on one aspect rather than another. He or she must 'encapsulate' software based on that aspect. Such encapsulation is essential in any software design process. 'Applications' are the result of designers choosing a business process or procedure—some set of closely related functions—as the focal point.

Intuitively, since the objects on the user interface must be independent, then it seems reasonable to base *our* encapsulation strategy on those objects. Experience has shown that this is an excellent design strategy. Thus instead of focusing on processes and functions, we should focus on the *things* needed by the user. This means encapsulating on the basis of things rather than functions.

And this brings us to object orientation. (A brief introduction to object orientation (OO) is provided in Appendix 1.) A fundamental principle of OO is encapsulation on the basis of data—or 'things'. Consider a 'customer'. A customer has data (or attributes)—a number, a name, an address, a balance, etc. A customer also has associated behaviour. It can be deleted, changed, created; it can be printed or displayed. It can be queried (e.g. 'What is your balance?').

OO encapsulates the customer by wrapping into one software unit first a definition of the data for any given instance of the class 'customer', and secondly the functions required to give the customer some behaviour. These functions operate on the data (the attributes of customer).

Now, object-oriented programming languages (OOPLs) apply object orientation to the components being used in the build process. They seldom (if ever) focus directly on the *thing being built—and which will be delivered to the end-user*.

We, on the other hand, need to *deliver* objects as independent executables. Thus we must apply OO to the unit of delivery. We call such a deliverable a 'cooperative business object'—a CBO. (To be absolutely precise, I mean, of course, deliver *classes* not objects. See Appendix 1 for an explanation of the difference.) Whether we use procedural or OO languages to *build* a CBO is beside the point, as illustrated in Fig. 3.4.

Now these objects need to talk to one another. For this, they use messages. Since the objects are produced as independent executables, the messaging mechanisms must be external to the objects, and this in turn points to the need for some form of run-time layer of middleware (infrastructure) software. This message externalization is a major difference between these objects and the sort found in OOPLs.

Of course, the infrastructure is the 64 000 dollar question. But if there were such an infrastructure, then the difficulties referred to above could be handled by that infrastructure. The result would be as shown in Fig. 3.5, where CBOs as deliverables can communicate happily with each other at run-time. Figure 3.5 shows a collection of CBOs, some written using an OOPL, others using procedural languages, and where one of the CBOs (CBO3) is remote. The figure indicates that

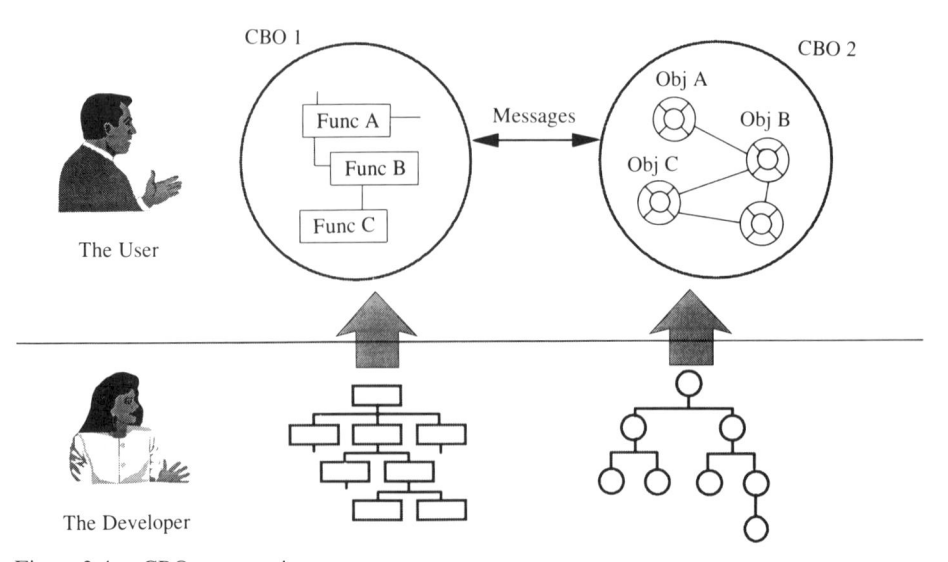

Figure 3.4. CBO cooperation.

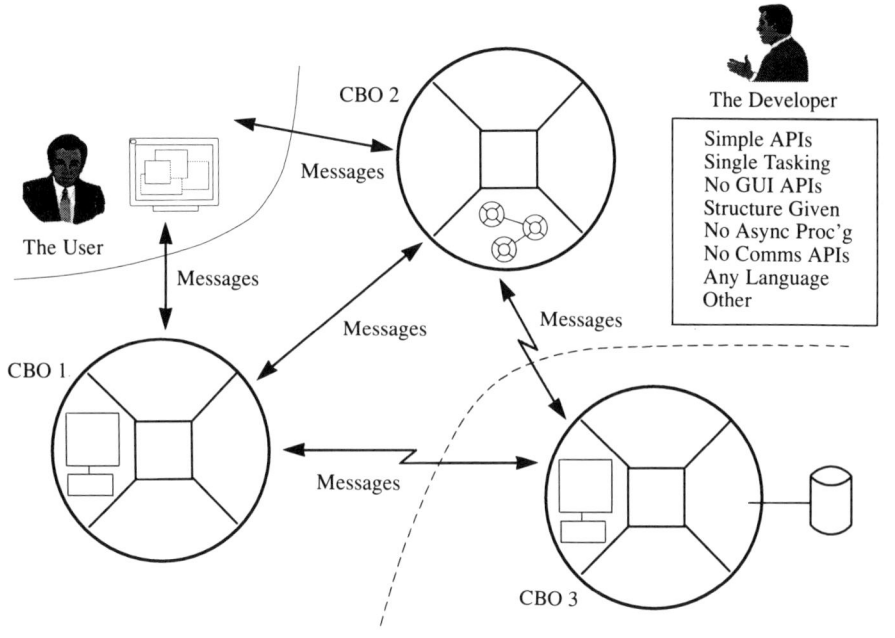

Figure 3.5. CBO integration.

the developer does not have to worry about system-level complexities. Multitasking, communications APIs, GUI APIs, cross-language considerations, etc. are all handled for the developer by the same middleware layer that handles messages.

This same middleware also converts *all* external events into the same messaging API, as well as providing all of the system-level GUI functions required. But what does CBO application code *look* like? Figure 3.6 shows (at a high level of abstraction) what a CBO programmer might write.

First, a CBO is event-driven. It is invoked by the infrastructure when a message needs to be handled by it. Secondly, the CBO handles the message (shown by testing for the message within a 'case' statement). If the message is not handled, then it is passed to the CBO's superclass. Note that a CBO may send a message to another CBO in order to complete the handling of the incoming message. The CBOs can each be written in different languages.

A CBO is not a kind of mini-application, running in its own address space. While that may on occasion be required, in general, several CBOs should be able to run in the same address space—perhaps in the same thread (or task). From the operating system point of view, this makes CBOs quite fine-grained units of execution. The underlying CBO infrastructure must enable this level of granularity as well as coarser levels.

Finally, we need to consider the data carried by messages between CBOs. Here we need some form of type-independent data stream, which carries information about the data itself. It must carry data labels, in other words. Performance is a prime concern here, so building and parsing this data stream must be exceedingly

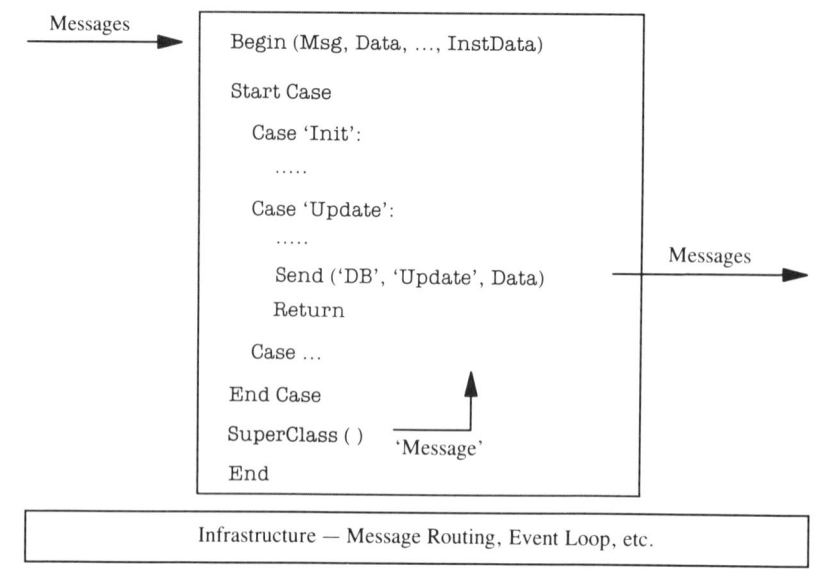

```
            Messages    ┌──────────────────────────────────────┐
         ─────────────▶ │ Begin (Msg, Data, ..., InstData)     │
                        │                                      │
                        │ Start Case                           │
                        │                                      │
                        │   Case 'Init':                       │
                        │      .....                           │
                        │                                      │
                        │   Case 'Update':                     │
                        │      .....                                         Messages
                        │      Send ('DB', 'Update', Data)     │ ─────────────▶
                        │      Return                          │
                        │                                      │
                        │   Case ...                           │
                        │                                      │
                        │ End Case                        ▲    │
                        │ SuperClass ( )   ───────────────┘    │
                        │                    'Message'         │
                        │ End                                  │
                        └──────────────────────────────────────┘
                        ┌──────────────────────────────────────┐
                        │ Infrastructure — Message Routing, Event Loop, etc. │
                        └──────────────────────────────────────┘
```

Figure 3.6. A cooperative business object.

efficient. This aspect of required CBO infrastructure is discussed in greater detail in Sec. 8.4.2.

3.3 A restatement

That a CBO is the end-product of a development process, rather than a component used within it, is so important that, in this section we restate what we have said already, but in a different form. If what we have said so far needs no restatement, please skip this section. If not, please read on.

Let us take the example of a financial institution, where a user is required to handle account transfer, customer enquiries and account maintenance (or update).

The question we now want to address is, 'How should we structure the application software in order to present this function—money transfers, customer enquiries and account update—to the user?'

We might have done a data entity analysis of this and related business areas, and we might have identified three base entities (using the term fairly loosely)—account, transfer (a relationship between accounts) and customer. Further, we might have done some process analysis that showed, among other things, that we needed to display four things to the user: customer, a list of customers, an account and a transfer slip. Treating the base entities as servers, and the others as clients (which might reside on the PC), we arrive at the conclusion that our application software must handle the things shown in Fig. 3.7.

Traditionally, when we build code to deliver business function through computer systems, what we do is to encapsulate a given process into what we call 'an

Items

[Customer PC]   [Cust List PC]   [Cust DB Server]

                                   [Accs DB Server]

[Account PC]   [Xfer Slip PC]   [Xfer Reg Server]

Figure 3.7. Example—items to be handled by application software.

application'. This is shown in Fig. 3.8, where we have wrapped the seven items we identified above into our three applications. Tidying up this picture gives us the situation shown in Fig. 3.9.

Here we see the major aspects of the application problem. How can we address this problem? The answer is not to encapsulate business function and processes in applications. Rather, it is to build CBOs—individual software executables that are compiled and link-edited separately.

The key here is to encapsulate on the basis of the data, not on the basis of the process or function. This, of course, is the idea behind object orientation. What is new here is the idea of developing and producing independently executable objects

Applications

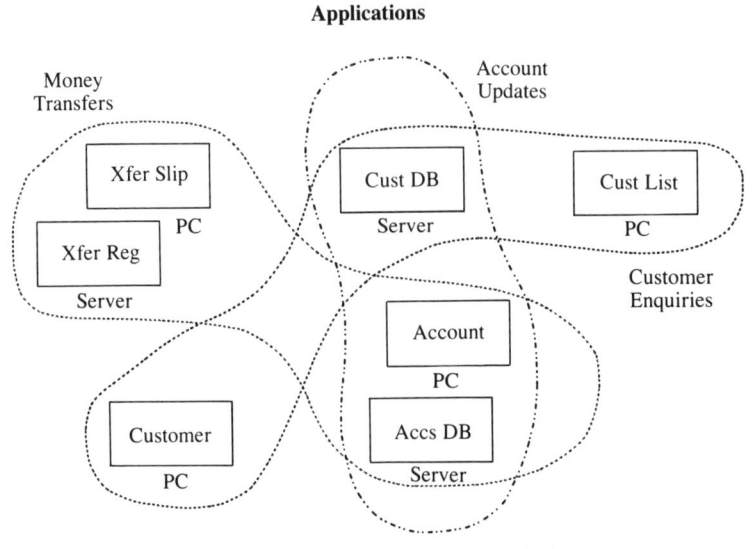

Figure 3.8. Example—applications by functional encapsulation.

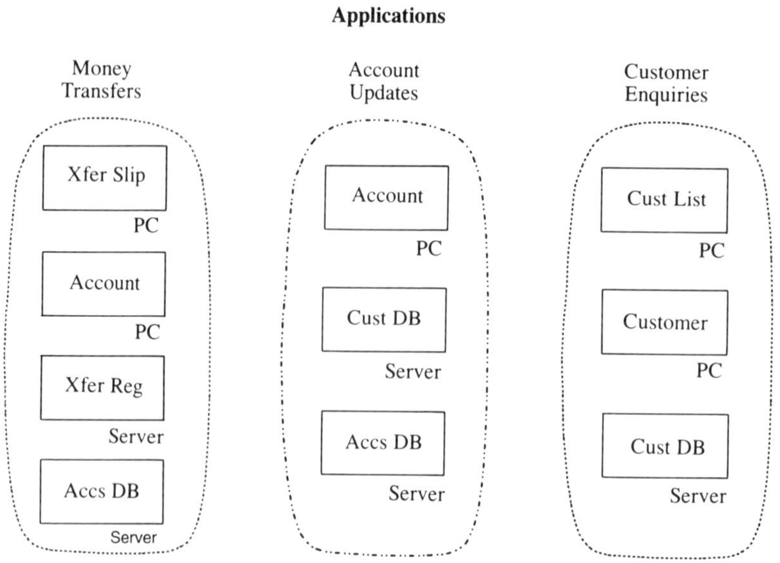

Applications

```
   Money              Account              Customer
  Transfers           Updates              Enquiries
```

- Money Transfers: Xfer Slip (PC), Account (PC), Xfer Reg (Server), Accs DB (Server)
- Account Updates: Account (PC), Cust DB (Server), Accs DB (Server)
- Customer Enquiries: Cust List (PC), Customer (PC), Cust DB (Server)

Figure 3.9. Example—duplication in applications.

rather than producing applications whose source code is organized on the basis of objects.

In building an independent software object of this sort, the developer *knows* that it is of limited use all by itself, and that its real use is to be used with other independently developed objects at execution time, communicating with each other through messages. This is quite unlike applications, which are generally built without any idea of communicating with other as yet undefined applications.

It is true that today's industrial-strength applications are almost always built with interfaces to other applications—either existing or planned. However, it is often the process of planning and managing such integration that causes so much of the delay, rigidity and complexity afflicting current application suites. Developers need to establish documents of understanding between each other; need to define interfaces; need to ensure change control, etc. CBOs on the other hand, being independently-developed, promise to allow much easier integration both with existing and planned developments, and—importantly—with those not yet conceived.

Figure 3.10 illustrates a set of such independent objects. Note that account maintenance required us to implement a customer object. Because the customer object was an independently developed object, then at run-time we also gain (for free!) three more capabilities—without development having built any applications:

- Customer service (elements of)
- Customer locate
- Customer enquiry

Independent Objects

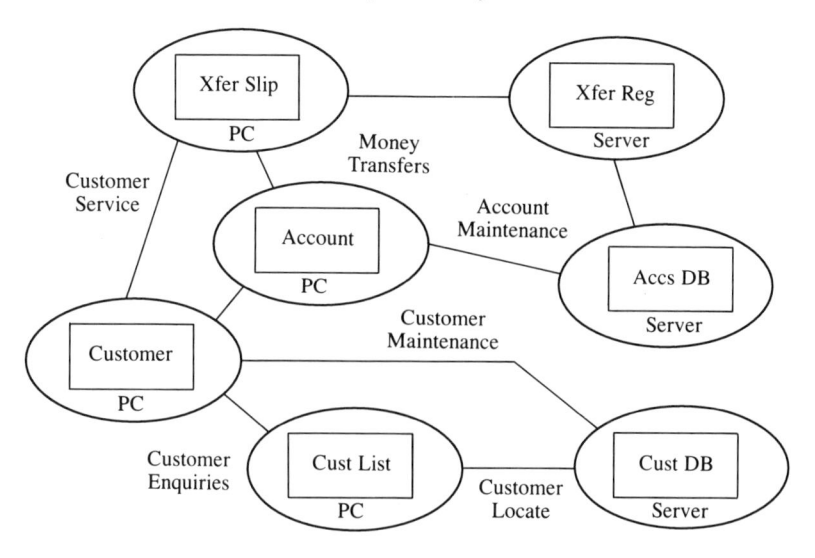

Figure 3.10. Example—independent objects.

The design point for independently developed objects is at the level of a business entity—such as a 'customer', an 'invoice', an 'account', an 'order form', a 'transfer slip', etc. This is why we call them *business objects*. To reflect the key point of their being independently developed, and hence their need (generally) to cooperate with each other to perform many business-related processes, we call them *cooperative business objects*—or CBOs for short.

So far, we have seen how borrowing the OO idea of encapsulation on the basis of data is very useful. Is there anything more we can usefully borrow from object orientation? Well, consider again our transfer slip object. Its behaviour is as follows:

- It knows about two accounts.
- It knows about an amount.
- It understands that the amount is to be transferred between two accounts.
- It has data (and probably an identifying number).
- It can send a message to a register log object to effect the transfer.

Now consider that we want to add another function for the user—a 'sweep', where an amount is transferred from account A to account B on a periodic basis (say once per month), if the balance in A is greater than some pre-set value. Would we have to write a new money transfer object?

Here we can draw on the OO technique of 'inheritance' (discussed in Appendix 1). What we could do is to build a subclass on our transfer slip CBO (remember that a subclass in OO terms, typically provides a *superset* of behaviour—the behaviour of the subclass *plus* the behaviour of its superclass, the object from which it is subclassed). Thus we might build a subclass that had this behaviour:

- It knows about how often the sweep is to be done.

The rest of its behaviour would be *inherited* from the transfer CBO. Thus just by adding a subclass of transfer, we get an object that:[1]

- Knows about two accounts—one to be debited, the other credited.
- Knows about an amount (below which the transfer should not occur).
- Understands that the amount is to be transferred between two accounts.
- Has data (and probably an identifying number).
- Can send a message to a register log object to effect the transfer.
- Knows about how often the sweep is to be done.

And since the subclass may be in a different language than the superclass, we see a level of software re-use that has long been desired, but never—until now—delivered.

The key to enabling this is to enable inheritance mechanisms across independently developed CBOs—which also means across languages. Thus we see another requirement on our infrastructure.

3.4 Summary

The cause of the *integration problem* is the very structure of code we have been building for the last 30 years or so. An 'application' is an island of function, devoted to a specific task. It hides the things in it—things that are needed to perform the function. Because of this hiding, it is very difficult to have applications inter-operate without each application having an intimate understanding of the internal workings of others. The solution is to build CBOs *instead* of applications.

If we build CBOs, then the picture would look like Fig. 3.11, where IT would first have done an object analysis of a given business process, and would then have built the CBOs needed by the user to perform that process.

Note, however, that if a CBO has already been built for another process, it is not rebuilt. It is not even included in other code (as would be the case with many object-oriented programming languages). The user would just re-use it (on the object-based user interface). This illustrates the principle of object re-use—*by the user*, and also by other CBOs.

Again, the use of CBOs rather than applications makes it feasible to do something about the departmental processes that are seldom addressed by AD departments. For instead of building trivial applications, the AD function could develop

---

[1]At the detail design level, this example is not quite correct. But it is certainly sufficiently valid at the level of the discussion to illustrate the point.

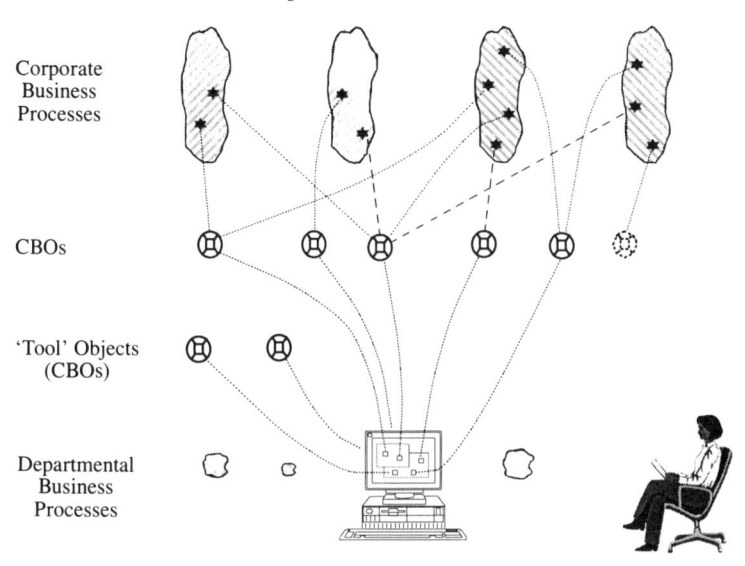

Figure 3.11. Business objects

re-usable 'tools'—such as a pad of Post-It notes, or a specialized container (some form of folder, perhaps). These would then be able to work with other CBOs.

Cooperation between CBOs is all-important to addressing user needs, and is achieved by CBOs sending messages to each other. Thus systems are built of independent CBOs, acting on messages sent to them, and in turn sending messages to other CBOs.

For these objects to live on today's operating environments, some form of 'middleware' or software infrastructure needs to be built. But, just as, if you want to build transactions, then a batch spooling system is the wrong software infrastructure, so existing infrastructures are wrong for CBOs. A new infrastructure is needed (as shown in Fig. 3.12).

We will discuss some of the characteristics of such an infrastructure later (Chapter 8), but first let us concentrate on the other great impediment to ease of programming—the client/server connection.

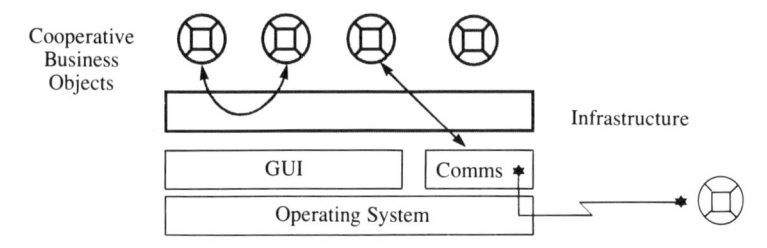

Figure 3.12. Business process integration.

Part Two
The programmer—application structures

In this part of the book, we develop a general application model of cooperative processing in client/server and distributed systems. (The term 'application' has come to denote two things. Used as an adjective, it denotes code that implements business function rather than system function. Used as a noun, it is often interpreted as an executable that encapsulates a business process. In the last chapter, we showed how building 'applications' (the second of these two meanings) was part of the integration problem, and that building CBOs was preferable. From this point in the book, we will use the term 'application' only in its first meaning—as an adjective denoting business as opposed to system function.)

The model is developed in terms of the desired *shape* of application code, and a cross-system (program-to-program) *structure*. The shape and structure together are aimed at delivering ease of programming.

We show how a shape combining messaging and 'event-loop' code best meets the aim. Further, this shape turns out to be a true subset of the structure of CBOs. Thus the shape of application code that best handles object-based user interfaces also turns out to be excellently suited to handle cooperative processing.

Our general model for cooperative processing in client/server systems identifies two major structural elements or 'domains'—the user interface domain, and the shared resource domain. Within these two domains, we identify a number of different *types* of CBO. These types, within the structure identified, prove to be particularly useful in addressing a number of the common design problems of client/server systems.

Cooperative systems are different

Real cooperative client/server applications have gained a reputation for being difficult to design and implement. There are broadly speaking two reasons for this:

1 *Programming difficulty* Building application code that cooperates across PC and mainframe has proved in practice to require very high skill levels in program design and implementation.

2 *Systems management* Viable systems are manageable systems. It is only recently that we have seen the introduction of systems management products that start properly to support distributed and heterogeneous systems.

In this book, we focus on the first of these problem areas.

Consider client/server systems in general. We can perceive these general characteristics:

- The essence of GUI application code on the PC is that it is event-driven. Events are generated by the user; the application code reacts to those events, does what is necessary and then quiesces, waiting for the next event.
- Shared resources such as data are normally located on systems such as mainframes, local area network (LAN) servers or minicomputers, which are accessed by many PCs concurrently. Corporate systems (even those of very small companies) seldom live entirely in a single PC.
- There will usually need to be application code on the server as well as at the PC.

Ah, you may say, what about distributed database? Then you can have all the application code on the PC, can't you? Well, on the face of it, that is true. But, as we shall see, it is not as true as it appears. In any case, and perhaps more importantly from our viewpoint, it turns out to make little difference to the application developer.

The inevitability of event-driven code at the PC means that the shared resource systems (the servers) cannot 'drive' the user interface. Rather, the system must be organized such that it is the servers that are 'driven' by the client PCs—but in such a way as to enable business rules to be enforced, and to protect the integrity of corporate shared resources.

So the first step to client/server wisdom is to recognize that the traditional roles of mainframe (or minicomputer) with character-based terminals are, *must* be, stood on their head. Instead of the mainframe/minicomputer containing code that drives a dialogue with the user through the terminal, with client/server the PC contains the equivalent of the 'dialogue' code, and drives an essentially passive 'server'—the mainframe.

Since there often needs to be application-level code on the server, this means that code on the client needs to be able to communicate with code on the server. We give the name 'cooperative processing' to the situation where two pieces of application-level code in different systems (or at least in different address spaces) need to communicate with each other to do some single piece of work.

Cooperative systems are difficult

The developer who first sets out to build cooperative business code meets a whole number of difficulties, from handling an advanced GUI on the one hand to understanding how to ensure data integrity on the other. The response to this is often to build some form of middleware to make the job of the application programmer easier.

In practice, it is often the case that each cooperative application developer has had to design and implement his or her own middleware. This is so in spite of products aimed at this area: some make programming simple, but do not allow full exploitation (or sometimes even partial exploitation) of the object-based user interface; some provide useful APIs for connection, but do not provide for other complex areas (such as multi-tasking); others provide a closed environment, often for a single language only.

The reason for this is that there has been no general model of what—in software structure terms—a cooperative processing system *is*. There has been no generally accepted notion of what it is that we would like application programmers to build—and hence no well understood appreciation of the services and facilities that should be made available to those programmers.

We need such a model because building a cooperative application is *different*. If we treat it like previous application structures, then we will find things difficult. If we accept that it is different, but do not have a *model* that explains the differences, then it will still be difficult.

One of the major challenges to ease of programming in client/server systems arises from what the average application programmer is confronted with, in terms of understanding and of APIs, when connecting code on one system to code on another. A programmer finds things easier when there is a generally agreed structural model that describes the *shape* of the software to be written. Thus, while it may take a week or so for someone new to transaction processing to understand the nature of the code that must be written, once that shape is understood, things become much easier.

Objectives of the model

The objective therefore is to construct a programmer's model that exhibits the following characteristics:

- A simple conceptual structure for the programmer
- Language independence
- Enables application integration
- Ease of programming
- Wide applicability

In this part, we develop a model that has been proven to meet these objectives. The context for discussion is a client/server system where the PCs have an object-based GUI and the servers have application code. This is probably the more complex case. Our model, however, will be equally applicable to other system shapes—for example, server-to-server and general peer-to-peer application code relationships.

It is important here to focus on the area of discussion. We are not talking about basic communication protocols, or of system mechanisms such as RPC (remote procedure call), or of systems management across a network, or of underlying safe store and forwarding of cross-system messages. What we are talking about is making it easy for the average application programmer to communicate with other (remote) pieces of application code in a way that hides system-level facilities such as the low-level communication APIs.

A major surprise is that we find that the structures that best allow us to implement the object-based GUI—CBOs—are equally useful in solving the ease-of-programming problem for connecting two (possibly separately developed) pieces of application code across a network. And just as 'transactions' (as a desired application structure) need an underlying software infrastructure to support them—a 'transaction processor'—so CBOs need an infrastructure.

We develop the discussion as follows:

- Chapter 4 develops the model as the application developer would see it, and provides an overview of the structure. In particular, this chapter introduces a most important design concept—the separation of application code to do with serving a single user from application code to do with handling shared resources.
- Chapter 5 looks in some detail at the first of these two areas—application code that serves a single user—and develops the concept of two *kinds* of CBO within this domain.
- Chapter 6 discusses the second area—application code that handles shared resources—and introduces three different kinds of CBO within this domain.
- On the face of it, it seems that having five different types of CBO does not lead to ease of programming. Chapter 7 shows how these five types represent a superset, which can be both subsetted and coalesced in many situations. In essence, the five types of CBO represent a way of thinking about design, rather than a rigid recipe.
- Chapter 8 summarizes the functions and facilities required by the infrastructure, and briefly discusses the importance of self-defining data.

4
Structural overview

In this chapter, starting from the viewpoint of traditionally structured application code, we develop the argument in favour of CBOs as the foundation for a general model. We do this by addressing three main questions:

- What are the *base requirements* for application structuring in a client/server system?
- What *shape* of application code should be written if ease of programming is to be achieved?
- What is the end-to-end structure of a client/server system?

Making programming easy is the crux of the matter. But unless there is a consensus about the general 'structure' of the application code—and what should be distributed where—then we cannot design a general-purpose application-enabling layer that will make it easy.

Given that CBOs are the right *shape* for application code, we further develop a *structure* based on the separation of 'user logic' from 'business logic'. We develop not only *technical* reasons for this separation, but also sound *design* reasons.

4.1 Base requirements

To begin the discussion, we propose the following four axioms:

1 There will be application code on the PC that handles the GUI, and thus serves the user. For the moment, we will call this code *user logic*.
2 In general, the user logic must be able to respond to keyboard or mouse 'events' within a tenth of a second or less (otherwise the GUI becomes well-nigh unusable).

   For example, suppose the user has requested some data, and then changes his or her mind and presses the 'cancel' button. The user logic code must respond to this straight away (if only to say 'please wait'). Again, for direct manipulation (drag/drop by the user), it is sometimes necessary to refer to the user logic code to see if one object is allowed to be dropped on another. This requires GUI-level response times within application code (i.e. the user logic). (Clearly this is not *always* the case. My point is that we must *allow* in our thinking and in our design for such response times.) Although not always required, such fast response time within application code must be provided for by our model—otherwise it would not be a general-purpose model.

3 There will be application code that accesses the shared resources needed by the PC user. We could call this code the 'shared resource logic'; but since the shared resource is mostly data, for the time being, and for ease of reference, we shall just talk about data. Hence we shall call this application code the *data access logic*.

4 The delay in accessing shared resources will generally be (much) more than a tenth of a second. In addition, such shared resources will not typically be located on the PC.

From these four givens, we can see a key design consideration: there is a significant difference in response time between the application code that handles the GUI—the user logic—and the code that handles the shared resource—the data access logic.

The user logic code must return to the underlying system-level presentation layer within around a tenth of a second. The data access logic, on the other hand, cannot be expected to respond reliably within this time. Indeed, we may be talking of tens of seconds (two orders of magnitude greater).

The only effective way to handle this difference is to separate the two pieces of code, such that they run at least in different threads of control (tasks), or in different processes (address spaces), or maybe on different machines.

Running the two pieces of code in different threads of control means that the connection between the two must be *asynchronous*. That is, code initiating a request from the user logic (managing the GUI) to the data access logic must not be held up waiting for the response. Here we have a key distinguishing characteristic of cooperative processing in a client/server environment: Cooperative processing applications require *asynchronous* requests and responses between user logic and data access logic. The top part of Fig. 4.1 shows this—the separation between the user logic and the data access logic by an asynchronous connection. This in turn means that we need a simple way for the programmer to handle asynchronous requests.

Notice that this model is insensitive to the placement of the data access logic. As shown at the bottom of Fig. 4.1, whether or not we are using distributed database makes no difference to the model. Placing structured query language (SQL) calls on the PC does not remove the disparity in response times between the user logic and the data access logic. It merely means that we have to do asynchronous connection *within* the PC. However, for ease of exposition, we will assume that the data access code will not be on the PC. This assumption makes no difference to the overall model—it merely serves as a useful vehicle for discussion.

Structural overview

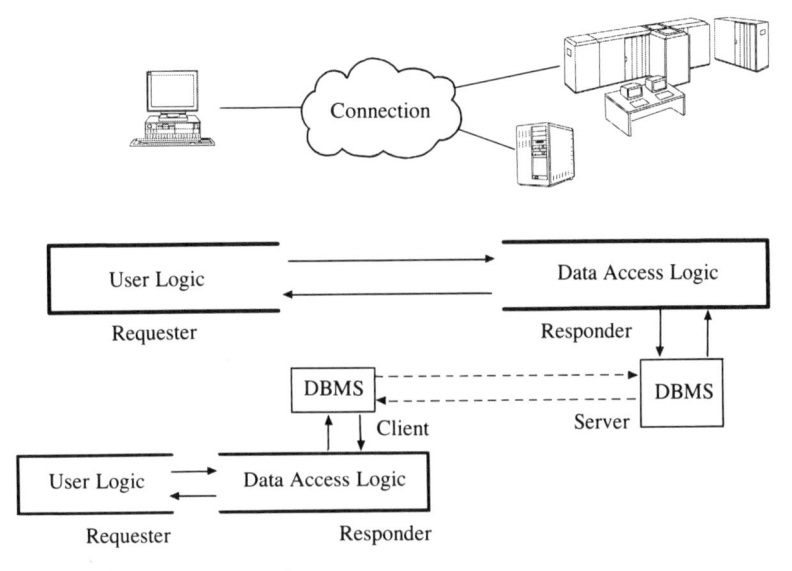

Figure 4.1. Client/server separation.

The key point here is that user logic must not be blocked while the data access logic is executing; otherwise the user interface will block.

Our model, then, must recognize that:

- There will be application code (user logic) that handles the GUI and is separate from
- Different application code that handles the shared resource (data access logic); and that
- User logic and data access logic must run in different threads of control, but in such a way that
- There is a simple mechanism provided for the application programmer to connect these two pieces of code.

These considerations give us the model shown in Fig. 4.2(a) (for clarity, the operating system components and their APIs are not shown). The thread boundary is shown as a vertical dotted line.

So far, we have talked only of the user logic (GUI) and data access logic. But what about the business logic? And what do we mean by 'business logic'?

Business logic

What people *normally* think of as 'business logic' is that application code which *enforces* business rules. For example, code that ensures that a customer order is either completely recorded on the database, or completely rejected, is business logic. 'Complete recording' of an order will often entail the update of several different database tables (e.g. order header, order detail, product and maybe

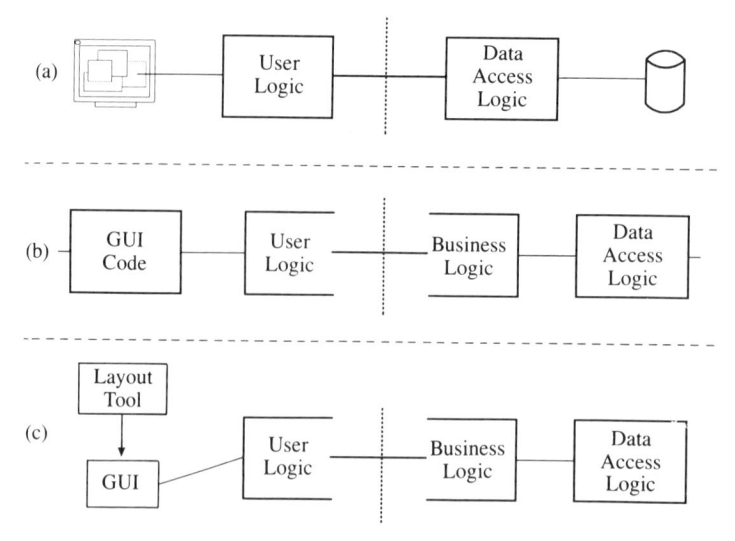

Figure 4.2. Cooperative processing model (1).

customer). In other words, 'business logic' is often associated intimately with commit scope processing.

We can distinguish this sort of logic from that required to access a single table or file (data access logic), or to do cross-field validation on data entry (user logic), and we call it 'business logic'.

Thus we introduce business logic as a separate thing from data access logic. But since it is normally dedicated to ensuring the integrity of data (and shared resources generally), and will typically not return with a 'yes' or 'no' until the data has been properly accessed, then it is placed with data access logic on the other side of the thread boundary from user logic.

An example that serves to show the difference is as follows. Code that checks whether a customer is over credit limit is business logic. On the other hand, code that displays a warning to the user that the customer is over credit limit is user logic. Again, code that reads a record from a file is really data access logic; while code that checks that if an order header record is recorded, then at least one order detail line must also be written, is business logic.

Consider an order entry process. Figure 4.3 illustrates the main actions within such a process (for simplicity, we exclude back-ordering, stock allocation and error conditions). Notice how many of the things that need to be done are primarily to do with accessing data, or supporting the user. However, the kernel of the process—the part that *must* be done (even if it is a batch process, where the 'user' parts would have been done via data entry and edit runs)—is business logic.

But where should this logic be?

We have said that business logic should be on the same side of the thread boundary as the data access logic. In general, the thread boundary defines the boundary

Action	Related to:
Identify customer (and credit limit)	Data
For each part required:	
Identify part required, and	Data
Capture quantity required	User
Find stock-on-hand of parts	Data
Assess if on-hand is sufficient	Business
If not, warn the user	User
Enter special instructions	User
Check if over credit limit	Business
If so, warn the user	User
Validate order	Business
Record order on database	Data
Commit order	Data

Figure 4.3. User logic, data logic and business logic.

between 'client' and 'server'. Often this boundary will be much more than just a thread boundary—it will be a communications link. Business logic is frequently associated with commit scope processing (that is, code effecting business rules which must be followed between receipt of a request by the server and its response to the client). In that case, the 'server' will normally be a shared resource system which is physically separate from the PC. On the other hand, where the data access logic is handled by a distributed database facility on the PC, then the business logic *and* the data access logic may be on the PC—but still on the other side of the thread boundary from the user logic. User logic (which will often include simple data validation) should be in the PC unless it is obvious from the nature of the logic that it should be done elsewhere. In building real systems, this is almost always a trivial and obvious decision.

In this categorization, we are not attempting to define rigorously the differences between the three types of application logic, nor to build a model with precise theoretical boundaries. What we have done here is to focus on the major differences between the necessary bits of code in the client/server system. Later, we shall give each part more precise responsibilities. For the time being, the important thing is the separation of business and data logic as the preserve of the server, and user (presentation and interaction) logic as the preserve of the client. Thus we can enrich our model by adding business logic, as shown in Fig 4.2(b). (For clarity, in Fig. 4.2(b) we omit the PC screen and the actual data (the disk storage). From now on, we will not show these.)

GUI code

But why have we also added another block called 'GUI code' in this figure? And why is the task boundary shown as being between user logic and business logic, rather than between GUI code and user logic?

Consider the GUI API provided by the system. Handling this API is generally complex and requires a very high level of C programming skills. We need to isolate the application programmer from this complexity if we are to achieve our ease-of-programming objectives. This is often done by providing a window layout tool, which generates the required low-level GUI code. We redraw the model to show this in Fig. 4.2(c), where we label the GUI code as just 'GUI', being produced by some appropriate window layout tool.

But what about the task boundary? Well, and this is an important point, often not fully appreciated, the task is as shown because, in the general case: The user logic on the PC must sometimes respond at GUI speeds to user events.

This does not mean, of course, that there *cannot* be a task boundary between the GUI code and the user logic; indeed, such a task or process boundary may be very useful depending on specific PC operating system implementations. What is being said here is that there *does* have to be such a boundary between the user logic and the business logic.

Thus there is a technical reason in addition to a design reason for separating user logic from business and data logics.

Before examining this separation in more detail, we now take a necessary detour to answer the question, 'How are the separate pieces of cooperative code connected?' How does the programmer access one from the other? This is perhaps the key question in enabling us to design easy-to-build code, and hence to define the underlying 'enabling' infrastructure required.

4.2 Application code structure

In this section, we address three areas of difficulty:

- What *kind* of connection—between two separate pieces of application code—should we provide for the programmer?
- What *API model* best implements the kind of connection chosen?
- Is there a specific *structure* for application code that delivers ease-of-programming more than any other?

4.2.1 Kinds of connection

Our focus here is a *single interaction* between two pieces of application software across a communications link. There are, in general, three different design approaches for such an interaction:

1 *Master/slave* This is where one end (the master) owns and drives the other (the slave), and usually implies a great deal of knowledge at the master end about the state of the slave end. The master controls and directs the whole process. An example of this is where code on one system drives a non-programmable terminal through the code on a screen controller. In this

case, the 'single' interaction is probably very long-running—from log-in to log-out.

2 *Peer-to-peer*   This is where each end of the link is of equal importance. Either end can initiate an interaction. Usually, peer-to-peer requires each end to know detail about the state of the other, and protocols are defined to communicate these states. An example of this might be a distributed database system, where, to ensure coordinated recovery, each database must discuss recovery, sync point and rollback matters with the other. Any of the databases can initiate this with any of the others. The single interaction here may be short or long duration, and is characterized by each end both sending and receiving within that interaction.

3 *Client/server*   Here, a 'requester' piece of code (the client) initiates a request to a 'responder' piece of code (the server). (Here we use the phrase 'client/server' in its 'connection design' sense; see the Glossary for the other two meanings.) Essentially the server is there to provide a service of some sort for any client that requires it. The server knows nothing about the state of the client. The server is (typically) passive. An example of this might be a credit check agency, which provides a 'server' interface to other companies' computers requesting a credit check. This design is based on the following principles:

(a) The client makes a request of a server; the server responds back to the client.
(b) In each completed interaction between client and server, the client sends one and only one request. This request starts the interaction. The server responds with one response (which may be in several parts). This response ends the interaction.
(c) No state information is retained in the client or the server about the state of the interaction. That is, each interaction between client and server is independent of other interactions. Of course, both the client and server may retain information about their *own* state across multiple interactions. What we are saying here is that, for any given interaction, there is no dependence on either previous or future interactions for that interaction to complete successfully.

This design is sometimes called a 'one-shot transaction', to imply that there is no continued conversation or dialogue between the client and the server. Note that servers can also be clients. The processing logic within a server could make requests of other servers. In that case, the requesting server would be a client to those other servers.

From these three, we choose the client/server design as the basis for connection between the separate pieces of cooperative code. The reasons a client/server design is preferable are:

- It is simpler than the others, owing to the lack of state information that needs to be held about the interaction.
- You get much looser 'binding' between each end of the interaction than otherwise. The looser the binding between two pieces of code, then the greater the potential for re-use. Thus several clients may use the same server. Servers can be re-used across application boundaries. Several servers may be accessed by a single client.

While this form of connection may not suit all occasions (for example, if the thing you are building is a distributed relational database, then it may be insufficient), it seems to suit most, if not all, of the situations met in commercial data processing—the 'core' or 'mission-critical' business systems. It also seems to suit many other situations. In particular, it is an excellent base for a *business* interaction, where several such interactions, at the business logic level, must be carried out between different pieces of application code.

4.2.2 Programming models

But what does a programmer actually have to *write* to effect the connection between two separate pieces of application code? Well, when a programmer writes code, he or she is actually doing two things:

- Implementing a concept—a *model*—of what he or she wants to do.
- Obeying some syntactical rules about how to implement that model.

The second of these is of much lesser importance. If the syntax is particularly tortuous, then it merely makes the thing the programmer wants to do more laborious. The first is much more important. If a programmer cannot easily conceptualize the effect that each line of code has, then the task is made extremely difficult.

In Fig. 4.4 we show on the left a number of different tasks that a programmer might want to perform. In each case, the programmer is easily able to visualize the effect of the code that needs to be written. This code is shown in the centre of the figure. Depending on the language, the programmer will either do a call to make something happen (as with the C language, for example), or there will be some built-in language syntax (as with COBOL), or there will be some statement that is pre-compiled into a call (as is often the case with EXEC SQL ...). Figure 4.4 shows examples of all three. Finally, down the right of the figure are the underlying system mechanisms that implement the code that is written. Note that the implementers of such mechanisms are usually also the designers of the APIs that access them.

In the first example, the programmer is reading a record from a file. The programmer is protected from all the underlying complexities of the file system by the design of the API to that file system. This allows him or her to write the simple statement READ FILE INTO RCD_A to implement his or her image of the process.

Structural overview

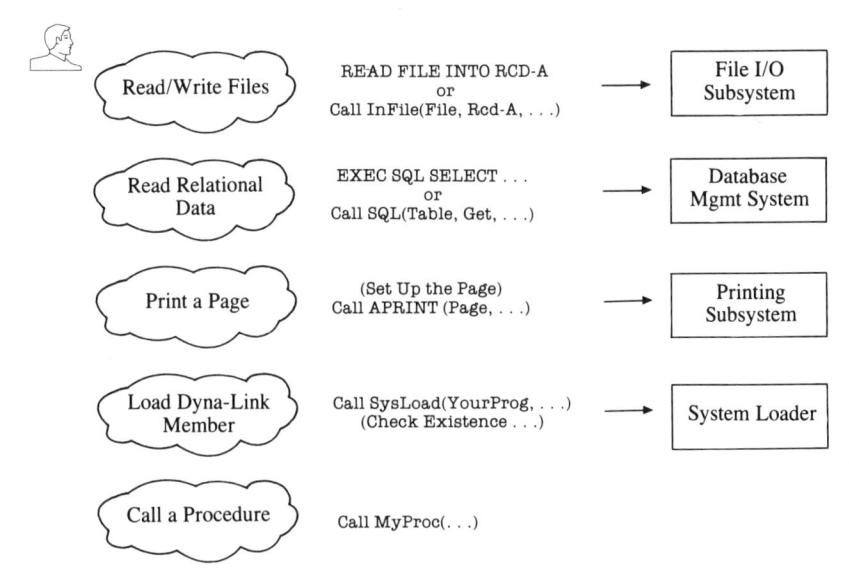

Read/Write Files	READ FILE INTO RCD-A or Call InFile(File, Rcd-A, . . .)	→ File I/O Subsystem
Read Relational Data	EXEC SQL SELECT . . . or Call SQL(Table, Get, . . .)	→ Database Mgmt System
Print a Page	(Set Up the Page) Call APRINT (Page, . . .)	→ Printing Subsystem
Load Dyna-Link Member	Call SysLoad(YourProg, . . .) (Check Existence . . .)	→ System Loader
Call a Procedure	Call MyProc(. . .)	

Figure 4.4. Models, APIs and implementations.

Thus the designer of this API ensured that the API corresponded to the programmer's model of what the programmer was actually doing.

Thus: Implementers of APIs for cooperative processing must first design the application programmer's *model*. Designers either do this explicitly or they do it unconsciously (because they cannot avoid it!).

Note also that the examples of code in the centre of Fig. 4.4 include a 'call' form (such as might be written in the C language). Self-evidently, although the syntax of each of these calls is similar, the programmer is doing quite different things, and has a different model of what is happening in each case. We will come back to this later.

In providing an API model for the programmer, we must above all else keep it simple. It must be easy to use. This means that:

- 'System-level' complexities must be invisible to the programmer. Such complexities include:
  —Getting across a task/process boundary to handle the asynchronous nature of the connection
  —Synchronizing application code with code running in the other task/process
  —The physical location of the other piece of business logic
  —Driving the underlying communications API
  —Initiating or loading the other piece of business logic
  —Routing the response back to the requester
- The API itself must be simple (a few lines of code at the most).

It is for these reasons that many currently available APIs are not suitable (e.g. pipes, sockets, redirected file input/output I/O). For example, none of these will get the programmer transparently over the task boundary.

Business objects

There are probably four different choices for an API model:

- Remote procedure call (RPC)
- Conversation
- Make the interaction look identical to some existing external facility (for example, like file input/output)
- Messaging

As we shall see, none of these is entirely satisfactory by itself. We will need to add a further factor—the *shape* of the code that deals with the API. Before discussing that, however, let us look at each of the four models.

Remote procedure call

The idea behind RPC is that the programmer merely calls a procedure (a subroutine) as usual, but the procedure is actually outside the program—in another process or address space, on either the same or a different system.

Figure 4.5 shows this. The programmer calls a procedure. The 'system' intercepts the call, and routes it to the remote procedure, which then executes. Meanwhile, the calling program waits—just as it would do if the procedure was local. When the remote procedure has executed, it returns control (together with any data and maybe a return code) to the 'system', which then returns control (with the data and return code) to the next sequential instruction in the calling program. If any code translation needs to be done (e.g. ASCII to EBCDIC, or one form of floating point to another), then the 'system' will do it automatically. A different form of RPC from that shown in Fig. 4.5 is where the programmer passes a handle that identifies the routine to be invoked by the response. In this case, the programmer has to work out what to do if, before his or her program can continue, the response is needed. Perhaps wait (if that is an option)—synchronously.

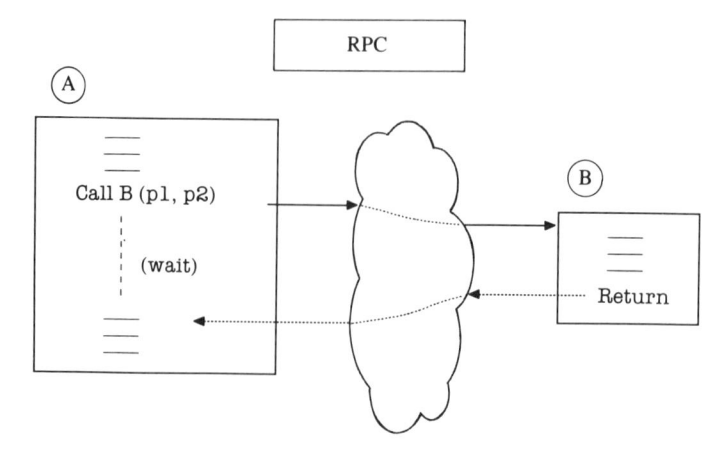

Figure 4.5. Client/server models—RPC.

Structural overview

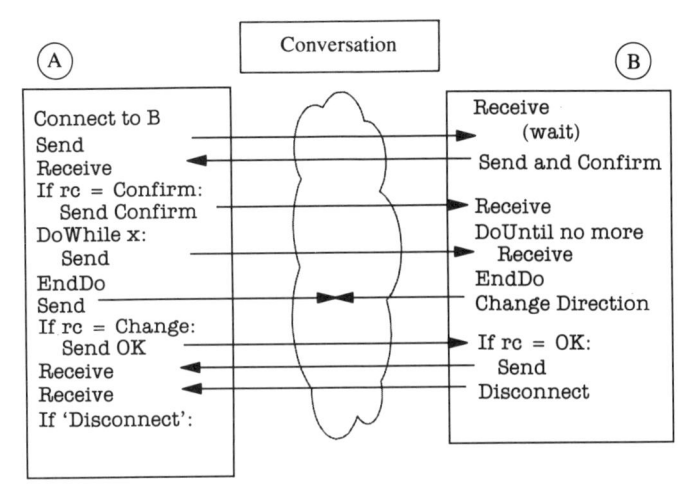

```
         A                Conversation                B

Connect to B                                    Receive
Send                                             (wait)
Receive                                         Send and Confirm
If rc = Confirm:
    Send Confirm                                Receive
DoWhile x:                                      DoUntil no more
    Send                                           Receive
EndDo                                           EndDo
Send                                            Change Direction
If rc = Change:
    Send OK                                     If rc = OK:
Receive                                             Send
Receive                                             Disconnect
If 'Disconnect':
```

Figure 4.6. Client/server models—conversation.

Conversation

The principle behind a conversation is that each end does explicit sends and receives. This implies that each end must be aware of the state of the other (at least whether it is expecting to send or receive). Figure 4.6 shows such an interface.

Note that, if both ends send at the same time, there must be a way to handle and recover from the resulting collision. Protocols such as CPI-C provide for such events.

Using an existing model

This means creating an API based on some existing and well known mechanism. For example, one could construct a cooperative processing API to look like file I/O, thus building on concepts already familiar to the programmer.

Messaging

Here, the programmer thinks in terms of sending a message to something (another piece of software), and of receiving messages from somewhere (other pieces of software—either the programmer's own, or someone else's). In procedural code, a messaging scheme might look like the one shown in Fig. 4.7. Notice that the programmer must be aware that a message will be returned.

Sending a message is inherently an asynchronous operation. Control is returned to the calling program before the message is delivered. Notice, however, that the receive is synchronous; the program issues a 'receive message', and waits until there is a message to be received. Thus messaging is *synchronous* at the receive.

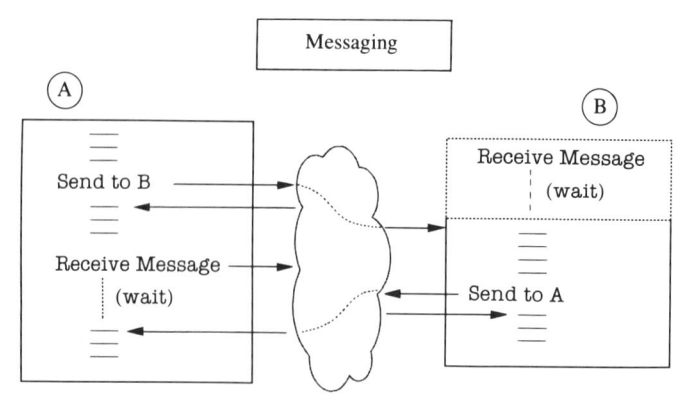

Figure 4.7. Client/server models—messaging.

4.2.3 Choosing a programming model

Before choosing between these four, remember that there are three different aspects of an API:

- What the programmer *thinks* he or she is doing.
- The *language statements* (and their syntax) that the programmer needs to write to make it happen.
- The underlying mechanism that *implements* those statements.

It is the second of these three that people normally mean when they talk about an 'API'. But it is the first of these three that is the most important to the programmer.

Let us consider the four types of connection in relation to our objectives—asynchronous messaging and ease of programming.

Remote procedure call

The great advantage to the programmer is that RPC appears just like an ordinary procedure call . . . or does it?

The problem with RPC as the basis for cooperative software across unreliable networks is that, in reality, it does not map to a normal local procedure call.

For example, after issuing a normal procedure call, the programmer is concerned only with:

- The data returned by the procedure.
- The return code from the procedure (which might indicate that the procedure found some error condition).

The programmer using RPC must be concerned with:

Structural overview

- The return code from the system (as opposed to that from the remote procedure)—telling the programmer (depending on the specific RPC implementation) such things as:
  —Whether the call failed to connect
  —Whether the called procedure exists
  —Not all the data could be returned
- Dealing with the wait if a call takes a long time (say more than 100 milliseconds).
- Dealing with the situation that not all the data was returned.
- The data returned by the procedure.
- The return code from the procedure (which might indicate that the procedure found some error condition).
- In addition, depending on the RPC implementation, someone must handle some or all of the following 'set-up' requirements:
  —Define the RPC bindings (for automatic data conversion at run-time)
  —Pre-compile the code 'stubs'—one for the client, one for the server
  —make sure those stubs do not have name clashes with other stubs
  —Ensure that the stubs are *available* in the appropriate development libraries

Even assuming that someone else does all the set-up, the programmer still has a problem with long-running calls, and with more than one chunk of data being returned.

And, of course, RPC does not handle the necessary asynchronous nature of cooperative processing (which we specified as a key principle)—it does not handle the 'long-running call'.

The long-running call

A long-running call occurs when the transmission of the call to the server takes a long time, or when the server itself takes a long time to process the request (for example, accessing a database), or both. Remember the RPC model—the calling code waits until the call returns. This is called 'blocking', as the wait 'blocks' other threads of control from using the code.

Now for a normal procedure call (or maybe for a very fast call across a high-speed LAN to a powerful server) the wait is very small, and the blocking effect is trivial. By 'small' we mean less than (say) 100 milliseconds. This is the maximum time a user should be locked out of doing anything with a graphical user interface—and hence (in the general case) the maximum time the business logic on the PC should have to wait.

The call may even block a whole address space. For example, if this call were done in a program that also handles the system-level GUI API, then, unless the programmer handles his or her own multi-tasking, the whole application—and maybe even other applications—will be blocked. And the user will *not* be happy as the screen and keyboard lock—for no apparent reason!

Now, the programmer's model for cooperative processing must include the idea of asynchronous connection. The RPC model excludes this. Therefore, RPC is not a good choice of model.

Telling the users to do their own multi-tasking to handle the long-wait problem does not smack of ease of use!

Conversation

Handling a conversational API model—even a simple one—is intrinsically complex. You might restrict the complexity by specifying a subset of capability (such as the 'CPI-C Starter Set' does). However, such a restriction will probably include only synchronous receives, which do not match our requirement for asynchronous operation. If asynchronous receives are offered, then this does not map to our requirement for shielding the programmer from handling task/process boundaries.

Using an existing model

The problem with using existing models is that they typically do not map easily to the essence of cooperative processing—a client making an asynchronous request of a server. For example, each file I/O call is synchronous—it waits until it completes. Also, with a file I/O model, you would have an open and close operation. But there is no obvious necessary analogy to this with cooperative processing.

Messaging

The standard messaging model looks as if it is by nature asynchronous. This, however, is misleading, since we need to handle *incoming* messages as well as outgoing ones. And this is important, as handling incoming messages imposes a synchronous element that is unwelcome for our current purposes.

Often I am told that this is no problem. 'Just spin off a thread', I am told. The problem is that the people saying this are usually highly experienced programmers for whom writing operating system extensions is a weekend hobby; or they are people who have little idea of the realities of application programming, and who imagine that 'spinning off threads' is something learned on day 2 of the standard COBOL application programming class.

So, we seem to have concluded that *none* of the models is suitable for our needs! None of them appears to make asynchronous connection easy to program, as they all have synchronous elements, so leaving the application programmer to deal with the difficult bits!

To repeat: What we are after here is ease of programming.

Happily, there is a solution. It lies, not in a connection model alone, but in the combination of a connection model and a particular kind of code *structure*—

Structural overview   59

'event-loop programming'. And since events can most easily be thought of as messages, then we will choose messaging as our connection model.

4.2.4 *Event-loop programming*

Event-loop programming is not new. We find it today in both the transaction processing environment and in the low-level GUI code on a PC.

Transaction processing

Most existing transaction processing systems are event-driven. For example, consider what happens when the user on a character-based terminal connected to a transaction processing system such as Customer Information Control System (CICS) causes an 'event'—perhaps by pressing the 'enter' key:

1 An 'event' is signalled to the terminal controller.
2 The terminal controller transmits that event (with any associated data) to CICS.
3 CICS wakes up a piece of application logic (a 'transaction') and passes the event (and its data) to the transaction.
4 The transaction processes the event and replies by signalling a second event, destined for the terminal, together with any associated data, back to CICS (e.g. 'Write this data to the screen').
5 CICS passes that event and data to the terminal controller.
6 The microcode in the terminal controller processes the event and takes appropriate action (e.g. updates the screen buffer on the terminal).

The above would be immediately familiar if we replaced the word 'event' with the word 'message'. There are two such messages—one in, one out. Hence what we have just described is the processing of a 'message pair'.

Figure 4.8 shows the similarity between transaction programming and event-loop programming. On the left are some character-based terminal-style transaction programs. On the right is the same code, but built in an 'event-driven' style. Indeed, the right and left parts of this diagram are in a real sense the same; the difference is in the packaging. For high-performance transaction processing systems like CICS and Information Management System (IMS), packaging is as shown on the left of the figure because of performance considerations or (in some cases) to improve maintainability and availability.

PC GUI code

It is the nature of GUI code (unlike code driving non-programmable terminals) that it must respond to a huge variety of user keyboard and mouse actions. It must

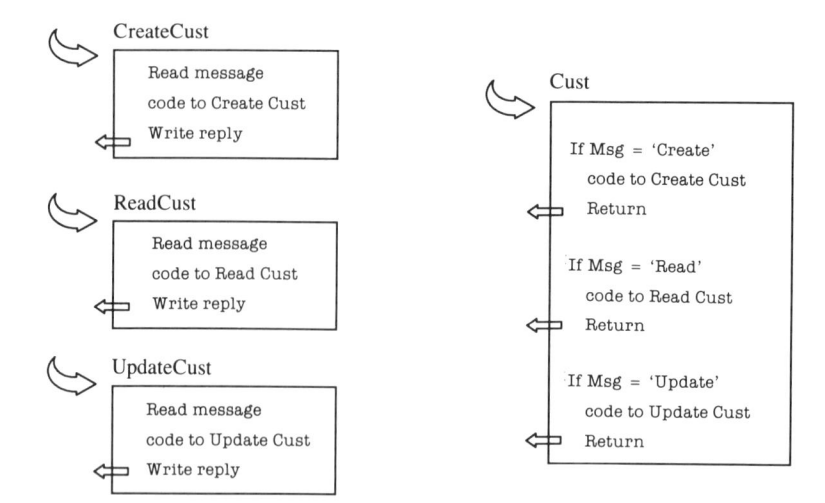

```
        CreateCust
    ┌─────────────────┐                       Cust
    │ Read message    │              ┌─────────────────────┐
    │ code to Create Cust │           │ If Msg = 'Create'   │
    │ Write reply     │              │   code to Create Cust│
    └─────────────────┘              │   Return            │
                                     │                     │
        ReadCust                     │ If Msg = 'Read'     │
    ┌─────────────────┐              │   code to Read Cust │
    │ Read message    │              │   Return            │
    │ code to Read Cust │            │                     │
    │ Write reply     │              │ If Msg = 'Update'   │
    └─────────────────┘              │   code to Update Cust│
                                     │   Return            │
        UpdateCust                   └─────────────────────┘
    ┌─────────────────┐
    │ Read message    │
    │ code to Update Cust │
    │ Write reply     │
    └─────────────────┘
```

Figure 4.8. 'Event-loop' programming.

also manage a vast array of GUI constructs such as push-buttons, scroll-bars, windows, icons, etc. This makes such code far more complex than character-based terminal code.

The way that much of this complexity is managed is to structure GUI code such that, instead of trying to drive the user interface, it merely sits back and responds to events. Thus GUI code is built as 'event-driven' code.

In contrast to traditional transaction programs, however, instead of having one piece of code for each event/message, GUI code is structured as larger lumps of code, each of which handles several different event/message types. Such code will loop around a 'get next event' statement—or will be woken up only when an event arrives—that is, something outside of the application code provides the 'get next event' loop and invokes the appropriate piece of application code. This is where the phrase 'event-loop programming' comes from.

In the PC, different performance considerations lead to packaging as shown on the right of Fig. 4.8. This is because the 'events' are much more likely to include GUI things—e.g. an event might be 'button "Apply Changes" pressed'—which have to be processed at very high speed (remember the tenth of a second response time requirement). Such events are not only swift, but also of wide variety. This means they cannot afford the overhead of code loading implied by transaction programming packaging, or—if transactions were to be pre-loaded for speed—the sheer number of such transactions that would be needed.

Thus in event-loop programming on the PC, the programmer expects to receive a message at the beginning of his or her code, to handle the message and then to return (to wherever he or she was called from). So the programmer's model is not that he or she writes a complete program (although in practice he or she has to do so!); what the programmer thinks of are independent modules—each relating to a given window on the GUI—which fit into a system-provided context.[1] That context is one of freely flowing messages. At a high level, this is broadly similar to transaction programming—although quite different at the detail level!

Conclusion

We can achieve ease of programming for asynchronous connection as follows:

- Adopt an event-loop program structure.
- Use messaging as the API model.
- Create an infrastructure to support the event loop (both of which are invisible to the programmer). When a message is received by the infrastructure, it will invoke the relevant piece of event-loop code. This will handle the message and return to what it sees as the system, that is, to the infrastructure.

It may seem odd, but today's operating systems do not support this kind of software structure for the average application programmer. The nearest to it are the various transaction processing systems (or the low-level GUI APIs such as those provided by Windows and PM). So we need some supporting software infrastructure that will do such things as:

- Handle the messages and the event loop.
- Dispatch the appropriate 'module' of application code by passing the message data to it and 'starting' it .
- Take over when the application module returns control after processing the message.
- Manage the thread or process boundary to provide asynchronous messaging.
- Route messages to the right place, and return responses to the requester.

With this structure, the application code might look as shown in Fig. 4.9, where:

- The code (high-level pseudocode) on the left of the figure (A) is invoked by some incoming message X (perhaps an 'apply button pressed' message from the GUI).
- In processing that message, A sends message Y to B.
- B processes message Y, and sends the response back to A in the form of message Z.
- A then processes the response to its initial message Y in the code which 'catches' message Z.

Well, that may be fine, but there is still one problem. Looking at the code in Fig. 4.9, it is hard to understand how an application (or part of an application) can be

---

[1]Although GUI subsystems such as PM, Windows and X-Windows all provide APIs that support a messaging model, they do so at a system level, they require a high degree of programming skill, they have a long learning curve and they do not support cooperative processing. Thus those APIs are unsuitable for our purposes.

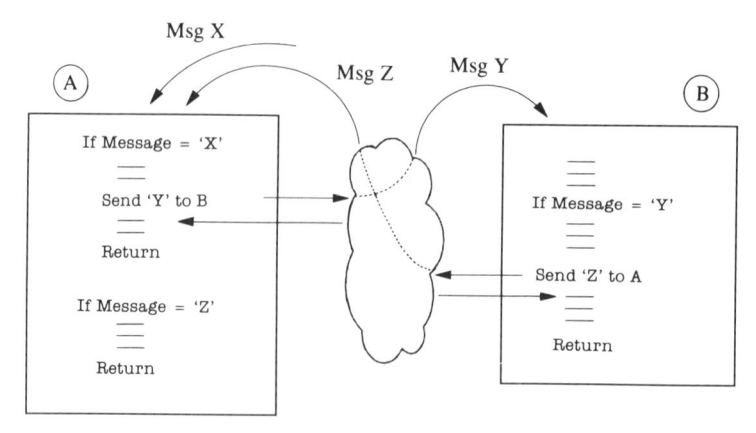

Figure 4.9. 'Event loop' with messaging.

written in that style. If we want to produce a module or program of that shape, then what is the basis of modularization? It is difficult to see how it can be functionally based.

The answer is to modularize on the basis of data—of things, of *objects*. But how might this work? Consider Fig. 4.10. On the left, we see two traditional transactions. We assume that the user enters one of two such transactions—'update customer' or 'enquire on order'. Each of these will invoke the appropriate function. The 'order enquiry' function will read the customer and orders (and, not shown, parts) databases, format the reply and return it (perhaps display it directly on a character-based terminal). Similarly, the 'update customer' function will write to the customer database.

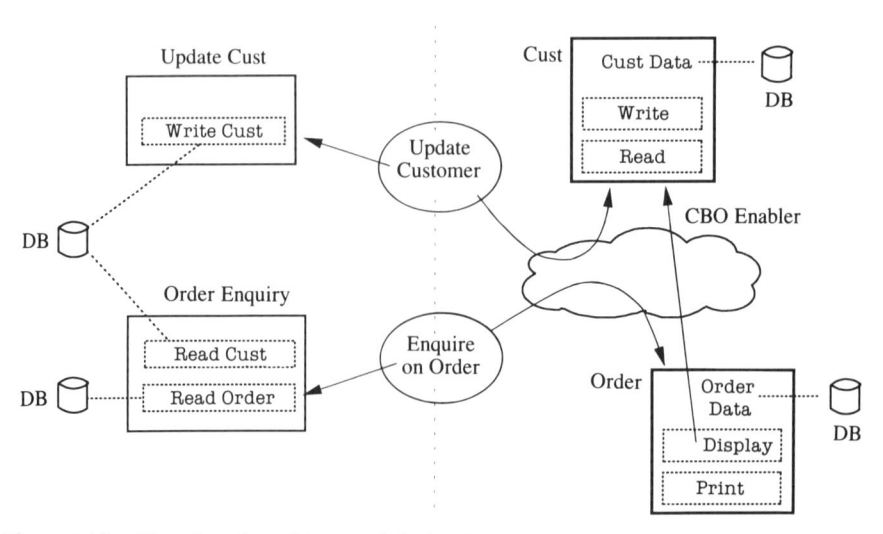

Figure 4.10. Functional vs object modularization.

Suppose we were to modularize on the basis of data (objects), and build a piece of event-loop code that dealt with all the functions done on customer data, and another that dealt with all the functions done against an order. This might look something like the right side of Fig. 4.10, and would work as follows.

Consider the two user transactions—'update customer' and enquire on order'. Let us assume that there is some infrastructure (middleware) code that will transform our user requests into messages. The 'update customer' action would result in a 'write' message being sent to the customer object, which would write to the customer database.

Now consider the 'order enquiry'. A 'query' message (or, perhaps better, a 'display yourself' message) would be routed to the order object. Now, an order object will typically not have, for example, the customer name and address in its data, although it will certainly hold the key (customer number) of the customer who placed the order. So how does the order object display the customer name and address as part of itself?

The answer is that the order object sends a message to the customer object, asking for its name and address. (Object-oriented readers may notice that this breaches encapsulation rather badly. If you prefer, let us say that the customer object returns an address object, which the order object then uses appropriately; or that the order object sends a 'display your address object here' message to the customer object.) The order is then displayed (maybe by sending a message across the network to a PC).

4.2.5 *CBOs again*

But have we not seen something like this before? Yes, in Chapter 3 we developed the idea of cooperative business objects (CBOs) as the answer to the problem of object-based user interfaces. A CBO looks very similar to the event-loop structure we have developed here. Indeed, in all its main aspects, it is identical. So we find that the idea of CBOs is much more generally applicable than just in the GUI area. It can apply to both ends of the client and server connection. Thus CBOs provide the structural base for a solution to the ease-of-programming problem for cooperative client/server systems.

What luck! CBOs solve not only the object-based GUI problem, but also the cooperative processing problem!

In subsequent chapters, we will examine CBOs in greater depth.

4.2.6 *Synchronous connections*

We have focused on the need for asynchronous messages, and have concluded that this can be achieved—with ease of programming—through a messaging API *plus* an event-loop style of program structure. However, there are many situations where a *synchronous* connection is required.

Why is this? Well, consider the event-loop code shown on the left of Fig. 4.9. Notice how, for each message sent, we provide a block of code to handle the response (the programmer will know that the response to the message Y will come back in the form of message Z).

Now, there are many occasions when, in processing some single message, the programmer will want to send several messages whose responses are required in order to complete processing of the first incoming message. If asynchronous messages are all that is available to the programmer, he or she will need to provide a piece of 'catcher' code for each different incoming message. Not only that, the programmer will have to manage the 'state' of things—the fact that processing of one thing cannot continue until the result of another thing has been received.

Now, while managing a limited number of states (two or three) is not too onerous, managing 10 (say) is extremely complex. This complexity can be avoided by allowing synchronous as well as asynchronous messages.

As described in Appendix 3, it is useful to provide the programmer with the ability—at the API level—to specify whether a message will be synchronous or asynchronous. Thus we might have a 'send' API for synchronous messages, and a 'post' (say) for asynchronous.

We can then have the underlying infrastructure *ensure* that—regardless of the location of the target code—the *behaviour* of the messaging system will always be the same. This leads to much easier programming. Consider, for example, the pseudocode shown in Fig. 4.11, which assumes that only asynchronous messaging is available.

Now consider the exact functional equivalent in Fig. 4.12, where both synchronous and asynchronous messages are available. This is clearly *much* simpler code than in Fig. 4.11. (The pseudocode shown in Figs 4.11 and 4.12 is focused on messaging, and hence omits other important things such as the handling of message data, scratch-pad areas, etc.)

While the availability of both synchronous and asynchronous messaging will not guarantee it, clearly ease of programming is *enabled* by the presence of both options. As always, bad program design can make anything messy; but good design is made infinitely easier if facilities that *support* that design are available.

What about the server end—the recipient of messages? How do we provide ease of programming if a given server might be 'sent' a message on one occasion and 'posted' a message on another?

One approach might be as shown in Fig. 4.13. However, since we need a messaging infrastructure anyway, why not have that infrastructure hide whether the sender sent or posted the message? This might work as shown in Fig. 4.14. In this figure, the complexity is hidden in the piece the programmer does not see—the messaging infrastructure. The server programmer writes the same thing (program C) regardless of whether a message has been sent or posted.

Also hidden in the messaging infrastructure are things not shown in the figure, such as how the message queuing works, and how task and/or process boundaries

```
/* Program 'A' */
StartCase(Message)
  Case 'Button_Apply'
    Post 'Msg_X' to B (reply 'B_Reply')
    Post 'Msg_Y' to C (reply 'C_Reply')
    Post 'Msg_Z' to D (reply 'D_Reply')
    Set State = 'Waiting for B'
    Set State = 'Waiting for C'
    Set State = 'Waiting for D'
  Case 'B_Reply'
    Set State = 'Not Waiting for B'
    ready = CheckState()
    if ready = 'Yes' then
      Post 'Request_Update' to E (reply 'E_Done')
  Case 'C_Reply'
    Set State = 'Not Waiting for C'
    ready = CheckState()
    if ready = 'Yes' then
      Post 'Request_Update' to E (reply 'E_Done')
  Case 'D_Reply'
    Set State = 'Not Waiting for Z'
    ready = Checkstate()
    if ready = 'Yes' then
      Post 'Request_Update' to E (reply 'E_Done')
  Case 'E_Done'
    If Data_in_Message = 'Updated' then
      Display message 'OK' to User
    else
      Display message 'Not OK' to User
EndCase(Message)
Return
procedure: CheckState
  if State = 'Not Waiting for B' and
     State = 'Not Waiting for C' and
     State = 'Not Waiting for D'
  then:
    Ready = 'Yes'
  else:
    Ready = 'No'
Return
```

Figure 4.11. Messaging with asynchronous messages only.

are managed. Finally, it is worth noting that the messaging infrastructure invokes the application programs directly. Now it may be the case—especially in the PC—that several such programs are loaded concurrently in a single thread (task). This means that the infrastructure must handle *both* intra- and inter-task messaging.

Of course, a synchronous message as shown in Fig. 4.14 is really the same as an RPC. However—and here is the difference—we can build very similar APIs for

```
/* Program 'A' */
StartCase(Message)
  Case 'Button_Apply'
    B_Reply = Send 'Msg_X' to B
    C_Reply = Send 'Msg_Y' to C
    D_Reply = Send 'Msg_Z' to D
    Post 'Request_Update' to E (reply 'E_Done')
  Case 'E_Done'
    If Data_in_Message = 'Updated' then
    Display message 'OK' to User
    else
      Display message 'Not OK' to User
EndCase(Message)
Return
```

Figure 4.12. Messaging with asynchronous and synchronous messages.

both 'send' and 'post', thereby presenting the programmer with a consistent messaging model. Notice that the programmer never sees queues. He or she merely *sends* a message, and knows that the returned data will be available on the next sequential instruction, or *posts* a message, knowing that a subsequent incoming message ('event') will carry the response (the programmer should always specify in the post statement the response message that he or she would like to receive).

Note that the asynchronous message is quite different from the form of RPC where the handle of the routine to be invoked by the response is passed with the request. With the asynchronous message, the programmer has nothing further to do. With RPC-with-handle, the programmer has to additionally handle such things as:

- What to do if the response is needed before the response routing is invoked

```
/* Program 'B' */
StartCase(Message)
  Case 'Msg_X'
    ... (process message - prepare response) ...
  If message was Sent then
    Return Response
  else /* Message was Posted */
    Post 'B_Reply' to the requester
  Case ' ... '
Endcase(Message)
Return
```

Figure 4.13. Server visibility of message type.

Structural overview

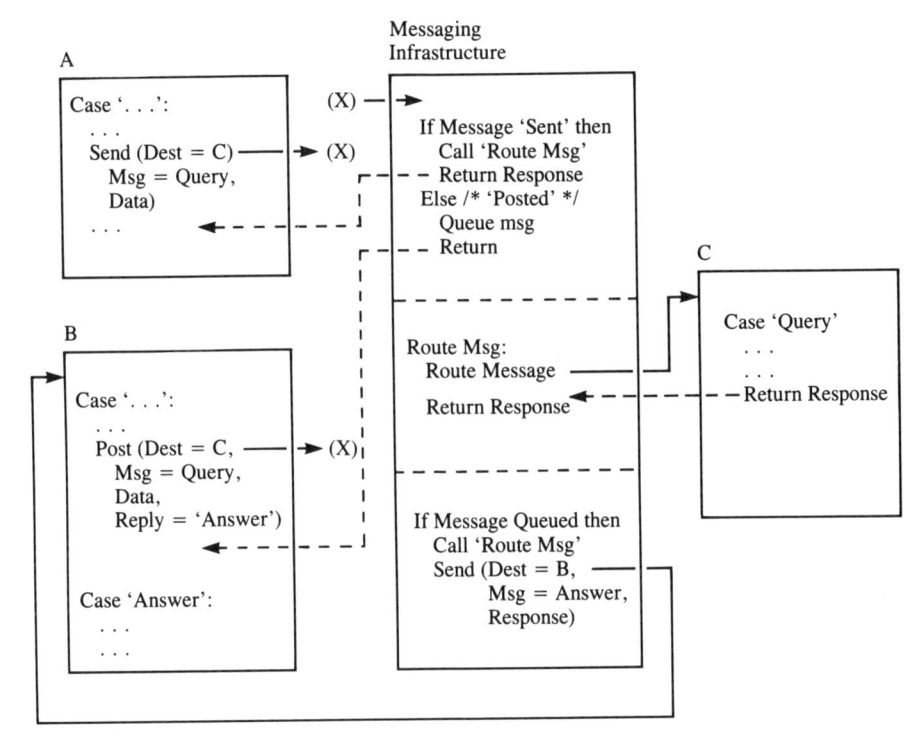

```
      A                        Messaging
                               Infrastructure
   ┌─────────────────┐  (X) ──┌──────────────────────┐
   │ Case '...':     │        │ If Message 'Sent' then│
   │   ...           │  (X)   │   Call 'Route Msg'    │
   │   Send (Dest = C)──────► │   Return Response     │
   │     Msg = Query,│        │ Else /* 'Posted' */   │
   │     Data)       │        │   Queue msg           │
   │   ...           │◄─ ─ ─ ─│   Return              │       C
   └─────────────────┘        │                       │   ┌──────────────┐
                              │                       │   │ Case 'Query' │
      B                       │ Route Msg:            ├──►│   ...        │
   ┌─────────────────┐        │   Route Message ──────┤   │   ...        │
   │ Case '...':     │        │   Return Response ◄───┼───│ Return Response
   │   ...           │        │                       │   │              │
   │   Post (Dest = C,────► (X)                       │   └──────────────┘
   │     Msg = Query,│        │                       │
   │     Data,       │        │ If Message Queued then │
   │     Reply = 'Answer')    │   Call 'Route Msg'    │
   │       ◄─ ─ ─ ─ ─│        │   Send (Dest = B,─────┤
   │                 │        │     Msg = Answer,     │
   │ Case 'Answer':  │        │     Response)         │
   │   ...           │        └───────────────────────┘
   └─────────────────┘
```

Figure 4.14. Server transparency of message type.

- How to re-synch if the response routine is invoked when in the middle of something else
- Checking if the response routine has been called.

Recursive messaging

Consider Fig. 4.15. Here, a message X is received by A (1). Processing of message X requires message Y to be sent to B (2). But B's processing of message Y includes sending message Z (back) to A (3).

In this case, the messaging infrastructure feeds message Z to A just as if it were any other message. However, remember that A started off by processing message X. But before it completes this processing, it has to handle message Z. Note that when it receives message Z, it has not received the response from B to the first message X.

This means that the same code (A) is entered twice. Although this is no problem for modern stack-based compilers, this requirement for recursiveness on the part of the language being used should not be overlooked.

The knowledge that the code may be called recursively (or, to be precise, re-entered by a second thread of control before the first thread has completed and returned) cannot be hidden from the programmer. Thus the infrastructure must

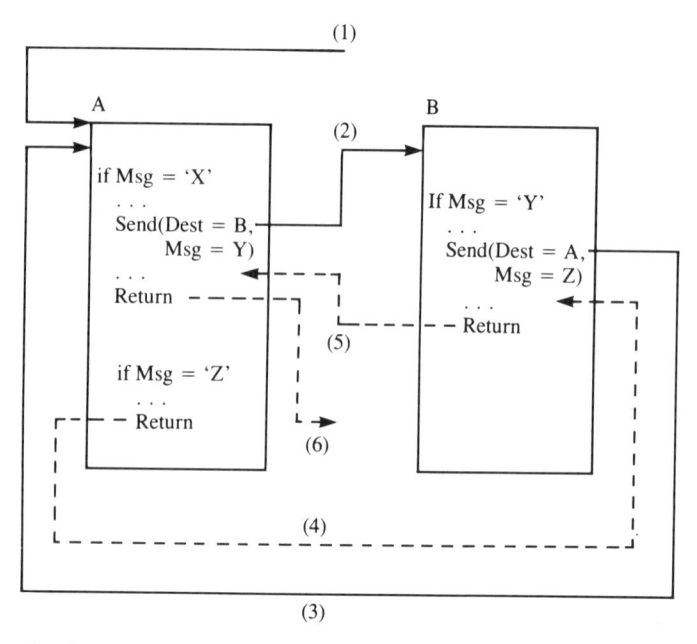

```
                              (1)
        ┌─────────────────────────────────────┐
        │   A                    B            │
        │  ┌──────────┐    (2)  ┌──────────┐  │
        └─▶│ if Msg='X'│───────▶│If Msg='Y'│  │
           │  ...      │        │ ...      │  │
           │ Send(Dest=B,──┐    │Send(Dest=A,─┤
           │     Msg=Y)    │    │    Msg=Z) │ │
           │  ...          │    │  ...      │ │
           │ Return ◀──────┤    │ Return ◀──┤ │
           │          (5)  │    │           │ │
           │ if Msg='Z'    │    │           │ │
           │  ...          │    │           │ │
        ┌──│ Return        │    │           │ │
        │  │      (6)      │    │           │ │
        │  └───────────────┘    └───────────┘ │
        │                                     │
        └──────────────(4)────────────────────┘
                              (3)
```

Figure 4.15. Synchronous messages and recursive code.

ensure serial re-usability between clearly defined points. In this case, the programmer should have no more difficulty than with similar situations in transaction processing. He or she does not have to deal with re-entrant code, merely with serially re-usable code.

GUI events

Turning to the PC specifically for a moment, we notice that system-provided GUI APIs are event-driven. So if we can have the messaging infrastructure present incoming GUI messages to us in the same way as other 'events', then we will add even more ease of programming, since the programmer starts to see *all* events in the same way—as incoming messages, all conforming to the same programming model, of the same format and having the same API.

Conclusion

Of the various connection models, we choose messaging to implement the client/server connection, for these reasons:

- It maps well to the necessary model of cooperative processing.
- It handles asynchronous requests in a natural way for event-loop programming (which is natural on the PC).

- The server can be of several different styles, and event-loop programming at the server is not forced.
- It provides a natural way to get over the task/process boundary transparently to the programmer.
- It does not always force asynchronous operation, and so can be used for synchronous messaging as well; however, the same API model can be used for both.
- It can handle a server responding to a request with multiple responses (multiple messages).
- It can be implemented (under the covers) with any of the normal mechanisms: RPC, message queuing, conversation, Inter-process Communication (IPC) mechanisms, pipes, etc.

Overall, then, a messaging API (both at the model and at the code level) provides an excellent balance between programming simplicity on the one hand and wide applicability on the other. This will be of vital importance in the further development of our cooperative processing model.

Meanwhile, we must pick up again the notion of separation of the user logic from the data logic referred to at the beginning of this chapter.

4.3 The user vs the data

Earlier in this chapter, we briefly discussed the separation of 'user logic' (application code on the PC that serves the user) from 'data logic' (application code that accesses shared resources). We then added 'business logic' (application code that implements business processes and rules) on the side of data logic.

This separation is a fundamental concept for client/server systems. For, although there are some similarities in required functions at a server and at a PC, the two systems are differentiated by their prime purpose. Thus:

- The PC is there to serve a user; to provide the user with a human–computer interface that will make it possible to *use*—to *exploit*—available IT resources, such that the user's business objectives can be achieved.
- The server is there to make valuable IT shared resources *available* to multiple concurrent requesters, while at the same time protecting the integrity of those resources, and ensuring that business rules are enforced.

These two quite different aims make the client and the server different in the facilities they must provide. For example, data commit and rollback would not generally be expected of a PC, while providing the user with a choice of fonts on a graphical user interface would not be expected of a server.

In today's client/server systems, *both* of these are equally important if full value is to be gained. Often the user aspects are said to be less important than data integrity and business rule enforcement. From the point of view of protection of invaluable corporate resources, this is true. From the point of view of *using* those resources to best effect, it is false. Client/server systems must not only *manage* shared resources, they must also provide the best possible *access* to them.

We formalize these two aspects into a general model defined in terms of a 'user interface domain' and a 'shared resource domain', as follows.

4.3.1   The user interface domain

The *user interface domain* (or UID) is the application code (CBOs) responsible for serving a *single* user. There will be as many UIDs in a given system as there are active users.

The key characteristic of the UID is that it has a user interface. Thus in the UID, CBOs will be focused on presenting data and function (from whatever source) to a single user, and allowing that user effectively to interact with it.

The UID has no responsibility for data integrity, nor for the enforcement of business rules. All operations on data (and other shared resources) that originate in the UID will be requested of the shared resource domain.

4.3.2   The shared resource domain

The *shared resource domain* (or SRD) is the application code (CBOs) responsible for ensuring the security and integrity of corporate shared resources such as data.

CBOs in the SRD will be concerned with things like concurrent update protection, accessing shared data (and other resources) and commit scopes.

The SRD will normally provide a number of specific 'one-shot' processes (such as 'change customer'), and ensures resource integrity by encapsulating the commit/rollback processing.

The boundaries of an SRD are defined by the boundaries of the underlying resource manager (such as a transaction processor and/or a database manager).

4.3.3   UID and SRD interaction

A simple example of UID and SRD is shown in Fig. 4.16, where a PC is connected (perhaps across a local area network (LAN), through a gateway and across a wide area network (WAN)) to a mainframe. Requests can flow both ways, and are always in the form of messages. One domain issues a message to the other; the other responds by sending one or more messages back to the requester. Normally, the requester will be the UID.

Our domain model admits of many other cases than this, however. For example, Fig. 4.17(a) shows the case of a distributed database management system (DBMS), where some or all accesses to the database are issued from the PC. In that case, the SRD extends from the mainframe to the PC. The PC contains a UID and part of the SRD.

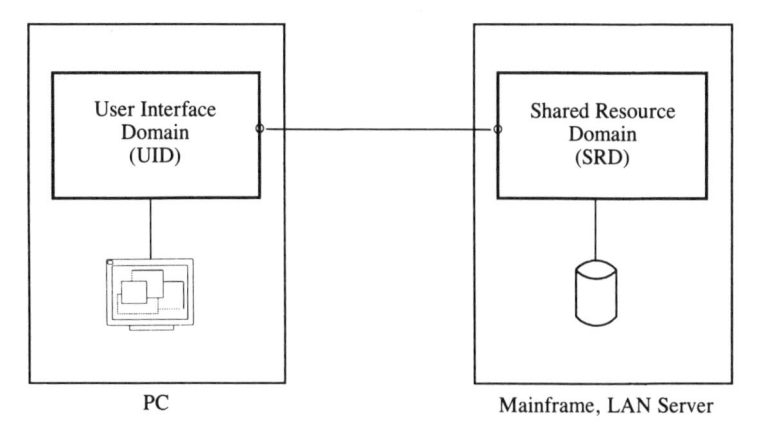

Figure 4.16. Cooperative processing domains (1).

Figure 4.17(b) shows the case of part of the UID being on a LAN server, with the SRD on both the LAN server and a mainframe.

Although each domain will have some similarities, they will differ at the detail level. In particular, the detail of the CBO code in each will be very different. For example, the SRD assumes the existence of an underlying resource manager (such as IBM's CICS with DB2, or one of the several DBMS that also have transactional capabilities), while the UID will be greatly concerned with the object-based user interface.

There will be as many UIDs as there are users. In addition, there may be more than one SRD (depending on the resource manager used). While the SRD is

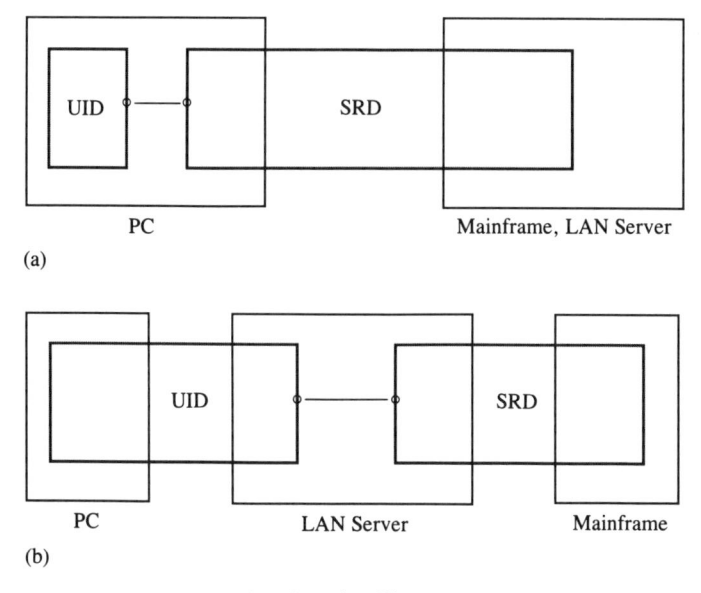

Figure 4.17. Cooperative processing domains (2).

normally the server, there will be occasions when something in an SRD needs to initiate a request of a UID. Thus the connection between the two, while always 'client/server' in the sense of request/response pairs, is more of a peer-to-peer nature. This is because both can be clients (that is, both can make a request of something else) and both can be servers (that is, both can receive requests from somewhere else).

An SRD may well access another SRD directly. For example, a UID on a PC may send a request to an SRD on a LAN server, which, to handle the request, may need to read some data from the mainframe server. Without an underlying distributed database, there would be two SRDs involved—one at the mainframe, one at the LAN server.

Both the UID and the SRD are implemented with CBOs. Within each domain, there are a number of identifiable *types* of CBO. The next two chapters discuss these different types.

4.4 Summary

In this chapter, we have identified and discussed the need for the following:

- *Ease of programming* to implement cooperative systems.
- *Asynchronous requests* between the two pieces of cooperative code.
- *A requester/responder design approach* for cooperative processing—that is, an atomic request/response interaction, where the responder (the 'server') knows nothing about the state of the requester (the 'client'), and where the responder, between invocations, does not retain knowledge of previous invocations.
- *Messaging* (as opposed to RPC or conversation)—together with an 'event-loop' style of programming—as the single approach that meets the ease-of-programming and asynchronous request requirements.
- *Synchronous requests* between different pieces of event-loop code.

We have also introduced the following concept:

- *Separation* of user-oriented and shared resource responsibilities into the 'user interface domain' (UID) and the 'shared resource domain' (SRD).

So we have seen how messaging, combined with event-loop programming, can potentially give us the best of all worlds—both synchronous and asynchronous requests with a single simple API and programmer's model.

This also gives us a way to handle incoming unsolicited messages. And, of course, the messaging infrastructure can cross the task/process boundary without the programmer being aware of it.

Furthermore, we discover that the structure of application code that best delivers ease of programming in this environment is the *same* structure that we found we needed to handle the object-based user interface. By applying the techniques of object orientation to event-loop code, we gain the benefits of *both* OO and cooperative processing. The resulting structure—the thing that the application programmer writes—we call a 'cooperative business object' (or CBO).

Finally, we see an important separation of function in client/server systems into the UID and the SRD. This separation is not only technically necessary (for asynchronous requests) but also hugely useful from a *design* point of view, as will become apparent in later chapters.

5
The user interface domain

In this chapter, we look in more detail at the area we called the 'user interface domain', or UID. In client/server systems, the UID is the province of the 'client' CBOs, and is located (either completely or mainly) in the PC. Since the UID is all about serving a single user, we focus in this chapter on the CBOs immediately behind the object-based GUI.

Consideration of the responsibilities of the UID leads to our finding that two different types of CBOs—the 'view' and the 'local model'—are needed. This is a refinement of a concept that has been around for several years, the idea of a 'view' object and a 'model' object. We find that, while a single model object may be adequate for stand-alone systems, it is not so for distributed client/server systems. Hence the introduction of a 'local model'. In this book, we replace the general notion of a 'model' object by specific types of CBO in the SRD—the 'focus' and 'entity' objects. These are discussed in depth in the next chapter. Appendix 4 discusses the difference between the 'local model' and the 'model' in some detail.

In the body of this book, the term 'model' is used exclusively to mean the local model (in the UID). For this reason, whenever you see the word 'model', you should take it as meaning 'local model'.

So, the UID is populated with view and model CBOs, and, between them, they contribute significantly to our overall objectives, which were:

- Object-based GUIs,[1] plus
- Cooperative processing, plus
- Software re-use and integration potential

---

[1] But what if we are not building an object-based user interface? In this case, the model presented in this chapter is still useful at some level of abstraction. Separation of function into the stuff to do with handling the user interface and the stuff to do with handling the entities that know where the real data is (in the SRD) is still useful. One can then see that the view objects (presentation modules) represent the several menus and panels one might want, while the model object (business logic) is the business logic.

Experience has shown that even with an application-oriented user interface, one gravitates towards presenting business-related 'things' in separate windows anyway. Thus this model is appropriate for both application- and object-oriented user interfaces.

all with:

- Ease of programming for the average application programmer

At this point, and before developing the main argument, I should like to interpose a brief note on what I call the 'mainframe culture'.

The 'mainframe culture'

Among some IT professionals today, there exists the notion that the PC end of a client/server system is merely a trivial user interface, of no import, and best left to some GUI layout tool whose selection, use and implementation should be assigned to the most junior and least experienced members of the IT department. I even heard someone say, within the last two years that, 'Advances in business modelling, data analysis and CASE tools have been such that we can now implement an entire system—right through to system test—without considering the user interface at all.'

Client/server developments where this impression has been dominant have *always* (in my experience) run into serious trouble. For such attitudes not only indicate a breathtaking arrogance (the user does not matter); they are also a sure recipe for disaster. At the beginning of a new technology curve, the system *as a whole* is the proper realm of the more senior and experienced IT professionals. This means understanding *equally* what is needed for both the UID and the SRD.

As it is, there seems to be a lamentable level of ignorance among many senior IT professionals about a key part of a client/server system—the PC. Test this for yourselves. Look around your own IT department. List the more senior and knowledgeable professionals—the ones whose technical judgement is trusted by senior IT management. Now list the people with acknowledged expertise in PCs. If there is more than 10 per cent commonality, you are probably well ahead of the game.

This is, however, more than just an attitude. It tends towards being a culture, and two conflicting corollaries can be observed. Sometimes, senior IT management can be overawed by someone whose experience is limited to the PC and LAN environment only, resulting in the person being over-valued in wider systems contexts. Alternatively, someone who understands PCs is often seen as thereby necessarily being inexperienced in other areas of IT expertise. I call this the 'mainframe culture'. It is not mainframes that are dinosaurs, but the *culture* of the mainframe.

PCs and the notion of client/server systems have been with us for some five years at the very least (I first met this idea some 10 years ago). The reason we have not yet got to grips with the shape of client/server applications is arguably because of the mainframe culture. It has been a significant failure of the IT industry. If this book helps, in any way at all, to change that failure to a success, then it will have served its purpose.

The truth is that the UID is *equally* as important as the SRD. After all, the whole reason for putting expensive PCs on users' desks instead of cheap character displays is to enable users to *exploit* the SRD. If this cannot be done, then why waste money?

It may well be that in five years or so, we will have discovered how to generate object-based user interfaces automatically. We may also have discovered how to generate high-performance databases and business logic in the SRD automatically as well. Until then, the serious designer of client/server systems must pay equal attention to both ends of the system. They are very different in their technical detail; but one without the other will severely decrease the value of the system to the business.

5.1 User logic

In the previous chapter, we developed our general model to the point shown as (c) in Fig. 5.1. We used the example of a PC connected to a shared resource system as the vehicle for discussion, and we now focus on the PC end of that system.

We begin by examining further the user logic part of the model. What do we mean by 'user logic'? Many people have the strong opinion that 'business rules' and 'business logic' (or 'application logic') have no place in a PC; for integrity reasons, it is said, such code must be restricted to the server.

Well, consider the following examples:

- Application-level logic may need to be run to handle some drag/drop situations. For example, a user may not be allowed to drop an item onto an order form if the customer is over credit limit.

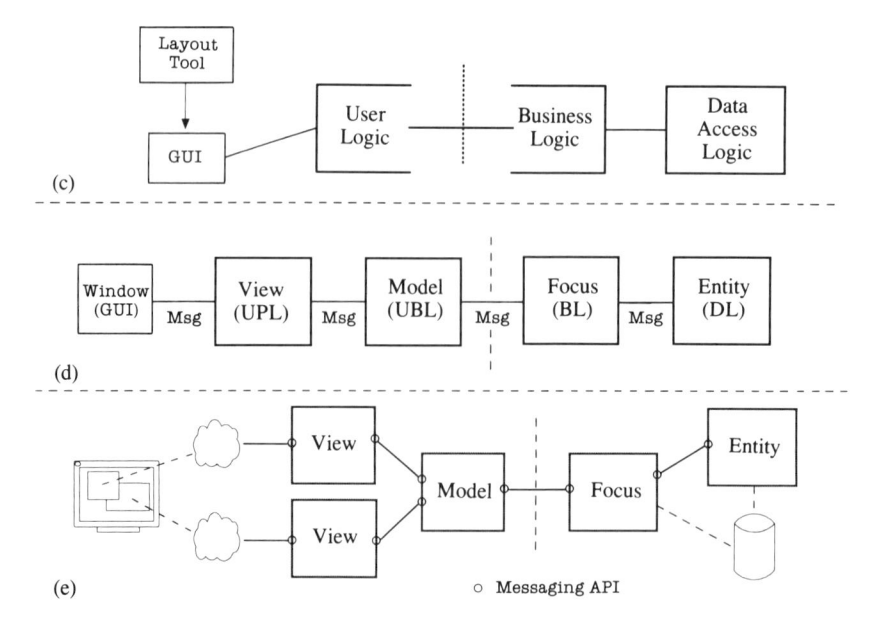

Figure 5.1. Cooperative processing model (2).

- An 'apply' push button on a window may need to be greyed out (made temporarily unavailable to the user) while a response is obtained from a server.
- A Post Code (Zip Code) keyed in by a user may need to be edited to ensure that it is at least in the right format.
- A request needs to be sent from the UID to an SRD to get some data that needs to be displayed.
- The current value of a customer order may need to be shown as items are added to it.
- Functions that are disallowed for users without appropriate authorization may need to be disabled.

All of these are things that will require application logic to be run; all of these are things that you really do not want to go back to the server to do.

For the first example, indeed, you *could not* go back to the server. The application logic to handle drag/drop needs a very short response time to satisfy user feedback requirements. The mouse pointer needs to change from 'OK' to 'Not OK' as the user drags the customer over the border of the order form. This means that the application logic that decides whether a drop is OK or not must certainly run in the PC.

The last example clearly requires some 'business' or 'application' logic, just as it may require the application of 'business rules' to calculate the correct total. And again, we do not want to go all the way back to the server just to accumulate a total!

The one thing that distinguishes all of the above examples is that they all serve the user in some way. They are not essential to the core business process; but they (and others like them) are essential in enabling a *person* using a PC to drive those core processes.

Whether we call such code 'business logic' or not becomes then a matter of definition. In the last chapter, we implied that business logic existed only on the server. We now amend this, and make the following definition: *Business logic* is all the code that is peculiar to specific business data and/or processes.

Thus code that greys out an 'Apply' button on the screen is not business logic; but code that applies a business rule to *decide* whether or not a button should be greyed out *is* business logic. An EXEC SQL statement that accesses the business' prime 'customer' data is not business logic; but code that checks whether the customer is over credit limit is.

However, we also differentiate between UID business logic and SRD business logic. Thus there are two kinds of business logic; that relating to the UID, which is there to assist a person (the user), and that relating to the SRD, which is there to assist the business as a whole.

Now, the application logic on the PC has to do two things:

- Handle the GUI (graphical user interface)
- Provide UID-related business logic, some of which will involve making requests from the UID to the SRD (typically across a task boundary)

Because these are quite different kinds of logic, it becomes very useful to split the user logic into two parts: the 'view' (or 'user presentation logic') and the 'model' (or 'user business logic'). This is shown in Fig. 5.1(d) (the 'focus' and 'entity' boxes on this diagram relate to the SRD, which we shall address in the next chapter). Thus:

- The GUI requests services from the view.
- The view responds to the GUI and requests services from the model.
- The model responds to the view, and makes requests of the server.
- The server responds to the model (and may make requests of other servers before doing so).

This 'model–view' structure allows us to separate UID code to do with presentation and interaction (that is, connecting to the tool-produced GUI code that drives what the user sees) from UID code to do with the business entity, and is illustrated in Fig. 5.1(e). Further, a view will be implemented as a CBO, as will a model.

But did we not imply that, for each object on the object-based user interface, there would be a (single) CBO? Well, yes, we did. But before we expand on this, let us look a little more closely at the idea of models and views.

5.2   'Models' and 'views'

Consider the kind of object-based user interface we discussed in Part One. Now an object on the screen (such as, say, a 'customer') can have one or more 'views'. Why is this? Well, consider the case of a user who needs to understand both a customer's mailing address *and* the physical location of that address. Such a user might well want to look at both a text presentation of the address, and at a map showing the *location* of the address. An example of this is shown on the left of Fig. 5.2, where there is an icon (the customer) and two windows. One window—or view—shows the address of the customer as a text description, while the other shows exactly the same data, but presented as a map of how to get there.

5.2.1   Multiple views

This is paradoxical; for inasmuch as both views are showing the same thing—the address—they are the same. But inasmuch as one is a graphical map-like thing and the other is a text-like thing with formatted fields of data, they are quite different.

We deal with this paradox by recognizing both the differences and the sameness in different bits of code. Thus the difference between the two windows is handled by structuring the code that handles each of them into two separate CBOs. This is shown on the right of Fig. 5.2, where one CBO deals with a map (which shows how to get to the customer's location), and another deals with a text window (which shows the customer's address in text). We call each of these a 'view' CBO, as each handles one visible aspect of an object—what the user can see (or view)—on the screen.

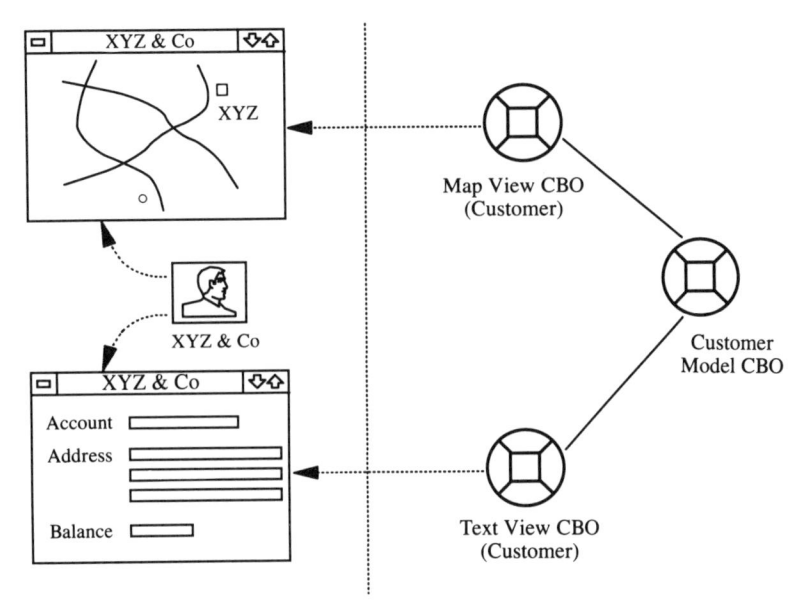

Figure 5.2. Model–view object structure.

But where is the code that deals with the customer *per se*? Again, we find it useful to separate the 'sameness' aspect of the two views into a separate CBO—which has no knowledge of the details of the views, nor of the fact that there is more than one. This we call the 'model' object, as it relates to the user's model of 'customer'. (The *terms* 'view' and 'model' are often attributed to the Smalltalk 'Model-View-Controller' framework, whose context is a GUI. In this book, the same terms are used but with expanded meanings to fit the wider distributed system context.)

Note that the 'customer model' CBO handles a particular instance of customer—for example, it will handle customer *Jones*, not the whole database. If it is required to handle other customers concurrently (for example, customer *Smith*), then there will be a second instance of the customer model CBO. Such multiple instances will be handled by the 'infrastructure' or 'middleware' code that is necessary to deliver the ease of programming for cooperative processing and advanced GUIs. As the discussion progresses, we shall add additional requirements for this infrastructure, and will summarize them in Chapter 8.

Thus we have expanded our general model in a way especially important for object-based user interfaces. The 'user logic' part in fact consists of two different kinds of CBO—views and models.

5.2.2 A single CBO?

Now let us come back to the question of the object-based user interface, and the idea that each object will be implemented by one CBO. Well, that single CBO is the model CBO. A model may have one or more views associated with it. Each view will be implemented as a separate CBO. The implications of this are:

- A model will not know how many views it has; but it will know that it *may* have views. Hence, on occasion, it may need to send a message to whatever views it may have (for example, if its data has changed, then it may need to have its views reflect that change).
- A view may not know what model it is viewing. This allows for general-purpose views, usable by several models (achieved through separation of class name from code—see Sec. 8.3.4).
- The linkage between views and models should be provided by the CBO infrastructure.

5.2.3 Model and view differences

We can best describe the differences between views and models by looking at their responsibilities.

The *view* is responsible for:

- Understanding what data—and in what format—is displayed in a window.
- Handling user interactions (such as understanding that a push button has been pressed, that check boxes have been checked, that data has been entered, etc.).
- Providing any business logic directly associated with a window on the screen. For example, the view would do simple edit checking, display error messages, or provide application-related dynamics beyond the possible knowledge of a GUI layout tool. For example, if the 'apply' button on a new installation form must be disabled if the customer is found to be over their credit limit, then it would be the view's responsibility to disable the button.

The *model* is responsible for:

- Handling business logic common to several views.
- Being the place to send messages to in the UID (other CBOs should not know about views). For example, if an order form object is interested in a specific customer object's address, it might get that address by sending the customer object an appropriate message.
- Providing other CBOs in the same UID with data or status (an order form may need to know the Post Code, for example; the order form CBO would send a request to the customer model CBO asking for the Post Code—not to one of the customer's views).
- Handling garbage collection. For example, a user might have looked at a given customer some time ago, and may have closed its views. The underlying infrastructure may send a 'discard yourself' message to the customer, since it recognizes that it has not been referenced for some time. That message would be sent

- to the customer model, which would then decide whether or not to discard itself. The implications of this are further discussed in Sec. 8.3.11.
- Handling initialization processing (for example, when a user drags a new order form from a 'pad' of order forms, it would be the order form model CBO that obtains the new order number).
- Handling requests that result in an interaction with the SRD. The model CBO is the object that knows how to 'talk' to the SRD(s).
- Handling consistency within the UID. (For example, a business rule might be that a change to a customer address initiated from a given UID should be reflected anywhere else in that UID where the address is in a view. In this case, the relevant model CBOs would handle things, then report to any views that a change had been made.)
- An object might be a 'background' object, with no views or icon. Such an object would be implemented as a model CBO.
- Handling user authorization, by communicating (probably) with some security and/or authorization object.
- If certain common user interface actions are disallowed (for example, making a copy), then the model object is the appropriate place for the corresponding application code.
- Handling application-related things within the user interface domain, and which are beyond the competence of a single view. For example, if the user drags something across a customer icon (an icon is not a window, and hence does not have a view CBO), the model would be asked if a drop is OK or not.

Model-to-model interaction

Clearly in implementing business processes, it will be useful—if not essential—for one model object to be able to 'talk' to another. For example, if the user wants to enter customer details on an order form, and if we have both an order form model object and a customer model object, then we would want the order form model object to talk to the customer model object so that, for example, the order form can display customer details in its view.

Thus model objects must be able to communicate with each other, as well as with their views. Figure 5.3 illustrates this. It also illustrates the model talking to the 'server', using the same API. We discuss this later, in Sec. 5.4.

5.2.4   Merging model and view

The idea of views and models discussed so far has a number of implications which, while not rules, are useful design guidelines:

- A single model can have several views.
- Any given instance of a view CBO has only one model.

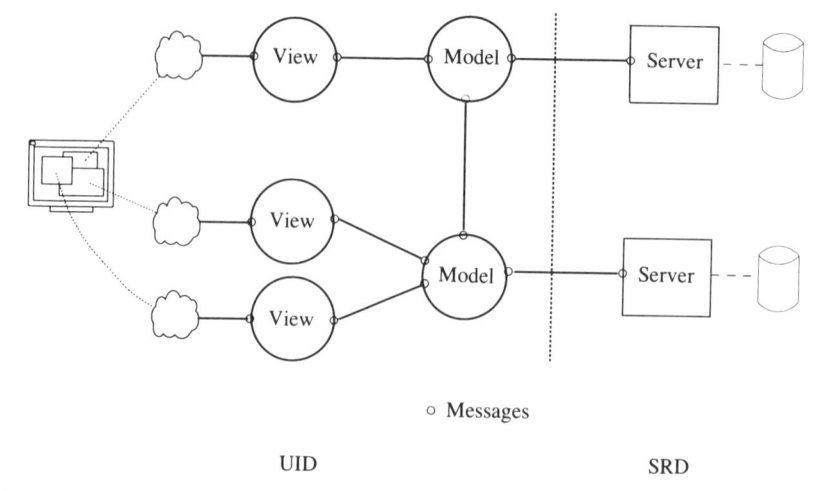

Figure 5.3.   Model–view and model–model interactions.

- The model knows where to get its data from. The view will get its data from its model.
- A view cannot exist without a model.

The last implication is interesting. What about the situation where the view encompasses all of the function required, and hence the model is extremely simple? Does that mean that we are *forced* to build two CBOs? The answer is no (certainly from the programmer's viewpoint). Where a single combined CBO is all that is required, then what is built is a single model that has lots of view behaviour. We call this a 'view model'.

By the way, note also that if you built a large view/model CBO, with several secondary windows, and which ignored all messages from other CBOs, then you would have something that looked very much like a traditional PC application.

5.2.5   Views and the GUI

Let us go back to views for a moment. For we have to ask, how does the view CBO relate to the system-level GUI API (such as Windows, or Presentation Manager)? For ease of programming, we can say that the view CBO programmer should not *have* to understand such APIs; he or she should be completely shielded from them.

The answer is to have some GUI layout tool and the infrastructure work together to produce the window layout in such a manner that:

- When the user does something to a window, the view CBO receives messages such as 'apply button pushed', or 'menu item "save" selected'—where those messages are exactly the same in format and structure as those received from other CBOs.

- The view CBO programmer can treat the window as if it were another CBO, and send it messages (such as 'write "Joe Smith" into the field "Cust Name" ').

5.3 The view 'layout'

This is an attractive solution, as it means that the view CBO does not *have* to understand the layout of the window, just what fields and controls or widgets are on it. ('Controls' in the context of GUI windows refers to units such as scroll bars, push buttons, check boxes, entry fields, title bars, menu bars, etc. A 'widget' is the equivalent in X-windows.) Thus if the layout is altered, the view CBO need not change.

Figure 5.4 shows how this might be implemented, where the window is an order form, and the view CBO is called the 'order view' CBO. At build time (on the left of the diagram), a WYSIWYG (what you see is what you get) window layout tool allows the designer to design the order form window. All windows on GUIs are driven through the system-level GUI API, and the layout tool would talk directly to that API. The output from the layout tool is a script file (or layout definition file)—the 'Order View' layout script. This script file is so called because it is a human-readable 'script' of the window layout. Mind you, not many humans would understand it. By 'human-readable', we mean that a knowledgeable human *could* understand it using a normal text editor to look at it.

At run-time, the 'window manager' part of the CBO infrastructure reads this script file, and talks via the GUI API to produce the window on the screen. Any events signalled from the GUI API to the infrastructure are filtered, and a useful

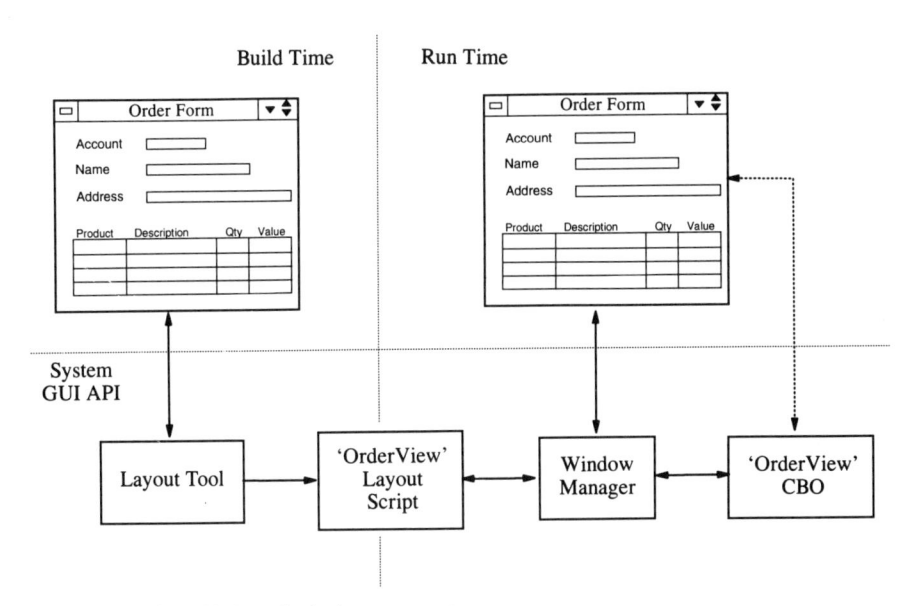

Figure 5.4. View CBO and window separation.

subset of those events are converted to CBO messages, and sent to the view CBO ('Order View' in Fig. 5.4). In turn, the view CBO sees the window as another object, and talks to it by sending messages to it. These messages are converted by the window manager into the required system-level GUI API calls.

This approach has a number of advantages in addition to those noted above:

No code generation

The window layout tool does *not* generate code. This means that a programmer using (for example) some high-level interpretive language such as REXX does not have to understand a development environment that may be quite alien to him or her just to be able to use the layout tool.

No code integration problem

Some layout tools that generate code have to deal with the problem of incorporating application logic into the generated code. *Not* generating code avoids this problem altogether.

Late binding of layout and view CBO

The layout script and the view CBO can be associated—or 'bound'—at run-time, thus allowing great flexibility during development (and maybe for the user as well—see Part Five). Run-time association means that we can, if we wish, move towards the idea of several layouts having the same view CBO. Again, since the view CBO is an object, we could place significant behaviour for different categories of windows into superclasses. (See Appendix 1 for a description of superclasses.)

Layout change without code change

Separation of layout and the view CBO code means that the layout can be changed without touching the code in the view CBO. Association of the two can be done through an external control file, or via some run-time utility CBO.

Dynamic layout creation

Although for simplicity Fig. 5.4 shows the layout script being read in by the window manager, in fact it would be read in by a view superclass which would be provided by the CBO infrastructure. This enables a view to build a layout dynamically at run-time if that is what is required.

To illustrate this, suppose there is a superclass called *SuperView* (not shown in Fig. 5.4), and what we are building is 'OrderView'. When the window manager detects that a window must be drawn (for example, the user double clicks on the customer icon, meaning 'please show me a view of this object'), it will send a 'QueryLayout' message to 'OrderView'.

Normally, the 'OrderView' CBO will ignore this message, and it would be passed to *SuperView*, which would read the layout script file into memory, and return the layout script to the window manager. However, 'OrderView' could override the 'QueryLayout' message, build its own layout, and return it to the window manager.

This design allows layouts to be generated either by an external layout tool, or dynamically by a view CBO itself.

Direct access to the GUI API

Figure 5.4 shows a dotted line from the 'OrderView' CBO, across the system GUI API, direct to the window. This illustrates that the 'power' programmer (for example, a C programmer skilled in the use of the system GUI API) is not locked out from doing advanced GUI work directly.

Thus, although the average application programmer need know *nothing* about the system-level GUI API, the knowledgeable programmer can use it if required.

Dynamic addition of new controls

The window manager component of the CBO infrastructure can be built such that new GUI controls (for example, a special kind of entry field that only allows entry of properly formatted part numbers—or a pink polka-dotted blinking blob, or whatever) can be added without changes to the infrastructure. This is hugely simplified if controls are treated as objects in their own right.

5.4 Connecting to the server

In addition to model–view and model–model interaction, we also need a way for models to communicate with the server. For ease of programming, we would like to use the same messaging model and API for *all* requests, whether local or remote (as indicated in Fig. 5.3).

In order to do this, we need to have the CBO infrastructure handle the low-level communications APIs. In this way, we achieve something rather attractive, in that the programmer of a model sees the server as just another CBO—with the infrastructure handling the requirement of getting over a task boundary.

Of course, the 'server object' here is not the server at all. It is something that adapts an object message sent to it into some form of communications code. This communications code routes the message to the real server. We call this object an 'adapter'. The model CBO, however, *sees* it as the real server.

Ideally we would like that routing to be done by the infrastructure code. Given that we will use messaging as the vehicle for models, views and servers to 'talk' to one another, let us have a closer look at the adapter.

The adapter object

The key point about an adapter is that the application programmer never sees it. The programmer of the model sends a message to what he or she sees as the server. However, the CBO infrastructure routes this message to the adapter, as shown in Fig. 5.5.

The main characteristics of an adapter are:

- It appears to a model object as just another CBO.
- It provides for getting over the task or process boundary (without programmer knowledge).
- It routes a request from a model to the server (using some system-level communication technology such as APPC (advanced program-to-program communications), RPC, the CICS OS/2 ECI, Named Pipes, TCP/IP, etc.).
- It routes responses from the server back to the requesting model object.
- It is *not* written by the application programmer.
- The adapter may itself be a CBO (which neither the user nor the application programmer ever see). That is, it can be an object, and can benefit from the usual inheritance mechanisms of OO. For example, there may be a general-purpose adapter that handles the multi-tasking or multi-processing aspects. A subclass of this might filter messages, such that only valid messages are sent to specific servers.

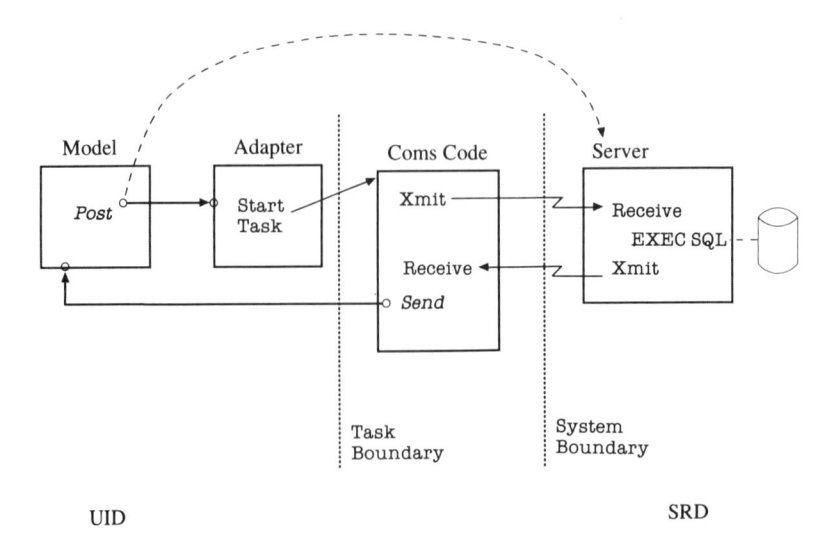

Figure 5.5. Model–adapter–server.

The adapter is built as a 'hybrid' object—displaying object behaviour and appearance to model objects, but driving procedural session-level communications code on its 'other side'. The essential idea here is that a message sent by a model to a 'remote object', such as, say, a 'customer database' server (which might actually translate to a CICS transaction), is mapped to a send/receive transaction by the adapter. This process would normally have the general shape shown by Fig. 5.5 (which illustrates the asynchronous case).

'Xmit' (transmit) in Fig. 5.5 indicates a communications send function (such as issuing a CPI-C (common programming interface for communications) 'CMSEND' verb—as opposed to sending the sort of message implemented for models and views). (There could be several transmits from the server; and, of course, in the communications code task there may be a loop round the receive. It is also sometimes useful to separate the communications send and receive into separate modules; this option is not shown in the figure.)

Finally, the adapter must maintain the semantics of the two ways of issuing messages from a CBO—send and post—as follows:

1 *Send* In this case, to allow for the situation shown in Fig. 4.15, the infrastructure must arrange things such that, although the message is synchronous with respect to the sending CBO, the sending CBO must *not* block. This is regardless of whether the communications link is synchronous or asynchronous. In addition, the data returned must be available at the next sequential instruction, even though it might have to be returned across a network. In this way, the programmer's model of what 'send' means, and what it does, is maintained regardless of whether the message is sent to a local or remote CBO.

2 *Post* The semantics of a 'post' require a return of control from the adapter as soon as it has initiated its communication to the server, even though the communications mechanism might be synchronous (such as some terminal emulations, or some RPC implementations). The adapter must also catch the response, and route it back to the requesting CBO as another message.

Messages are routed from the model object to the adapter by a routing function in the infrastructure code. It is worth noting that there are really two different routers at work here:

1 The message router, which picks up a message sent from a CBO and routes it directly to another CBO *in the same system*—for example, from the model to the adapter (or to another model) and from the adapter back to the model.

2 The piece of communications code, which sends the message *to another system* and catches the response(s).

If the receiving end is a CBO, rather than a traditional transaction program (say), then of course the CBO infrastructure must provide a 'listening' function, and also an initiation function such that the receiving CBO can be identified and (if not already loaded) loaded into memory. The incoming message can then be routed correctly to the receiving CBO.

There are also other considerations here: suppose messages for (say) 20 remote objects are all to be carried on the same APPC LU–LU link. A way must be provided for routing messages to any of the 20 remote objects through the same adapter, which should handle multiple sessions concurrently (assuming an independent logical unit (LU)), each in a separate task. Thus a form of 'aliasing' is required (preferably table-driven).

5.5 Summary

In this chapter we have explored further the user interface domain—the area in which the user presentation logic, and that business logic which assists a single user, reside.

We determined that it is useful to create two separate types of CBO to handle the two areas of programming logic—a view CBO (user presentation logic) and a model CBO (user business logic).

Each model object may have several views, allowing the user to view an object in several different ways. Where a single view only is required, and where the application code is simple, then the model and view may be combined into a single CBO (the 'view model').

We discussed how a view CBO could communicate with a window on the GUI via a 'layout' (a definition of the window layout), and how a model could communicate with a server via an adapter object in such a way as to provide the programmer with local/remote transparency.

Throughout, a central theme has been making things easy for the application programmer, and we have defined the functions required of a software infrastructure (middleware) to achieve this. Such a definition is not academic; it has been proven in practice. The infrastructure defined, and the structure of CBOs, is designed specifically to make the production of cooperative application code much easier than it has been previously.

6
The shared resource domain

In this chapter, we examine the structure of the shared resource domain (SRD)—the server end of a client/server system. The context for discussion is that of core business systems (mission-critical systems), where the server contains transaction processing and database management software. The transaction processor and database are together assumed to provide an environment within which concurrent transactions can each be either entirely completed (and any changes made to shared resources committed) or, in the case of a problem, rolled back (and any changes backed out so that resources are restored to their pre-transaction state).[1]

First, we discuss the *nature* of the SRD. We then define the *design points* for the SRD. The most important of these is that, to protect resource integrity, a single request to the SRD should be entirely handled within one interaction, so that the response to the requester (typically a UID) reflects committed work, or some error (implying that no changes have been made).

A *structural overview* of the SRD structure is then presented, in terms of traditional transaction programs. Just as the UID consists of a number of different elements, so the SRD consists of:

- A front-end, which hides the programmer from underlying communications complexities.
- Focus modules, which focus on the commit scope, such that a transaction is handled properly.
- Entity modules, which manage a specific logical entity.
- Resource modules, which manage a specific resource (these are very often combined with entity modules).

Each of these *components* is then discussed.

---

[1] The context is important for the analysis presented here. Other contexts are possible. One such is an emerging concept of object integrity, which promises a high degree of integrity across multiple different database and transaction systems. However, at the time of writing, I know of no large-scale core business system implementations of this approach.

Finally, *building the SRD with CBOs* is discussed. Having CBOs in the SRD raises the question of the concurrent object (an object through which multiple transactions run concurrently), and this—in the context of CBOs—is discussed.

We find that CBOs can indeed be used profitably at the server end of a client/server system (though for transaction processing systems, some technical questions are still outstanding). We also find that there is a distinct difference between the user interface area on the one hand, and the area where shared resource integrity is essential on the other. This leads to a specific set of design guidelines, which ease considerably questions such as 'Where does the function go?'

6.1 The nature of the SRD

A high-level view of the cooperative processing model developed in previous chapters is shown in Fig. 6.1, where each box is application-level code, the lines linking them are messages, and the 'task boundary' shows where messages *must* be asynchronous.

At a high level of abstraction, this model is one of PCs connected to systems that manage shared resources. The view and model are to do with the user interface, and have nothing to do with accessing shared resources. The 'server' is the code that accesses shared resources (such as a database). Often the 'server' will be on a mainframe or a LAN server. However, even in the case of a distributed DBMS with APIs available on the PC, this design still applies (but in this case the 'server' might be located on the PC).

With this separation, we can talk about the 'user interface domain' on the one hand and the 'server domain' on the other. However, using the term 'server' here now becomes difficult, as it can easily be confused with the same term used elsewhere (e.g. 'client/server', 'file server'). What we are really talking about is the 'shared resource domain', or SRD (introduced in Sec. 4.3.2). In the SRD, shared resources are accessed by application-level code (the 'server' module in Fig. 6.1), and managed by system-level resource management code (such as is found in IBM's CICS and DB2 products).

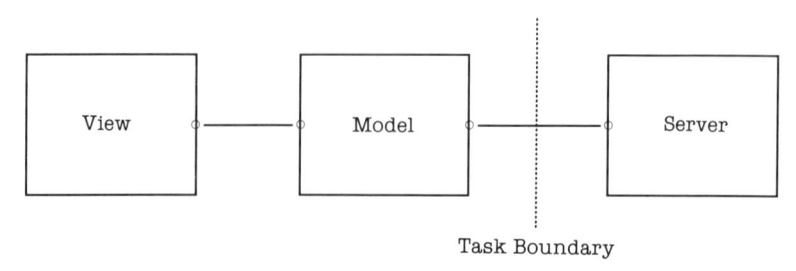

Figure 6.1. General model for cooperative processing.

Now, an overriding imperative in the design of any system that provides access to shared resources is to ensure resource integrity. In general, this means using the available capabilities of the system-level resource manager, and conforming to any constraints it might impose. (We do not want to write our own two-phase commit function!) From the point of view of the cooperative processing designer, there are two important aspects of these capabilities that must be taken into account. These are:

- The scope of the resource manager (single system, distributed, etc.)—that is, the scope over which it can manage multiple concurrent and recoverable units of work.
- The commit scope as seen by the programmer (not always the same as the scope of the resource manager).

6.1.1 Resource manager scope

A good example of what we mean by 'shared resource' is a database accessed concurrently by more than one user, where a system resource manager provides concurrency control, back-up and commit function, perhaps logging, etc. For example, IBM's, CICS and DB2 products are both good examples of resource managers.

The essence of a resource manager is that it keeps resources secure. This means not only that there is adequate back-up and recovery, but also that resources are kept in a consistent state when errors occur during changes. This means that database changes are either rolled back to the previous consistent state, or they are committed. In transaction processing systems, the unit of consistency is typically the transaction. The scope of the commit may be a single database, several databases (not necessarily in the same machine if there is a distributed DBMS), or both databases and some other resource (such as a communications link). It is the resource manager provided by system software that defines the commit scope.

For simplicity, we shall in general assume that the shared resource is always a database. This does not affect the essential argument.

Concurrency is typically controlled through serialization of changes by the underlying resource manager. Application-level code should not see this serialization. The first transaction to request the start of a commit scope (sometimes done simply by virtue of the transaction starting) will lock the resources required by that transaction, and commit (again, sometimes automatically) at the end of the transaction. While the database is being changed, it is locked to other transactions (or at least the records or rows in question are locked against changes by other transactions). These other transactions are (normally) queued, or serialized, by the resource manager.

The scope of the resources controlled in this way by a resource manager we will call the *resource manager domain*.

Thus when considering DBMSs (database management systems), the resource manager domain is the area that the DBMS controls. If the DBMS is distributed, then this area may extend over several physically separate systems.

However, there is an additional constraint on commit scope as it applies to the designer of application code. Consider a single business process that requires two databases to be updated, one on machine A and one on machine B, where both A and B are managed by a single (distributed) DBMS. This operation could potentially be written in two ways:

- A program could be written on machine A that updates data on both machines A and B.
- A program could be written on machine A that updates data on A, then calls a program on B to update data on B.

Many distributed DBMSs limit the effective commit scope to a single program—or a transaction that runs (as far as the application code is concerned) on a single machine—even though that single program can, through the DBMS, update data on several physically separate databases. In this case, to ensure data integrity, only the first option is available to the application designer. The second option is only possible where the DBMS (or DBMS and transaction processor working together) allows code in several different machines to participate in a single controlled transaction.

Thus although a DBMS may give the programmer access to data on several machines (the resource manager domain), it may impose limits on where he or she can place code to access that data. The area within which this code can be placed such that a recoverable unit of work can be initiated, run and completed, we call the '*shared resource domain*' (or SRD).

If a transaction (a 'commit scope') is further limited on some system to a single process or address space, and that machine can run multiple processes concurrently, then there would be multiple SRDs on that one machine.

Here is an example to illustrate the concept of 'shared resource domain'. A certain computer system provides a single (non-distributed) database resource manager, accessible by all concurrently running programs. We would say that the resource manager domain is bounded by that system. Further, each program runs in a different process (address space, partition, task, job, etc.). Now assume a system-imposed rule: that, for any given unit of work (transaction) to be recoverable, all database accesses within that unit of work must be issued from a single process or address space (that is, from a single program).

In this example, the resource manager domain is the entire system. The SRD, on the other hand, is a single process—or application-level code running within a single address space.

This would mean that the designer would have to ensure that all server code handling a given recoverable transaction *must* run within a single address space.

6.2 SRD design points

The requirements for on-line transaction processing (OLTP) are perhaps more stringent than for most other forms of cross-system connection. We will therefore consider the design of code within the SRD with OLTP in mind. Requirements on SRD design from less stringent environments we find are often a subset of the OLTP requirements.

In designing SRD application code, the following design points should be taken into consideration:

1 *'One-shot' interactions*   The first and most important rule for the SRD is this: An incoming message is treated as a *single unit* of work by the SRD. This rule enables commit processing in the SRD to be properly completed. By 'commit processing' is meant the ability of the SRD either to update resources and commit those changes, or to roll back changes to the state that was obtained before the message was received.

   There should always be at least one response message sent back to the requester. This will contain a return code indicating the success of the request, plus (maybe) some data. When a large amount of data must be returned, there may be several response messages sent back to the requester.

   Experience in the client/server area suggests that, even when an OLTP can manage multiple interactions within a single commit scope, design and programming are made much easier by implementing this 'one-shot' approach. In addition, the binding between the SRD and UID is made more loose.

2 *Messaging*   We adopt the messaging model for interaction with the SRD.

3 *No 'dialogue' state information*   Servers are atomic; they do not retain knowledge of any user conversation, dialogue sequence, or data, between invocations. This implies that the SRD never partakes in dialogues with requesters. However, it does not mean that the SRD is always 'passive'. It means that it is passive with respect to a requester (which might be a UID or another SRD). An SRD can itself send messages to other SRDs—and to UIDs. Some of these situations are discussed in Chapter 10.

The above may seem somewhat restrictive. However, they are not hard-and-fast rules—they are an extremely useful set of 'rules of thumb'. They can be broken—if the designer knows exactly what he or she is doing.

Finally, it is worth noting that the SRD can be accessed from a different kind of UID—one that knows nothing about PCs, but implements dialogues for character-based terminals. This is especially useful where both PCs and older non-programmable (dependent on the main computer) terminals must be supported by the same SRD code. In that case, a separate UID for the dependent terminals would be built. Both PC UIDs and character-based terminal UIDs would request services of the SRD application code. In this way, SRD code can be used for both client/server and centralized environments.

6.3 Overview of SRD structure

In Fig. 5.5 the server (the SRD) was shown as a single module. However, we need a little more than shown there. In particular, we do not want the application programmer to have to write communications code. Thus we provide a 'front-end', which handles the communications code and various other related matters. This front-end will be an essential part of the client/server software infrastructure.

The server end of the client/server link, then, is as shown in Fig. 6.2 (which also shows a model object in a UID for completeness). In this figure, the server of Fig. 5.5 has been split into a focus part and an entity part. (Terminology in this area is developing. The term focus derives from the BSDM system development method. Other terms sometimes used are 'control' and 'business process'. The *entity* is also sometimes referred to as the 'CRUD' (for 'create, read, update, delete'—a term first used in E/R modelling, where processes are mapped to entities in a CRUD matrix).

The focus provides the commit scope for an SRD transaction. It is the 'focus' of the transaction, and will reflect a defined atomic process against some entity or group of entities. The idea of the entity is to have a single place where handling of a given database (or perhaps a given logical view of several tables) is done. Other code, if it wants to access data from that database, would make a request of the relevant entity module. In general, for each data entity, there will be one entity module.

Often the SRD requirements will be handled by a single (coalesced) focus and entity. We might call this the server(!). This is reflected in Fig. 6.2, where both the focus and entity are seen issuing I/O against a shared resource (shown by EXEC SQL).

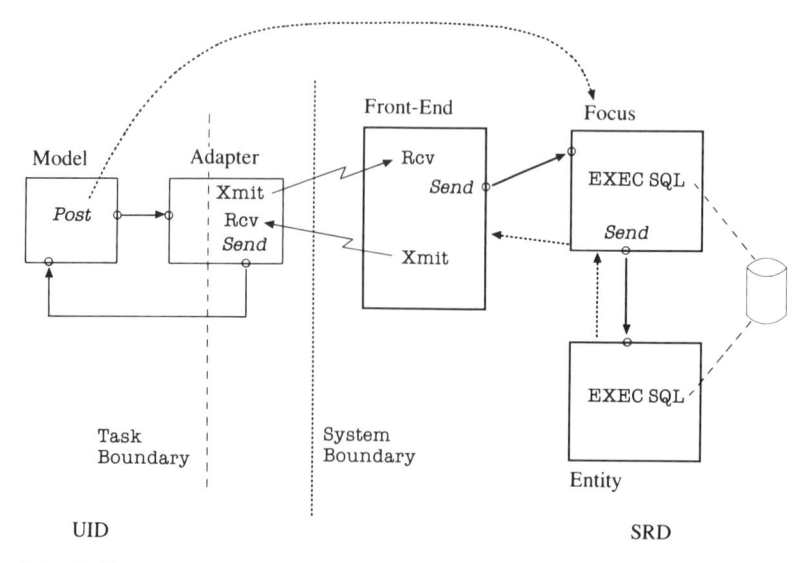

Figure 6.2. SRD structure.

The general idea with this model is that the programmer should only have to build the view(s), the model, the focus and the entity. In practice, we find that the SRD parts can generally be built independently from the UID elements. The adapter, the communications code and the server front-end are part of the underlying infrastructure, and should not be seen by the application programmer.

Figure 6.2 shows a messaging connection between the focus and the entity. In the general case, such a link is required if SRD components are to be the clients to other SRDs (which may themselves be on yet another system).

An important implementation point here is the precise nature of this link. It should be designed so as to allow both synchronous and asynchronous messages—and also to allow multiple responses (messages sent back) to a single message. It should also be designed to use the same messaging API as at the PC end—at least at the programming concept level. Finally, it must also be designed such that the commit scope is retained (that is, all messages between server components for a given request must be in a single SRD).

An example of how this could look to the application programmer is shown in Fig. 6.3. As can be seen, each of the three modules addresses application-related logic (rather than GUI or communication details). This simplicity derives from two key aspects of the model:

- Use of code structured for event-loop processing.
- Availability of both synchronous and asynchronous messaging.

Clearly, to enable this level of simplicity, our infrastructure code must provide a wealth of function. But it is not until we have defined the *user's* view—that is, what the average programmer would like to be able to do to handle both advanced user interfaces and cross-system cooperative processing—that we can fully define its characteristics.

Finally, since in essence our model defines a general easy-to-program messaging

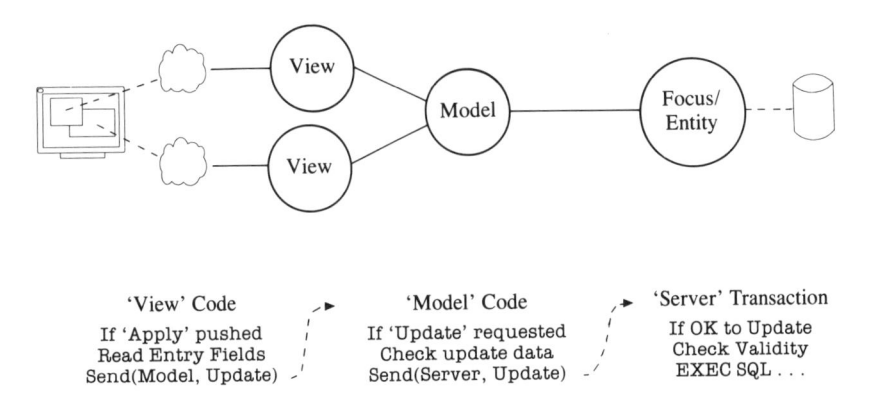

```
'View' Code           'Model' Code            'Server' Transaction
If 'Apply' pushed     If 'Update' requested   If OK to Update
Read Entry Fields     Check update data       Check Validity
Send(Model, Update)   Send(Server, Update)    EXEC SQL . . .
```

Figure 6.3. Programming simplicity.

mechanism between independently developed event-loop software modules, it can address many different systems scenarios, including:

- Stand-alone PC.
- Stand-alone mainframe (with non-programmable terminals).
- Interconnected systems where messages flow freely between systems.

6.4 SRD components

Experience suggests that the design of server code is made considerably easier when an object analysis and design approach is taken. This is so for both CBO design and non-CBO design. For this reason, the SRD components discussed in this section are referred to generically as 'modules'. Later, we will consider CBOs in the SRD (Sec. 6.5).

6.4.1 The 'front-end'

The major responsibility of the SRD 'front-end' is to hide communications coding and protocols from the programmer. It receives incoming requests (as messages), routes them to their destination (a server) and routes responses back to the requester. As such, this is part of the SRD infrastructure rather than part of the SRD application-level code.

The front-end will also handle such things as:

- Invoking one or more servers, in the correct sequence.
- Translation of data representation (e.g. ASCII to EBCDIC) and code pages.
- Access authorization.
- Version levels (where a system might have—at any one time—two or more versions of PC and/or server application code).

In invoking the appropriate server(s), the front-end may use a routing table, or may assemble a set of requests dynamically from the incoming message. From a design point of view, it seems better that the incoming requests be for a single service. The front-end may then decide to invoke several servers to process that request (within a single transaction). This approach better encapsulates the SRD as seen by requesters.

Tibbetts and Bernstein (1992) describe the front-end as a 'function dispatcher', and describe its function in some detail.

Finally, it is worth noting that the front-end code may be more or less complex depending on the system environment. For example, if there is a transaction processing system in the server system, then the front end will be considerably simpler than if there is none.

6.4.2 The 'focus'

The 'focus' module is responsible for ensuring the integrity of all shared resources involved in a single request from a client (that is, from a UID or perhaps from another SRD). The focus knows where shared resources are located, and manages the commit scope (assuming, of course, an underlying commit manager such as is found in CICS and/or DB2).

To clients, the focus is the server, and as such does not retain state information about clients outside of a single client request. Therefore a client cannot have a dialogue with a server.

The focus encapsulates a given atomic business process (such as 'add a new order'). This should not be confused with a business process as seen by a user. The kind of 'process' implemented by a focus module is one where a given single entity is being changed, but, as a result of that change, business rules require that one or more other entities also need to be changed.

Consider, for example, an incoming message requesting the creation of a customer order. Clearly data must be written to the orders database to reflect the new customer order. But it is normally the case that business rules require other data to change because of the addition of a new order. And these other changes must be done within a single commit scope. The 'process' encapsulated by the focus might then look like this:

- Update the customer balance outstanding.
- Create the new order (order header and order detail lines).
- For each item ordered, update that item's stock-on hand.

Often a single transaction would do all of these. But it is sometimes useful to separate out the individual data accesses into separate modules. Then they can potentially be re-used by other focus modules. Now data is often organized in a way that reflects an entity analysis; for this reason, the separate modules are called 'entity' modules.

To handle our example, then, we might build an 'order' focus module that would use several entity modules—the customer entity, the order entity and the item entity. The order focus module would provide the start and end of the commit scope, and run any business rules peculiar to the order as a whole.

The main objectives of a focus module are:

- Encompass the commit scope for the entire server request.
- Understand which resources are to be accessed, and how to access them.
- Package up the response to be returned to the client, and return it (to the infrastructure, for the infrastructure to deliver).[2]

---

[2] In some implementations, this is a logical responsibility; in fact, responses are gathered together in the form of a self-defining data 'blob' by entity modules, so that the focus just adds to its own information, rather than being responsible for formatting and packaging the lot.

- May handle referential integrity (if not handled elsewhere).
- Apply any business rules which apply to the transaction as a whole.

When a focus does not have to apply business rules, the focus can be seen as a general-purpose 'transaction shell', possibly combined with the front-end. In this case, the client must compose a 'package' of requests, which are unpacked by the focus and sent to the appropriate entity modules, all within a single transaction.

6.4.3 The 'entity'

The *entity* module is responsible for accessing some specific instance of a shared resource, such as a given data table. Typically it will act as a server to one or more focus CBOs. One entity CBO might handle a single physical table, a logical view (i.e. a database (DB) view), or perhaps several tables where each table is really part of a whole (example—a 'supplier order' entity might manage both a supplier order header table and a supplier order detail table).

Entity modules handle specific data entities in databases (e.g. 'customer', 'account', 'order header'). For some incoming messages (e.g. 'read customer record for customer number A1234'), the entity modules will provide all of the server function needed; in that case, the single entity module encompasses both focus and entity roles.

Entity modules can be re-used in various different business process areas. This is really an extension into application-level code of the idea of having a single database, accessible to all applications that need the data.

Some of the characteristics of entity modules are as follows:

- Referential integrity—if not handled by the DBMS (much the better option)—will be handled in the entity modules.
- Unless we can be sure that incoming messages are *always* received from a secure and trusted environment, then entity modules will also re-run key business rules, to ensure not only update integrity, but also business integrity.
- Entity modules may invoke other entity modules (e.g. an order entity may invoke order header and order details entities—assuming that the latter are required as independent entities for some reason). Entity modules may also be invoked as servers in their own right—for example, a customer entity module may be invoked from a UID to handle an update. In this case, the entity must play the role of a combined focus and entity. This dual role may be constrained by the underlying resource manager. Some resource managers require the programmer to issue explicit start and end commit scope instructions, and others provide implicit commit scopes. If explicit start and end commit statements are required, and if an entity is to play a dual role, then the underlying resource manager must allow nested commit instructions. This is because the entity module should not have to determine how it is invoked, and so decide whether or not to issue commit instructions.

Occasionally, the data access function implicit in an entity is broken out into another kind of module, which I call the 'resource' module.

6.4.4 The 'resource'

The *resource* module is responsible for providing transparency as to the underlying resource manager to the entities. The resource module issues the SQL, or does the VSAM I/O, etc. If resource manager transparency is not required, then the resource module function would be collapsed into the entity.

Resource CBOs can, in some circumstances, be an extremely useful agent for lessening the impact of change. The entity CBO applies business rules; the resource CBO issues the I/O. Encapsulating the I/O in the resource CBO can help where:

- It is planned to move from one form of DB access to another (e.g. chained files to relational).
- Several different kinds of data access must be catered for (each will have a different resource CBO; but the entity CBOs should be the same).
- Several different SQL dialects may have to be catered for.

To those who have a single dialect of SQL as a corporate standard, and who do not intend to change, then an approach that encapsulates all the SQL into one kind of CBO—well away from the application logic—may seem odd. Suffice to say that such an arrangement is an option, not a rule. Where a single database (DB) API is certain to be persistent for the foreseeable future, then one would not bother with separate resource CBOs.

6.5 SRD CBOs

Previously, when discussing the UID, we showed how building cooperative business objects (CBOs) instead of applications provides a much closer fit to the problems of cooperative processing than more traditional approaches, and also opened up dramatic new potential for software re-use—for the user as well as for the developer. In particular, we showed that:

- CBOs provide *ease of programming* to the average application programmer for both synchronous and asynchronous requests between the two separately developed pieces of application code, with local/remote transparency.
- CBOs (and the required middleware or infrastructure) provide a superior design for the PC end of a cooperative system.
- The functional requirements for CBO-enabling middleware had many similarities with those provided by transaction processing systems (such as IBM's CICS):
  —Task management
  —Program invocation

—Storage management
—High-level APIs
—Communications management
—Concurrency management

The question now is whether CBOs show similar advantages for the server end of a client/server system—or, to be more specific, for the SRD. Since a transaction-based SRD, with concurrent update requests and resource integrity, is perhaps the more challenging of the possible SRD environments, we will address this question from the point of view of transaction processing servers.

The remainder of this chapter discusses CBOs in a transaction processing environment. First, in the next subsection, we list the potential advantages of CBOs. Then we illustrate these advantages with an example. This example is used to generate key questions about CBOs and transactions. Subsequent subsections discuss answers to these questions.

6.5.1 CBO advantages

There are a number of advantages to using CBOs rather than traditional structures in the SRD:

- CBOs provide all the advantages of object orientation, including re-use, incremental development through inheritance, encapsulation of data (reducing code redundancy) and reduction of the scope of changes.
- CBOs map well to the emerging ideas of 'networked objects'—the idea of networks of free-flowing messages, unconstrained by connection protocols, and providing ease of programming for the average programmer. The existence of a standard messaging protocol and formats between CBOs (not the same as between systems!) will enhance open interchanges.
- CBOs can form the basis for a market in objects. A given CBO (perhaps a 'customer order', for example) may even by purchased by several different companies from the same specialist software house. Using inheritance, the CBO purchased might be specialized without IS touching the bought-in CBO (no recompile, no relink). The other CBOs could be built, or bought in from other vendors.
- CBOs can substantially improve customization of software. For example, suppose the corporate CBO department (located overseas) develops an account object. If some local legal constraint requires the behaviour of this CBO to be modified, then a subclass can be built. This can avoid any need to modify the code delivered by the corporate CBO department. It also makes maintenance of that code much easier (the modifications do not have to be reapplied). (This approach requires class names to be assigned at run-time rather than at build time—another requirement on the CBO infrastructure.)

The shared resource domain

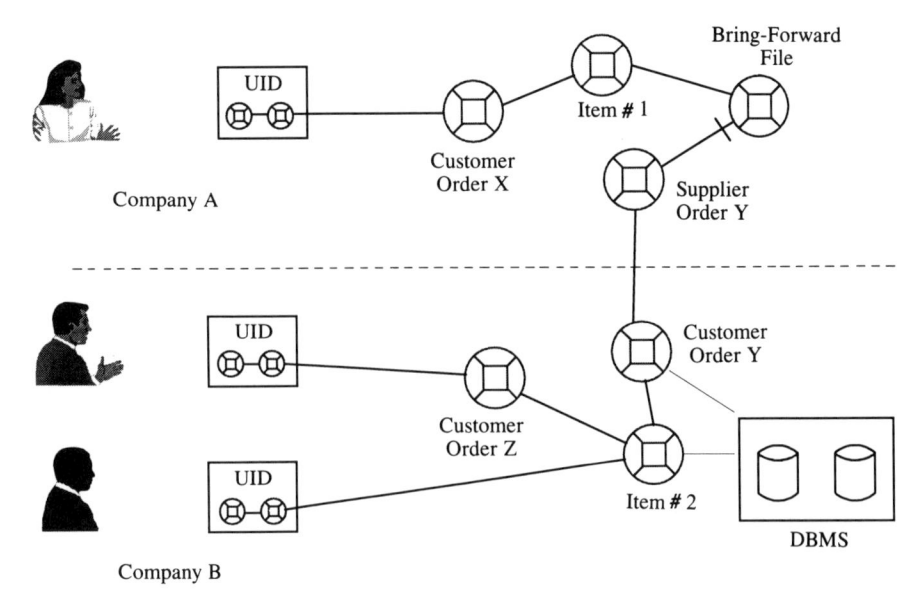

Figure 6.4. Networked CBOs.

Suppose we could execute CBOs within one of today's transaction processors, such as IBM's CICS. Figure 6.4 shows how this might look. We see two companies, A and B. Assume that B is a supplier to A. In company A, a user places an order for one of company A's customers. The order is built in the user's UID, involving several UID CBOs. One of these sends a 'create order' message to an SRD, and here is what happens (note that, for clarity, only a few of the CBOs that would be involved in this process are shown, and the focus, entity and resource CBOs are not shown separately):

- The Customer Order X CBO sends a message to the Item #1 CBO to decrement stock-on-hand. Assume that on-hand falls below reorder level.
- The Item #1 CBO sends a 'Place Supplier Order (for me, on company B)' message to a 'Bring-Forward File' CBO. For present purposes, we assume that it is the Item CBO that has the responsibility for knowing from whom to replenish itself.
- Some time later (indicated in the figure by a bar across the message line), the Bring-Forward File CBO issues a 'Create New Supplier Order (on company B)', which results in the creation of the Supplier Order Y CBO.
- The Supplier Order Y CBO sends itself to company B, by sending a 'Create New Customer Order' message across an Electronic Data Interchange (EDI) link to company B. This results in a new Customer Order Y being created in company B.
- The Customer Order Y is for Item #2 (this is company B's item number for the product that company A calls 'Item #1'). During processing, Customer Order Y sends a 'Decrement Stock On-Hand' message to the Item #2 CBO.

Meanwhile, a user in company B is also placing an order for Item #2, using the same customer order class (a different instance—Customer Order Z), which in turn sends a 'Decrement Stock On-Hand' message to the Item #2 CBO. Another user in company B is enquiring on the stock status of Item #2.

Several questions arise from this example:

- What is the difference between a UID 'model' CBO (say 'customer order') and the SRD 'customer order' CBO?
- If the SRD is implemented with a transaction processing system, how are the CBOs mapped to transactions and tasks?
- Is there a single instance of the Item #2 CBO being accessed by three transactions concurrently? If not, what is happening? How is commit scope retained?

We now address these questions.

6.5.2   CBOs—UID vs SRD

In the previous chapter, we saw 'customer' objects, 'order' objects, etc., in the UID. Now we see them again in the SRD. Are they identical, and, if not, why not?

A common confusion

SRD CBOs will often be implemented as focus and entity CBOs. For example, the 'customer order CBO' in Fig. 6.4 would probably be implemented as an order focus CBO, an order header entity CBO and an order detail entity CBO. However, when discussing the SRD in general, those three CBOs will often be referred to as a single object—'the order CBO', or as just 'the server object'. To make the confusion worse, at this level of abstraction, a 'server object' is sometimes referred to as the 'model' object.

If this terminology is used, then, when discussing the client/server object structure, there seem to be two 'model' objects. Clearly (the argument goes) there can only be one, and it must be in the SRD. Therefore, it is concluded, the model cannot be in the UID. This conclusion leaves only view objects in the UID, and can lead to implementations that are unnecessarily complicated.

To avoid this confusion, and possible undesirable consequences, we can use the term 'local model' to refer to the UID model, and focus and entity (or just server object) to refer to the SRD 'model'.

Different responsibilities

The major differences between UID and SRD objects are as follows.

A *UID local model* object:

- Provides the user with a representation of something he or she needs to do their work.
- Does not have any knowledge of sharing data, but provides a local surrogate for the SRD object, filtering requests from views and routing some of them to the SRD.
- Has very fast response times (may often have to be less then 100 milliseconds for trivial interactions such as drag and drop).
- Will often reflect changes to other objects in the UID (depending on user interface requirements).
- Is single-user, with no need to take concurrency (from multiple users) into account.
- Will be long-running and conversational (to avoid the overhead of program loading).

A *SRD server* object:

- Provides the organization with a representation of a valuable shared resource.
- Is responsible for enforcing business rules, for providing access to shared resources and for cooperating with resource managers to ensure resource integrity.
- Is not constrained by the same order of user interface response-time requirement; this means it can (for example) issue SQL requests within their methods. UID models are generally designed to avoid this.
- Understands that data is shared.
- Can reflect changes to other objects in the SRD (depending on business requirements).
- May be accessed by multiple users, and must take this into account.
- Will often be short-running, and, if so, would be 'unloaded' between transactions (by the infrastructure, and transparently to the programmer).

One might say that these differences are somewhat pragmatic, and, in the future, they may become less important. Nevertheless, with today's resource manager, network and database response times, the pragmatics dominate, leading to a requirement for different objects depending on whether they live in the UID or the SRD.

On the other hand, even with infinite computing resources, the differences in responsibility between (say) a 'customer' object that is built to satisfy UID requirements, and one built to live in an SRD, seem sufficient to justify a separation. We will discuss this further in Chapter 13.

6.5.3 *Mapping CBOs to transactions*

When we look at the messages flowing between objects for a given piece of work, we find that the flow is kicked off at a given object by some external event (such as an incoming request), passes through several other objects and finally ends up back at the starting object. I call this set of messages a 'flurry'. (Flurry is defined in the *Concise Oxford Dictionary* as: 'gust, squall; commotion, excitement; nervous hurry, agitation; sudden burst of activity'.)

If we then look at what is required for a flurry to run in an SRD, we find that many underlying infrastructure capabilities are required—such as multi-tasking (we might run each flurry in a separate task). Interestingly, when we match these required capabilities to a transaction processing system such as CICS, we find that many of them are already there.

There is a distinct similarity, then, between a flurry and a transaction. From one point of view, indeed, a flurry is really the same as a transaction. We give it a different name to avoid confusion with the usual structure of 'transaction programs'. Why should there be any confusion? Well, thinking in terms of a 'flurry' helps with discussing the next question: is there a single copy of any given CBO instance (e.g. Item #2), or are there multiple copies of that single instance, one per SRD? (See Appendix 1 for an introduction to the concepts of classes and instances.)

6.5.4 Single vs multiple instances

Suppose several users access the same customer data concurrently. Is there a separate instance of the customer object in the SRD for each transaction? Or is there a single instance that is shared between transactions?

In other words, just as with traditional transactions programs, a separate 'copy' or instance of a transaction program is run in each transaction (although, of course, only a single copy of the code is loaded), should we have a separate 'copy' of the customer object for each transaction? Or, just as there will only be one record on disk of the customer record in question, should there also be one single object through which all transactions accessing that data run?

This question is of key importance in implementing CBOs for shared resource domains, and its answer leads to two quite different design approaches (and to different infrastructure requirements) as follows:

- Create a separate instance within each transaction, and so have *multiple instantiations* of the same object. This is feasible today with little extension of the transaction processing environment.
- Create a single instance that is shared by several transactions, and so have a *single instantiation* of the object. This approach requires additional infrastructure capabilities to handle the concurrency.

To explain the difference, we will consider each approach in turn, and then discuss the outstanding technical challenges.

Multiple instantiation

'Traditional' design

The top part of Fig. 6.5 illustrates a traditional approach to implementing an order creation transaction. *Server 1* is invoked by an incoming 'create order' message, and issues DBMS calls (e.g. SQL) directly to the DBMS. Note that the transaction will be designed such that all of its code runs within an SRD.

Server 2 at the bottom of the figure shows a focus/entity implementation of server 1. The focus will invoke the appropriate entities. The entity modules would then issue the appropriate DBMS calls.

Whatever the connection between the focus and entity modules, the designer will have to ensure that all the invoked code stays within the SRD—else the commit scope will be lost.

Suppose server 2 is invoked at the same time as server 1. If the same item was ordered on both orders, then there would be two update accesses (one from each transaction) to the same specific item row or record in the item database. There would be two (essentially) identical pieces of code accessing the item database (DB), and the concurrent update problems are those which face any on-line transaction processing system. (These are discussed in some detail in Sec. 10.3.)

CBO design

Now consider how this same design might be implemented using CBOs. The essential thing here is to run transaction—or activity—within a single SRD. The CBOs might look as shown in Fig. 6.6.

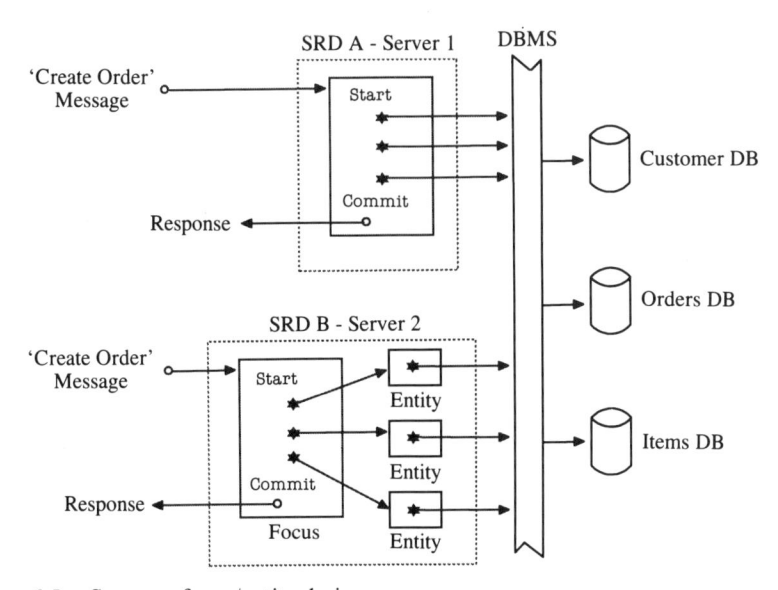

Figure 6.5. Server vs focus/entity design.

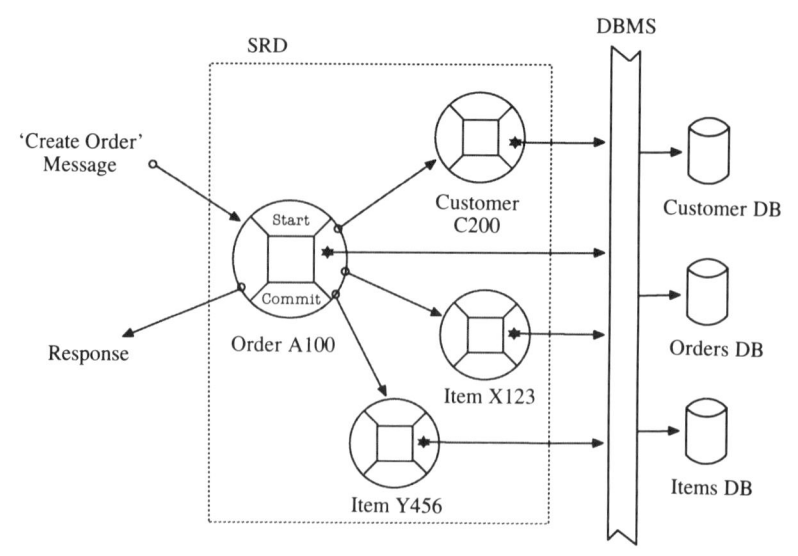

Figure 6.6. CBO 'server' design.

Here, the incoming message is for the order object (specifically, instance A100 of the class 'order'). This object sends messages to the customer object (instance C200 of class 'customer') and to the two item objects (instances X123 and Y456, both of the class 'item'). The order, customer and item objects all call the DBMS (an example of a focus CBO handling DB access). All four objects are instantiated within the same SRD.

What would have happened if another message had been received concurrently that also wanted to update item X123? In that case, another transaction would have been started by the transaction processor, and a second instance of object item X123 would have been instantiated—within the second transaction.

This is shown in Fig. 6.7, where we see two identical instances X123 of class 'item' within the same system (for simplicity, we assume a single transaction processing system—such as a single CICS region). The problem of data integrity is effectively the same as for the traditional approach, and again details can be found in Sec. 10.3.

Implementing this approach requires additional infrastructure functions over and above those provided by today's transactions processors. They include:

- Object instantiation
- Message routing
- Superclass handling
- Storage management (for instance, data)
- Code loading (depending on the specific transaction processing system)

All CBOs within a transaction would lie within one and only one SRD.

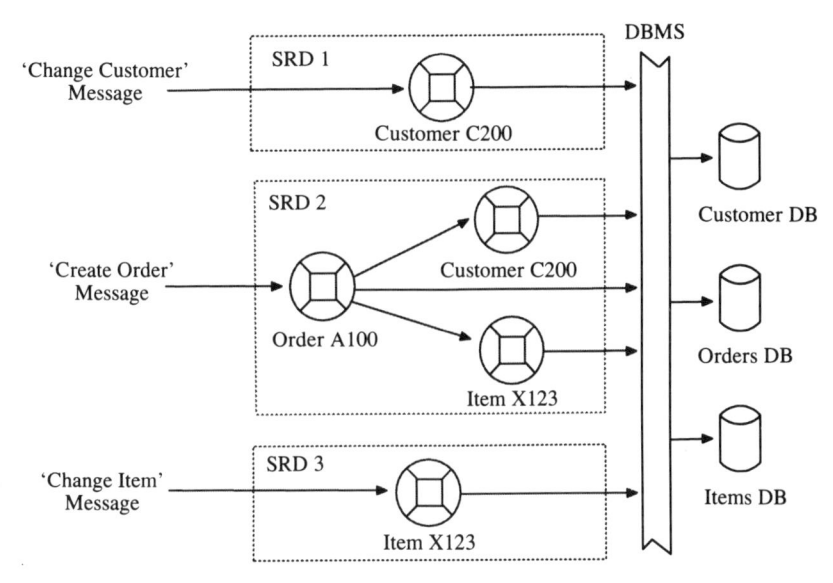

Figure 6.7. CBO concurrency—multiple instantiation.

Single instantiation

The 'single instantiation' approach says that there will only ever be one instance of a given class at any one time. If two transactions both needed to access the same instance, then the infrastructure would have to:

- Provide for multiple concurrent access to an object (without the CBO programmer having to handle the complexity).
- Provide some form of 'activity token' so that multiple activities accessing the same instance could be identified.

The single instantiation approach is shown in Fig. 6.8, where we see three transactions. The customer C200 CBO instance is accessed concurrently by two transactions, as is the item X123 CBO instance.

Since a single instance implies a single copy of data in storage, then we would have multiple activities all accessing the same (in-storage) data. However, if this occurs, then one transaction may see inconsistent data.

If we then add the notion that we might like a given instance to be located remotely (in the network) from some other CBO—but have both within the same SRD—then we can see significant problems in implementing the single instantiation approach.

Currently, work is being done on at least two approaches to these difficulties, but it would be premature to report more fully on them at the present. One consideration for a partial solution is that, if one transaction had to change an instance outside its SRD, then the commit scope would be lost. However, as long as the

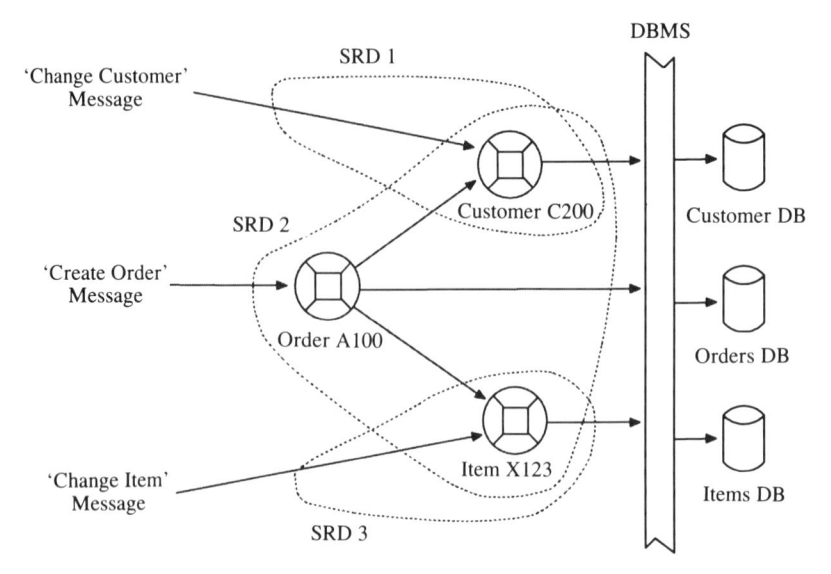

Figure 6.8. CBO concurrency—single instantiation.

infrastructure can at least report a 'not fully committed' error, then this may be acceptable in some circumstances.

The reasons why the single instantiation approach is likely to be the more fruitful in the long term include the potential to:

- Locate object instances anywhere in a network.
- Allow better for a future blurring of the current difference between DBMSs and CBOs—and hence provide a migration path (where appropriate) towards possible future 'active' OODBMSs.
- Avoid a possible need for pre-execution 'binding' of objects into a single transaction.

Full support for two-phase commit across any set of objects will require not only object concurrency but support for a network-wide SRD by the resource managers.

In brief, the conclusion is that CBOs can run in today's transaction processing systems (given, of course, the CBO-enabling infrastructure) using the multiple instantiation approach. More work is required before we can say that the full single instantiation approach is viable.

Today, we can move towards CBOs in systems like IBM's CICS by designing focus and entity modules (and maybe resource modules) to run in a single transaction.

6.6 Summary

In this chapter we have further explored the shared resource domain—the application code responsible for ensuring the security and integrity of corporate shared resources. Specifically, we defined the difference between the resource manager domain (the scope of resources controlled by a resource manager such as a transaction processing system) and the shared resource domain (the area within which a programmer can place code such that a recoverable unit of work can be done). Within the SRD, three different kinds of CBO can be identified:

- The focus—responsible for ensuring shared resource integrity
- The entity—responsible for accessing a specific resource.
- The resource—responsible for providing transparency to the entity by understanding the precise system-dependent resource access mechanisms.

We then discussed whether separate SRD CBOs should be created for each transaction, or whether a multiple instantiation approach was better. The single instantiation approach appears to provide several benefits, but more work is needed before it is known if the advantages outweigh the additional infrastructure functions required.

7
End-to-end summary

In this chapter, we summarize the discussion in the preceding two chapters, showing an 'end-to-end' CBO model of client/server.

7.1 Domain interaction

There will be as many UIDs as there are users. In addition, there may be more than one resource manager domain (depending on the resource manager used), and hence, for a given client/server interaction, more than one SRD. While the SRD is normally the server, and the UID the client, there will be occasions when something in an SRD needs to initiate a request of a UID. Thus the connection between the two, while always 'client/server' in the sense of request/response pairs, is more of a peer-to-peer nature. This is because both can be clients, and both can be servers (in different situations).

Again, one SRD may well access another SRD directly. For example, a UID on a PC may send a request to an SRD on a LAN server, which, to handle the request, may need to read some data from a mainframe server. Without an underlying distributed database, there would be two SRDs involved.

7.2 Components of the end-to-end model

Both the UID and the SRD are implemented with CBOs. (Although the model is presented in terms of CBOs, it is also generally applicable to non-CBO application structures. In particular, the separation of UID and SRD is a generic concept, and not limited to CBOs.) Within each domain, there are a number of identifiable types of CBO. The overall structure is shown in Fig. 7.1. In the figure, solid boxes are CBOs, dotted boxes are infrastructure (middleware) components. There are two types of CBO in the UID (the view and the model), and three in the SRD (the focus, the entity and the resource).

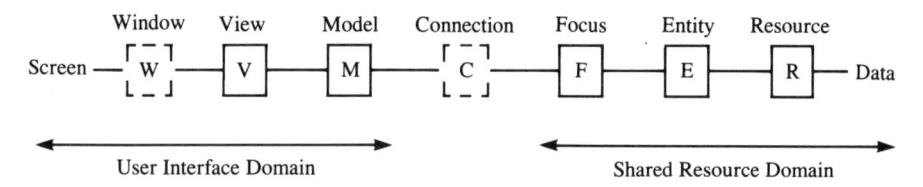

```
         Window    View    Model   Connection   Focus    Entity   Resource
          ┌ ─ ┐                     ┌ ─ ┐
Screen ───┤ W ├────┤ V ├────┤ M ├───┤ C ├────────┤ F ├────┤ E ├────┤ R ├─── Data
          └ ─ ┘                     └ ─ ┘
```

```
         ◄──────────────────────────►              ◄─────────────────────►
                User Interface Domain                  Shared Resource Domain
```

Figure 7.1. End-to-end-structure.

7.3 Component behaviour

The various CBO types interact in certain ways, and design guidelines restrict this interaction as follows.

1. *Component interaction* The following defines inter-component request and response behaviour:
   (a) Requests from one CBO to another (also between view and window, CBO and connection) are made by sending messages. Messages may be synchronous or asynchronous.
   (b) Message routing is done outside of the CBO application code by CBO infrastructure or 'middleware' code.
   (c) CBOs in the same machine may be in different address spaces or the same; in different threads of control or the same.
   (d) The programmer writes CBOs, which are event-loop code entities such that the loop handling is done by the infrastructure. This means that concurrency handling for asynchronous messages can be done by the infrastructure, and the programmer does not see this complexity. CBOs are also true objects (to be precise, they are classes) in the OO sense. One CBO class can inherit behaviour from another CBO class.
   (e) Data in messages is in self-defining format (containing metadata—data about data—as well as data values). This approach makes for extremely loose binding between components (effectively at the level of data labels), and makes CBOs insensitive to data types and data positions within a message. This does, however, trade loose binding for execution cycles.
2. *Component restrictions* In the model presented, we can define some restrictions on the CBO types that can 'talk' to other CBO types. While these are not necessarily technical restrictions, nor hard-and-fast rules, they have been found to be useful design guidelines and are:
   (a) A view can only talk to its model (by 'model' we mean 'local model').
   (b) A model can talk to its view(s), to another model, or to a focus.
   (c) A focus can talk to entities, and to models.
   (d) A focus can talk to another focus in a different SRD.
   (e) A model can talk directly to entities if the entity encompasses the required commit scope (that is, if the entity is also a focus).

112   Business objects

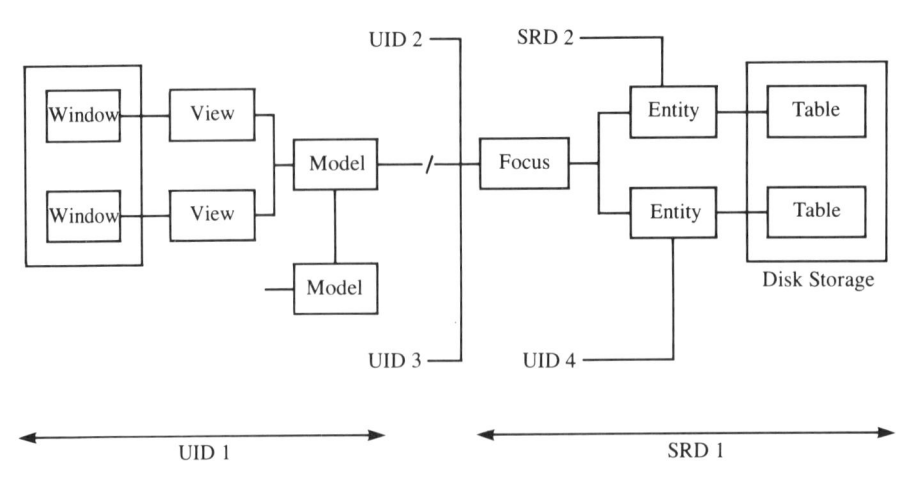

Figure 7.2. Generalized client/server CBO model.

(f) An entity can talk to resources.
(g) A resource can only talk to an entity.

With these behaviours and restrictions taken into account, a slightly more general picture can be generated from that shown in Fig. 7.1, and is shown in Fig. 7.2. In this figure, the different CBO types are shown in a typical situation. Note that:

- The focus is talking (perhaps concurrently) to three UIDs.
- One of the entities is being talked to from another SRD (perhaps a read; if a change is being requested, then this implies that this entity is also a focus).
- One of the entities is being talked to by a UID (again, if a change is requested, then this entity is also a focus).

7.4   Model subsets

It should not be thought that this model defines an over-rigid separation of CBO types. There will be many instances where one or more different types can be merged, or collapsed, into a composite type. Thus subsets of the general model can be defined. For example:

- Resource and entity can be combined.
- Focus and entity can be combined. The result would be very similar to a traditional server-style transaction.
- A view can never exist without a model. If there is only one view for a given model, then view and model can be combined. The result is a model that also has view characteristics.
- A model can exist without a view.

- The model (that is, local model) and the entity can be combined. This results in what is essentially a 'remote model'.

Note also:

- If all possible subsetting is done, then the result is a single component in each of the UID and the SRD. If two systems are involved, the connection component is included with the application code, the result is today's typical cooperative processing structure—for example, a PC application talking to a CICS application (perhaps using APPC).
- If the SRD is exceedingly trivial, then both the SRD and the UID can be combined. The result is a typical PC stand-alone application. Note, however, that in the typical client/server system, the UID and SRD should *never* be combined; the boundaries between them should never be mingled. Indeed, from a design point of view, even when CBOs are destined to run stand-alone on a PC, I have found it useful to build separate UID and SRD CBOs. The SRD can then be designed as a trivial subset—a shared resource domain shared by one person(!). But if ever a need arose to share for real, then only the SRD CBOs might have to be rewritten.

8
The CBO infrastructure

At various times in the previous chapters, reference has been made to 'the CBO infrastructure'. In this chapter, we now discuss some of the more important aspects of such an infrastructure.

The code that implements a CBO infrastructure is certainly 'system-level' code, and is something of a challenge to build. Until very recently, such software was not available on the market. At the time of writing, it is just starting to become available in industrial-strength products. (One such, called 'Newi' (New World Infrastructure), is produced by Integrated Object Systems Limited, Newbury, UK.)

This chapter is in seven sections:

- First, we define what we mean by 'infrastructure', and review why it is necessary.
- Then we discuss the common elements of a client/server infrastructure, suitable for both CBOs and more traditionally structured applications.
- Following this, we look at the specific requirements of a CBO infrastructure.
- So far, we have completely ducked the question of the data within a message. In real systems, this turns out to be an extremely important consideration, and in the fourth section we show how a self-defining data mechanism that carries metadata (data about data) is required.
- When there are several different types of computers in a distributed system, data conversion (e.g. ASCII to EBCDIC) becomes important. We look at some of the lessons learned.
- Then we briefly discuss how the infrastructure might handle connection of CBOs to a non-CBO environment, so enabling higher levels of integration.
- Finally, we look at some of the operating system implications for the design of the infrastructure. For example, should each CBO run in its own address space, or not?

8.1 Why an infrastructure?

In a real system, there are several interlocking infrastructures, including:

- The hardware, operating system and networking infrastructure.
- A systems management infrastructure, which would handle such things as software change management, user access authorization, directory services for cross-system names, etc.[1]
- An application enabling infrastructure, which supports a given 'model' of how application code should be structured, and provides significant ease of programming for that model.

This chapter addresses the last of these, one that supports the CBO model.

We often find in practice that each client/server application has had to design and implement its own software infrastructure. This is so in spite of products aimed at this area; some make programming simple, but do not allow full exploitation (or sometimes even partial exploitation) of the object-based user interface; some provide useful APIs for connection, but do not provide for other complex areas (such as multi-tasking); others provide a closed environment, often for a single language only.

The reason for this is that there has been no general model of what—in software structure terms—a cooperative processing system *is*. There has been no generally accepted notion of what it is that we would like application programmers to build—and hence no well understood appreciation of the services and facilities that should be made available to those programmers.

We need such a model because building a cooperative application is *different*. If we treat it like previous application structures, then we will find things difficult. If we accept that it is different, but do not have a model that explains the differences, then it will also be difficult. The concept of CBOs developed in the previous chapters provides such a model.

An analogy is that: At the end of the sixties and beginning of the seventies, it became apparent that, if you wanted to build an on-line application that exploited the new character-based terminal technology, then the thing you really wanted to build was 'transactions'. But this required much non-application code, which did things like task and storage management, screen handling, transaction initiation, etc. This code was not only difficult to write, requiring high design and programming skills; it was also reinvented for each application.

Over time, it was realized that, to make programming easy, all the non-application code should be provided in common for each application through a layer of middleware—of software infrastructure—which sat on top of the operating system. You needed this layer because the operating systems did not provide it. Thus transaction processing (TP) monitors such as CICS, GCOS, IMS and CCP

---

[1] Other things managed by this level of infrastructure would include alerts and problem reporting (automated), configuration, performance monitoring, system administration, communications APIs such as RPC and APPC, security, user profiling, data compression and encryption, printing, error handling, store and forward processing, commit scope, routing services, naming services (directory) and translation services.

(on the System/3) were introduced to provide the required function. Today, systems such as OS/400 (the operating system on IBM's AS/400) provides this transaction environment as an integral part of the base operating system. (The IBM System/34 was an excellent example of one of the first systems to provide a degree of transaction processing built into the operating system.)

For interactive applications (such as decision support), much the same argument applies, and we saw the emergence of systems such as CMS (the VM interactive operating system) and TSO. Today, systems such as OS/2 and UNIX provide this interactive environment as an integral part of the base operating system.

Figure 8.1 illustrates this. A printout is shown at the bottom left. If that is what you want to produce, then a batch application seems ideal. In turn, the batch application requires an operating system upon which to run. If the thing you want to produce is an on-line system, then the things you need to build and deliver are transaction programs (T1, T2 and T3—each writing to an SPA or scratch pad area). Transaction programs require a transaction processor to run. Likewise an interactive application (such as a spreadsheet) needs an interactive computing (IC) environment. CBOs in turn require a CBO infrastructure. Thus the general 'shape' of the software you want to deliver (batch suite, transaction, interactive application, CBO) determines the services and functions you need to provide either in, or on top of, the operating system at run-time—*if you want to make programming easy!*

One very good example of the kind of run-time support required is drag and drop (direct manipulation). The real business benefit of drag/drop lies in its application integration potential. It is the mechanism whereby the user can introduce

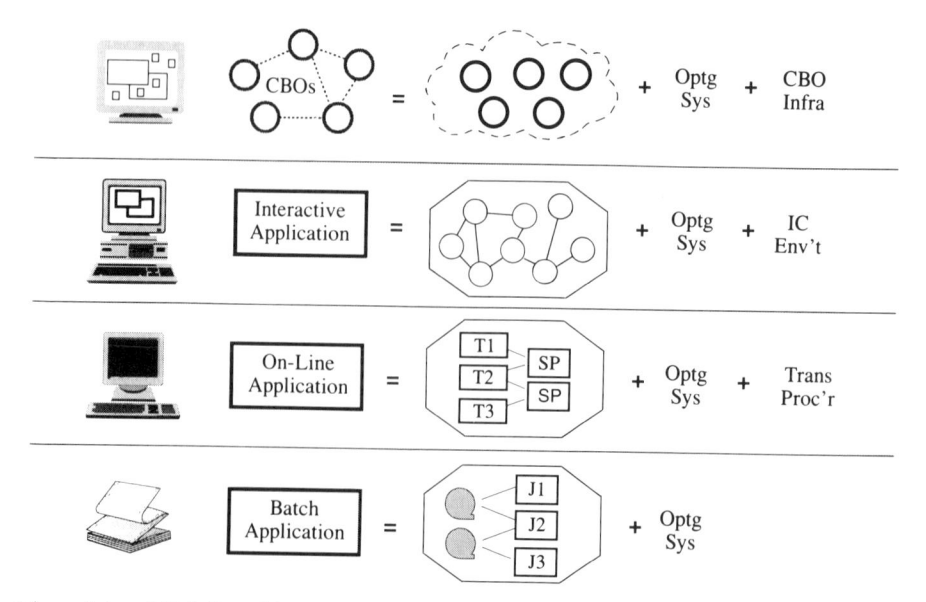

Figure 8.1.   AD deliverables.

two objects—behind which are two pieces of software—that have been separately developed. CBOs, and the CBO infrastructure, allow this *inter*-application function to operate easily.

8.2 Common components

Much of the discussion of this section applies to non-CBO application function. However, the assumption is made that the application code, whether CBO or not, communicates by means of messaging.

8.2.1 *The UID*

We can summarize the user requirements (the expected characteristics of an effective UID on a PC) in terms of *flexibility*. That is, no rigid screen dialogue constraint, the ability to conform to an unstructured customer dialogue, and so forth. This translates into a number of capabilities that the GUI should enable, including the ability to:

- Handle several business processes concurrently
- Jump from object to object (and window to window) as required
- Display multiple instances of one thing (e.g. two customers) concurrently

These required capabilities can be equated with specific desired PC characteristics; in particular, aside from how the GUI is designed, they imply that the necessary 'background' access to servers should be as non-intrusive as possible. This in turn points to:

- Concurrent sessions
- Queuing of requests when sessions are all busy
- Separation of GUI code from the communications code, so that windows are not 'frozen' while relatively long-running communications are happening—in other words, asynchronous connections to the server

Thus one of the first requirements of the infrastructure is to enable application code to make simple requests of the server. This can be done through an infrastructure-provided 'request sender', as shown in Fig. 8.2. At the server end, there is a matching 'request catcher'.

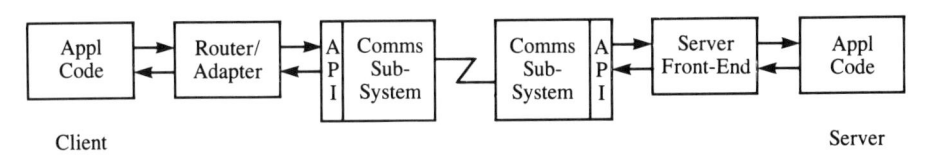

Figure 8.2. Request sender and catcher.

Business objects

In considering these key usability aspects, together with some important ease-of-programming factors, the following requirements arise:

- Concurrent requests for access to the SRD should be honoured, even though the number of communication 'sessions' may be less than the number of outstanding requests. This means that such outstanding requests must be queued.
- Access to servers is often, from the PC GUI response-time point of view, a long-running function. For example, with a slow network, or an overloaded server—or just a large request—access to the server may take (say) 10 or more seconds. An asynchronous connection between the UID (client) and the SRD (server) should therefore be provided. Otherwise, the user interface may block, producing for the user an unacceptable 'freeze' of the window.
- A response to an asynchronous request needs to be routed back to the requester. (The response could be returned to a piece of code other than the requester; but this would break the client/server model—a response would arrive at code that had not issued a request! This would lead to greater complexity in design and programming.)
- Different communications protocols required to access different servers should be hidden from the CBO application code.
- Drag/drop between objects on the screen must be effected by some function external to the CBO application code. The CBO should see only incoming messages.
- CBO-to-CBO messages must be provided (for example, to allow CBOs to exchange data after a drag/drop). Although this can be done with system function (e.g. Dynamic Data Exchange, DDE), for ease-of-programming reasons, such facilities should be 'front-ended'.

For the UID, these considerations lead to an expansion of the 'request sender' function shown in Fig. 8.2 to the set of functional components shown in Fig. 8.3.

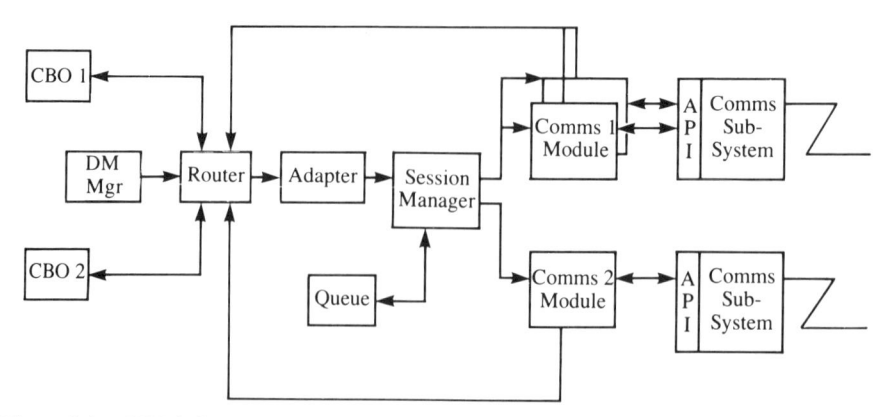

Figure 8.3. UID infrastructure components (PC).

Note that this figure shows function as opposed to actual software detail design and packaging. The components illustrated in Fig. 8.3 are as follows.

Router

The router catches requests sent out from application code and decides where they should be sent. Thus the API that the application programmer sees is that provided by the router. In some cases, requests will be sent to other application code on the same system; in other cases to a different system.

Adapter

The adapter is so called because it adapts message requests to some communications mechanism in order to send them to remote servers. It is responsible for mapping the destination name specified by the application to a specific communications route, and sending it on its way through that route to the server. In this way, aliases can be provided for remote objects—which might indeed not be objects at all, but, for example, transaction programs. The sending CBO does not need to understand the transaction name; as far as it is concerned it is talking to another CBO.

Session manager

The session manager knows where the communications code is running (in another thread or process) and how to pass the request data over to it. It also knows whether a communication session is busy, and hence whether to queue a request until the session is available. (Some communications implementations—such as APPC—handle session queuing themselves.) Should the particular communications module (or subsystem) provide an API that can be run against it from different threads or processes, then the session manager will handle a pool of threads or processes. The session manager also handles things like communications error logging, any retry strategy, etc. In general, on an error, the session manager should return to the requesting application (via the router) an indication of failure only (rather than all of the communications-level sense codes, etc.).

Queue

A queue is where outstanding requests are waited. This is only required for communications subsystems that are not themselves queued. By 'queued', I mean that, if there are n sessions available, and there are $n + m$ concurrent requests made, then the communications subsystem is able to accept all the requests, returning to the requesters when a session is available. How the subsystem deals with the outstanding requests is immaterial; it appears to queue them. An example of a queued communications subsystem is SNA's LU6.2 (with its APPC interface definition and its CPI-C API). An example of a non-queued subsystem is a terminal emulator, where the communications API interacts pretty directly with a logical terminal screen (in-storage). If all terminal sessions are busy, then the emulator does not 'queue' a subsequent request, but will return 'busy' and leave it to the caller to work out what to do. For a non-queued subsystem, when a communication session comes free, the session manager interrogates the queue to see if there are any outstanding requests.

Communications module

One or more communications modules handle the actual communications protocols. This really refers to the communications mechanisms offered by the operating environment, such as APPC, terminal emulation, sockets, RPC, message queuing, etc.

DM manager

In addition (at the left of Fig. 8.3), the DM manager (direct manipulation manager—or drag/drop manager) provides a layer of function on top of any system-level capability, such that high-level direct manipulation messages can be sent to the appropriate application code. In the figure it is shown doing this through the router.

8.2.2 The SRD (server)

The major difference at the server end is that the SRD is multi-user. That is, it must be able to handle multiple concurrent requests from one or more UIDs (and, indeed, from other SRDs).

Now, while PC UID environments are generally very similar in their facilities and capabilities, typical SRD (server) environments can range from that same PC being used as a LAN server all the way up to the largest of mainframes. But, more importantly for present purposes, we find that the system facilities are widely different. However, we can identify two different system environments for servers; one where there is a transaction processor, and one where there is not.

Since the essence of the server is to handle what are really transactions, then an environment without a transaction processor—or effective transaction management in the database manager—will have to have the required transaction processing elements built.

So let us now consider the case of a system without a transaction processor. Assume we have a typical server program, say a customer update module. This might look like this:

```
Start
  Get Request from Client
  Validate the Request
  If OK, then
    Perform the Update
    Return 'OK'
  Else
    Return 'Error'
End
```

Now come the difficult questions:

- How is this application program loaded into memory? What piece of software does the loading?
- Is it loaded once for each request, or does it hang around waiting for the next request?
- If it hangs around, what software wakes it up—and how?
- Who queues or schedules or otherwise handles the second of two concurrent requests?
- How does the second line (Get Request from Client) actually work—what underlying software is behind the 'Get'?

These questions are referred to by Orfali and Harkey (1992, p. 1077) as '... an area that can really get wild'. However, if there is no transaction processor, then someone has to answer these questions, and build the code needed to implement the answers—either as part of the application, or as middleware. In effect, they would be building some aspects of a transaction processor. As someone (else) once said, 'If you're processing transactions, then you need a transaction processor'.

It might seem that distributed database is the answer. Then you can just put the above code on the PC. But this only moves the problem (although it does answer the multi-user aspects—assuming that the DBMS provides concurrency control). Something still has to initiate the code, pass the request to it, etc. Then again, with an object-based user interface, it is not impossible that two CBOs may concurrently make a request of the same server. Certainly such an event needs to be catered for in a general-purpose solution (which is why even with a stand-alone PC application, it is still useful to separate UID and SRD).

Because of the wide disparity of likely server environments, there are few definable components that are common across all. Even mainframe transaction processor environments differ widely. For example, the infrastructure components required for CICS and for GCOS are quite different. Perhaps the main common component is the communications front-end; after that, there are a number of considerations, the structural answers to which may vary widely.

The communications front-end

As shown in Fig. 8.2 a 'front-end' is needed to separate the server application code from the code containing the communications API. Note that the underlying communications subsystem may itself address a number of problems to do with code initiation (for example, APPC can automatically initiate the transaction program required).

The major function of the communications front-end is handling incoming messages, and returning responses. It should also handle such things as:

- Sign-on or other general access authorization (as opposed to specific resource authorization).
- Invocation of the appropriate SRD server or servers.
- Version control—where the incoming message may be checked for its version, and the appropriate SRD application module invoked.
- Conversion of data formats where they differ between machines.

Other considerations

Besides the communications front-end, the infrastructure at the SRD must also consider:

- Commit scope management. If the SRD consists of several independently developed transaction programs, then some way has to be devised to invoke them all within a single commit scope. This may require commit scopes to be embeddable.
- Storage management of message data passed between transaction programs.
- Implementation of a router function may be required.
- Megadata. This is about handling the situation where a great deal of data needs to be returned—either in a single response, or as a series of messages sent back. Additional considerations are discussed in Chapter 11.

Object design

At its simplest, an SRD may be little more than a set of transactions, running under the control of a transaction processor. If each transaction maps to a single transaction program, then the communications front-end may be little more than a subroutine called by each transaction program.

Whether this is the best design approach is arguable. However, it has been found that even such simple design schemes as this can benefit greatly from taking an object approach to transaction program design. That is, design objects and implement them using normal transaction programs.

In this way, since objects are essentially event- or message-driven, the resulting transaction programs have a high probability of being reasonably good servers. They will not make assumptions about clients that use them; they will be complete; they will exhibit the required ACID (atomicity, consistency, isolation, durability) properties. This is so even though the various attributes of CBOs (inheritance, encapsulation, etc.) are not provided.

8.3 CBO aspects

A CBO infrastructure does not only support CBOs. It must also support the concept of peer-to-peer messaging between CBOs, as well as the more traditional client/server interaction. Thus a CBO infrastructure is also a distributed object manager.

One of the first such infrastructure offerings (if not the first) has recently been jointly developed by IBM and Softwright joint venture company Integrated Object Systems Ltd (in Newbury, Berks, UK). Much invaluable experience has been gained over the past few years through some leading-edge projects in applying this technology. From these projects, we have excellent indications as to the benefits of CBO technology; we know that it works.

An exhaustive discussion of the internals of the CBO infrastructure is beyond the scope of this book. However, in this section, we mention a number of facilities needed, and discuss further a few of the more important of them.

8.3.1 CBO support

In the course of previous chapters, we have identified a number of the services required to support CBOs. These include:

- A high-level messaging API (together with appropriate message data architecture)
- Message handling and routing (both synchronous and asynchronous)
- Storage management for class and instance data
- High-level standard messaging 'wrapper' for low-level GUI functions
- Code initiation
- Task (thread) management
- Communications management
- Table-driven aliasing scheme for routing over networks
- Object persistence (over power-off, for example, and over code unloading)
- Object management (multiple instances of classes, instantiation, inheritance, etc.)

Other aspects not so far addressed are:

- Separation of class and its associated code (sometimes called the class's 'implementation')
- Code loading and unloading
- High-performance message routing
- Message data storage management
- Retaining messaging semantics regardless of source and target object locations (a key aspect of distributed object management)

- Differing communications structures depending on whether there are CBOs or more traditional servers at the remote end
- Peer-to-peer (unsolicited messages)
- Multi-tasking and concurrency support
- Support for self-defining data streams to provide for dynamic data binding at run-time
- Object instantiation
- Garbage collection
- Dynamic class name allocation (essential for ease of customization)
- Infrastructure administration

On some systems, a transaction processing subsystem can provide some of these facilities. However, even when the facilities are in the right place, and usable in the way required for CBOs, they still need software 'glue' to provide the ease of programming required, and to provide the object and GUI management. On the PC, typically most of these facilities are not present to the level required, and so have to be provided by the infrastructure.

IBM's 'system object model' (currently available on OS/2 Version 2 and on AIX for RS/6000, and often referred to as 'SOM') should in future provide some of the system-level facilities that will make building such an infrastructure easier. We anticipate that all these facilities will eventually be provided by (or as an adjunct to) the operating system.

8.3.2 Synchronous or asynchronous?

Any discussion of synchronicity must state to what that synchronicity refers. In this section, we discuss briefly the major aspects of this question.

To the programmer

To start with, consider the user of the infrastructure—that is, the programmer. To him or her, the question of synchronous or asynchronous is always with reference to the application code. Thus, for example, a program statement 'Send', which the programmer has been told is synchronous, should not return until the request has been responded to. Also, the response data must be returned with the return of control (that is, must be available at the next sequential instruction). This should apply regardless of the location of the target CBO, and of the nature of the communications mechanism. The infrastructure should provide for this.

If the request takes a long time (e.g. more than a few milliseconds—or less!), then the infrastructure should prevent blocking while the request is being satisfied. A brief discussion of this can be found in Appendix 2.

A program statement 'Post' (which the programmer has been told is asynchronous) should always return control immediately at the next sequential instruction (without the response, of course), with some indication as to whether the message was sent on its way correctly. The response should arrive at the CBO that issued the Post as an incoming message (which will invoke the CBO).

A good way of allowing programmer control over the specific message to be received with the response data is to specify it in the Post statement. This behaviour must apply regardless of whether the target CBO is local (even if it is in the same thread/task as the sending CBO) or remote.

A brief discussion of send vs post is provided in Appendix 3.

To the infrastructure designer

To the infrastructure designer, the question relates to the communications mechanism, and refers to the request sender. Thus if the designer starts a task that will do the communications business, he or she gets control back into the request sender before the communications task has returned the response. This is an asynchronous connection.

If on the other hand, he or she does not start a separate task, but issues communications statements from within the same thread as the request sender, then this will be a synchronous connection.

In either case, the infrastructure designer must ensure:

- That the semantics of send/post are preserved for the CBO programmer, regardless of whether the target CBO is local or remote
- That CBOs are not blocked while a synchronous connection completes

The latter requirement can be particularly difficult to design into the infrastructure; but it can be done.

8.3.3 Name space for objects

For performance reasons, an object ID (identifier) is an internal token, often only of meaning to the system in which it is used. But a given CBO cannot always be expected to know the object ID of the CBO to which it wishes to send a message. So how does it send the message? The answer is to have a scheme such that the infrastructure can construct the correct object ID from an external name, such as class 'customer', instance 'A123' (the instance name in this case is the customer number).

Similarly, the infrastructure must be able to provide the programmer with class and instance names given an object ID.

8.3.4 Class name vs code

By 'code' I mean the code that implements a given class. It might be thought that code for a given class of CBO cannot be separated from the class. However, consider the following:

Code for a class 'Customer' is developed. It includes methods for display, update, etc. Another class 'Account' is also developed. The code for the two classes was developed independently; each code module is separately executable.

Within the 'Account' class code, assume that a message is sent (by name) to an instance of the class 'Customer'. Both customer and account classes are used together by some set of users. So far so good.

Now assume that code for a third class is required by another set of users. This class is called 'Customer_1', and is intended to be a subclass of 'Customer', adding (say) a delete method. If this second set of users also use the 'Account' class, then it would appear that 'Account' cannot interact with 'Customer_1', since it sends messages only to instances of class 'Customer'. Thus the code for 'Account' needs to be changed for the second set of users.

This conclusion is unwelcome. In particular, if you wish to build CBOs that can be customized by building a subclass, it means that you cannot do it—because the customizers would also have to change code in other CBOs that send messages to the class that is being subclassed.

A solution is to have the infrastructure separate class names and the code that implements classes. Let us assume that class customer is implemented by code called 'Cust', Account by code called 'Acct' and Customer_1 by code called 'Cust_1'. The infrastructure might read a definition file relating classes and implementations at start-up. Each set of users would be provided with a different definition file, as shown in Fig. 8.4.

In this figure, 'Code' means the name of the executable (on disk, in some library) that implements a given class. 'Super' is the name of the class's superclass (from

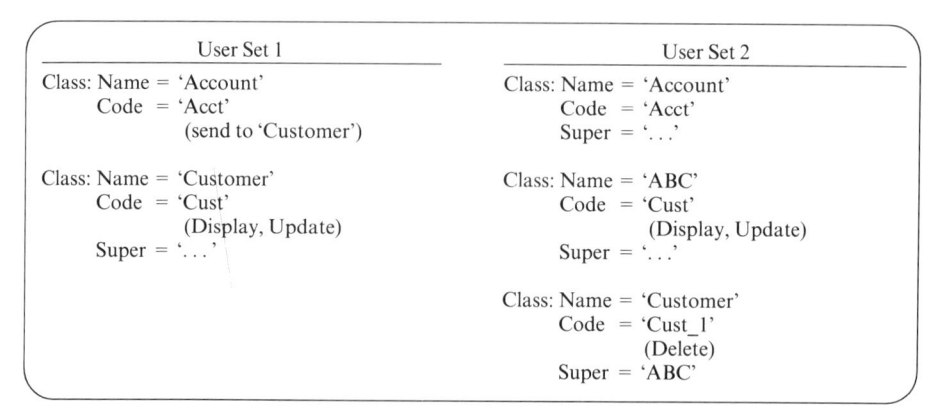

User Set 1	User Set 2

Class: Name = 'Account'
    Code = 'Acct'
        (send to 'Customer')
	Class: Name = 'Account'
	    Code = 'Acct'
	    Super = '...'

Class: Name = 'Customer'
    Code = 'Cust'
        (Display, Update)
    Super = '...'
	Class: Name = 'ABC'
	    Code = 'Cust'
	        (Display, Update)
	    Super = '...'

	Class: Name = 'Customer'
	    Code = 'Cust_1'
	        (Delete)
	    Super = 'ABC'

Figure 8.4. Class vs implementation.

which it inherits behaviour). As can be seen, the second set of users have a definition file where the class Customer is implemented by the code 'Cust_1'. The Customer class has 'ABC' as its superclass. The code for ABC is 'Cust' (which for the first set of users is the code for class Customer).

In this way, the code 'Acct' successfully sends to class Customer for both sets of users—without modifying any code. However, the behaviour of class Customer is different for each set of users (the second set has a delete capability).

Again, where several views have the same *behaviour* (regardless of differences in their appearance on the screen), then a single 'view' CBO could be coded. By assigning several classes to this code—'CustomerView', 'ProductView', etc.—the same view code can be used for several different model CBOs.

We could indeed go further than this, and similarly separate code from version, so providing for different versions of the same code.

Thus we can separate class name from the code that provides the implementation of a class. Such flexibility is essential for CBOs, in particular to enable customization. The CBO infrastructure must support this.

8.3.5 Systems management

We have defined systems management to be a separate aspect from the CBO infrastructure. However, since the infrastructure will be the object of systems management, then it must support, or at least enable, a number of facilities. These include such things as:

- *Alerts* The infrastructure must not only log out-of-line events, but must be able to route defined log messages to an alert handler (probably a systems management CBO), which can then pass the message as an alert systems management system.
- *Hooks* From time to time, a systems manager (or an automated systems management function) may wish to query the infrastructure. Thus the infrastructure must provide for accumulation of statistics of various kinds, and make available information (such as what classes, and what implementations, are loaded currently). This might be done via an infrastructure-provided CBO, so providing a 'hook' into itself for the systems management system to use.
- *Change management* An important aspect of change management is the ability to regress after a change proves to be unfortunate(!). This can be effected through a versioning mechanism (as briefly mentioned in the discussion on class names and code).

8.3.6 Language neutrality

The infrastructure must be neutral with respect to the language used to build a CBO. Further, CBOs should be able to be written in as wide a choice of languages as possible. A given CBO will normally be written in a single language; that is, inter-language capability at below-CBO granularity is not part of the CBO definition, nor a required infrastructure capability.

The infrastructure, then, must be written in such a way that different programming languages can call its functions—or interface with its objects—without necessarily having to have special interfacing code written. For example, the infrastructure might provide its interface in terms of C structures and C function calls.

For languages that can call such functions and deal with such structures through built-in language facilities (such as C++, or some COBOLs), then the only thing required is some macros or preprocessor statements to enable ease of programming.

Languages that cannot directly call the infrastructure functions (such as REXX) will require a layer of support code. The infrastructure should provide a 'slot' for such support code, which will map things like messages in and out, instance data, registration services, superclassing and various service functions.

A major consideration will be re-entrancy (how local variables are handled by the language when code is re-entered recursively). Another major consideration will be the language's storage management of local variables.

8.3.7 'Ghost' objects

A 'ghost' object is one that looks to the user as if it is there, but really is not. This is required as part of the solution to the megadata problem (see Chapter 11).

Suppose a user is looking at a list of 200 customers. We then have some conflicting requirements:

- The user should see each item in the list as an object.
- We do not want to instantiate 200 objects (and get the data from a remote database) just in case the user uses one of them.

Thus the infrastructure should allow for the programmer to manipulate objects that are not instantiated; and whose implementation may not even be on the same machine (see Sec. 11.2.3 for further discussion).

8.3.8 Message content

A major requirement for CBOs is that the message structure be rich in information. Experience has shown that content of a CBO message (as seen by the CBO programmer) should include such things as:

- The message name
- Data sent with the message
- A space for the receiver's reply

- The object ID of the sending CBO
- The user ID

The last two of these should not have to be provided by the sending CBO; they should be inserted into the message automatically.

In addition, the infrastructure must define the format of data sent and received. If left to the programmer, then the binding between CBOs is tightened to a degree that will probably negate many of the advantages of CBOs. This is further discussed below, in Sec. 8.4.

Reply space

But why do we include a reply space? Well, consider a programmer, Bill, who sends a message. Suppose to do this he writes:

```
MyData = 'Account_Balance'
x = Send(TargetId, 'Query', Mydata)
```

In this example, Bill is sending the message 'Query' to a CBO whose object ID is in the variable TargetId. The thing he is querying is the value of 'Account_Balance', so he provides that information as the data sent with the message.

Now, Bill needs two pieces of information to be returned from his send instruction:

- A return code (indicating for example whether the infrastructure managed to route the message OK, or whether the target object did not like the data sent).
- The result of his message—that is, the target's account balance?

In the example above, is *x* a return code or the account balance?

Now consider the programmer, Sue, of the target object. She might have written something like this (for simplicity, we assume that the only thing allowed to be queried is the account balance):

```
Method 'Query'
   If Message_Data = 'Account_Balance' then
      return Balance
   Else
      return Error
   End_If
End_Method
```

But this is not good. If Error is numeric, then Bill has no way of knowing whether, after his send, his variable *x* contains the account balance or an error return code. Clearly we need to separate the two. Remember also that the two CBOs are separate and independent executables.

Experience with this problem suggests that the following is a useful solution. The first programmer, Bill, writes something like this:

```
MyData = 'Account_Balance'
rc = Send(TargetId, 'Query', Mydata, HisReply)
If rc = 'OK' then
   ...
```

where the variable `HisReply` contains the account balance after the send (if return code *rc* is 'OK').

The second programmer, Sue, writes something like this:

```
Method 'Query'
   If Message_Data = 'Account_Balance' then
      Message_Reply = Balance
      return OK
   Else
      return Error
   End_If
End_Method
```

where the variable `Message_Reply` is made available to her as a parameter of the incoming message (parsing of that message is not shown). The infrastructure will ensure that the content of this variable is passed back into Bill's variable `HisReply`.

With this approach, neither programmer is in any doubt as to which is returned data, and which is the return code. However, this lays some requirements on the infrastructure, including:

- Storage management of the message data and reply spaces.
- Returning both message reply and return code across networks if the target is remote.

Send/post transparency

As was discussed in detail in Sec. 4.2.6, in order to achieve our goal of ease of programming, we would like the infrastructure to understand whether a message was 'sent' (synchronous with respect to the programmer's code) or 'posted' (asynchronous with respect to the programmer's code).

The programmer of the target object need not then be concerned with whether a message is sent or posted to it. Both can be dealt with in the same way; the target object would always place the response into the reply space (provided to it by the infrastructure). And the infrastructure would take care of returning the response (if the message was sent) or issuing another message back to the sending object (if the original message was posted). The effect of all this is to make send or post transparent to the target CBO.

User ID

The user ID (identifier) is the ID of the user 'logged on' at the sending UID or SRD where the event originated. The infrastructure must either provide a mechanism for the user ID to be entered in the first place, or (preferably) link in some way to a separate security system—perhaps operating-system-provided—so that the user ID can be obtained and plugged into messages.

In general, the user ID associated with a message is the user ID applicable at the point where a given request was originated. Suppose some message X is sent from UID_1 to SRD_1. Suppose also that, as part of handling message X, SRD_1 sends a message to SRD_2. The user ID on all messages resulting from message X, including those between the two SRDs, should have the user ID of the original message X.

In addition to the user ID, the message can also carry some token representing the user authorization profile.

8.3.9 Frameworks

The infrastructure should support various 'frameworks'. (In object orientation, the term 'framework' is normally used to indicate a set of predefined interactions between two or more classes. Subclasses can then be built that together inherit the inter-object behaviour. Wirfs-Brock *et al.* (1990), when discussing the kinds of software that can be re-used, define frameworks as 'skeletal structures of programs that must be fleshed out to build a complete application'. They are '... white boxes to those that make use of them'. The frameworks discussed here do not have to be fleshed out.) By this is meant a set of functions provided by the infrastructure (probably in system objects, and/or in system-provided CBO superclasses) that provide behaviour that is either:

- Not difficult, but very common
- Difficult, whether common or not

In this way, the CBO programmer is relieved of what would otherwise be much tedious and error-prone effort.

The following are among the frameworks that have been found so far to be of great use to CBO programmers:

- Drag/drop (direct manipulation)
- Object persistence
- Model/view
- Notification
- GUI independence

One framework that is being investigated at the time of writing is a 'transaction' framework, also referred to as a 'CBO generator' framework.

Experience with view, model, focus and entity CBOs has suggested a significant degree of commonality in the things a CBO programmer has to do. This suggests the possibility of automatically generating the required (base) CBOs from (say) an entity or data analysis. Data names (entity attributes) must be already defined.

Some initial work in this area looks promising. Now that we know what it is we want to build, we can start thinking of CASE tools. The infrastructure would provide a small number of superclasses to handle the common code. A CASE tool would generate appropriate subclasses, which a developer could then choose to enrich (or not). Again, there are tentative suggestions that during development, because of the structure of a CBO (a set of methods), modifications to generated code may be able to be made persistent. That is, the case tool can 'see' them when the CBO is regenerated, and can ensure that they are reintroduced in the regenerated code.

Direct manipulation

The most important point about direct manipulation (or 'drag/drop') is the infrastructure designer's model of what the CBO programmer should see. Some current low-level drag/drop protocols are very much bound to the idea of transferring files between applications, and providing rendering mechanisms for different file formats.

CBOs, on the other hand, need an 'introductory' concept, where the purpose of drag/drop is to introduce two objects. Indeed, the whole notion of direct manipulation can be subsumed into the more general concept of an 'introductory' protocol. This can be used, where appropriate, without the need for any user involvement.

Once two CBOs are introduced, that is the end of the drag/drop process. In this model, it is after the introduction that the objects interact to (for example) exchange data, or change their state, or whatever.

The infrastructure can provide CBOs participating in direct manipulation with a rich set of information. This can include information about context. For example, suppose some object is in a container object, and the business rules state that the object should not be moved out of the container except to another container of the same type. The context for the object is the type of container that it is in.

In this (admittedly complex) case, there are three objects involved in the drag/drop:

- The 'draggee'—the object being dragged
- The 'source context'—the container that originally contains the draggee
- The 'target'—any object over which the draggee is dragged

A fourth object that could be involved (but is not in this example) is:

- The 'target context'—an object that contains the target

The infrastructure can provide information about the drag operation to each of these. For example, the draggee can be told that it has been picked up, and that it is being dragged over a specific object; the target can be told what is being dragged over it; etc. Each of the objects involved can then provide a boolean return code (yes or no), which indicates whether the drag-and-drop operation can continue. If any returns no, then the infrastructure can change the mouse pointer to a 'no entry' sign, so telling the user that a drop is not allowed.

If the operating system provides some system-wide drag/drop mechanism, then the infrastructure should use it. However, it must ensure that the much looser messaging described above is effected. The reason that the system-level mechanism should be used is to provide for drag/drop from non-CBO stuff (e.g. a word-processing application that does not run as a CBO) to CBOs, and vice versa.

Some of the characteristics of CBOs in the direct manipulation domain are as follows (where we illustrate with user-driven direct manipulation). If a user picks up A and drops it on B, then:

- A does not have to know that it has been picked up; but it can find out if it wishes.
- Before the drop, the system tells B that A is being dragged over it by sending B an appropriate message. B responds with a 'yes' or 'no'. The system uses this response to set the mouse pointer to 'no entry' or not. B is given (via the data in the message) the following information:
  —A's object reference
  —A's class name
  —A's instance name
  —Whether this is a requested move, copy, reflection, etc. (which the user would have requested through use of 'modification' keys on the keyboard)
- If B replies 'yes', and the user then drops onto B, then B is sent a second message, containing the same data as in the 'drag-over' message.
- A and B then communicate to action the user's direct manipulation request.

In addition, multiple objects dragged at once must be catered for, with the target CBO able to find out details of all the objects being dragged.

Object persistence

If there are a large number of objects in storage but not being executed, then significant system resources can be consumed. It is often necessary to clean things up—to retrieve storage being used for instance data by inactive objects, to unload code, etc.

Thus the infrastructure needs to be able to unload objects, and reload them when necessary (typically when a message is sent to one of them). Again, when the user closes the system at the end of a day, the CBOs being used should not be destroyed;

rather, when the user starts up the next day, they should be automatically reconstituted.

In other words, the infrastructure should provide object persistence for CBOs.

While this should be transparent to the CBO programmer, he or she should be able to understand when an instance or class is being deactivated (unloaded) and activated (loaded). The infrastructure should send an appropriate message to any objects being so treated. If the programmer ignores the message, then an infrastructure-provided superclass should handle the message.

Model/view

When a user double clicks on an icon (an object), then a view CBO may need to be instantiated. Further, it will need to populate the controls on the window that is the user's view of the object. To do this, it must ask the model object for the data.

Again, if the user updates something on the window, then the view CBO must read data from the window, and request of the model that the changes be kept (how, and whether they are accepted, would typically be up to the model, not the view).

Normally, the infrastructure will provide view and model classes that programmers will use as superclasses when they build their own model and view CBOs. There is a significant amount of to-ing and fro-ing between a view CBO and model CBO in these operations; but the code required is usually the same. Thus a model/view framework can be provided in the infrastructure-provided 'model' and 'view' classes. Since programmers use these classes as their superclasses, the effect of such a framework is to relieve programmers of much if not all of the work involved.

Some aspects of the model/view framework are:

- A model CBO should be able to be designed, built, tested, distributed and used independently from any view object.
- A view CBO requires that a model CBO exists—both for its testing and for its use. However, it should be able to be distributed independently of the model.
- The infrastructure provides for a 'view—model' class when only a single view is required, and the model is very simple. This single class 'collapses' the view and model attributes into a single CBO—a model with view attributes.
- When a second view is requested, the model object does not initiate the view. This is done by the infrastructure. This implies that the developer defines a view object as being a view of a given model object. That is, the developer defines a view class as being for a given model class. The system deals with tying up instances.

Interest registration

Often one CBO needs to know when a given event occurs at another CBO. The first is said to be 'interested' in the second. However, the programmer of the second CBO should not have to be aware of that interest.

This can be done by infrastructure-provided superclass function. Thus the first CBO might send a message 'I am interested to know when your state changes' to the second. When the second changes its state, then it sends a message that its (infrastructure-provided) superclass picks up, checks who has registered an interest and sends them a message.

Note In OO applications, this function is sometimes implemented using a separate 'interest registration' object. For CBOs, this approach is sub-optimal, as the first CBO may be remote from the second. A separate interest registration object can easily increase the network traffic.

GUI independence

By 'GUI independence' is meant independence, on the PC, from system-level GUI presentation APIs such as those provided by presentation manager, Windows, X-Windows, etc. Such independence is essential if we are to meet our ease-of-programming objective. It also enables a high degree of portability of CBO code across different GUI platforms. This independence can be achieved as shown in Fig. 8.5.

On the left is what the user sees—a window showing an order form. The programmer writes a view CBO—'OrderView', subclassed from the infrastructure-provided 'View' CBO. The window layout (entry fields, push buttons, menus, etc.) is defined in an external layout script (window layout definition) file—'OrderView', which is processed by the infrastructure-provided 'view' class. Interaction between the view object and the window is translated from/to the system-level events and GUI APIs by the infrastructure-provided window manager. Such interaction can be provided both by CBO messaging and by a high-level API. The programmer then has a choice of which to use—messaging or API.

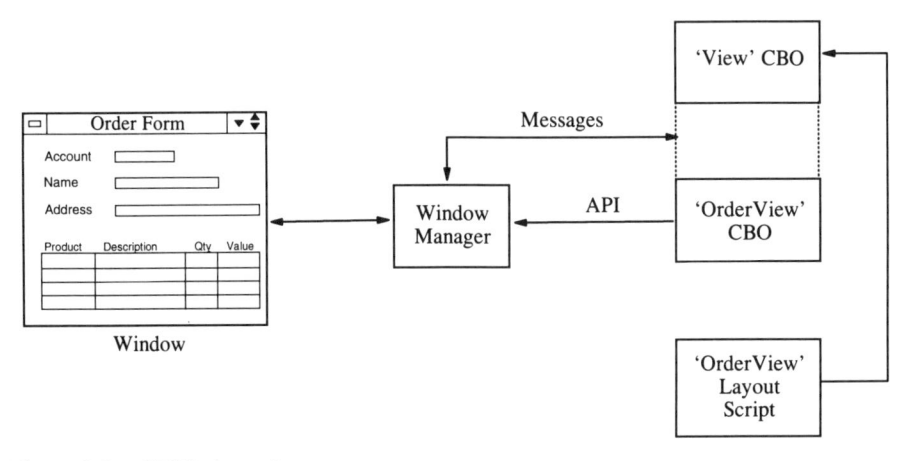

Figure 8.5. GUI independence.

Note that the layout script is optional. The view object could build this dynamically, since its superclass (the infrastructure-provided 'view' class) actually just asks itself for a lump of memory containing the window layout definition (this message flow is not shown in Fig. 8.5). The view superclass also provides a method to read the file itself if its subclass does not override this method (this is shown).

The window is built dynamically on demand, rather than being precompiled. Thus, by changing dynamically the content of the layout script, the layout of the window can be changed dynamically also.

Using this structure, the programmer of the view CBO ('OrderView' in our example) need know nothing about the underlying system-level GUI API complexities, and can write a CBO that will be extremely portable (at the source level) to other environments.

Not shown in Fig. 8.5 is the ability of a knowledgeable programmer to issue his or her own low-level presentation interface calls; these are not locked out (but clearly the CBO would become that much less source-portable).

Finally, note that the programmer does not have to do anything to drive the icons that represent the model. Their behaviour is handled entirely by the infrastructure.

8.3.10 Performance

Clearly, the infrastructure must not only do all of the things so far discussed, but, where necessary, do them very fast. In particular, very fast messaging is vital, as is very fast self-defining data handling (see Sec. 8.4.2).

The separation of the router from the adapter code (for connecting to other systems) is important. This allows the router to be connected only with a single system—or perhaps preferably a single address space.

For this reason, the router will not normally ask if the target CBO is remote or not; it will always route to a local CBO. This may turn out to be an adapter that handles the communications to send the message to its real destination in a separate thread of control.

8.3.11 Garbage collection

In Sec. 8.3.9, we said that objects should be persistent. This may be eminently reasonable in a server, where the objects represent shared resources that should be persistent! In a PC, however, there needs to be some mechanism to clean up the UID—to destroy CBOs that are no longer needed. (This whole issue seems to be primarily a UID issue. I have not yet come across an example where objects should be 'cleaned up' in the SRD.)

There are two situations in which a CBO may become 'garbage'—i.e. when the infrastructure can destroy it without impacting anything else. These two situations arise from the idea of local model ageing and from view ageing. We look briefly at these two areas. Further, since garbage collection involves deleting objects, there is the question of what 'delete' should mean. There are in fact several different meanings—we examine them. (We use the term 'garbage collection' in a subtly different way than is used by OOPLs (object-oriented programming languages). An OOPL will garbage-collect during execution. We use the term to apply to persistent objects that have outlived their usefulness.)

Local model ageing

Suppose the user causes an object (for example a customer CBO) to be instantiated on a PC (in the UID). So far so good. But now assume that, after instantiating the customer object, the user closes all views of it, and removes it from all containers (including the desk-top) in which it was placed.

The user now has no way of accessing that object (other than reaccessing it from the server). Now, removal of this sort does not necessarily imply that the object should be destroyed. But if the user is not using it (cannot use it), and other CBOs have no interest in it, then it will just hang around, using up system resources (memory, control blocks, disk space if the persistence mechanism has written it out there, etc.) for ever!

Clearly the CBO infrastructure must recognize this situation, and be able to remove such objects that have not been overtly destroyed, but have become 'garbage'—of no further interest to anyone. Note that this does not mean getting rid of shared data; it just means cleaning up resources in a PC—in the UID.

A further consideration that requires the application of business rules is discussed in Chapter 13.

Note There are situations when a CBO should not be discarded by the infrastructure, even when no other CBO is (at that instant) interested in it. Thus the infrastructure must provide support for a CBO to make itself non-discardable. This might be done by a configuration option.

View ageing

Normally, the position of a view (that is, of the window that the view CBO manages) should be maintained by the infrastructure (either through superclass behaviour, or through some other means). This is because an object-based user interface often requires that, if the user opens a view, moves the window to a new position, then closes the view, then the next time the view is opened, the window should appear at the new position (where it was when the user closed it).

Again, this memory of position should be able to be maintained over PC power-off and power-on.

If this behaviour is required, then a problem arises. If the user opens the view two seconds after closing it, then it is very reasonable, and user-friendly, to have the view reappear in the same place as it was when closed. However, suppose this is a view of (say) a customer, and there is a six month gap between the user closing the view and reopening it. Having it appear in the same place as six months previously is a less obvious requirement.

Now, the infrastructure must remember where the view was (this is not something that the CBO programmer should have to be concerned with). But for how long should it remember? There must be support for a time-out on view position memory. This may be a configurable option, or a piece of infrastructure-provided superclass behaviour.

Remove vs discard vs delete

It is necessary to distinguish between three kinds of deletion. We examine them from the point of view of the CBO infrastructure in a UID.

- *Remove* The user may wish to get rid of an object from a container. The same object may exist in other containers. This operation is a purely user interface operation, which should have no effect on the object itself (except that, if it is not in any other container, and not referenced by any other objects, then it becomes eligible for garbage collection).
- *Discard* The user may wish to get rid of an object from the PC, regardless of what container it might be in on the user interface, and regardless of whether it is referenced by other objects. Clearly, if getting rid of the object impinges on some business process or rule, then the user should be so informed. At least a warning of the consequences should be given. Again, this operation should result in a message being sent to the object, so that the CBO programmer can override it. Some superclass might perform the actual destruction of the object. This mode of destruction does *not* affect the SRD—it involves only the UID.
- *Delete* The user may want to initiate a transaction from the UID such that some item of shared data (which the user sees as an object) is destroyed. The infrastructure typically has no part to play in this, as such processes are almost always surrounded by business rules and authorization issues. Of course, once the transaction has been completed, then the CBO responsible for the unit of work would normally be expected to discard corresponding objects in the UID. Note that, in the trivial case of the data being on the PC, and not being shared, then a delete may be combined with a discard.

Note The usage of the terms 'remove', 'discard' and 'delete' to distinguish the three different situations is not standard.

8.4 Binding

By 'binding' I mean what is known as 'coupling' in the area of structured design. Coupling is a measure of the strength of interconnections between software modules; and as Yourdon and Constantine (1979, p. 85) state, 'Obviously, what we are striving for is loosely coupled systems—that is, systems in which one can study (or debug, or maintain) any one module without having to know very much about any other modules in the system.'

Brad Cox (Cox and Novobilski, 1991, p. 13)[2] defines 'binding' as '... the process of integrating functionality from different suppliers [of software] into a consumer's code'. Binding can be early (things are fitted together at compile or link time) or late (things are fitted together at load or execution time). Cox and Novobilski (1991, p. 17)[3] define another concept, 'surface area', as 'the number of things that must be understood and properly dealt with for one programmer's code to function correctly in combination with another's'. The less surface area the better. This is the equivalent of coupling.

In this section, we use the single term 'binding' to mean both coupling or surface area. Loose binding means less surface area; tight binding means more. CBOs by definition are bound late—at execution time (in fact, at message time).

The real question at issue here is how do we achieve loose binding? That is, how do we ensure that the CBO programmer needs to know as little as possible about message data and reply data? Remember that CBOs are independently compiled and linked. This means (for example) that we cannot use the compiler for type checking of message data across two CBOs. The six main issues are:

- Data types (character, integer, etc.)
- Data structures (e.g. location of a specific integer in the message data)
- Data sizes or lengths
- Extraneous data (e.g. a programmer may have got some data from some source, and in it is data that must be sent to another CBO; can he or she just send the lot and hope that the target CBO can sort it out?)
- Semantics (how the programmer can find out what a given piece of data is—is the integer '2 3' a person's age, or a house number?)
- Method of data definition (how can the programmer of one CBO 'publish' the data types and structures expected in message data so that another programmer can successfully send a message to the first CBO?)

Let us look at the problem in more detail.

8.4.1 The problem

Suppose a given method in a CBO expects to receive three values in the message data:

---

[2] Pages 13–29 provide an excellent discussion of this area.
[3] Here, Cox mentions a number of different factors that can influence software surface area.

140   Business objects

Name	Type	Length	Value
Name	Character	30	Arthur Jones
Balance	Integer	4	42000
Age	Integer	4	35

The following problems arise:

1 *Data format* If we just send the data values, then we must provide it in exactly the same format as the receiver expects:
   (a) Same types (character and two integers)
   (b) Same position (character first, then two integers)
   (c) Same lengths (first is 30 bytes, second and third each four bytes)
2 *Extraneous data* Suppose we want to include another data item in the message—which might be of interest to the target class's superclass? Where would we place that data in the message? Again, what if a given CBO needs to query (say) three other CBOs, make a single package from their responses and just pass it to a fifth CBO? That implies that the first CBO has to understand all the data formats of the other four. Finally, what if a new version of the receiving object that requires a further parameter were built? Would we have to update all instances of the code, and all instances of the possible clients of that code, at the same time?

   All of these examples imply, unless something is done, that the receiving (and maybe the sending) objects will have additional things—outside their proper responsibility—to handle and understand. This significantly increases the tightness of the binding—and vastly increases the sensitivity to change.
3 *Semantics* The receiving object has to understand the semantics—that is, that the first parameter is a name, the second a money balance and the third a person's age.

Forcing programmers to understand all of these three things would result in very tightly bound CBOs. In particular, they would be highly sensitive to change—even changes in versions. Suppose the length of the name had to be changed to 35 bytes. It would be essential for all CBOs using that data item in messages also to be changed—all at the *same* time!

Happily, a solution is available that removes many of these problem areas.

8.4.2 The solution—semantic data

A 'semantic data stream' (SDS) is a way of making binding extremely loose. With SDS, the above example might look something like this:

```
[Name] <James Harris> [Bal] <250> (Int) [Age] <33> (Int)
```

The labels of the data (metadata, or data about data) are carried within SDS. So is the data type (the type as it is within the SDS). In the example above, we assume the default type to be character.

To the programmer, the SDS is just a blob, from which he or she fishes data by name. Thus to retrieve the name and balance, a programmer might code something like this (given that the SDS blob is in the variable Message data[4]:

```
Define 'Name'    40 CHAR
Define 'Balance' 10 PACKED_DECIMAL
...
Name    = GetFromSDS( MessageData, 'Name')
Balance = GetFromSDS( MessageData, 'Bal')
```

Note that programmers do not have to understand the internal format of the SDS blob. Rather they use an API (or if coding in an OO language, they see SDS as being a class). Type conversion to and from defined types can be provided within the API. Depending on language, programmers may have to indicate the type in which they would like the data to be retrieved.

Thus SDS solves the four problems referred to above:

- Data types can change. For example, the sender may send the balance in floating-point form. The code above does not change. Private data types can be accommodated as long as the supplier of the private data type also provides his or her own conversion routines.
- The position (structure) of the data items may change. The code above does not. Thus the position of a particular item in the SDS blob becomes irrelevant to the programmer. The code can contribute/extract only his or her own data from/to the blob, without worrying about what else might be in there, or where his or her own data is located.
- The size of the data can change, since SDS holds data in variable length form. The code above does not change (although if data is made longer, then the receiving programmer may lose the end of a character string or bit string if the return codes are not checked).
- If the sender also includes another data item (or another hundred) anywhere in the SDS blob, the code above does not change. This means that version matching is not nearly so stringent as it would otherwise be. For example, if version 1 of some CBO only looked for the three data items in the example, but version 2 looked for an additional one, then both versions would continue to work when the sender placed four items in the SDS blob.

---

[4] This example is, of course, somewhat abstracted. For example, in REXX, the programmer would have no declarations to do; in C, the function call would give lengths, and might indicate the target type for under-the-covers type conversion; in C++, the SDS blob might be an object, and the programmer would use C++ language messaging rather than using a function call.

The examples shown above are abstracted. A real SDS implementation would provide for such things as:

- Internal formats, so that data labels were not held necessarily as strings, but as tokens (to save space)
- Placing one SDS blob inside another
- Concatenating SDS blobs

In addition, the set of APIs provided would address not only retrieving, but also adding and replacing, blob handling, concatenation, searching, etc.

The overall effect of SDS is that the programmer often has to know only one thing—the name of the data item.

In effect, SDS becomes a common language for message data sent between CBOs. Thus, instead of each CBO having to know about the detailed data structures required by each method in each other CBO with which it communicates, it has to know only two things:

- SDS
- Data labels

This is what makes for very loose binding—the very small amount of surface area exposed.

8.4.3 Performance

Clearly the performance of building and parsing SDS blobs is vital. However, the incredibly loose binding provided by SDS is essential for full exploitation of CBOs—for the realization of the advantages of OO.

Tight binding gives high performance. But such performance requirements are typically met where tight data type and position binding is also required. This is often found within an executable, when it is built using an OOPL. CBOs, as independent executables, must be much less tightly bound than the kind of OOPL objects found within an executable. This means that they can afford a bigger overhead in message handling.

Having said that, it is nevertheless very clear that excellent performance of SDS build and parse is vital.

8.4.4 IDLs vs SDS

IDLs (interface definition languages) have come into vogue recently as a way of providing a language-independent way of mapping data types and structures. IDLs are much more than documentation, however. They are used (by, for example, RPC and object request broker implementations) as machine-readable files that aid the programmer significantly in connecting with another piece of code that might have been written in another language. IDLs are normally used at build time. If an IDL changes, then the chances are high that other code that uses that same IDL must be relinked or even recompiled. This is appropriate where performance is key—such as when dealing with small objects, or subroutines. With CBOs, we trade execution cycles (but not too many!) for the looser binding provided by SDS.

Again, if a CBO was built from an interpretative language such as REXX, then it may be difficult for the average programmer in those languages to handle IDLs (they would have to be dynamically built at run-time, thus reducing their performance advantages). Remember that many people who code in interpretative languages do not have access to compilers, linkers, etc. And if they did, they might well not know how to use them.

Finally, it is worth noting the IDLs may be sensitive to changes in an interface. If a change in one interface means that all using objects/functions must also change—at the same time—then this strongly typed and structured interface may be extremely difficult to manage across large networks.

Having said that, it is clear that, certainly for small domains where tighter binding may be desired, although SDS and message-time data type binding appear a more useful and flexible approach than IDLs, there is no *a priori* reason why a CBO should not publish an IDL, so that non-CBO software entities can use the build-time advantages of IDLs; and vice versa. This is an area currently being researched, and we can expect a growing degree of compatibility as time goes on.

8.4.5 Data typing

The debate over typed vs untyped programming languages still goes on. For a loose binding such as SDS provides, one would ideally prefer a typeless approach (which really means a single-type approach).

Experience suggests that single-typed data in SDS does not perform adequately, as type conversions at execution time are frequently required. A fruitful approach is to define a small number of generic types for SDS, together with facilities for automatic conversion. This means that high performance can be obtained through the programmer matching in-program types to the types delivered in any given SDS. At the same time, where performance is less of an issue, another programmer can use what types he or she likes, and have the SDS facilities perform a type conversion if necessary at run-time.

SDS should also provide for user-defined types, and should provide a framework for handling type conversions provided by the provider of the non-standard type.

8.4.6 SDS advantages

The major advantage of SDS lies in its being an extremely 'soft' interface. Thus it:
- Requires a minimum of knowledge on the part of the programmer (it has small 'surface area').

- Is tolerant of unbalanced change—it provides for different software versions to coexist in a network.
- Can be used by interpretative languages (such as REXX) by people without compilers and linkers.

8.5 Code page and data conversion

The preceding discussion had as an implicit assumption that the CBOs involved were on the same system. If on different systems, then they still use SDS, but something may well have to do some translation if each CBO is to see the SDS data and labels in terms of its own machine architecture.

It is useful to consider the conversion problem in two parts:

- Graphic character conversion (e.g. ASCII to EBCDIC)
- Non-character data type conversion

Here are some considerations, presented in the form of general guidelines.

The CBO programmer should not be concerned with conversion

The CBO programmer should not have to be concerned with message data conversion. If a message is received from a remote CBO, where the sending CBO is running on a machine with a quite different architecture, then the translation to the receiving machine's architecture should be done by the infrastructure, not by the CBO programmer.

Conversion routines should not have to understand application-level data formats or semantics

System-level conversion routines should not have to understand about application-level data formats. For example, they should not have to understand that for message X the first to fourth bytes are character, the fifth to sixth are an integer, etc. Where they do so, then the level of complexity rises sharply, and the change management load can very quickly become insupportable. To prevent this, a self-defining data stream should be used.

Country differences should not be forgotten

This is all a question of code page conversion. Briefly, a 'code page' (an IBM term), is a table of byte values together with their associated graphic characters. The point to remember here is that this is not merely a case of converting ASCII to EBCDIC. Different countries often use a specific code page. Normally, there is some set of characters (A–Z, a–z, 0–9, plus some special characters such as comma, parentheses, etc.) that, regardless of country code page, always have the same code points. That is, a given character graphic has the same byte value in all code pages. Other graphics will have different byte values in different code pages. Some graphic characters will exist in some code pages, but not in others (for example, accented characters).

Even if two systems both use ASCII, they may use different binary representations for special characters (typically above value 127). This can be expected when systems communicate across national boundaries.

An example of the kind of problem that can arise is this. Consider the dollar symbol ($) and the pound sterling symbol (£). The following shows how these two symbols are represented in three commonly used code pages[5]:

Symbol	Code Page		
	US EBCDIC	UK EBCDIC	PC ASCII
$	X'5B'	X'4A'	X'24'
£	-	X'5B'	X'9C'

Assume we are in the UK. In converting from EBCDIC to ASCII, you cannot just convert X'5B' to X'9C' (the ASCII pound sterling code point). If the message arrived from a US EBCDIC-based machine, what you would be doing would be to convert, for example, the string 'You owe me $100' into 'You owe me £100'—which is quite wrong!

All this means that the infrastructure should insert the sending system's code page into the message data somewhere, so that the receiving system can convert if necessary. There are, of course, many further considerations—such as right-to-left languages and double-byte character sets—in handling fully the various country differences.

Graphic character conversion should be done (all other things being equal) at the receiving end

If conversion is done at the sending end, then each sending system must have knowledge of the specific graphic character architecture of each of the possible receiving systems. For example, suppose a system at some location X is changed from an ASCII-based machine to an EBCDIC-based machine. Suppose also that there are 1000 systems that send messages at some time to whatever system is at location X. If conversion were done at the sending end, then 1000 systems would have to change in some way, so that they now converted to EBCDIC instead of ASCII. And all the changes would have to be implemented at the same time.

If done at the receiving end, then the receiver only needs to know the architecture of the graphic characters in the message, regardless of that of the sending system (which, if it has merely passed on the message transparently, may not be

---

[5] The EBCDIC code pages used for this example are the standard IBM System/370 code pages typically used on US and UK machines. The PC ASCII code page used is code page 437, which is commonly used in the many countries that use the Latin alphabet—including the USA and the UK.

the originating system). In the example above, if all conversion was done at the receiving end, then (assuming that each of the 1000 other systems already understands how to translate EBCDIC into their own graphic character architecture for messages received from location X) nothing need change.

Hence less knowledge is required, making for easier systems management.

All other things are seldom equal, however. In particular, where there are many PCs talking to few servers, it may be that, for performance reasons, it is decided that all conversions will be done on the PCs. In that case, each PC, when it first contacts any given server, should send a message to the server asking for its graphic character conversion table. The PC then uses that to convert at the sending end.

This approach avoids the systems management problem of providing all PCs with the conversion table in case they will talk to any given server. The cost is the additional network time required (which may be very small).

Sending in a common format

Suppose there were, among the various systems in the network, 10 ways to represent the single type 'integer', eight ways to represent the type 'floating point', etc. If each system sent data in a message in its own format, then every system would have to know how to translate every other system's data format—for each of the possible data types.

One way of avoiding this problem is to convert to a common form—into a kind of Esperanto—that all systems will understand. Of course, this would not apply to 'as-is' formats, such as an image, or a spreadsheet; in that case, the data would be sent as-is at the sending end. One such common form is character string (leaving only the code page conversion to be done). ASN (abstract syntax notation) is another. Note that SDS can be cast into character form.

The disadvantage with character form is that it takes much more space—more bits—than formats such as integer or float. This has to be weighed against the advantage of simplicity. Again, compression techniques can be used if performance requirements allow it.

Sending an object by sending its instance data

How does one send an object to another system? This is a particularly complex area. However, a start can be made, using SDS as the basis. Let us assume to start with that the code is not sent (although this could be done—especially with interpreted languages). What we can do is send the instance data as an SDS blob. The receiving system can then invoke the correct implementation (code) and 'plug in' the instance data. To the newly moved object, this implies an activation rather than a creation.

One objection to this is that encapsulation would have been breached. However, if the object itself chooses to hold its instance data in SDS form (or cast it into SDS form on receipt of some message from the infrastructure), then it is not strictly speaking breaching encapsulation any more than the mechanics of object persistence are. Clearly, however, the infrastructure would have to play a major part in the mechanics.

8.6 'Alien' objects

The infrastructure manages the dispatch of both intra- and inter-address space messages. The receiving code may be a CBO, a piece of language support code, or an adapter. Hence the infrastructure provides for CBOs to talk to non-CBO software (and vice versa). Such non-CBO application code can be accessed through an adapter, which provides (from the point of view of the CBO) an 'object wrapper'. Thus it appears as an object, but really is not one. It is an 'alien' object.

Since either end of a message flow may or may not be a CBO, one view of the infrastructure is that it is a general 'software bus' between pieces of application code. This leads to the notion of the infrastructure being a 'process aid'—a 'friend' of any piece of application code—as long as the infrastructure is well behaved—as long as it does not demand ownership of the address space or any of the operating system resources within the address space. For example, a well behaved infrastructure, on being loaded in another's address space, should not assume ownership of the stack(!).

This lends weight to the view of the infrastructure being a lightweight piece of code, rather than as a heavy piece of code with a cross-system view of things, and control over multiple address spaces.

The conclusion is that a CBO infrastructure can provide integration possibilities to much more than CBOs. As well as enabling CBOs, it can also enable inter-application integration.

8.7 Operating system implications

This section comments briefly on some important aspects of infrastructure's internal 'shape'.

One of the most important aspects of infrastructure design is the decision as to where the application code that uses the infrastructure will run—in its own address space (process), in its own thread (task), or sharing either threads or address spaces with other application code.

Another important design aspect is whether the infrastructure itself 'owns' the address space in which it runs, or whether it can run in an address space owned by something else.

In this section, we briefly discuss the first of these questions. Traditional applications often run in their own address space. Transaction programs often run in a thread, where the process is owned by the transaction processor.

Some operating systems do not provide a thread structure—only different address spaces. Thus a CBO infrastructure intended to run on many operating systems must be designed such that the CBO programmer does not have to be aware of whether the CBO will run in a thread by itself, in a process by itself, etc.

But what is the best way for a CBO to run? Some have suggested that all instances of a given class should run in their own 'class' address space; others that each instance should run in its own thread. However, probably the best design is one that aligns the flow of control as the computer sees it with the operating system facilities to isolate that flow from other flows.

But what, with objects, is the flow of control? Well, the flow of control is the flow of messages, and messages go from one object to another. Thus it is not obvious that placing each class (or even instance) in its own address space or thread is the best approach.

In fact, the flow of messages always starts with some external event. In an OO system, there is no 'controlling' application that is given control by the operating system when it starts, and which then manages its own flow of control. This is particularly so for a CBO system. Typically, once loaded, objects will wait until some external event (a user action, a timer, an incoming message, etc.) occurs. The infrastructure responds to this event by sending a message to some object. Then there is a 'flurry' of messages among objects, until control returns to the first object invoked, and then back to the infrastructure. The infrastructure then waits for the next external event.

Probably the best approach for aligning tasks and address spaces is with that 'flurry' of messages that results from the external event. This flurry is very much like a transaction, by the way. If we elevate the word 'flurry' into a technical term, then we can talk about 'flurry-based packaging of CBOs', which would imply an infrastructure that placed (packaged) CBOs such that a flurry was aligned with operating system address spaces or threads.

A further question is whether a given instance of a CBO class should be able to participate concurrently in more than one flurry. Detailed consideration of this is beyond the scope of this book.

Another question is whether flurries should always have an address space or thread created for them, or whether they should be allowed to occur in a pre-existing address space or thread. Probably the answer to this will be determined by the detailed implementation of the infrastructure.

One aspect determining this is the design philosophy behind the infrastructure. Infrastructures can be of two sorts (by design):

- *Lean and mean*   The infrastructure is minimal, does not own the address space in which it runs and does not manage other address spaces (but may manage threads). In this case, there may be several infrastructures in a given system.
- *Big and fat*   The infrastructure manages multiple address spaces and knows a great deal about what is going on in the computer system as a whole. In this case, typically there will be one infrastructure in a given system.

I prefer the former. That is not to say that it is the best (although I would argue that it is!). Time will tell. One implication of the lean-and-mean approach is that, within a system, each infrastructure must be able—preferably automatically—to 'learn' of the others, so that messaging across address space boundaries can take place (transparently to the CBO programmer).

An implication for SRD infrastructures is that the management of flurries should be able to be handled by an underlying transaction processor.

Part Three
Design issues

This part of the book discusses some of the design problems that, from experience over the past several years, have shown themselves to be the most common when starting out on client/server design. Much of the discussion is independent of whether you are implementing CBOs or not.

In line with the rest of this book, we confine ourselves to those problems which, loosely, fall in the application developer's domain. Thus this part does not address the problems of sizing, of network design, or operational robustness, of systems management, etc., which must also be considered in implementing client/server systems.

Many design problems I have found to be more tractable when considered in the light of the general model developed in the previous part. This part, then, unashamedly exploits those concepts. In effect, we illustrate how the framework of thinking implied by the model can be profitably used to solve some apparently difficult problems. Such problems include:

- How to protect the integrity of data against multiple update in a cooperative processing environment. This is essentially a discussion about how to create viable commit scopes.
- Where the point of control of a process should be, especially when the commit scope must be in the server, and the control of the process is on the PC.
- How can we distribute data? Is there a natural location for data of a given type? What do we mean by 'data of a given type'?
- How relevant are current or future advanced technologies such as object-oriented database and distributed relational database?
- How should we handle data that is out-of-date in the face of the user interface demand for object persistence.
- Should business logic be placed on the PC?

This framework of thinking, this mental model, this 'paradigm',[1] can be summarized as follows:

- When data has been retrieved from a given SRD into another domain (either another SRD or a UID), that retrieved data does not *have* to be kept in 'sync' with the original data. This is a most important concept, and is discussed further in Chapter 10.
- In client/server systems, there is never a single application that must be split across two systems. There is only ever a single application for one of the two domains—the UID and the SRD. The fact that many people start off with one business process in mind does not alter this. Previously, the UID and the SRD were mixed together—not seen separately. This was so (in general) even when the dialogue part of an application was separated from the 'business logic' and the 'data logic' parts.
- Data integrity should never be addressed as an attribute of the UID. It is always an aspect of the SRD. There will often be more than one SRD.

Many of the issues discussed here are not unique to CBO-based systems; they apply equally to more traditionally structured code, in client/server systems. The first two chapters of Part Three address data integrity, and the others cover design issues and concerns.

Data integrity

Resource integrity in computer systems is a large subject covering data validation, referential integrity, backup and recovery, hot standby, concurrent update protection, two-phase commit, concurrent batch and on-line update, access authorization, transaction management, database management, etc.

In this book, we are primarily interested in this as it relates to application structuring, and to ways of thinking—conceptual models—that will ease the application designer's load. (I do not claim any theoretical rigour for these concepts; merely that—so far—they have proved very useful, and—also so far—they have not been misleading.) The design issues and concerns of this perspective seem to break into two crucial areas—data location and data integrity (here we are talking about data on disk (in databases) rather than program data or object instance data).

The majority of problems in this area arise from the dichotomy inherent in client/server. On the one hand, a major aim is to make shared resources easily

---

[1] I came across the word 'paradigm' in the mid-seventies, in the first edition of Stafford Beer's thought-provoking *Brain of the Firm* (see Beer, 1981). Beer defines paradigm as 'An exemplar or pattern; a basic way of doing something recognizable beneath many superficial variations' (Beer, 1981, p. 403). Some speak of a 'paradigm shift' when referring to object orientation. Hofstadter (1979) sees such things, not as rare events, but as pervasive. Hofstadter suggests that '... real science does not divide up into "normal" periods versus "conceptual revolutions"; rather, paradigm shifts pervade—there are just bigger and smaller ones, paradigm shifts on different levels'. I see the shift in thinking caused by client/server together with OO to be one of the bigger ones.

available to clients; on the other, an overriding concern is to maintain the integrity of those shared resources.

This dichotomy—and the subject matter of the next chapters—is best defined by the sorts of questions that arise most commonly when people first consider client/server systems. These are all of the 'How do we ...' variety, and are the following. How do we:

- Handle distributed data?
- Keep data copied to a PC in sync with the database from which it was copied?
- Manage a unit of work when it crosses several user interactions—and often several separate pieces of application code (CBOs)—on the PC?
- Update the data on the PC when the remote database is updated?
- Handle conflicting update requests from several PCs concurrently?
- Handle an update across several SRDs?

These questions define a number of problem areas, as follows:

- Data placement
- Data currency
- Unit of work management
- Update control (single SRD)
- Update control (multiple SRDs)

In Chapter 9, we introduce some concepts that help to handle the notion of the same data being on both the PC and the server.

Chapter 10 deals with the problem of ensuring integrity while dealing with a multi-system environment where there is no all-embracing distributed resource manager. An opinion sometimes expressed is that client/server is not feasible until such a universal resource manager, with distributed two-phase commit, is available. This chapter discusses techniques for ensuring data integrity in a client/server system *without* a distributed resource manager. The purpose of these two chapters is to discuss concepts that make the problems outlined above more tractable.

Other design issues

Other design issues include how to access very large amounts of data from a very small PC system, how business processes and rules are retained and enforced on an object-based user interface, and different approaches to design methodologies and techniques. (Although we include some discussion of methodologies and techniques, the presentation of a complete design method for client/server and CBOs is beyond the scope of this book.) Specifically, this part, after discussing data placement and integrity, is structured as follows:

- In a client/server system, a user can make a request that could result in thousands of responses from a multi-million-row database server (for example,

'show me all the Jones'). However, often neither the network nor the PC, nor the user, can handle such volumes. This is called the 'megadata problem', and the problem, together with some solutions, are discussed in Chapter 11.
- The subject of business processes and business logic arise frequently. First, there is the question of how, on an object-based user interface, do we show a business process? Secondly, a common question is, where do we split the business logic, and should any business logic be placed on the PC? Chapter 12 discusses both of these questions, and presents answers that have proved to be useful in real systems.
- In Chapter 13, we discuss a number of the design lessons learned over the past several years. In particular, we look at the usefulness for design of the concept of the separateness of the UID and SRD. This chapter is not a comprehensive guide to good design; rather it records a number of findings, and ways of thinking, that have proven useful in design. They all involve specific issues, topics and concerns that have a habit of raising their heads whenever client/server and CBO-based systems are designed.

9
Data placement

In this chapter, we discuss several concepts that can assist with data placement decisions. We also provide a framework of thinking about data that has proved to be useful in considering not only placement, but also data integrity.

Our prime concern is dynamic shared data, which will be accessed and/or changed by more than one user concurrently, rather than (for example) how to distribute static data—such as a rate table—to many PCs in a distributed system. The latter is generally more a question of systems management than of data integrity.

There are two questions here:

- Can we locate part of a database locally?
- How do we keep data copied to a user's PC in sync with the database?

A major concept that helps with these kinds of questions is the concept of the *scope* of data.

9.1 Scope of data

The scope of a given entity[1] is the number of users who access it.

Figure 9.1 illustrates this, where we see an organization chart, together with an indication of three data entities (represented by a star, a square and a diamond). Since the 'star' data is used by people across the organization, we can say that its scope is that of the enterprise; this data is of 'enterprise scope'. Similarly, the square data is of location scope, and the diamond data is of department scope.

Now, a very important rule about data scope is this: When data is *copied* from one scope to another, then it is *no longer the same data.*

---

[1] Pragmatically, we think of 'a given entity'—or business entity—as being the complete set of instances of some entity, and we also think of this set being held on some database. Strictly speaking, each instance of a given entity can be said to have its own scope. Also, a given business entity may be implemented as two or more data entities, each with a different set of attributes, possibly held in different logical locations. For example, a 'customer' entity might be held in two relational tables: a 'party' or 'legal entity' table, and a 'customer relationship' table. However, these considerations do not affect the argument presented here, so we content ourselves with the simplifying assumption that all instances of a given business entity are in a given 'logical' database, and have the same scope.

Figure 9.1. 'Scope' of data.

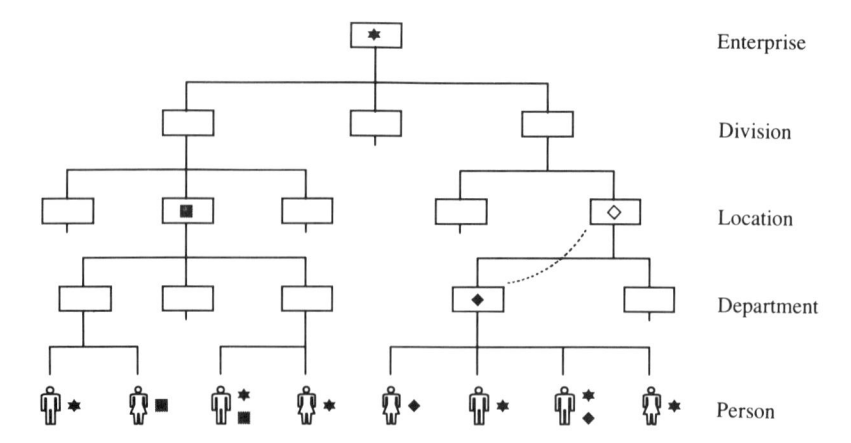

* Enterprise Data
■ Location Data
♦ Department Data

Thus, when data is retrieved by a PC from some database (DB) server, then that data becomes data of 'personal scope'. That is, the data on the PC is not expected to be accessed by more than one person (the user of the PC). Suppose that the original data was of enterprise scope. Since the scope of the data on the PC (which might remain identical in content to the original data for some time) is different (personal as opposed to enterprise), then we know that, regardless of content, it is not the same data.

This is shown in Fig. 9.2, which also illustrates that data on the PC—in the user interface domain—can validly be regarded as being work in progress.

It may well be that, for some specific business process, we are interested in knowing whether or not the two pieces of data become different in value. However, the important conclusion derived from the above principle is: Just because we make a copy of enterprise data does not mean that the copy and the original must be kept in sync.

Put another way, this conclusion reads: Just because we have created some personal scope data by copying from enterprise scope data does *not* mean that they *have* to be kept in sync. Since the copy is not the same, there is no compelling need to keep it in sync with the original data. (Of course, there may be times when you want to do so, and in some situations this may be very desirable.)

Let us check this against what we know of data in traditional transaction processing systems, where the user interacted through a character-based terminal. In this case, the UID encompassed those parts of the transaction programs which handled presentation of menus and/or panels.

Suppose a user retrieved some data (say customer name and balance) at time T_1. Also suppose that, at time T_3, the user had not done anything further, and so the

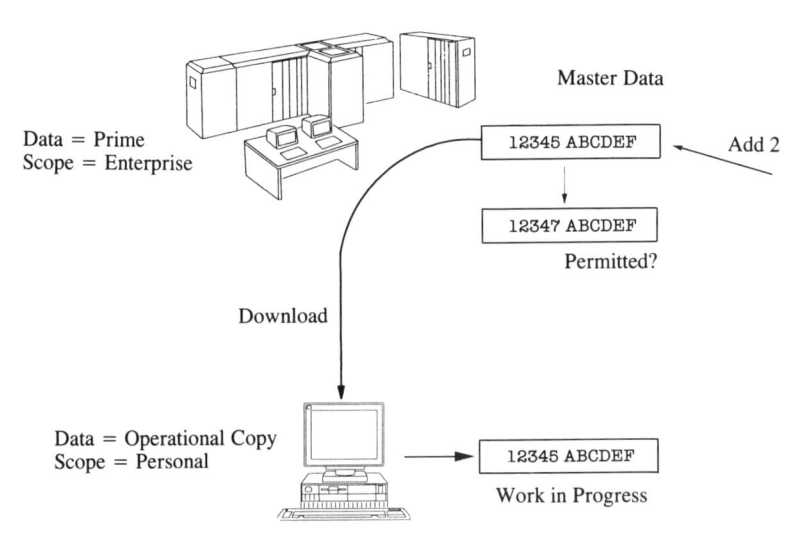

Figure 9.2. Different scope is different data.

balance of (say) £150.00 was still displayed. Now suppose that at time T_2 (before T_3, but after T_1) another user had updated the balance by £20.00. What would we now say about the now out-of-date amount showing on the first user's screen?

Well, what we would not have said was that the data should immediately be changed! (Of course, there may have been some situations where that is exactly what we would have said—in a dealing room, perhaps, or in a process control system maybe. However, these situations are not typical of the average commercial data processing system.)

9.2 Kinds of data

Suppose that the corporate data being copied to the PC was historical—say last year's sales figures for some product. In this case, the question of keeping things in sync becomes almost irrelevant. Suppose now that it is a customer's current account balance that is copied to the PC, and the user will use the data to make some legally enforceable business commitment to the customer. Suppose also that another user may enter some transaction that updates that customer's balance between the first user getting a copy of it and using it. This case is clearly quite different. The difference is caused by the different nature of the data. In the first case it is static (historical, unchangeable); in the second it is not only dynamic (is changing) but it is also vital that the user has the latest copy when making the commitment.

So there are different kinds of data, and we can categorize as follows:

- Prime data
- Business copy data
- Operational copy data

(The categorization of data types presented here is not intended to be definitive; but it is certainly proved to be very useful. The concepts presented here are from an internal IBM paper (Schofield, updated). This paper included detailed guidelines on data placement; such detail is beyond the scope of this book.)

9.2.1 Prime data

The term 'prime' data (also sometimes referred to as 'master' data) means the most current and trusted committed instance of each data entity.

By 'trusted' is meant that the business will point to that version (if there are several such) as the one in which they have most faith as to accuracy and currency.

Prime data is almost always shared data, which is updated interactively. Even if only one user accesses it, it may also be accessed (perhaps concurrently) by batch processes. However, it is valid to consider data of scope 'personal' to be prime. For example, if a manager maintains a small database on a PC of employees' birthdays, so that they can be sent a card, then that data is prime data of personal scope.

Prime data, as the only or most trusted version, must always be adequately secured. That means that it must be backed up, and that it should be able to be restored. In general, the degree of IT professionalism required for its management is directly proportional to its scope and its importance—in other words, to the cost of recovery were it to be lost or corrupted. Even data of departmental scope (say) can benefit from protection against multiple update, if the cost of a transaction processor is less than the cost of recovery. Remember that recovery also includes recovery from errors made between the time that the data became corrupted, and the time that that corruption was discovered.

Placement

In general, prime data should be located on a server at the same level as its scope—or higher. Thus data of department scope should be placed on a department server, or on a 'higher' server, such as a location or divisional server. There are two related things here:

- Scope of data—a logical attribute of data
- Level of sharing—a physical attribute of processing—the machine(s) on which the data is stored and from which it is accessed

For example, suppose that the scope of shared access to some given data is the set of users in a certain factory. In that case (at least as a first-cut design decision) the data should be held on that factory's server.

If prime data is placed on a server at a lower level than its scope, then the implication is that adequate access to that lower level is available from outside the lower level.

Data placement

Sometimes (by design and happenstance) a system structure does not have a machine large enough to be able to hold all of the prime data for some given (wide) scope. In general, there are two solutions to this:

Use a lower-level scope system as the higher-level server

For example, consider the factory mentioned above. Suppose now that the business grows and/or changes, and users outside the factory, in other locations, need to access the data. In that case, the data may be left where it is, as long as the outside users have access to it.

This may seem simple; but often, if the other users are connected to other systems, it may be something of a challenge—and may in any case be unacceptable from a performance point of view. In any case, where there are more than a few (say 10 or more) systems involved, this approach will probably require some message routing software to route requests from the various systems to the one at the factory.

Partition the data among the lower-level servers

The is an interesting approach, which implies dividing the data up into chunks such that each chunk effectively becomes of a lower-level scope. This can only work well if there is some acceptable algorithm to use, to define which data goes into which chunk. It also must mean that users cannot access data outside their own scope.

For example, suppose a manufacturer has 10 warehouses, and wishes to have a server at each warehouse. Further, suppose that any user can commit any stock from any warehouse, as long as he or she can 'see' that stock. Let us assume that the company does not want a central server to provide stock details to all users in all warehouses. Finally, suppose that a user at one warehouse cannot access another warehouse's system. (I have actually met this situation—it is not academic. The company that implemented this scheme had very good reasons for doing so, and are proud of their distributed data architecture. They say it saves them a lot of money.)

This can be done as follows:

- Each warehouse has a stock items database that contains all the items across all warehouses.
- Free stock (stock available for allocation to a customer order) for any given item is an array of 10 values. Each array element is the free stock for that item from one warehouse.
- On a regular basis, a batch run is made in each warehouse. This applies some algorithm to determine how much of this warehouse's stock—for each item— should be 'seen' by each of the other warehouses. That information is then

transmitted to the other warehouses, and their stock items databases are updated (again in batch).

The down-side of this approach is that, on occasion, a user will tell a customer that there is no stock available when in fact there is. The up-side is that the company may be able to right-size to a cheaper IT system than otherwise.

It is clear that the algorithm used to divide up the data is of utmost importance.

It is also very clear that this approach will not work in some situations. For example, suppose a bank branch were to tell you that, although you have £1000 in your account, they can only give you £20 of it due entirely to an internal IT structure decision. Your account, I venture to guess, would not stay with that bank for long!

9.2.2 Business copy data

'Business copy' data refers to snapshots of prime data. Business copies are read-only. They are often summaries of some kind (e.g. first quarter sales) or time-frozen information (e.g. balances as at month end). Two examples are:

- Copies that provide a static base for query and decision support (management information) functions.
- A 'shadow' of some prime data, such as conference (computer conferencing), or tools repository.

Business copies may also differ from prime data in that:

- They can contain derived data (e.g. aggregations).
- They are normally refreshed regularly (either by increment or by replacement).
- Versions may be kept to provide historical references.

Business copies may themselves be subsetted, and those subsets distributed. Since this is static (unchanging) data, there is no synchronization requirement. Hence copies can be made and distributed to any level of scope (as long as the IT system can manage whatever load is implied, of course).

The placement of business copies is largely determined by the IT strategy for handling this kind of data. For example, it might like to maintain all this data centrally, so that it is available to all authorized users. Alternatively, it might distribute defined subsets to different locations, depending on which users want which data.

Sometimes, a business copy may form the base for prime data. For example, a subset of a customer database (prime) may be snapshotted, and then used as the basis for prime data of a different scope. In general, this is not particularly effective, as the new prime data will increasingly diverge from the original prime data, and will probably be of decreasing usefulness.

Finally, remember that the scope of a business copy may be wider than that of the prime data from which it is derived. If the prime data is held on (say) a location server, then there may be a requirement to copy some subset of it to provide part of a business copy of greater scope.

9.2.3 Operational copy data

An 'operational copy' is a copy of prime data taken with the aim of improving some level of service such as response time or availability. An operational copy is a duplicate. Whether it must be kept in sync as a direct consequence of being a duplicate will depend on its scope.

Some examples of operational copies as they affect PCs or small PC-based workgroups are:

1. *Static data* Copies of small tables (e.g. rate tables). This is very similar to a business copy. Such data is read-only, regularly refreshed.
2. *Prime subset* Copying a subset of prime data to, for example, a location server. This data is maintained at the location, and is read-only to other users outside the location. Updates to the local copy are logged, and the logged changes fed as transactions back into the prime data.
3. *Work in progress* Copies of prime data for use during a PC-based unit of work. Changes are accumulated during PC processing, and, after an explicit prompt has been answered affirmatively by the user, are committed by sending a single transaction to update the prime data (see Sec. 10.3 for integrity considerations). For example:
   (a) Taking a customer record to a PC, changing it, then sending a transaction back to update the prime data.
   (b) Copying an engineering drawing to a PC, working on it for some time, then storing back the changed version.
   (c) Retrieving an application development component, updating it, then putting it back into the prime data.

Other examples include copying to a remote site for disaster recovery, and copying to another SRD for some reason. The latter is possibly the most complex, as it implies having a single data item in two locations. In that case, the two must be kept in sync, within a time delay defined by business requirements.

9.3 Local data and availability

In this section, we consider a design aimed at providing greater system availability through locating prime data at a level lower than its scope. We use the example of a bank branch holding its own copy of prime data, when that data is of corporate scope.

The branch will have some number of customers who see that branch as their branch. Perhaps 80 per cent of all accesses to those customers' details will be made by people within the branch. So why not hold that data locally? In addition, if the data is held remotely on some corporate server, then how does the branch continue working if access to that data is removed (for example, due to a communications line failure, or the server going down)? This is a question of availability. Why not use the computing resources in the branch to provide greater availability?

Well, there are many reasons why not—including access from other branches, backup, recovery, etc. (often it is a requirement that branch personnel should not need to be trained to engage in computer administration such as backup and recovery).

Indeed, there is an argument that says that a client/server system must be less reliable than a traditional character-based terminal and mainframe/minicomputer system, since the number of components in the link between the user and the data is greater. Can the client/server architecture be used to increase availability rather than reduce it?

Let us see how we can square this circle.

The essence of the design is that we make no changes to our thinking about prime data and scope. First, a copy of the branch's customer details is made from the prime data (located on the corporate server), and is copied to the branch system, where it forms the branch customer database. This situation is shown in Fig. 9.3.

What we then have is an operational copy on the branch system. All read requests from the branch are sent to the branch customer database. But how are changes handled? The principle is that all changes must in the first instance be made to the prime data, through the appropriate authorized transaction ('Update Customer Transaction' in Fig. 9.3). How is the branch system kept in sync?

The best way to think about this is that it is not. Rather, it is refreshed—not on a regular basis, but rather on a 'relevant transaction' basis. What this means is that, whenever the prime data is changed—regardless of the source of the change—then the change transaction also (possibly as part of the same commit scope) sends an update message to the relevant branch system. Prime customer details will include what branch system holds the operational copy of that particular record. This process is illustrated in Fig. 9.3.

The effect of this is to provide both branch users and branch-based CBOs with the appearance of a local copy of their prime data. But how does this help availability? Consider the situation when the corporate server is (for whatever reason) unavailable. This is shown in Fig. 9.4.

In this case, the branch system software recognizes that the prime data system is unavailable, and does the following two things:

- Update requests are logged within the branch system.
- A 'Read' request is satisfied by a merge of branch customer DB data and update log data. This means that if some customer data is changed, then a subsequent read will return the changed data—but the branch customer DB has not been changed.

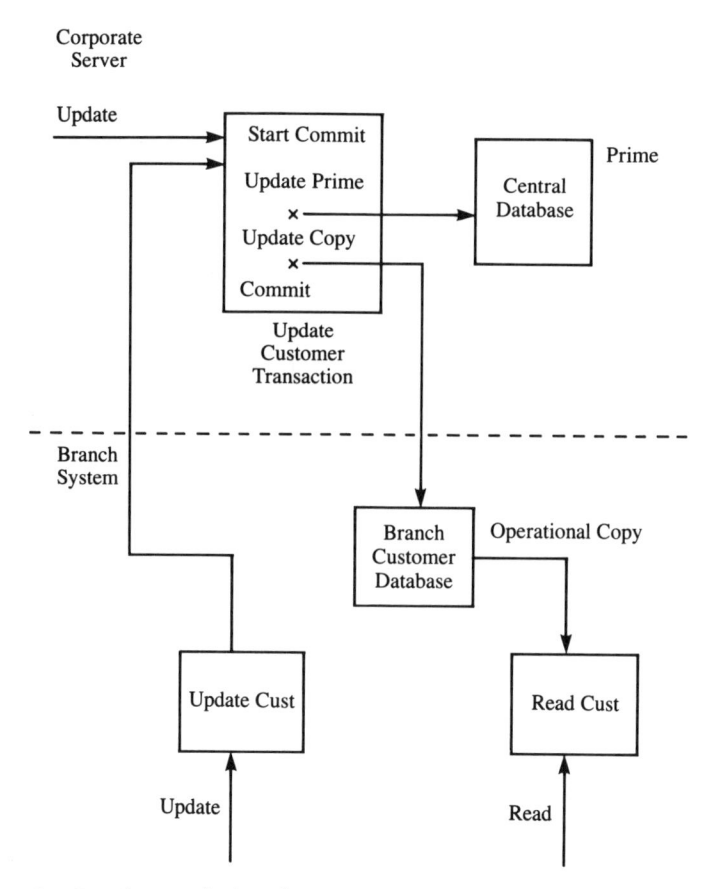

Figure 9.3. Local copy of prime data.

This merging of data is done 'on the fly', and the whole design approach is sometimes referred to as the 'merge-on-the-fly' approach.

When the corporate server becomes available again, the branch system uploads the transaction log (quite possibly as a set of normal transactions), so that updates made while the line was down can be applied—and the branch customer DB refreshed.

One question remains. Suppose that the corporate server is unavailable owing to a communications failure in the connection to the branch. What happens if the branch's customer details at the corporate server are changed by someone outside the branch?

There are (broadly speaking) two types of changes to data:

- Replacement (for example, changing an address).
- Increment (for example, adding to an account balance).

This is where business rules come into play, and the whole 'merge-on-the-fly' approach cannot work unless business rules can support it. For example, there

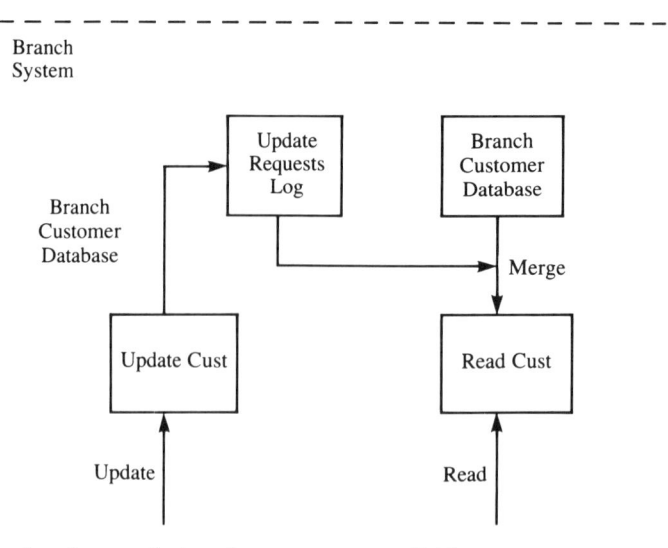

Figure 9.4. Local copy of prime data—server unavailable.

would have to be a business rule that defined what to do about replacement-type changes, if they are not received in chronological order.

Increment-type changes are more difficult, as often business commitments depend on receiving changes in chronological order. For example, suppose a given customer has a balance of £100, and that he banks at Branch X. He has no overdraft arrangement. His account is joint, in his and his wife's names. The business rules state that no account can become negative unless there is an overdraft agreement. Now assume the following sequence:

Time   *Event*
11:00   The communications link from the corporate server to branch X goes down. Account balance according to prime data (on the corporate server) and operational copy data (in the branch) both say £100.
12:00   The customer's wife draws £60 from branch Y in a nearby town. Prime data balance is now £40; operational copy is still £100.
13:00   Customer goes to branch X, asks how much is in his account, is told £100, and draws £70 of it. This seems OK because the operational copy says his balance is £100, and so funds appear to be available. Prime data balance is £40; operational copy is £30.
14:00   The link is restored, and the £70 withdrawal transaction is sent to the prime data. The prime data is updated to show −£30, and the transaction is fed back to the operational copy, which now also shows −£30.

Here we have an example of breaking a business rule, owing to a technical fault (the line going down). Clearly, if the business rule is sacrosanct, then this design will not work. However, some companies are happy to define a business rule that says that a given limit should not be exceeded by some agreed amount. In this case, suppose the business rule said something like: If no overdraft arrangements have been made, then account balances must not become negative; except that when the prime data is not available, they must never appear to go negative, and not more than 50 per cent of the apparent balance may be withdrawn.

If this rule had been in place, then the customer would have been told that, owing to system problems, he could not draw £70, but could withdraw £50.

Where rules of this general kind are acceptable, then operational copies can be used to enhance availability substantially.

10
Data integrity

This chapter examines various aspects of data integrity as found in client/server systems. Again, the major emphasis is the CBO programmer's view of this question, rather than the whole topic in its entirety.

The context for discussion assumes a resource manager that provides a domain in which multiple concurrent requests against shared data are handled, and commit scopes maintained. That is, a request is either completely and successfully completed, and all changes caused by that request are committed, or any changes are rolled back, and the shared resource is restored to its pre-request state.

Examples of such resource managers include transaction processing systems and database management systems.

Given such a resource manager, experience suggests that the main problem areas from the developer's viewpoint are as follows:

- The status of PC data that is outside the resource manager scope.
- Handling a unit of work that extends over multiple user interactions.
- How concurrent updates can be handled such that they do not interfere with each other. This is a question of locking strategies.
- Managing a unit of work that extends over several separate resource managers.
- How to inform all interested parties about a change to shared data.
- How to coordinate commitment of changes to multiple CBOs in the UID when those changes are all within a unit of work?

Before discussing these areas, let us briefly recap on a couple of concepts introduced in Chapter 6. First, the 'resource manager domain' (or RMD) defines the scope over which the resource manager can handle coordinated (two-phase if necessary) commits. For example, a distributed DBMS might handle a single coordinated commit across several heterogeneous systems. Secondly, the shared resource domain (SRD) defines the scope within which application code must be written in order to be within a single commit.

Data integrity is always an attribute of the SRD, not the UID (by definition). A question sometimes asked is, what about a stand-alone PC application, which accesses non-shared data on the PC? I have always found it useful, even in this situation, to structure things such that there is a separate SRD component—even though the SRD is 'shared' by only one user. This has clear advantages for subsequent (unplanned) expansion to more than one user; it is also an excellent basis for decomposition in the solution domain.

Now let us look at the above questions.

10.1 Data on the PC

The general question is, can data be held on the PC, and, if so, what is its status?

We first need to differentiate between data on disk (prime data) and operational copies (see Chapter 9). If the question is about prime data, then it is really one of data placement, which we addressed in Chapter 9. Here we can add that such PC placement of prime data certainly requires an effective RMD that encompasses the PC.

In this case, both the UID and the SRD will be on the same PC. The real question is usually about data that is outside the RMD scope. It most frequently arises in the context of operational copies where the copy persists on the PC. The main concern is the currency of the data.

10.1.1 *Data currency*

With a GUI, a user can change from one task to another. This means that a task may be forgotten—or at least put aside for some considerable time in a half-way-through state. Again, with object-based user interfaces, often the GUI is required to look the same when powered on in the morning as it did when powered off the previous evening.

Both of these situations mean that, if data has been retrieved at the start of a piece of work from a server, then by the time the user picks up the task again, the data may be out of date. (We deal with what happens when the transaction is submitted and data is out of date in Sec. 10.3.)

The question is how to handle this situation. We are helped by observing that this is not a new problem. With character-based terminals, a user could start a transaction that displayed some data on the screen, and then leave the screen to go to lunch. On return, the data on the screen may well be out of date.

With PCs, the only difference is the length of time data can be left 'hanging around'. Potentially, data may become significantly older than it can on a character-based terminal—since the terminal user cannot 'park' a job half-way through—he or she has to complete it or cancel it before starting anything else.

The start of addressing this problem is to realize that the data in question is all data held in the UID. This means that it is really work in progress (see Sec. 10.2). As an aid to users, it may be backed up periodically (for example, overnight), but it will be backed up as a UID backup—nothing to do with the prime data from which it was derived.

Treating this data as work in progress simplifies the problem. We now have a simple question of currency.

There are only really four approaches to the problem of data currency in the UID:

1 On making the operational copy to the UID, always lock the prime data, so that the UID data is forced to be current. This means that the prime data is not available to other users—which may make this approach untenable.
2 Regardless of how long data has been held in the UID, whenever it is actually used, refresh it from the prime data. Aside from introducing a significant network and server load, this does not work; for as soon as the data is refreshed, it is potentially out of date.
3 Whenever the prime data changes, refresh the operational copies wherever they may be. This implies that a record (which may change second by second) be kept of all operational copies. Note, however, that with CBOs, together with the kind of interest registration framework described in Sec. 8.3.9, this may not be as onerous as it otherwise sounds.
4 Accept that the data is out of date as soon as the operational copy is made. If the prime data changes, then decide what to do about it only when a transaction based on the now out-of-date data is sent to the relevant SRD. This approach is entirely in keeping with the data being work-in-progress data. It also matches well the real separation of responsibilities between the UID and the SRD.

Of these four approaches to solutions, the last two, in general, seem to be the best—the last certainly being much preferred for non-CBO SRDs. Additional considerations to do with 'ageing' CBOs in the UID are discussed in Chapter 13.

10.2 Units of work

In the context of an RMD, a 'unit of work' (UOW) generally means a set of changes that are committed or rolled back as one.

Now, a very useful guideline for client/server systems is: An RMD unit of work should be initiated by a single message to an SRD.

In other words, a unit of work in an SRD should not involve multiple messages to and from another domain (typically a UID). Note that this is a guideline, not a rule. Sometimes, this guideline will be enforced by the transaction processor used in the SRD, and the designer will have no choice (this is common with some mainframe systems). At other times, it will be a design option—other approaches are common on some minicomputers, for example.

Although this guideline is a good 'first-cut' design rule, and makes for simpler designs, there are other approaches. In general, we can define three approaches to the unit-of-work question:

1. *The classical server* A classical server is initiated by a single request, and responds with a confirmation of either completion or complete rollback at the end. In other words, a classical server corresponds with what one might call a 'classical transaction'. This approach results in 'atomic' servers. Such servers have no knowledge of the state of any other unit of work, have no interaction with anything outside themselves during the UOW and do not retain state information between different invocations.

2. *The journal entry* There are occasions where the classical server approach is desired (or forced) for several separate transactions, but where a commit by one transaction must be able to be 'undone' because of some business situation met by another transaction. This is typically not a technical failure situation, but rather a genuine business need to reverse an already committed change.

    In this case, application code must be invoked in order to effect the 'undo', which, to the resource manager, will be just another transaction (another invocation of a classical server). The term I use for this situation is 'journal entry', taken from book-keeping, where an error is never erased, but is corrected through an additional balancing entry. These balancing entries, which do not relate immediately to an external event such as a customer payment, are called 'journal' entries.

3. *The conversational server* This is where an SRD is allowed to conduct conversations with domains outside itself between the beginning and end of the UOW.

Before discussing these, however, it is necessary to recognize that there are two units of work involved in client/server—the UOW as seen by the user, and the UOW managed by the resource manager. This is an important principle for client/server systems: There are *two* quite different units of work—the user unit of work, and the SRD unit of work.

10.2.1 The user unit of work

A unit of work as it appears to the user, and a unit of work as it appears to the resource manager in a SRD, will often not be the same. For example, consider an order entry process. The single user unit of work might start when a customer rings up to place an order, and end when the user says goodbye to the customer—after getting confirmation from the computer that the order has been successfully placed on the system. Thus the user unit of work could look like this:

1. Answer phone
2. Get customer details
3. Check stock for items requested
4. At end, inform customer of total amount of order
5. Place the order

User actions	SRD functions invoked	RMD involved
1. Answer phone		
2. Get customer details	A. Read customer details	RMD 1
3. Check stock for items requested	B. Read item details	RMD 1
4. Inform customer of total amount, and of new balance outstanding		
5. Place the order	C. Create order Update customer balance; Update items' stock-on-hand	RMD 1
6. Ask about time to next order		
7. Say goodbye and hang up		

Figure 10.1. UID unit of work vs SRD unit of work (1).

6   Ask if customer would like to be reminded to place their next order (based on ordering frequency)
7   Say goodbye and hang up

This is shown on the left of Fig. 10.1. On the right are three SRD (server) functions—A, B and C (maybe methods of CBOs). For simplicity, we assume no customer locate function. Each of A, B and C are SRD units of work (even though the first two are trivial inasmuch as they do not change anything), which occur in the same RMD (RMD 1). There is only one user (UID) unit of work, however; it starts with the user picking up the phone and ends with it being hung up.

Note that, within the UID, the operational copy of the customer data is changed so that the user can inform the customer what the new balance outstanding will be (step 4). One can imagine a customer details window on the screen that shows this new balance, having been updated automatically as the order lines were entered.

This update is done within the UID—and hence is nothing to do with the SRD. Such an update may well be required by a business rule that says that the user must inform the customer when an order takes the customer over credit limit—and must disallow any further items being ordered.

Clearly this kind of thing is a UID thing. Since the order has not yet been committed, the balance outstanding is not actually over credit limit. It is just potentially so.

This is a good example of the usefulness of performing 'business logic' in the UID, and introduces another important design guideline: Updates in the UID are always updates to work in progress, and do not necessarily have to be updated concurrently in the SRD.

Now let us turn to the three approaches mentioned above.

10.2.2   The classical server approach

The example in Fig. 10.1 illustrates well the classical server approach to data integrity in client/server systems. In the example, three classical server transactions are done. The first two are reads. Changes are all accumulated in the UID, until the entire user UOW is sent—as a single transaction—to the SRD in RMD 1.

Suppose, however, that the balance outstanding (prime data) had been changed by some other user while the order was being taken, such that the customer was now over credit limit? In that case the response to user action 5 from server function C in Fig. 10.1 would have caused the user to be informed that such was the case. The order would then have had to be amended. This is fine, as long as the business rules (constraining the user to the way the company wants to run its order entry function) accept this mode of operation.

There are several points of note here:

- The order creation, as a separate transaction (C), is done entirely within a single SRD.
- Transactions A and B could well be re-used in other user units of work.
- If the user decided to enter the items before identifying the customer (if business rules allowed that), then there would be no change in the SRD (except trivially that B would be invoked before A was).

In essence, the above example well illustrates the basic design approach of UID and SRD interactions—design the UID unit of work such that all requests of the SRD are read-only, until the user is ready to say 'do it'; then do it (request an update) once, at the end.

Attractive though this may be as a design approach, however, it will not always work.

10.2.3 The journal entry approach

The example in Fig. 10.1 shows the user checking stock availability (step 3). However, the prime data is not updated with the amount requested by the customer. Suppose that another user had got in first—between the SRD functions B and C—and placed an order that took the stock level below that requested by the first user's customer. In that case, when the first user's order is placed (SRD function C), the customer would have to be told, and invited to take a lesser quantity or accept a back-order.

Suppose now that the business rules change to say that, when a user says there's stock available, then it must continue to be available when the whole order (of several items) is placed (this is a similar situation to airline reservations).

In that case, the scenario would change to that shown in Fig. 10.2, where an extra step has been added—UID step 3a, and SRD step B1. This SRD step is still a classical server transaction—the allocation is a single UOW in the RMD. (Several users may be doing order entry, and may be accessing the same item concurrently. A single total of allocations (not yet committed) might be accumulated for each item. Each increment to the allocated total would be done by a classical server transaction. However, if a technical error occurs (e.g. a line goes down), then it is

User actions	SRD functions invoked	RMD involved
1. Answer phone		
2. Get customer details	A. Read customer details	RMD 1
3. Check stock for items requested	B. Read item details	RMD 1
3a. Allocate quantity requested	B1. Record amount allocated	RMD 1
4. Inform customer of total amount, and of new balance outstanding		
5. Place the order	C. Create order Update customer balance; Update items' stock-on-hand Release stock allocated	RMD 1
6. Ask about time to next order		
7. Say goodbye and hang up		

Figure 10.2.   UID unit of work vs SRD unit of work (2).

not possible to reverse just that user's allocations. Thus a separate record needs to be kept of allocations per order.)

Subsequently, and before the user has 'placed' (committed) the order, the amount allocated for a given item may have to be changed, or the entire order may be cancelled by the customer. This may occur if, for example, the customer goes above credit limit, or just changes his or her mind.

In this case, the change will be via a classical server transaction (not shown in Fig. 10.2). Those transactions must reverse the already committed allocated stock. Such application-driven (business rule-driven) changes, which reverse already committed prime data (as far as the SRD is concerned) within a unit of work (in this case a UID unit of work), are what makes this approach a 'journal entry' approach.

10.2.4   *The conversational server approach*

Suppose that it was decided to write, for the business process illustrated by Fig. 10.2, a single transaction program to run in the SRD. In that case, the commit scope (the SRD unit of work) would extend over interactions outside the SRD (in this case, with a UID).

This approach is often taken in smaller transaction processing systems, and can be very effective, as long as the implications are understood. Briefly, two of the main implications are as follows:

- Data may be locked over user interactions. If the user goes off for coffee (or on holiday!) in the middle of the transaction, then resources can be locked for a long time. In the general case, some time-out is required in order to detect hanging locks, unlock them and roll back the hanging transactions.

    The idea of a user going off on holiday is rather silly in the context of traditional systems with character-based terminals—the user would turn off the screen, the transaction processor would trap the resulting 'lost terminal' signal, and would (hopefully) abort the transaction. With client/server, on the other hand, the PC may well be designed to cater for persistence of state over power-off (see Sec. 8.3.11).

Where this is so, it may be required not only that is there time-out function in the server, but also that the UID function may have to have function to detect a PC closedown request in the middle of a user unit of work, and take appropriate action (for example, disallowing close-down, or sending an abort action to the SRD).

- Unlike the classical server approach, or the journal entry approach to stock allocation, a conversational server will often place long locks on the data. This requires either a DBMS that supports a 'read with update intent', or application-provided marking of records.

  The only problem with application-level marking of records is that all applications that access those records must check the markers in the data. Structuring server code into entity CBOs (or entity-style transaction programs) can provide an effective control over this.

10.3 To lock or not to lock

In Fig. 10.1, we saw data being read by one transaction (e.g. the read of item details by SRD function B), and being updated by a separate transaction (C). Also, we saw the read and update separated by several user interactions. But suppose another user caused the same item data to be updated between the first user's read and update? How do we protect against conflicting updates, which, if not protected, might break the business rules?

This problem is *not* new; it is the problem of concurrency control, and we have had to handle it since the advent of on-line processing against shared data. However, let us take a moment to spell out the essentials of the problems.

To illustrate, suppose item X has a reorder level of 100, and a stock-on-hand of 200. Suppose then that the first user places an order for 70, and (concurrently) a second user places an order for 80. Figure 10.3 shows what could happen (in time sequence) if a 'replacement' approach to updating is taken. Such an approach replaces the old value on the database with the new value (quantity on-hand in our example).

The problem here is that, while an address change may be a proper candidate for a replacement approach, transactions that are really incremental are not. The reorder level should have been broken by the second transaction (and a reorder triggered)—but it was not. We could fix that by sending the increment to the server transaction.

Let us look at incremental updates, this time in terms of the customer balance outstanding. Assume both users were (unknown to them) accepting an order from the same customer. Then, even with incremental updates, the business rules (this

174   Business objects

User A	User B	Item X On-hand	Reorder
		200	100
Read item X; On-hand = 200 Reorder = 100			
	Read item X; On-hand = 200 Reorder = 100		
Deduct 70; On-hand = 130			
	Deduct 80; On-hand = 120		
Update item X on hand = 130			
		130—No reorder	
	Update item X on-hand = 120		
		120—No reorder	

Figure 10.3.   Integrity violation (1).

time about credit limits) could be broken, as shown in Fig. 10.4 (where the credit limit is 400).

In this case, the second user (user B) should not have been allowed to complete the transaction without being warned of a credit limit violation, since that user's transaction brought the balance outstanding above the credit limit.

The point here is that, in the general case, there must be a common way to protect against such concurrent updates—to reject transactions that break the business rules, or which leave the data in an inconsistent state—even though the transactions looked OK to the users while they were being entered. The answer is to organize things such that either:

- The second user cannot start until the first user has completed or
- The second user sees his or her transaction rejected

These two approaches are sometimes called the 'lock' and 'no-lock' approaches. (There are two kinds of locking—the first is that done under the covers by the

User A	User B	Cust X Bal O/S	CredLim
		200	400
Read cust X; Bal O/S = 200 CredLim = 400			
	Read cust X; Bal O/S = 200 CredLim = 400		
Order value = 170 Bal O/S = 370 (OK)			
	Order value = 180 Bal O/S = 380 (OK)		
Update cust X bal O/S = +170			
		370	
	Update cust X bal O/S = +180		
		550	

Figure 10.4.   Integrity violation (2).

DBMS, the second is the kind that has to be considered by the application developer. The boundary will depend on the precise facilities of the DBMS. For example, some DBMSs provide a lock when a 'read with update intent' is performed; others have no such concept, and it is therefore up to the developer to manage a read with update intent.) Which approach is chosen will depend on many factors. For the present, this is how (in general) each approach is typically implemented:

The 'lock' approach

Here, following the initial read, you (the programmer) write a 'data unavailable' marker into the data. Many DBMSs do not provide for this, so the marker is actually (as far as the DBMS is concerned) just another data field in the record (column in the row). When another read is done by someone else, this field is checked, and if the marker is set, then the read may not be allowed (sometimes reads are OK, and only changes disallowed), and an appropriate 'fail' response is returned.

This approach is also known as the 'check-out' approach. It allows data to be locked over user interactions, and relies on the last transaction in the user unit of work to reset the marker to 'data available'.

The 'no-lock' approach

On the initial read, you (the programmer) are given a token of some sort. Often this is simply a date/time stamp (of the last change), which is recorded in the data as just another data field or column. (Some DBMSs handle this automatically for you, with either timestamps or other mechanisms. In general, the concept of not locking on read, but checking if things have changed under you on the write, is called 'optimistic locking'.) When a subsequent update is requested, you:

- Check whether the token you got on the read is still the same as that now recorded in the database.
- If yes, then you generate a new value for the token, and record it in the data. (During the update, of course, the data is locked automatically by the DBMS.)
- If no, then it means that someone else has got in and changed the data between your read and update requests. The update may go ahead, or be rejected, depending on the business rules. For example, a change of address may be acceptable even though you know that another change has been made since your initial read.

Note that 'replacement' updates may not be required to check the token. Thus many companies accept that for some data attributes, such as an address, since there's no business rule they can formulate to decide which is 'correct', the principle is that the last transaction wins. This implies that the code that performs the update (issues the DBMS I/O) should be sensitive as to which attributes (fields) are token-sensitive and which are not.

The determinant of which approach to use will depend on the type of data, its volatility and any applicable business rules. These considerations provide constraints on design freedom.

Since many DBMSs today do not typically support these kinds of locking operations across transactions, they have to be implemented by application-level code. The danger is that a programmer could forget (or may not realize that he or she needs) to check for markers or tokens.

Having said all that, an essential design principle is this: Since the DBMS will perform serialization of changes such that, with the commit scope provided by the DBMS, data integrity and consistency are protected, then the developer should design things (within the constraints noted above) such that as little serialization as possible is done outside the DBMS. Further, any such application-domain serialization should be done as close to the DBMS as possible—certainly in the SRD rather than in the UID.

10.4 Commit scope start and end

It is worth noting briefly that different transaction processors and DBMSs have different ways of designating the start and end of a unit of work—of designating the commit scope. Here are some common approaches:

- A transaction processor may force the start of a UOW to be the point when a message is received, and the end of the UOW to be the point when the transaction program ends (having sent a response to the message). This approach makes for extreme simplicity for the developer, at the cost of less design flexibility.
- A transaction processor may provide an automatic start UOW when a message is received. However, several interactions with the requester may be made by the transaction program before it ends. When the transaction program ends, the transaction processor automatically commits (or rolls back) all changes.
- A transaction processor provides explicit 'start commit' and 'end commit' statements to define a UOW. However, only one UOW can be processed in one address space at any one time.
- A DBMS may provide specific 'start commit' and 'commit' statements to define the boundaries of a UOW. The 'start commit' will return a token, which represents the transaction. Calls to the DBMS between the start and end of the UOW must provide the token as an input parameter. This approach allows several transactions to flow through the same code running in the same address space (or even in the same thread). This gives greater flexibility to the developer

than the previous approach, at the cost of being forced to take concurrency into account.

As can be seen, there are several approaches to managing units of work, and hence commit scopes. The important point to be made about designing CBOs in the SRD is that the developer must be fully aware of which approaches are provided by the underlying transaction processing and/or DBMS software.

Again, an important question for CBO design in the SRD is whether nested commit scopes are allowed by the underlying transaction processor or DBMS. If they are, then both focus and entity CBOs can issue start and end commits. If not, then some other design approach may be necessary (for example, by providing the start and end commit either explicitly or implicitly in some 'front-end' piece of code).

10.5 Update control (multiple SRDs)

There are two common situations whose chief characteristic is the presence of more than one SRD. The first involves a single UID UOW that requires access to two or more SRDs. The second is where one SRD must access another in order to complete its UOW. These two situations are illustrated in Fig. 10.5.

10.5.1 UID and two SRDs

Figure 10.6 illustrates a not-uncommon situation. The situation is identical to the example shown in Fig. 10.1, except for one thing. For some reason, the business requires a work record to be kept of the number of orders placed by a given department (or user), together with any notes made by a user while talking with a customer.

We assume that, for some reason, the existing server code handling order entry cannot be changed. We also assume that there are two RMDs—RMD 1 and

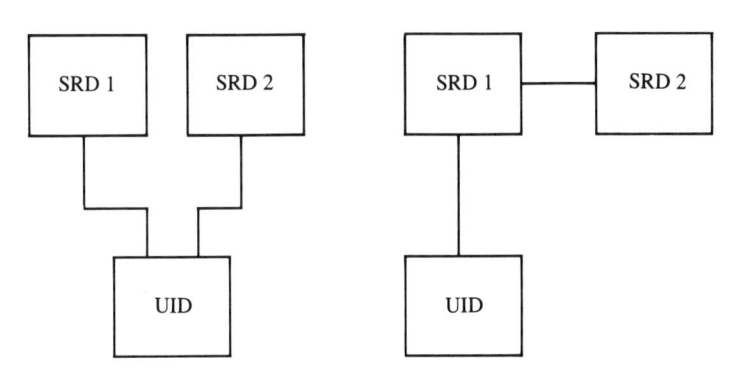

Figure 10.5. Multiple SRDs.

User actions	SRD functions invoked	RMD involved
1. Answer phone		
2. Get customer details	A. Read customer details	RMD 1
3. Check stock for items requested	B. Read item details	RMD 1
4. Inform customer of total amount, and of new balance outstanding		
5. Place the order	C. Create order Update customer balance; Update items' stock-on-hand	RMD 1
	D. Increment department work record	RMD 2
6. Ask about time to next order		
7. Say goodbye and hang up		

Figure 10.6. Example of multiple SRDs.

RMD 2 (perhaps one is on the corporate server system, the other on a departmental server). SRD functions A, B and C are managed by RMD 1, while the department records (SRD function D) are managed in RMD 2. (The update sent to RMD 2 (to add to the departmental work record) is a completely separate invocation of a classical server. This is exactly the kind of local 'customization' that can be effected through having CBOs rather than traditional applications. The IT department would probably have produced an order form CBO, which knew nothing about departmental work recording (or about RMD 2). Another person could have written a subclass (perhaps in a friendly interpretative language such as REXX) of the order form class. This subclass could have intercepted the apply message, invoked its superclass (which would send the completed order to an SRD in RMD 1), then sent a message to the SRD in RMD 2. It might even have 'sent the message' by shelling a process in which a 4GL database access mechanism updated the local departmental server—RMD 2.)

By definition, since there are two RMDs, there is no common DBMS or transaction processor to provide a cross-system coordinated commit.

But what if it is determined either that both should be done, or that, if the second cannot be done, then the first should be undone? This sounds like a candidate for the journal entry approach. Perhaps so; the question is, how should it be managed? Experience has shown that:

- One system should provide the point of control.
- That system should be the one containing the UID.

In other words, the point of control—the place where knowledge of the status of the unit of work should be—is on the PC (in the UID). Since the UID must track the unit of work anyway (so as properly to support the user), then that is the obvious place to put an understanding of the status of the two SRDs. If that knowledge was also placed in an SRD, we should be faced with the unenviable task of maintaining sync between two states—one in the UID, one in an SRD.

This provides us with a handy design guideline: If two or more SRDs are accessed within one UID unit of work, then the UID should manage knowledge of the status (success or failure) of the two SRDs.

10.5.2 SRD-to-SRD access

Consider the situation where a given SRD (say SRD 1) needs to access some other SRD (SRD 2) before it can complete its UOW. If the access is read-only, then the situation is trivial. The complexity arises when the access is for update.

Suppose that SRD 1 is invoked by some UID. But the UID has no knowledge of the internal workings of the SRD it invokes (Fig. 10.5). In that case, the access to the second SRD cannot be managed by the UID. So the questions are: Who manages it? How is it managed? This situation is always complicated, but may be made more tractable if one of the following two approaches can be taken:

- *Move the access* to SRD 2 to the UID. There are several implications in this—and it may not be possible, in any case. It will almost certainly involve a more complex design in the UID, and may prejudice the cleanness of the code design in SRD 1. Whether this can be effectively done or not will depend entirely on the situation. It may be necessary to place the management of the two SRDs in SRD 1.
- *Decouple* the SRDs. It may be that SRD 1 needs only to deliver an update request to SRD 2, rather than requiring data to be returned from it before it can continue. If so, then by definition SRD 1 does not need to know whether the update was successful or not—only that the request was delivered. In this case, the message to SRD 2 can be posted (sent asynchronously) rather then sent (synchronously). If the thing that handles the posted message can commit the message within SRD 1—that is, assure the code running in SRD 1 that the message will be delivered—then this will effectively decouple SRD 2 from SRD 1's unit of work.

11
The 'megadata' problem

A common problem that arises in client/server design is accessing large amounts of data in one computer (the server) from a much smaller computer that cannot hold all that data (the client). We call this the 'megadata' problem, and its implications are wider than one might think on first glance.

This chapter describes the megadata problem, presents its various implications and discusses some solutions.

11.1   The problem

11.1.1   Definition

The 'megadata problem' arises as follows. A key objective of client/server design is to hide from the user—as much as possible—differences among the various systems to which the user's PC is connected. However, the system environment generally implies:

- Large amounts of data are available at the server.
- Technology constraints prevent the delivery of all of that data to the PC screen.

Hence there is a conflict between design aims and technical feasibility, and any solution to the conflict will be a compromise between:

- Allowing the user to access as much data as he or she likes (assuming access is authorized).
- Presenting data to the user in such a way as to minimize the appearance of system constraints such as bandwidth, storage, etc.
- Minimizing the impact on system resources such as network and server capacities.

To illustrate the problem this presents to designers, suppose that:

- A user makes a request that results in 5000 hits on a customer database at the server.
- The data is to be presented as a list (a view of the 'customer list' CBO).

- Each entry in the list has 60 bytes of data associated with it (say customer number, name and town).
- The user has made the request in order to identify one particular customer and view that customer's details. (Clearly, and where appropriate, we would encourage the user to make specific requests—say by customer number—to avoid searches of this nature. Often, however, the user has to search generically.)
- All details for one customer are 600 bytes in size.

In this example, we might consider just returning all 5000 hits. Although that might take a long time (say 60 seconds[1]), when they arrive we could hold the lot in memory (300 000 bytes) on the PC and feed them into the customer list view as required.

However, the following design questions arise:

- Do we return all 5000 hits, or only a subset, making it clear to the user that there is more? And if we do this, then how do we tell the user that more data is available? (There are some subtle GUI design implications here.)
- How much data do we ship down to the PC for each hit? Do we return a complete customer row/record (because the user will want to display details for at least one customer)? Or do we return just the customer number, name and town, and then make another request when a specific customer is selected for display? Even if we choose to return only 200 of the 5000 hits, the amount of data per hit is still important. If we return number, name and town only (60 bytes), then we will be moving 12 kilobytes across the network (200 × 60). If we return 200 complete records of 600 bytes each, then we will be moving 120 kilobytes in one client/server transaction. What will that do to network loadings?
- Is some form of pre-fetching viable, especially since the user (by dragging the slider down a scroll bar with the mouse) can outperform most current networks?
- Where should received data be stored? A design that holds data in storage only is not robust. The design should allow for spilling on to disk (which introduces new problems of available disk capacity).
- What if the search had given 50 000 hits rather than 5000?
- How do we *present* the data on the GUI?
- How can we present an effective progress indicator to the user, since we have no indication on the PC of the amount of data being returned?

---

[1] Assuming 64 kilobyte lines, and a medium-sized mainframe as the server, this might take around a minute—45 seconds line time, 2.5 seconds database access, and a bit for turnaround and path length through controllers. This rather naive back-of-envelope calculation assumes unloaded systems, and zero path length on the user's PC.

In this illustration, then, we see the essentials of the 'megadata problem'. In general, the megadata problem is a problem of scale, and is characterized by:

- Requests for large amounts of data.
- System constraints (bandwidth, PC storage, etc.) that prevent us from managing the data on the PC as if it were local—that is, in such a way as to
  —Maintain the responsiveness the user expects (if he or she does not get immediate—that is, 0.1 seconds or less—response to a simple scroll operation, the user will be sure there is something wrong).
  —Present data effectively (for example, a list of one million items is probably not much use to the user—even if it performed adequately!).

In Sec. 11.2.3 we discuss further considerations resulting from the retrieval of only part of the data for each hit, and from having large numbers of objects shown on the screen.

11.1.2 A philosophical point

On PCs today, it is common to see users (especially PC developers) scrolling rapidly up and down large files (for developers, it is source code). Files of even 10 000 lines can be scanned, paged through and scrolled with immediate responses. This is done by loading the entire file into storage at the start, so file manipulation is all done without disk I/O.

Again, there are PC programs that allow for this kind of instant response without loading the entire file into storage. Such programs have pre-fetch algorithms, to 'feed' the user from local disk storage.

Now, the question is, can we present large corporate databases—of perhaps millions of 'lines' (rows)—in the same way? This is an aspect of a wider philosophical design question: Can we present to the user all the resources of the entire corporate information system in such a way as to enable the user to see them as an integral part of a desk-top PC?

My answer to this question is that, with today's technology, we cannot. Here are a few reasons why not:

- File access—we cannot feed a PC from all remote shared databases at the same speed, and with the same consistency of response time, as from a private PC file.
- When an 'apply' button is pressed on completing a transaction, the system may reject the transaction (see Chapter 10)—something that would not happen on one's own PC (in the absence of a technical failure).
- Travelling users may, while the PC is not connected to the server, enter a transaction and receive an 'OK' response. But they would be bold to assume that, on connecting with the network later to feed the transaction in, it will always be accepted.

In client/server systems, it is generally wise to encourage the user to think of the system as being a duality:

- Mine (the realm of the user's own PC).
- Other (the realm of the rest of the computing resources accessible from the user's PC).

This approach makes for much simpler design.

The notion of what some call a 'single system image' (encouraging the user to think of his or her PC as being in some sense indistinguishable from the rest of the distributed system) can lead to significant design complexity. It is normally not a useful avenue to go down. Experience so far suggests that it is mostly a blind alley, whose exploration can cost a great deal.

Note, however, that there is a great difference between, on the one hand, deciding that the disparity of distributed resources in accessibility and response times will be 100 per cent hidden from the user, and, on the other, trying as far as possible to hide that disparity but telling the user that such a disparity exists.

Thus there is absolutely nothing wrong—and everything to be gained—by attempting to preserve a 'single system image' as much as possible. It is just that it almost certainly will not be fully achievable, and so the user must be educated on the duality.

So, if we take the mine/other route, we can take the best design approaches to each separate realm, and have the user understand easily the underlying differences.

11.2 Approaches to solutions

Solutions to the megadata problem must address two separate but related areas. These are, the retrieval and management of large amounts of data, and the presentation of the data to the user. Solutions will inevitably be a compromise between maintaining the responsiveness the user expects and system bandwidth (including both network and CPU delays). There are perhaps three different aspects to possible solutions:

- Data selection and retrieval
- Displaying the retrieved data
- 'Ghost' objects

11.2.1 Data selection and retrieval

There are a number of approaches to selecting and retrieving data. Here are some of them:

1   One apparently attractive solution is to design the problem away at the requirements stage. This works if the end-user is expected to handle a small (and

probably personalized) number of entities only. For example, an order entry clerk may have a small list of say 200 customers to deal with. The list is only ever 200 lines long. However, even here, disallowing generic searches on the whole customer database is probably not a good thing, as it could impact customer service. So the megadata problem reappears (but in smaller volume)!

2   Design the server object such that, when it is asked to return more than n rows in response to a search request, it returns the first n, followed by an 'index' comprising the 2nth, the 3nth, the 4nth, etc. Present this index if the user scrolls past the end of the first n.

3   Model the telephone directory: build a high-level sparse index (the names at the top of the pages of a phone book) in a periodic batch run, and download this index to a LAN server. Then the user selects from that index. The response is a list of entities between the index item selected and the next index item. In the batch run, arrange for the number of entities to be n (where I would suggest that n is 200 or less). This has the problem that the user cannot search on the index and find an entity between two index items without first retrieving all the entities for the first index item.

4   Have the client object send a value n with the request. The server object then performs the algorithm shown in Fig. 11.1 (this is an overview of the real algorithm). This approach has a number of advantages. First, if the number of responses is large, it spreads the responses returned over the entire range of possible responses; and secondly, it allows for a cut-off at a level well above what the average user can manage, but below ridiculous numbers.

The responses can be prepared as a sparse index (similar to approach 3, except that the index is built dynamically instead of in batch). The user can opt to look at the entries between others (this will generate an additional transaction). Clearly with an object-based user interface, various different requests

---

1. Establish the number of items found by the request (r)

2. If $r \Leftarrow n$ then
   Return r items
Else
   Calculate m as some function of n
     (say the square of $n - 2$)
   If $r > m$ then
     Return a 'Too Many' message
   Else
     Return the first item
     Return every ith item (where $i = m/n$)
       between the first and last items
     Return the last item
   EndIf
EndIf

Figure 11.1.   Algorithm for data selection and retrieval.

for intervening groups can be presented as different views of the same object (the list). This enhances the idea in the user's mind that there is a list, which can be viewed through a number of different concurrent views.

Also, this approach requires the host server to count entries before retrieving them. This overhead needs to be considered in overall system loading analysis; and it may require database indices to be built and maintained that otherwise would not be needed.

5   Download n, and indicate to the user at the end of the list that there are more hits; allow the user to get the next lot (and show something at the top of the list that there is a previous lot).

In general, approach 4 seems to be the most useful. Other solutions may, however, be preferable in specific situations.

An important question is whether or not to retrieve detail data with the list of hits. In general, it seems better not to do this, because of the implications for system loading.

11.2.2 Displaying the retrieved data

For object-based interfaces, it is generally much better to present the user with two objects—the thing itself and a list of things. For example, if 'customer' is an object on the screen, then how does the user retrieve some specific customer? Customer locate is best done through a separate customer list object. Then the user can select the required customer from the list.

The PC provides us with the opportunity for some imaginative design. Here are some possibilities, which almost certainly do not stretch the PC capabilities (and hence show how design in this new world is often limited, not by the technology, but by our imagination).

A list—all entries

If all hits are brought down, and if the number of hits is less than some small number (say 200), then a simple list may be the best approach. This would be presented to the user as (for example) a 'customer list' object.

If the number of hits is larger, and you design such that, when the user scrolls past the last entry (or back above the first entry), you bring down the next lot of entries from the server, then you will be building a particularly unfriendly system. The reason for this is that on a PC the user can scroll faster than most current cooperative systems can deliver data. Hence you would be introducing delays at a point where the user does not expect a delay.

Note that pre-fetching is almost certainly not a solution to this—the user will be able to outperform you—and hence will see unnatural delays.

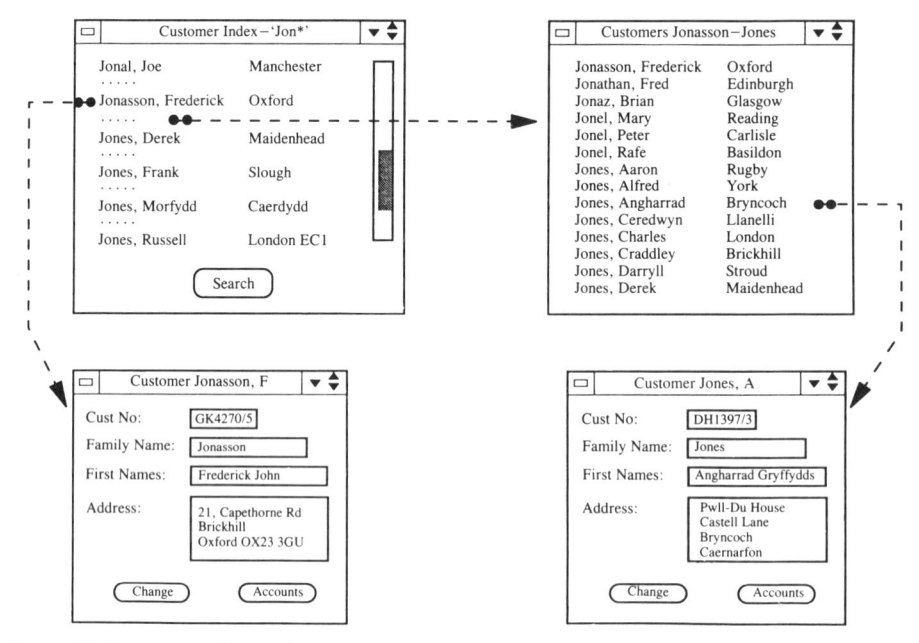

Figure 11.2. Indexed megadata.

A list—grouped index entries

Indices can be shown in lists. For example, if data retrieval approach 4 in Sec. 11.2.1 is used, then Fig. 11.2 shows how the list might look. (The list boxes shown are representational—they could well be icon containers.) Figure 11.2 also shows the result of the user double clicking on a group of 'missing' items, and of double clicking on a specific customer to view customer details.

A tree hierarchy

A tree hierarchy like the Windows and OS/2 File Manager and Drives object respectively is possible. This may be appropriate where an index is brought down—especially where the data is linked (for example, a customer list where the user can view customer orders, and from there view part details). Opening a specific index entry will result in a server interaction—but the delay is at a natural point (as opposed, for example, to a delay half-way through scrolling a list box).

A tree hierarchy is particularly effective when you want to show graphically the multiple relationships that an object might have with other objects.

A tabbed binder (or notebook)

This may a good way of displaying indexed megadata (as described in approach 3 in Sec. 11.2.1).

A combination drop-down box

A list might contain index entries such that an expansion of the index group could be displayed using a combination drop-down box.

A 'phone book' index

This design builds on the observation that, whenever someone looks up a phone book, they are (in a way) handling a megadata problem. The idea is to present an index that looks like a collection of the tops of phone book pages. Each entry gives the first and last entries in that group (page). This could be used for the index in the second option above in this subsection.

A network

Also possible is a network in which the nodes can be expanded (creates more complex network). In addition, each node can be 'opened' to show the detail of the 'node'. This approach may be useful where data has complex associations (or links, or references), and where the user is required to navigate these relationships.

11.2.3 'Ghost' objects

Consider a list of customers, where only sufficient data to populate the list has been retrieved from the server. For an object-based user interface, we would like the user to be able to treat each entry in the customer list as an object—a customer object—which can be looked at by 'opening a view' of it. Now a view of a customer object must show much more detail than appears on the list. But we have not retrieved that data.

On the other hand, we do not want the CBO programmer of the customer list object having to worry about whether or not the data for an individual customer is actually there or not. After all, that is a responsibility of the customer object itself; not of the customer list object. Ideally, we would like the CBO infrastructure to handle the opening of a view of a customer object from the customer list object.

The solution to this is to have the infrastructure handle the fact that an item in the customer list is actually a customer object. Further, we would like all concerned (the user and the CBO programmer) to be able to treat that item as an object—even though the object's data has not been retrieved, and the object is not instantiated.

This is what is meant by a 'ghost' object—one that appears to be there, but really is not. Provision of such a facility is a CBO infrastructure requirement, and enables the user to see the results of database searches without the network, gateway, LAN and PC spending too much time/resource handling data that the user might never look at.

There is another major aspect to this problem, which arises from direct manipulation (drag and drop). Each object in the customer list can be dragged over by some other object; and something somewhere needs to tell the system whether a drop is allowed—so that the system can change the mouse pointer to show the user whether a drop is allowed. This decision often requires access to the code. For example, dropping a stock item onto an order form may depend on whether the customer is above credit limit or not. This means that, in the general case, a static side table defining all the possible combinations of what can drop onto what is insufficient.

Does all this mean we have to instantiate 100 CBOs, just in case the user might look at one of them, or drag over one of them? If we instantiate all 100, we not only use up PC resources, we also (and more importantly) will have to get the data for each via a request to the server. But if we do that, then we might as well have got the data when we retrieved the list in the first place.

One approach to this problem is to have the infrastructure partially instantiate each object in the list. This means that the object is there as far as the infrastructure is concerned, and so can receive messages (e.g. drag/drop messages). It just has not retrieved its instance data yet.

Experience has shown that this approach, which sounds attractive on the surface, in fact leads to complicated programming. In effect, every method in every CBO has to check whether it is partially instantiated or not.

A better solution is to send the message to the class, rather than to the instance, of 'customer'. The class can then decide whether it can handle the message, or whether it needs to instantiate the specific instance.

One problem with this approach arises when the infrastructure provides for truly distributed CBOs. In that case, the code that implements the class may not be on the user's machine. Possibly the only thing to do in that case is to show the user a 'don't know' indication on the mouse pointer instead of a 'Yes' or 'No' indication. This in turn needs additional infrastructure support.

12
Business processes

In the past, we have tended to divide the application development domain into data (things) and processes. The discussion of an object-based user interface, however, tends to concentrate on things—on the user perception of data entities such as customers, products, etc.

This focus then prompts the question, what about the process side—the business processes? Where have they gone? Again, having discussed amodality, concurrency, drag/drop, etc., there may be an impression left that what we are talking about is a free-for-all, where the user can do what he or she likes. This prompts the question, where have the business rules gone? How does this freedom equate with the reality that business rules and business processes must be enforced and followed?

In this chapter, we discuss various aspects of this question, and show how these concerns can be addressed. The aspects covered are:

- How a required business process is enforced on an object-based user interface in a way that does not necessarily force the user through a predefined set of menus and panels.
- How units of work (UOWs) can be managed in this apparently unstructured environment.
- The extent to which CBO thinking can contribute to workflow management.
- We have talked about an object—for example, a 'customer' object—as if it will look and behave identically anywhere in the corporation. This, of course, is not always the case. Business rules require that different aspects of, for example, customer be shown to different types of user.
- How much business logic should be on the PC and how much on the servers.

12.1 Objects and business rules

Consider an office; any office, anywhere in the world. There is one thing that you will never, ever, see. That thing is an 'application'. Yes, there will be forms that have written on the back how to fill them in (that is, the business process). But what you *see* is a form. And, yes, there will be administrative manuals that describe how to do things; but what you *see* is a manual.

A corollary to this is that only in the realm of IT organizations is an 'application' a concrete thing—a controllable asset. Other parts of the organization may *use* that asset to manage their *own* assets.

I do not want to push this argument too far. It suggests that an application is entirely an artifice of the IT world, imposed on users who would otherwise prefer to use something more concrete, more allied to their world. But in many cases there are and have been classes of user who do only one thing—one process. For them, the IT application encompasses, supports, drives and assists their entire working day. For those users, the application is a real thing—usually called 'the computer'. Nevertheless, in this decade, most users are moving or have moved to a new style of work, where they are required to address a much wider range of business function, in a much less structured way, than hitherto. For this kind of person certainly, the appearance of an application as we have traditionally built them—as encapsulations of a given process—can become increasingly a hindrance.

So, if we move to an object-based user interface to provide the increasing flexibility required, then where is the application—as in 'business process'? Is there a valid object we can surface on the user's screen that encapsulates a business process? The answer is yes. The principle behind surfacing business rules and processes on an object-based user interface is: To the user, a business process is a *form* or a *folder*.

Forms

Let us first consider forms. In the example introduced in Chapter 2, we first saw order form, customer, customer list, product catalogue and order history objects (as shown in Fig. 2.2). In that case the business process was encapsulated within the order form object itself.

But care must be exercised when designing suitable forms. For example, if the user wished to create a new instance of the class customer, should we just show a blank customer object and have the user fill it in? In some companies, this might be an acceptable solution. In others, creating a new customer requires more than just filling in the details. It requires credit checking, market classification, etc. Hence it is often the case that a form—a 'new customer form'—is the appropriate object to surface on the user interface.

A slightly more complex situation arises when you have two objects that do not themselves encapsulate a business process, but an interaction is required between them in order to perform some business process or function. The two-account problem is a classic example. Money is to be transferred from one account to the other. On the object-based user interface, which account should be dropped on which, and which one issues the update request to the SRD? As shown in Fig. 12.1,

> The 'two-account' problem is this: A user in (say) a bank wants to transfer money from account A to account B. The system should either complete both the debit and the credit, or should do neither.
>
> In a traditional transaction processing system, the user might be presented with a screen on which to fill in the two accounts and the amount. On pressing Enter, a transaction would be started that would update both accounts (or back out if there was an error).
>
> In a cooperative system comprising a PC with an object-based GUI and a shared-resource server, this is often seen as a problem for the following kinds of reasons:
>
> - If there are two account objects on the screen, which one does the updating of the database?
> - How do you retain the whole unit of work (across both PC and mainframe) within a single commit scope when the two account objects on the PC are both changed?
>
> The answer to the first question is that neither of the account objects does the updating. Instead, we introduce a third object—a 'transfer slip'. The answer to the second question is that the unit of work is designed to be entirely within the SRD. The view/model code, and associated data, are looked upon as 'work in progress'. The overall process, then, might be something like the following. The user:
>
> 1. Tears a 'transfer slip' from a pad of slips (the pad is presented on the screen as another object).
> 2. Completes the transfer slip by entering the account numbers (perhaps by using drag/drop if the appropriate 'account' objects were already on the screen) and the amount.
> 3. Presses the 'apply' button (or some such) on the transfer slip to action the transaction.
>
> On 'apply' being pressed:
>
> 4. The transfer slip CBO in the PC (in the UID) sends a message to a server CBO (or transaction program) in the SRD.
> 5. The server CBO starts a recoverable unit of work, updates the two accounts in the accounts database, commits the changes and sends back a completion message.
> 6. The completion message is displayed as a message of some form to the user, reflecting the success (or otherwise) of the transaction.

Figure 12.1. The 'two-account' problem.

the answer to the problem is to introduce a third object—a form to effect the business process—a transfer slip.

If it is required to show a graphical (or textual) view of the process itself, then that will be one of several possible views of the object available to the user.

Folders

But now let us consider a process that cannot be encompassed by a single form, such as an insurance claim. Insurance claims normally have a number of related items associated with them (letters from the claimant, damage assessments, references to policies, etc.). In addition, the process flows from one person to another. How is this surfaced in terms of realistic objects on the user's screen?

The answer is to show it as a 'customer'—as a folder, a case folder perhaps. A container or folder is an object that contains other objects.

This approach also answers the problem of making changes to the objects within a folder, but not committing those changes until a whole piece of work is done. For example, suppose the user, in the course of completing a part in the claims process, changes the customer record, updates the claims history record, and adds a note to the folder? How does the user signal that the set of changes is complete? And how does the developer ensure in his or her design that the set of changes can be collected into one unit to be sent to the SRD as a single recoverable transaction?

The following approach to a solution builds on a number of items covered previously in this book. The developer places a push button or menu item on the view of the claim folder. When the button or menu item is actioned, it means (to the user) 'commit all the changes done up to now'. The claim folder might send a query to all objects involved and which are in the same UID (the claim folder object knows what it contains). Each object that has changed responds with an SDS 'blob' (see Sec. 8.4.2) containing the changed data. The claim folder collects these together in a larger blob, and sends the lot as a single message to the SRD.

Note that, owing to the nature of SDS, the claim folder object does not have to understand the data formats of the objects it contains, so retaining the essence of OO encapsulation (and the reality if the SDS blobs are objects in their own right).

These objects—forms and folders—are really 'business process' objects. However, I am extremely loath to call them such. The reason is that, unless the developer is experienced in UID object design, and has a full understanding of what the name implies, and what it does *not* imply, there is a great temptation to think of a business process object as, for example, a 'create order' object, which quickly becomes an 'order processing' object, which quickly becomes an application, and the user model is hopelessly broken—quite aside from it being more difficult to design and build!

Finally, a common design question is to decide what can drop on what (using direct manipulation). Designs of significant complexity can arise through over-use or inappropriate use of drag/drop.

The above discussion, from the viewpoint of drag/drop, exhibits a possible thread that may help with this question. Indeed, there may be a general principle here. For the time being, we can express it as a useful design guideline—what we might call the 'droppability' guideline. If there are two kinds of local model object in the UID—just for now let us call them 'data' objects (for example a customer object) and 'process' objects (for example an order form, or claim folder)—then: Always allow a data object to be dropped on a process object. A data object should not accept a process object, or another data object.

This is not to say that there will *never* be times when it is required to drop a data object on another data object. For example, if dropping a customer onto a property can *only* mean a house move, and the drop operation pops up an appropriate 'move details' form, then it may be useful. Again, there may be times when it is required that a process object accept another process object. One example is putting a form (a process object) into a container (which is also a process object). Again, business processes often also include other processes (which may be re-used in further processes).

A further consideration

In the preceding paragraphs, we have discussed how forms and folders can encapsulate the business processes that might, at first glance, appear to be missing from an object-based user interface. We should not forget, however, that 'data' objects (such as a 'customer') can encapsulate their own business rules.

Indeed, there is an argument to the effect that an object-based user interface can present business function to the user *better* than an application-oriented user interface. This is because objects do *not* encapsulate common cross-process function such as custom locate (this would be handled by a separate object—perhaps a customer list object). Hence objects such as customer or product—neither of them forms or folders—are more focused on the real processes and rules unique to themselves, and so exhibit better modularization. (An object such as a customer, which apparently does not encapsulate a process, often will in fact do so—at least as far as enforcing business rules about, for example, what constraints there are on updating customer details.)

12.2 Processes and units of work

An object-based user interface generally invites one to concentrate on things such as 'customer', 'insurance policy', 'account', etc. However, when these interact in some way, and several of them change in the UID within a unit of work, it is not at all clear how we ensure a coordinated commit in the SRD. In Sec. 10.2, we proposed the guideline that one RMD (resource manager domain) unit of work should be initiated by a single message to an SRD. But if a single request should flow, then which of several changed objects in the UID should issue that request?

12.2.1 The 'unit-of-work' object

One approach to this question is to introduce a 'unit-of-work' (UOW) object in the UID. This would be used as follows:

- At the start of the UOW, an object in the UID would send a 'start UOW' to the UOW object, which would return a token of some sort.

- Each object involved in the UOW will send any changes to the UOW object, which will store all the changes in a temporary queue.
- The end of the UOW will be signalled to the UOW object by some other object involved, upon which the UOW object sends all the changes as one message to the SRD.

This approach is not unknown in some traditional transaction processing implementations—database changes are stored across several user interactions, and applied as the last step in the process.

In a CBO-based solution, a single object would normally be responsible for sending the 'start UOW' and 'end UOW' messages to the UOW object, and for propagating the UOW token to other objects involved.

12.2.2 Encapsulated units of work

An alternative approach is to encapsulate the UOW in one of the participating objects, rather than having a separate UOW object. We discussed above how a unit of work can always be surfaced to the user as a form, or a folder. For example, a money transfer between two accounts can be presented as a 'transfer slip'; the processing by one user on an insurance claim can be presented as changes to objects *within a folder*. In both cases, when the user presses 'apply' on either object (the form or the folder), then the unit of work can be said to be completed, and a suitable transaction sent to the SRD.

Thus the UOW is encapsulated within the business object.

Consider the example of an insurance claim, presented to the user as a folder. This folder could contain a 'to-do list' as well as such things as claim letters, policies, notes made by other people in the organization, damage reports, assessor's reports, etc. The to-do list tells this particular user what to do, and (if necessary) the sequence in which it is to be done. Again, the to-do list could be presented, not as a separate object, but as an attribute (a view) of the folder itself.

This to-do list is part of the defined process for an insurance claim. It may show what has been done already, quite possibly by other people in the organization. It may have the appearance of a checklist—or of a page from an administrative procedures manual. It is the thing that makes the folder an active process rather than a passive collection.

Once his or her work on the various items in the claim is completed, the user indicates that he or she is done, and hence the UOW is completed. The folder object then sends a 'query' message to each of the objects it contains. Each will reply with an SDS 'blob'. The folder object then concatenates the blobs (without having to have any understanding of what is in them) and sends the resulting single blob to the SRD focus CBO.

From this discussion, we can elucidate some design guidelines:

- An SRD UOW should be surfaced to the user as a form or a folder.
- For a UOW involving several objects, the form or folder should send the single change request to the SRD.

Suppose, however, that the user starts (and completes) another UOW while the first is in process? Suppose further that the second UOW changes some object that is a participant in the first? Do we not need some form of concurrency control in the UID to handle this situation?

Well, remember that the UID is entirely work in progress. This means that we do not *have* to take account of the second UOW in the first. If we do not, the the worst that might happen is that the first UOW may be rejected—because of the second UOW—when sent to the SRD. If we would like to take account of changes to one UOW caused by another concurrent UOW—in the same UID—then we can do this through an infrastructure-provided 'interest registration' mechanism (see Sec. 8.3.9). The form or folder object in the first UOW would register interest in change events with all the other objects associated with that UOW. If any of those objects change, because of a second and concurrent UOW, then the form/folder will be informed, and can reapply business rules if necessary.

So it seems that in many situations we can handle concurrency in a UID without complex concurrency control. But suppose the request to the SRD is rejected because of other factors (e.g. other users having caused a change to the prime data that invalidates our own UOW)? In this case, we will have a number of objects in the UID that are showing an updated (work-in-progress) state, but which should be 'rolled back'. This rollback should not be to the pre-UOW state. It should be to the current state of the SRD. The simplest way to do such a rollback is to have the form/folder object send a 'refresh' message to each object involved. Each object will then refresh its data from the SRD independently.

Note that this design approach requires zero knowledge in the form/folder object of the state of the objects affected. It only requires that the form/folder CBO knows the names (IDs) of the other CBOs involved.

12.3 Workflow management

Workflow management is a large subject. This section confines itself to a few notes on the possible utility of CBOs in making workflow management systems more tractable. It does *not* attempt to discuss workflow management in general.

The traditional workflow management system is aimed at *controlling* the flow of work around an organization. It understands the status of many work items, and directs each to the next appropriate stage (perhaps to an automated batch system, or to a user's work queue).

As a director of flows, it is rather akin to an autocracy, where each item is told what to do, and where to go, next. Further, since there are very many items in progress, of many different forms, the workflow manager is necessarily a complex system.

Now, we can observe that there are perhaps two major aspects to workflow (this is, of course, an extremely abstracted view, and takes no account of detailed functions required of workflow such as event triggering, parallel execution and required rendezvous points, etc.):

- Directing items to the right place (based on an understanding of current status, of events occurring and of required process steps).
- Providing information to management about work item progress, out-of-line situations, etc.

Now consider a CBO—an object. In discussing encapsulation, and business processes, it is apparent that a given CBO is responsible for understanding much about its state. The word 'responsible' is important. In effect, encapsulation is all about understanding what an object is responsible for, and (equally important) what it is *not* responsible for. (The concept of objects having responsibilities is well established, and is an important design technique—see Wirfs-Brock *et al.* (1990, pp. 31–4, 61–85).)

Further, an object not only reacts to messages as a server, it also *initiates* actions by sending messages to other objects—as a client. Thus an object is given certain authorities (the authority to initiate some action of another object by sending it a message, and the authority to encapsulate certain functions) in order to discharge its responsibilities.

This congruence of responsibility and authority is entirely in line with good management theory and practice.

Now consider workflow management. What is it that is responsible for deciding where a given work item should go next, and what set of conditions within it determine that it should move? Surely the responsibility for deciding that it should move is encapsulated in the object (a folder or form). And if this is so, why not give the item the authority to move itself?

This kind of thinking is entirely in line with the concept of a system world populated by CBOs (as opposed to applications). There is no reason why a CBO should not 'send itself' from one place to another. As it does so, it can also report to some other object (e.g. a 'workflow manager') what it is doing. Of course, if the object 'knows' that it should go to a given department or skill group, it can send a message to that department or skill group asking to which individual user it should send itself.

This approach makes the controlling aspects of a workflow management system entirely the province of the CBOs themselves. Thus the workflow management system becomes a CBO that understands the status of things, what has happened and what should be happening, so that it can fulfil its management reporting responsibilities. The *direction* of work items is entirely the responsibility of the relevant CBOs (an insurance claim CBO, an order form CBO, etc.). Note that, although I use the user interface names for these objects, I am, of course, thinking about both the UID and SRD objects (in particular, the focus object, which will correspond to a UID form or folder CBO).

Of course, this does not invalidate a rules-driven approach to workflow management. On the contrary: the rules for a given process can be the class data of a specific 'procedure manual page' class, an instance of which could be owned by each form or folder object. Further, an expert system 'object' can provide support to the form/folder object, as long as the expert system software is 'embeddable'.

Again, CBOs can provide for graphical design of workflow processes. This can be particularly useful for processes that invoke non-CBO functions such as a word processor, or a batch job, etc.

Finally, some aspects of the CBO infrastructure provide necessary services for workflow encapsulation within CBOs:

- Use of the infrastructure-provided interest registration mechanism means that changes in one CBO can be 'seen' by other CBOs without continual polling.
- Object persistence means that an object can be deactivated over several days (say), and will only be activated when a message is sent to it. This prevents an object from taking up system resources while waiting for something to happen to it.
- A 'timer' object can provide time and wake-up services. This might surface in a given implementation as, perhaps, a 'diary' CBO, or a 'brought forward file' CBO.

12.4 Aspects of objects

There are perhaps two situations when an object—a CBO—is not what it seems. These are:

- When an object such as a 'customer' object is in fact a very big thing—much too complex to implement as a single class.
- When an object should behave differently according to the 'context' in which it is being used.

12.4.1 Very big objects

The obvious answer to very big objects is to decompose them into smaller objects. However, some objects are not obviously decomposable. Of course, from an object-oriented programming point of view, such objects are always decomposable—right down to elementary data types if required. But what we are discussing here is independently-produced business objects—CBOs, not their components. A good example is the typical 'customer' object. Not only will this have many data attributes, but, more importantly, it will have different responsibilities—and hence different behaviour—in different parts of the organization.

A customer service representative may see a customer as a person (or group of people) who represent(s) many different aspects of the customer organization. A delivery manager may see a customer as something that exhibits location and availability characteristics (e.g. 'goods in' is only open between 9 a.m. and 5 p.m). A salesman may see a customer as a series of orders and revenue, together with notes about future potential business. And so on.

In other words, different people will want to see varying characteristics of the same business entity. We can say that they have different 'abstractions' of that entity. Booch (1991, p. 39) defines abstraction as follows: 'An abstraction denotes the essential characteristics of an object that distinguish it from all other kinds of objects and thus provide crisply defined conceptual boundaries, relative to the perspective of the viewer.' Booch (1991, p. 40) further suggests that: 'Deciding upon the right set of abstractions for a given domain is the central problem in object-oriented design.'

However, in our case, what we would ideally like to do is to design a single 'customer' object that can be re-used across domains. In other words, we would like to achieve domain independence for our objects.

This is difficult. On the one hand, the last thing we want is a huge monolithic object that does everything to do with 'customer' across all domains. On the other hand, traditional OO techniques such as subclassing do not seem to help a great deal. While this problem remains one of the more difficult design challenges, an approach to a way of handling it is suggested by the client/server model presented in this book.

The problem becomes much more tractable when approached from the standpoint of entity, focus, model and view CBOs. Thus:

- An entity CBO (perhaps plus some subclasses) may encapsulate (for other CBOs) the persistent 'customer' prime data.
- Several focus CBOs may provide for different processes against the customer entity.
- Model and view CBOs will probably vary widely, given the differing views of customer that users in different parts of the organization wish to see.

In this way, using both the distribution of CBO type and the more traditional OO inheritance mechanisms, the very large object can be decomposed into peer objects, each of which encapsulates a specific responsibility. One view object may be responsible for displaying a map of how to get to the customer's location (and this CBO may itself be a subclass of a more general 'street map' object). Another may present several 'pages' of textual information about the customer. One focus CBO may provide for additions and changes to the set of customers held as prime data. Another may provide for referential integrity on deleting a customer record.

Not infrequently, a given object is required to behave differently in different contexts. This will now be considered.

12.4.2 Varying behaviour

A given object may be required to vary its behaviour depending on circumstances. There are perhaps three ways in which this may be accomplished:

- Context
- Role
- Self-learning

The last of these—objects that adapt their behaviour automatically, and to situations not foreseen by the designers—is the subject of on-going research, and is beyond the scope of this book. The first two reflect techniques used today.

Context

Consider again the example of an insurance claim. One of the objects in the claim folder could be a damage report. Let us assume that the business rules for the UID state that a damage report that is tied to a specific policy in a specific claim case should not be moved (by the user) out of the claim folder. It can be opened, and reflections (shadows) made, but it must not be moved out.

Now, let us assume that the damage report was prepared in the first instance by a user tearing off a blank from a damage report template (a 'pad' of damage reports). At this stage, it may not have been placed into a claim folder; it is merely work in progress, perhaps filed by the user in some general 'day's work' folder. At this stage, it is outside the claims folder, can be moved to other places, and that is OK. But as soon as it is moved *into* the claim folder, it is required to become 'fixed' to it. But technically, it is still the same object, with the same set of methods (at least, let us assume that this is the desired design). The question is, how can the damage report exhibit this different behaviour just because it has been put into a claim folder?

One answer to this is to use the notion of *context*. Thus the damage report object is built to recognize its current context. In this case, it is either in, or not in, a claim folder.

As long as the CBO infrastructure (in the UID anyway) can provide information to an object about what other object it has been dropped into, then the notion of context is viable. In fact, the ability to implement this concept is a particularly useful detail design facility.

Another way of recognizing context is from the user ID and profile that is sent with each CBO message. When looking at (say) an insurance claim, it may be that different people should see different views. A claims clerk may be limited to seeing the current details of the claim case only, whereas a claims supervisor may see the history of the claim, and perhaps reports of risk assessments as well. Thus on opening the claims folder, different people may see different things. The folder itself can assess the context in which it is being used from the user profile, and can dynamically modify the things it allows to be shown.

Note that dynamic behaviour modification on the basis of context is quite different from the sort of static recognition of context provided by subclassing. Such a static approach was discussed in Sec. 8.3.4.

Role

Now consider the claimant in our insurance claim example. Let us assume that:

- The claimant is a person (rather than, for example, a company).
- This person is also an employee of the insurance company.
- Employees and claimants have different behaviours (methods).
- The designer prefers to have a single 'person' class rather than separate 'employee' and 'claimant' classes.

The problem is, how do we separate the different behaviours inherent in employee and claimant, when they are really the same class? (In other words, the user wishes simply to deal with 'people' on his or her screen, some of whom may be employees, some claimants and some both. Intuitively you may feel the way to design for this is to have a person class, and then have two subclasses of person—employee and claimant. However, this could result in the user seeing two objects on the screen—a claimant and an employee—for the same person. This is not what is required for our particular example.)

One possible approach to this is to implement multiple inheritance, so that 'person' might be a subclass of both 'employee' and 'claimant' classes. But multiple inheritance is not simple. Essentially, the problem is that it can be difficult to program, and difficult to design. Someone somewhere has to decide which superclass should be activated for each time the class invokes its superclass—or if both are to be invoked, then which should be invoked first.

Another approach is to have 'role' objects. Thus when a person is a claimant, then an instance of 'claimant role' is created, and owned by the person object. When a person object is being used in some personnel domain, then an instance of 'employee role' can be created, and owned by person. If person is being used in two situations concurrently (probably by different users), and the SRD person object needs to be updated, then the SRD person object can have two concurrent roles—employee and claimant—which map to the real situation.

Role objects, then, may be able to expand the behaviour of other objects, and effectively appear to modify their behaviour.

12.5 Location of business logic

The degree to which business logic can be placed on the PC as opposed to the server is an extremely moot point, depending as it does on one's definition of 'business logic'. Here, we accept the definition given in Sec. 5.1, which was: 'Business logic is all the code that is peculiar to specific business data and/or processes.'

By this definition, there will certainly be business logic on the PC. Likewise, we will definitely have business logic in the SRD. However, suppose that we have a system environment that provides full distributed relational database, so that *all* of the SRD COBs can be placed on the PC. Is there then any case for putting business logic on the server system(s)?

Aside from the many platform-specific and implementation tool constraints, there are perhaps two main reasons why placing business logic on the server systems is preferred—or even essential:

1. *Performance* A designer of a client/server system will normally have the client send a single message to the server for a single transaction. In this case, both the network and the server will see one request flowing. Application code in the server will then issue perhaps many I/Os against the database.

    Distributed database software will not always collect all database requests into a single compound request, and may therefore use substantially more network and server resources.

    For this reason, it may be necessary or desirable to place the SRD code on the server, rather than use—on every occasion—the distributed database facilities.

2. *Untrusted environments* If PCs are provided to people outside the company (perhaps to agents who sell on behalf of the company, but who are not company employees), then there is a risk of malicious modification of the application code. A knowledgeable person could perhaps place a hook into the comms code on a PC, and, by updating the comms buffer just prior to a send, provide himself with additional discounts, etc.

    One way of preventing this is to rerun the business rules at the secure server location. Such a rerun would almost certainly mean different code from that provided on the PC.

13
Common design concerns

13.1 Introduction

This chapter brings together many of the design concerns that have been touched upon in other contexts elsewhere in the book. It discusses further the important concept of the separateness of the UID and the SRD. The focus is on design issues that arise commonly in client/server systems. The UID/SRD concept, and the way of thinking it implies, can be particularly useful in simplifying some of the more apparently intractable design problems that are often met.

A major theme to be developed is that, while user actions at the PC may appear to cross several objects within one transaction, and sometimes to handle several transactions concurrently, it is generally possible to map this activity to relatively simple client/server interactions that protect data integrity.

The chapter is in four sections. First, we discuss this concept of separateness. Then we define the characteristics of SRD CBOs, focusing on their role as servers. Thirdly, a number of common design concerns that centre around the role of the PC (the UID) in client/server systems are addressed. Finally, we comment briefly on design methods that may be useful in supporting client/server and the separateness of the UID and SRD.

13.2 UID vs SRD

Simplicity in design is always a worthwhile goal. However, it may not always be achievable; no matter what abstractions are made at the early stages of design and analysis, at some stage design comes face to face with all the awesome intricacies of reality. This chapter presents a way of thinking about client/server systems that can lead to relatively simple designs. This way of thinking, or approach to design, revolves around the essential difference between the UID and the SRD.

Many of the design problems common to client/server systems can be resolved once there is an understanding of the degree to which the UID and SRD are separate. The kind of problems that arise are to do with a perception that transactions (recoverable units of work) must be handled as a unit across both the UID and the SRD. While this may be the case in some situations, it is almost always true that a robust and rigorous design can be achieved by adopting the following simple rules of thumb: The UID and SRD are separate. UID CBOs and SRD CBOs are separate. Design of UID CBOs and SRD CBOs is separate.

This means that the problem of 'where to split a client/server application' is in many cases an irrelevant question—since you will not be splitting anything. Rather, you build SRD code and UID code separately. The SRD provides a defined interface to client code, and hence can be designed and built without considering the UID.[1] The converse is not true, since the UID code must conform to the interfaces provided by SRD code. That is, it must know what methods are provided by SRD CBOs, and what data should be sent when invoking those methods.

Here is an analogy that illustrates the separateness of UID and SRD:

- I decide to buy a stereo system, so I check if I have enough money by looking at my bank account statements.
- I see I need to move money from one account to the other, so that I have enough in the second account to write a cheque.
- I write to the bank, asking them to transfer some money from one account to the other.
- The bank replies, saying they have done it.

Mapping this example to client/server, then I am the client, the bank is the server. The client/server transaction starts with my letter being posted, and ends with my receiving the bank's response. (We assume that the bank account statements were provided by some other client/server transaction, or some server-initiated process.)

Note that there is nothing to be gained, and much to lose, by insisting that my processes (checking if I have enough money, etc.) should be tied into the bank's processes (making the transfer as long as funds are sufficient). Note also that, in spite of this, I still have to abide by the bank's business rules. If I have no money in either account, then asking for a funds transfer will waste my time and resources (the postage stamp)—and will not work. It is to my advantage to understand the bank's business rules.

We cannot drive this example too far; but it does serve to illustrate the degree of difference between UID and SRD responsibilities—and hence code.

13.3 Design in the SRD

13.3.1 *Designing servers*

Perhaps the most important design decision one can make at the server end of a client/server system is whether or not to design what might be called 'classical'

---

[1] Clearly this assumes that the client/server infrastructure is in place, and that project management has handled the scheduling of SRD CBO interface definitions. These are not always trivial assumptions.

servers. Such servers are units of executable code that encapsulate a single unit of work, and have the following characteristics:

- A server is invoked by a single incoming message (from a UID or from elsewhere, such as another server).
- The server encapsulates a single unit of work, which is either fully completed and committed, or fully backed out.
- On completion (or rollback) of the unit of work, a response is returned to the client. The response consists of one or more messages or returns of control (at least one message back is required to indicate the success or failure of processing at the server).
- There is no interaction with the client other than the initial message and its response.
- Servers are atomic; they do not retain knowledge of any conversation, interactive sequence, or data, between invocations; however, a server may retain knowledge of its own internal state over multiple invocations.
- A server may act as a client to another server.

The implications of this are as follows:

- The unit of work is performed entirely within one SRD—that is, within the commit scope provided by the underlying resource manager.
- The server never holds dialogues with a requester. (This statement is above all a *design* statement. As such, it is a rule of thumb. Experience has shown that this guideline is extremely useful in designing viable client/server systems. However, it can be broken—if the designer knows exactly what he or she is doing. This is further discussed in Chapter 3.)
- The server has no knowledge of the status of the requester, nor does it maintain state information about its requesters across interactions. It may, of course, maintain its own internal state across multiple interactions. This means that, while a given client may invoke a server twice in succession, on the second invocation, it cannot expect that the server will have any knowledge of the previous invocation.

One advantage of non-conversational servers that is sometimes overlooked is that, where static SQL is used, then the plans are likely to be smaller (perhaps significantly so) than with conversational servers.

13.3.2 Server CBOs

Previously, we identified two major types of CBO in the SRD—the focus and the entity (a third, less important, was the resource CBO). The main difference between focus and entity CBOs is whether they primarily relate to a business process or to a data entity. However, the exact responsibilities carried by each type are often a detail design question. Here, we briefly discuss this question with reference to the 'two-account' problem detailed in Fig. 12.1.

We could handle this problem (transferring money from one account to another—with integrity) in several ways. The following three approaches are perhaps more natural for CBO design than for transaction program design.

- A 'transfer slip' CBO could be the focus, sending messages to two instances of an 'account' entity.
- If we kept a register of such money transfers in a database, we might have a transfer register entity in addition to the two account entity CBOs. The transfer register database would be updated directly by the transfer register entity CBO, which also acts as the focus for the transaction.
- Where no business logic outside of the entity objects concerned is needed, then the SRD can provide a general-purpose focus transaction. The UID would send it a message whose message data would contain messages to be sent to appropriate entity CBOs. The function of the general-purpose focus transaction would be to provide a single transaction (within which the other SRD CBOs involved would run), and to unpack the incoming message data and send the contained messages to the identified SRD CBOs. Since the message data sent from the UID would be in self-defining form, the general-purpose focus transaction need know nothing about its application-related content.

As can be seen, the key to the difference between entity and focus CBOs is whether they primarily relate to a business process or to a data entity.

Note that, if the focus and entity objects are design-level only, and the code is implemented as transaction programs, then we might consider having a 'transfer slip' focus CBO, which sends two messages to a single 'accounts database' entity CBO to update the two account records (debiting one and crediting the other). While this approach is not particularly 'pure' from an object design point of view, it might be useful as a basis for designing more traditional transaction programs.

Note also that, where static SQL is used, then the need to bind plans to a transaction may limit the object design.

The entity CBOs may also act as focus CBOs. For example, suppose a request to change the maximum permitted overdrawn amount on an account was sent. To where would the client send it? The obvious answer is to the account. This implies that the account must have its own commit scope.

Where explicit start/end commits are issued by the programmer, the implication is that such commit scopes must be embeddable. Thus when the account is within a money transfer transaction, any commits it issues must be subsumed within those of the focus CBO. Whether this is allowed or not is a characteristic of the SRD (that is, of the underlying resource manager), and must be taken into account during detail design.

When all CBOs run in a single transaction managed by a transaction processor, and the transaction processor provides its own commit processing, then this problem is unlikely to arise.

The possibility of communications failures can also determine the design of SRD CBOs. Consider a user entering a customer order. Suppose stock allocations are made in the course of entering the order, and before committing it. Now suppose that, before the order is committed, the PC (or the communications link) falls over. In this case, it will be necessary for the server to know that that particular client has lost contact so that the allocations can be backed out. Such backout does *not* necessarily imply locking over client invocations (from the same PC). It implies:

- A log being made of the allocations as they are made (these would be 'trial' allocations).
- Something in the server recognizing that the client had lost contact, and sending a message to the SRD CBO involved, so that the log could be used to decrement the allocations.

13.3.3 UID-to-SRD mapping

The discussion so far has not mentioned the UID other than as one source of server requests. However, from this discussion we can derive the following:

- *User interface objects (on the screen) will often* not *map with entities or database tables*   For example, entity modelling may well have produced the two entities 'party' (or 'legal entity') and 'customer relationship'. These may be implemented in the SRD as separate CBOs. However, these two entities will almost certainly be shown in the UID as a single 'customer' object.

13.4 Design in the UID

We now move to the PC—to the UID. Probably the single most important issue here is how to interact with servers in such a way as to preserve data integrity, while at the same time giving the user as much freedom as possible through an object-based user interface.

This question has a number of implications. These are often voiced as questions, the most common ones being:

- If 'the user is in control', that means that business rules cannot be enforced, does it not?
- Units of work—If the user touches a whole number of objects during a single unit of work, how do I preserve data integrity without having to have conversational servers?

- Data on the PC—If things are to appear persistent to the user, then this means storing data on the PC. But this is not the right place to store data. Again, if data is held on the PC, that implies cross-system two-phase commit, does it not?
- Change and timeliness—What happens when the data on the PC gets out of step with the data on the server?
- Multiple SRDs—Which server should manage recovery when a unit of work that crosses multiple servers fails?
- Single system image—How do we present a single system image to users?—Do we give them the impression that their PC is the entire system?
- Direct manipulation—What does the user drop on what to have some transaction performed?
- What goes where—Where should the business logic be located?
- Recovery and availability—Surely recovery design is incredibly complicated in client/server systems? And how do I get greater availability from the system?

Much of the time, the answers to these questions seem to depend on looking at things from a different angle, rather than on some specific new design technology. The design approach characterized by separating clearly the UID and SRD is such a different angle. All the approaches to answers revolve around the notion that all work done in the UID is work in progress, and that we need to organize the UID such that, when the user says 'do it', then a single request is sent to some SRD object. We begin with this.

13.4.1 *The user in control*

The phrase 'the user is in control' has been widely used in describing graphical user interfaces—and in particular object-based user interfaces. It has also been widely misinterpreted as meaning that business rules cannot be enforced. What it means is really two things:

1 Given that the user interface reflects the things required by the user, rather than a predefined and enforced sequence of functions, then the user controls the sequence in which things are done. However, those things allow things to be done *only as far as is permitted by the business rules.*

    For example, in entering an order, the business may be neutral as to whether customer details or product details are entered first. The user may be left to control that sequence. However, the business rules will certainly require that both product and customer details be entered before the order is submitted. In other words, the business process includes the notion of completion criteria, as well as some required sequencing. In that case, the user is certainly *not* in control, and the CBO code must enforce those sequences and completion criteria.
2 The user can switch at any time from one process to another. The things being used for the first process are 'parked' by the user. This must be unexception-

able, since that is how people can manage all other things they deal with. From a business rules perspective, however, it may be that the process should not remain parked for more than some specified time. This can be built into the behaviour of the appropriate CBO, via a 'wake-up' or timer message.

A more serious concern is that data locked on the server at the start of the process will stay locked for too long. This is a real concern. Many 'long-lock' design approaches today assume that, once started, a given unit of work will be completed quickly. Such designs do not envisage the user parking that process while he or she gets on with another. This is one of the main differences between terminal-oriented systems and client/server systems. In general, there are two solutions to this:

(a) Somehow enforce the completion of the parked process (perhaps via some form of wake-up mechanism).
(b) Change the server end to a no-lock approach (see Sec. 10.3).

From a data integrity point of view, the work on a PC should be viewed as work in progress—if you like, it may be viewed as a form of data preparation. This viewpoint leads to designs and data conceptualizing that map well to reality. It also tends to lead to a no-lock approach being taken at the server.

So—yes, the user is in control of those things where the required business processes are neutral about sequence and completion criteria; and yes, the *system* is in control where the business requires it. The system (the code in the CBOs) applies business rules about completion criteria being met, and only controls sequence where the business—but not the technology—demands it.

13.4.2 Units of work

We have mentioned 'unit of work' (UOW) in the context of a recoverable unit at the SRD. However, we must also talk about units of work at the user interface. A key point to note is that they are not necessarily the same. Indeed, in general, it is useful to specify which UOW one is referring to—a UID UOW or an SRD UOW.

This is because, no matter how long it takes for a user to perform some unit of work, the commit transaction (typically) does not take place until the end of the UID UOW, when the UID sends a single message to the SRD. This message signals the start of the SRD UOW.

In the previous chapter, we discussed how an SRD unit of work could be initiated from a user interface object such as a form or a folder. The corollary is that work done up to the point of pressing the 'apply' button is merely work in progress. This means that any changes made to things on the PC prior to pressing 'apply' are by definition uncommitted.

For example, in order entry, the user may well see a unit of work as starting with the initial customer contact, and as completing with a verbal confirmation to the customer that the order has been placed. At the server end, the unit of work will not involve the interaction with the customer, and will probably be limited to adding the order to the orders DB and updating any related data (for example the parts DB).

It is with this design approach that we can provide for single-message atomic servers, and hence simplify the whole matter of units of work, commit scopes, etc. Thus an important design concept is: Data in the UID is work in progress only.

Of course, as a convenience to the user, such work in progress may be safe-stored at a server overnight. This does not change its scope; it just makes it safer.

13.4.3 Data on the PC

But suppose the data on the PC is actually shared by three people on the office LAN, and by no one else? Or accessed by a single person, but with the possibility of sharing with others sometime in the future? In that case, the data is prime, with a scope of office. This means that there must be an SRD to handle it—even if the concurrency control is merely an operating system's dislike of having a file open by two processes at the same time(!).

Thus there may be two kinds of data on a given PC:

- Instance data in CBOs that is saved on disk so as to present the user with the appearance of persistence at the user interface.
- Data that is a repository of valuable information, regardless of how or through what user interface it may be accessed.

If there are these two types of data, then it is useful to treat the PC as containing *both* a UID *and* an SRD, and to design accordingly. This, of course, may lead to building a single piece of code (a single CBO) that encompasses both the UID and SRD. That is OK. However, building a single piece of code because the essential differences between the UID and SRD are not understood is a different story, and can lead to significant difficulties if the code ever has to be revisited to allow it to support more than one person.

13.4.4 Change and timeliness

Suppose that user A retrieves customer X's data at 10:00, and at 10:10 changes the address, and requests an update. Further suppose that user B retrieves customer X at 10:03, changes the address and updates the prime data at 10:07. Should we have automatically updated user A's PC at 10:07? If not, should we have informed user A that his or her data was out of date?

The general question, which often arises, is, 'How do we keep things on the PC up to date when the data at the server changes?' The simple (and in general workable) answer is, 'don't try.' But just wait a minute . . . . We must keep things in step . . . .

Rather than continue this distinctly non-Socratic dialogue, let us step back and consider what happens today with terminal-based systems.

Consider a character-based terminal, at which a user has just summoned up a customer record. The user then pauses to think. One second into the user's thinking time, the customer data in the database is updated. In general, what we do not do is immediately to refresh the data on the user's screen. (Note that sometimes an immediate refresh is a requirement. It is generally so in trading or dealing rooms. That we do not design the average on-line commercial system in the same way as we design trading-room systems reinforces our comment about not immediately refreshing the user's screen. However, having said that, we note further that with a system consisting wholly of distributed CBOs, it becomes technically much simpler to keep the UID data refreshed dynamically from the SRD. In the future, this may open new design avenues for exploring this problem, as long as human factors at the user interface allow it.)

What this says is that data on a terminal screen—and also on a PC—is a snapshot at a certain point in time. It is a copy of the prime data made at a given time. It is a part of the work in progress of the user's unit of work.

If it is important that the data be refreshable, then either the user will be provided with a 'refresh' function, or—after a given period of time—it will be automatically refreshed from the prime data. A dealing-room system uses the latter approach, where (conceptually) the data is refreshed after a period of zero seconds.

The essence of this approach is to admit that, as soon as data is read from a database, it is out of date. If this is accepted, then the only question left is how long it can be allowed to remain visible to a user in its out-of-date condition. This is a matter of business rules. It is not a technical question.[2]

In particular, this means that one should *not*, in general, plan a design that has all PCs being updated just because the prime data changes. This may be OK for a small LAN; but such a design does not scale up—quite aside from probably breaching the principle of least astonishment at the user interface.

This approach, however, leads to a quite different problem, and it is this: A distinguishing characteristic of object-based user interfaces is that objects should be persistent—including over controlled shutdown and power off. Power-off will often happen every night, so the CBO infrastructure must provide a persistence mechanism using hard disk.

---

[2] Several years ago, a design team working on a proposed system at a bank were rather worried that, given the network loadings and mainframe capacity, data displayed on a PC in a bank branch could not be guaranteed to be less than 30 seconds out of date. Clearly this would not do. When they presented their design to the business management, they admitted that the data on the PCs would be out of date. The response was that the company were not about to pay a great deal of money for out-of-date data. Having up-to-date information was a major rationale for the system. When asked how much out of date the data would be, the lead designer answered truthfully. 'Thirty seconds at the most', he said, putting the best face on it. 'Thirty *seconds*!' came the response, 'If you'd said *hours* that would have been OK. I thought you meant *days*. Many of our branches are currently working on data that's two *months* out of date!'

Suppose a user retrieves the data for a particular object (say customer X), puts it in a folder on the screen, then forgets about it, until a year later that user again has to look at customer X's details. In order to support persistence at the user interface, the object will have been stored on disk (quite separately from the prime data).

Now, while a business may be happy for users to use data that is 30 seconds out of date, it will not be happy if the data is one year out of date. Somewhere between 30 seconds and a year, the data must be refreshed or removed. On character-based terminals, this is achieved as a by-product of the user completing the transaction. On a PC with an object-based user interface, however, the problem is more complex.

The solution is to have the CBO infrastructure at the PC include effective aging and garbage collection mechanisms. Business rules about the length of time a given CBO can remain in a UID, and when it must be refreshed or discarded, must be able to be set.

An important design point here is this: Persistence of objects in the UID must not be confused with persistence of prime data on the server. One is to support an individual user. The other is to support the business.

13.4.5 Multiple SRDs

There are several occasions when a given unit of work must access more than one SRD. This means (by definition) that the unit of work cannot be entirely completed within a single commit scope, and hence may not be automatically recoverable if something goes wrong.

Two situations when this can happen are:

- The PC sends messages to two SRDs as part of a single UID unit of work.
- A single transaction includes accessing another SRD (perhaps across an EDI link).

These two situations are discussed in Sec. 10.5.

13.4.6 Single system image

Not infrequently, designers voice a wish to have the user's PC seem to the user to contain the entire IT system. The idea is that the presence of servers in the system should be totally transparent. In general, this is a mistake—because such a view cannot be totally upheld.

A good illustration of why this is so is found in the notion of 'deleting' something, as follows. Let us assume that a user is updating a customer's address. While doing this, the user is interrupted, and asked to do a new piece of work that uses the same customer object. To do this work, the user creates a temporary work folder and makes a 'reflection' of the customer object in the work folder. (A 'reflection' is a user interface term. An icon is said to be a reflection of another when they both refer to the selfsame object; one is not a copy of the other. The user will normally have been through a brief education class that would have taught him or her the basics of an object-based user interface, including the difference between a reflection (or 'shadow') and a copy. This is akin to learning to drive. Once you have passed your test, you can drive on any road.)

Further, let us assume that the user also has a product object on his or her screen. The purpose of having the product object is because that particular product has been withdrawn, is obsolete, and must be removed from the product database (on the server). The user is required to complete the delete processing for that product.

Now consider the following actions taken by the user:

1   The interruption is completed, and the user wishes to remove the customer object from the temporary work folder (but keep the folder for a bit longer for some reason). Thus the user must be provided with some function that deletes an object from a folder, but does not affect any other reflections of that object elsewhere on the screen. This clearly does not mean 'delete from my PC', nor does it mean 'delete from the database'. Let us call this kind of delete a 'removal'. The user *knows* that this will not affect other reflections.
2   The user now completes the change of address on the customer, and wishes to delete all reference to that customer from his or her desktop (screen). Clearly this is more than a 'remove', and is less than deleting the customer from the database. Let us call this kind of delete a 'discard'. The user *knows* that this does not delete the customer record on the database.
3   Finally, the user does whatever is necessary to complete the business process of deleting the product from the database. We will call this a 'deletion'. The user *knows* that, after this, that product will not be able to be found (on the user's IT system) again.

In this example, the user has to be aware of three different forms of deletion. A system that provides only one form—deletion from the database—could be built. But it would not be very friendly at the user interface. In general, the user *must* know about things that affect his or her PC (removal and discard) as opposed to things that affect shared resources (deletion).

Thus we see that the user *must* be made aware of the yin and yang of client/server—the 'thisness' and 'otherness'—which exists in the IT system. 'This' is the user's PC. 'Other' is the rest of the IT system. Designs that try to hide this may quickly become hugely complicated, and will probably be unworkable. That is not to say that one should not hide the differences as much as possible. Where they can be hidden, they should be. Where they cannot, they should be surfaced to the user.

13.4.7 *Direct manipulation*

Direct manipulation (drag/drop) is often over-used. In general, if it is not quite clear to the user what will happen when he or she drops A on B, then drag/drop is probably not appropriate.

Consider (again) the two-account problem shown in Fig. 12.1. I have often been asked how the user chooses on which account object to drop the other in order to perform a money transfer, and which of the two should handle the resulting client/server interaction with an SRD object. I have also been told that drag/drop will not work for real business systems because of the indeterminacy implied by this question.

Let us look at this in another sphere, then come back to the two-account problem.

For example, suppose the user sees a customer object and a product object. The customer wants to order the product. Should the user drop the customer on the product, or the product on the customer? What does either *mean* anyway? A user who is interested in both handling customer orders and recording any known losses to competition could interpret dropping customer on product (or vice versa) as one of two things:

- The customer has ordered the product.
- The customer has not ordered our product, but has ordered a competitor's version of our product.

Sometimes a pop-up dialogue is presented to ask the user what he or she means—which of several interpretations does he or she want to choose. On choosing one, the user is then taken through some further dialogue, ending with a commit of some sort. Here, it is not clear to the programmer what object encapsulates the transaction, and it may be difficult to collect all the data needed for the transaction.

A better approach may be to have the user choose a form (or folder), then drop both the customer and product onto the form. Then it is quite clear what the drag/drop operation means—both to the user and to the programmer. In addition, we now have a distinct object—the form—within which to encapsulate the transaction. By that I mean that the form itself will, when the user says 'do it', or 'apply', send the single request to an SRD CBO.

Now let us come back to the two-account problem. We can now see that the answer to the question of which account should be dropped on which is: 'Neither—they should both be dropped on a third object, a transfer slip.' However, this begs an important question: how does the user find the transfer slip?

Mapping a transaction in the SRD to a single message sent from a form/folder requires that such form/folder objects exist, and there are likely to be many of them. How does the user find them? Three answers suggest themselves:

- Give the user a 'stationery stores' object, within which are all the forms, together with help in finding a particular one.
- Give the user a general 'finder' object.
- On each object that is not a form/folder (e.g. customer, product, etc.), provide a facility to find the forms common to that object. For example, the views for

both customer and product objects might have a menu item that enables the user to materialize an order form.

Note that all of the above should include a help facility that enables an object to be materialized on the screen. For example, if the help assists a user to discover that a transfer slip is what is required, the user should be able to materialize one straight from the help.

13.4.8 What goes where?

With client/server systems, the question is sometimes asked, 'Why not put all the application code in the PC?' Although this may sometimes be appropriate, there are three common situations where it is not:

1. There may not be an appropriate fully distributed resource manager available. Without this, the required commit scope domain would not extend to the PC. This would mean that updates and changes to corporate data—if done directly by application code at the PC—could not be guaranteed.

Even assuming the existence of distributed resource managers, it may be desirable to separate UID and SRD CBOs into different machines. Two common reasons for so doing are:

2. Performance issues may dictate issuing the SQL from the server rather than using the distributed facilities of the DBM. For example, a single transaction may require (say) 10 network interactions with a distributed database; issuing those 10 SQL statements in the same machine as the data will require only one request to a focus CBO.
3. The PC may not be a 'trusted' environment. For example, it may be in another company, perhaps giving suppliers direct access to some server function. In this case, some application code must be duplicated—placed on both PC and server. This is because the business rules must be enforced.

   For example, business rules might say that customer type X must not have a discount. Now calculating a discount should be done on the PC (it is absurd to think of shipping a transaction all the way up to the server just to do a simple multiplication!). However, if the PC is in an untrusted environment, then that calculation must be rerun at the server, and the PC result checked against the server result. If they are different, then the transaction must be rejected.

13.4.9 Recovery and availability

Recovery

In this section, we discuss recovery from failure in the server, or the link to the server.

Recovery is most often interpreted as essentially a technical issue. However, it also has its human aspect. Indeed, in designing recovery, the business requirements are often forgotten—or not ascertained. This can result in recovery strategies that are over-engineered. Here we suggest some 'rule-of-thumb' design approaches to recovery.

The user

The end-user should only be concerned with knowing whether something worked or not. In addition, he or she should never be left 'hanging'. Sometimes there may be doubt as to whether a server update was actually committed or not (for example, if the link fails after data has been committed, but before an 'update done' message is returned). In this case, and following the precept of 'keep it simple', it may be perfectly acceptable, when the link comes back up, to ask the user to check the status of prime data. The user should be told by the system that there is doubt.

This is very similar to business as usual with many terminal-based systems. However, we can add code to record an in-doubt situation, and inform the user on demand or at some appropriate time.

Design for automatic resynchronization when communications are restored is usually difficult. If the business requirements do not demand it, why do it?

However, this does not mean that we do not log errors and report them as systems management alerts; it just means that we do not design complex automatic recovery unless it is really defined *by the business requirements*.

The requesting CBO

The UID CBO that sends a message (a request) to a server should expect one of only three possible responses:

- A positive response from the server—it worked, and here is the response data.
- A negative response from the server—it did not work.
- A negative response from the infrastructure—there has been a failure somewhere; we do not know if it worked or not; in any case, there is no response from the server.

For some requests, there may be a large response (lots of data), which may be sent back to the client CBO as multiple messages. In this case, it is probably simplest to make each message one of the above, and leave it to the client object to work out what to do if there is a failure in the middle. This implies that there is some way for the client CBO to tell that more messages are expected.

It should be unnecessary to include code in the client object to check for a 'hang'. This code should be somewhere else (in the adapter). If there is a failure within the PC such that the client CBO is left hanging, then it may be acceptable to leave it to the user to recognize and deal with it. This may require provision of some form of 'forced close' mechanism.

The adapter

The connection component in the PC (part of the adapter) should be the primary identifier of failures (assuming that most failures will be at the line or session level). Essentially, a communications failure (however caused) could be treated as follows:

- Log the failure (use a timer to detect hangs).
- Return a 'failed' message to the client CBO.
- If the link comes back up and data for the client CBO is received *after* the 'failed' message is sent to the client object, then throw away the data received. After all, if you do receive anything after a 'failed' message has been sent to the client CBO, what are you going to do with it? Note also that this process applies to a hang that was not really a hang . . . . So if hangs are detected by a timer, then it is important to get the timer interval right for the specific system!
- If the failure is such that you do not know if a commit was completed or not (such as a failure in the receive), then send a 'failed—in doubt' message to the client object. Do the same if the failure is within the PC—if for example, code translation cannot for some reason be done.

Availability

In general, availability decreases as more components are put into a path. Client/server systems typically have more components in the end-to-end path than older terminal-based systems. This means that, for the same component reliability, and if the operation of the UID is dependent on server and link availability, then client/server systems must have lower availability.

Probably the key phrase in the above was '. . . if the operation of the UID is dependent on server and link availability'. By using the intelligence in the PC, designs can be built that provide greater availability than traditional terminal-based systems. One such design was outlined in Sec. 9.3.

An important question, therefore, is whether to design for high availability, or to accept lower availability. Of course, a vital consideration is what is meant by 'lower'. The answer to the question should depend on specific business requirements.

13.5 Methodologies and techniques

A full discussion of formal methodologies[3] and processes that can be used to design complete CBO-based systems is beyond the scope of this book. Indeed, such

---

[3] By mentioning specific methodologies in this section, I do not mean to imply that they are the *only* ones appropriate to CBO design.

methods are not yet mature. In this section, I merely mention a few of the things that seem important in the methodology area, and which are certainly food for thought. They are:

- A methodology must map well to client/server systems and to objects (this may seem obvious, but some methodologies do not seem to consider this overtly).
- Two different methodologies are required—one 'top-down', the other 'bottom-up'.
- The place of prototyping.

13.5.1 Choice of methodology

An analysis and design methodology will generally have some notion built into it as to the shape of the code that will eventually be produced. Often these notions will not be explicit. Some existing methodologies do not acknowledge the concept of client/server, and hence become difficult to use once past the problem domain analysis phase. Others do not consider objects.

What is needed is a methodology that explicitly acknowledges the two aspects of client/server and objects. Before using a methodology, one should ensure that the methodology and its associated processes and techniques will produce a thing whose shape conforms with the shape of the thing you want to build. If you do not know what it is you want to build, then there is not much point in choosing a methodology.

Two examples of those methodologies that do map to client/server and to objects are IBM's Business System Development Method (BSDM) (IBM, 1992a–e) and Ivar Jacobson's use case analysis (Jacobson *et al.*, 1992).

BSDM

BSDM is aimed at providing as wide a possible view in the early analysis phase, looking at the business rather than at a specific application (that comes later). Today, BSDM does not explicitly address objects. It has an entity-based approach, but one that maps well to SRD objects. This is because, through its concept of focus as an aid to identifying key business processes, it enables an early handle to be got on focus CBOs (as well as entity CBOs).

If I may paraphrase, the essence of the focus concept as it relates to focus CBOs is that, by focusing on a specific entity, and by understanding its life cycle—and the other entities that must change for any given state change in the entity being studied—then the essential business processes can be identified.

Jacobson

Jacobson calls the focus object a 'control' object. Basing their approach on a well proven technique called use cases, Jacobson *et al.* (1992, p. 135) say, 'Typically such functionality unique to one or a few use cases is placed in a control object. This is similar to the BSDM concept of focus.

However, Jacobson also addresses the dichotomy between UID and SRD in his concept of object types being categorized into interface (the UID), entity and control (the SRD CBOs). In analysis and design terms, it is extremely useful to have a method that explicitly recognizes and supports these three areas.

13.5.2 Different methodologies

Experience to date indicates strongly that design of the SRD (server) is quite different to, and can be treated quite separately from, design of the UID.

Inevitably, the first client/server application will require code in both domains. However, if (and it is an important *if*) the server parts are designed as independent servers, capable of handling client requests from various business process domains, then we find that these server functions (whether provided as CBOs or not) can be re-used for other application areas.

As suggested earlier in this chapter, there is much to be gained by splitting SRD design from UID design. Note that a UID design cannot be done without understanding the interfaces provided by the SRD objects. SRD CBOs, on the other hand, can be designed without consideration of the UID, as long as the designer is absolutely sure that his or her analysis has captured what real users and their managers expect from the system.

Of course, design of any one part by itself will not deliver business benefit. Both are needed. The point is that they can be designed and built separately.

Having said that, one should note that, particularly for the first two or three client/server systems built, it is advantageous—and sometimes required—to evolve the two in parallel. It has been known for design of the UID to identify entities that formal entity analysis did not find. Conversely, proper design of the SRD components can materially assist the identification of CBOs in the UID. As time goes by, successive UID designs should start to re-use SRD CBOs. Also, some of the UID CBOs themselves should be able to be re-used in different business areas.

I strongly suspect that each domain (the UID and SRD) will need different methodologies. SRD CBOs should be designed from a 'top-down' perspective. By that I mean from as high a level of abstraction as possible with regard to the organization as a whole, rather than any specific application area.

The UID should be designed using a 'bottom-up' approach. This means starting with specific groups of users, and finding out what things on the user interface they would like to use to do their jobs. Note that this approach is user-centred, not application-centred. It is no use asking a user about an application when the things you are trying to build are objects that may well be re-used across different business processes.

The top-down and bottom-up approaches meet at the interface between the local model CBO in the UID that requests services of a focus CBO in the SRD. And it should be the SRD focus CBO that defines that interface.

One reason for having different development methodologies is that the objects defined by one are not necessarily all (and only) the objects required by the other. For example, SRD CBOs representing a customer might be twofold—a 'party' (or 'legal entity') CBO plus a 'customer relationship' CBO. These would not be much use in the UID, where an explicit 'customer' CBO would be required. Again, no amount of entity analysis is likely to derive a Post-it Note object, whereas this may be a strong requirement in the UID.

13.5.3 *Prototypes*

A common requirement in client/server systems is to build prototypes—either as part of a more complete development method, or as a precursor. To support this, a process (together with some useful techniques) has been developed that is specifically aimed at designing *quickly* a prototype of the UID. This is detailed in Appendix 5.

It seems that prototyping has become an important part of the development process. Indeed, there has been much discussion over the past few years around 'prototyping to production'. Certainly, early experience with CBO-based systems has suggested that it is quicker to build a prototype *and* a system than to build a system alone. This is because mistakes are made during the prototype stage, and the lessons learned are applied to the system build. Without the prototype, mistakes are made *during* the system build, and lessons learned are only applied in expensive and lengthy re-work.

Part Four
Management implications

This part of the book focuses on the implications for IT management of moving towards client/server and CBO-based systems. While I do not pretend to address all of the implications, those covered here have shown themselves to be among the most immediate, the most obvious, or the most important.

Change can be said to have three aspects:

- Technical changes involved in moving to a new system structure
- Changes required in people-oriented aspects (skills, organization, etc.) that result from the technical changes
- Getting started

These three aspects make up the shape of this part of the book.

Many of the implications deriving from the adoption of CBOs have been dealt with in the course of the preceding chapters. In Chapter 14, we discuss some of the major technical issues that arise, but which are not central to the technical theme of this book.

Chapter 15 addresses implications for organization, skills, etc. It also presents some of the potential pitfalls and blind alleys.

Finally, in Chapter 16, we identify a number of possible starting points in terms of system structure, and suggest a process that, with minimal risk in terms of initial investment, can get you started.

Sometimes, a technical change does not require a supporting change in people skills or in organization. Client/server systems require both. Further, while adoption of CBOs does not necessarily mean taking on board new programming languages, it certainly requires new design skills and a new approach to organizing for re-use of code.

14
Technical implications

In this chapter, three technical implications are discussed:

- The need for a single end-to-end application-enabling software infrastructure.
- How network bandwidth can be affected, and the need to focus network capacity monitoring and planning on the implications of different client/server application designs.
- Changes in systems management, especially the need for both 'push' and 'pull' mechanisms for software distribution, and the implications for version management.

14.1 Client/server infrastructure

Experience of client/server to date has suggested that an application-enabling infrastructure is required. Even if simply implementing traditional PC interactive client applications that talk to traditional transactional server applications, an infrastructure is still required.

In such situations, we have seen the application developers of the first client/server system developing an 'ease-of-programming' infrastructure. This is referred to by several names, for example, 'Comms front-end', 'Call API', etc.

Now this infrastructure is bounded by the budgets, goals and organizational missions of the particular application development project. This means that it is seldom considered to be the general 'IT' client/server infrastructure.

The second client/server application then builds its own infrastructure. And before you know it, there are two or three different infrastructures—each bound tightly to a different application—in existence. And further, since building such an infrastructure is not easy, each application project will probably have seemed much more difficult and costly than envisaged.

Clearly what is needed is a single infrastructure that can be used by all application development projects, and that is capable of providing connections to other applications built without it (for example, bought-in PC applications). The promise of client/server is unlikely to be realized across the depth and range envisaged without such an enabling infrastructure.

The CBO infrastructure discussed in this book is only one part of the overall client/server infrastructure needed. Such an overall infrastructure will include:

- System management
- User training and help centres
- Development methods, processes and techniques
- An end-to-end process for developing new application areas
- An overall strategy for managing rapid technical change in the face of (hopefully) relatively constant IT goals

One danger in developing such an infrastructure is that it can become disassociated from the real business of IT—delivering robust and relevant function to users. When a separate strategy group is set up to address the cross-application infrastructure area, it has to be funded and missioned separately from specific application development projects. It must not, however, become irrelevant to those projects. One way of managing this is to have the strategy group measured on its ability to support front-line development projects in a way that the development projects themselves see and agree is useful.

Too often we see a strategy group beavering away at some grand plan that the people cutting code for an urgent business requirement see as wholly irrelevant. Any strategy group must be pragmatic, and must at least encompass what is there already, if not build directly upon it. A strategy group whose skills do not encompass the systems, tools and techniques being currently used is probably not going to achieve much. The best strategic thinkers, other than a few gifted and rare individuals whose feel for computing transcends the churn in computing systems, tools and techniques, are those who keep in touch—through self-starting acquisition of personal experience—with emerging technologies.

14.2   Network considerations

14.2.1   Traffic patterns

An important aspect of client/server systems is that they will tend to exhibit a different network traffic pattern than older terminal-based systems. In general, it would appear that:

- The transaction rate may decrease (per application area).
- The volume of data moved across the network may increase.
- The bandwidth demanded may increase.
- Transaction rate, data volume and bandwidth may be highly sensitive to the precise user interface design, rather than to the number of message pairs (transactions).

However, even more important is the impact that the design of the PC end can have on the network loads. To illustrate this, let us take an example. First, we shall look at a traditional terminal-based system, then at a client/server system that increases the required network bandwidth by a factor of 10(!), and finally at a more balanced client/server design.

The example is of an order entry task, with 1000 concurrent users. For ease of calculation, we (blithely) ignore network queuing effects. This does not affect the overall conclusion that PC design can have a significant effect on the network, and so must be done in conjunction with load estimates.

Terminal-based

With 1000 people using character-based terminals, we see the familiar network characteristic of a high rate of small transactions. Let us assume that:

- Each user's unit of work (say entering a customer order) comprises seven message pairs (transactions), and takes one minute to complete.
- The required response time is 2 seconds.
- The amount of data per message pair is 500 bytes (100 bytes sent to the mainframe, 400 bytes returned).

Now, for 1000 users, the network approximate traffic characteristics from that one application area are as follows:

- There will be $(7 \times 1000) = 7000$ transactions per minute which equals 117 per second.
- Total volume of data on the network (excluding protocol overhead) is $[(100 + 400) \times 7 \times 1000]$ bytes per minute $= 3.5$ MB per minute.
- Bandwidth required is determined by the need to transfer 500 bytes in 2 seconds. Let us assume that this 2 seconds is made up of 0.25 seconds mainframe process time and 1.75 seconds network time. Further assume that protocol, line propagation and turn-around time overheads can be accounted for by assuming 10 bits per byte of data. Then the bandwidth required is $(500 \times 10/1.75$ bits per second $= 2857$ bits per second. Let us call it 3000 bps.

This is shown in Fig. 14.1(a).

Client/server (1)

Now let us consider a possible client/server design. Here, most of the work is done on the PC. We assume that the parts database is small (say 25 000 rows of 400 bytes (10 MB plus indices)), and a read-only copy is held on a LAN server. The prime copy is on the mainframe, as is the customer database. The process might be as follows:

Terminal-Based
For Each User
 1 Task per Min
  (7 Msg Pairs)
 100 bytes in, 400 bytes out
  per Msg Pair
 2 Sec Response Time
 Data = 7 × 500 = 3500 bytes

1000 Users: 117 Txns/Sec   3.5 MB/min   Bandwidth: 3K bps

(a)

Client/Server (1)
For Each User:
 Download Part of Cust File
  (100 × 1K records)
 Upload Order (400 bytes)
 1 Task per Min
 10 Sec Response
  (2 sec host, 8 sec n/w)
 Data = 100 400 bytes/min)

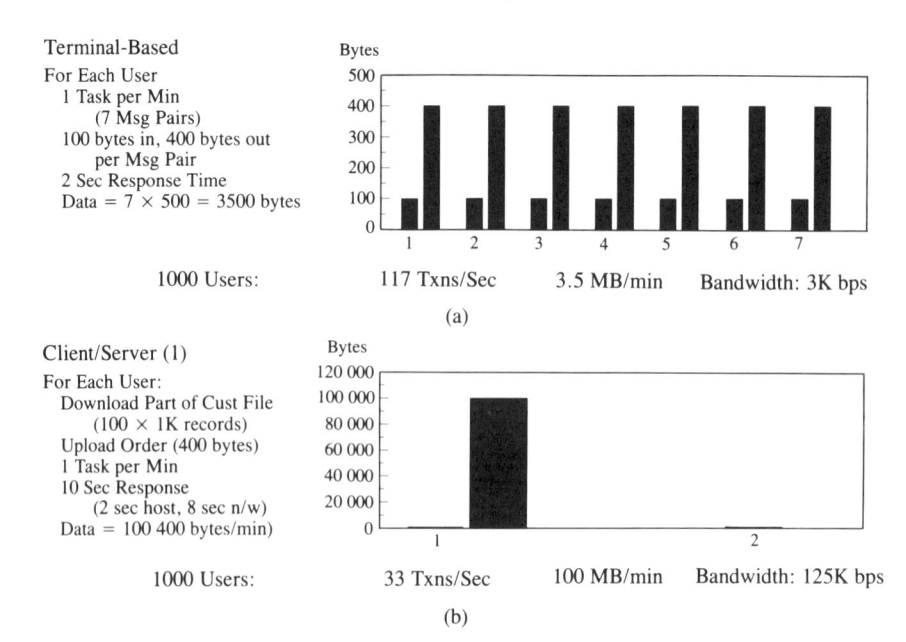

1000 Users: 33 Txns/Sec   100 MB/min   Bandwidth: 125K bps

(b)

Figure 14.1. Network traffic.

- The user starts off by searching by name for the correct customer record on the PC, and to support this the application downloads a small subset of the customer database to the PC—say 100 rows. Each row is, say, 1000 bytes. Let us assume that the required response time for this operation is 10 seconds.
- The order is then made up, referencing the read-only parts database on the server.
- At the end, the order is sent to the mainframe (assume 400 bytes) for stock checking and pricing, and an OK sent back if no errors (assume we can ignore this). The OK response serves as confirmation of the mainframe commit.

The kicker in this example is that the PC design requires all relevant parts of the customer record to be downloaded as part of the initial list. This means downloading 100 × 1000 bytes in a single transaction. Assume that the required response time for this operation is 10 seconds (2 seconds mainframe time and 8 seconds network time). Then, using the same assumptions as to bandwidth calculation as above, the single message pair to retrieve the customer data will require a bandwidth of 125 000 bps (100 000 × 10/8). The data volume will increase dramatically. For 1000 users, performing this operation once per minute, the data volume is 100 000 × 1000 = 100 MB per minute! This is shown in Fig. 14.1(b).

This load, remember, is caused by a particular design on the PC, which supports a very specific user interface design. The idea behind this design is to have a user model that says that, once the user sees a customer on the screen (in a list), then this means that subsequent references to that customer are at GUI speeds. This design must mean getting all the required data for all the customers in the list on the first access—just in case the user might like to look at one of them.

Let us see if we can improve on this.

Client/server (2)

If we tell the user that, on requesting a particular customer's details, there may be a delay while those details are retrieved, then we can have a design like this:

- On the initial search, only (say) 40 bytes per customer (maybe customer name and reference number) are downloaded from 100 customer records.
- Then, when the user selects the specific customer from the list, the rest of the row is retrieved (1000 bytes).
- At the end of the order, 400 bytes is uploaded, as before, for the order to be committed.

Now, for 1000 PC users, the network traffic characteristics from this one task are as follows:

- There will be three transactions per user (get list, get details of customer, send order) = 3000 transactions per minute (3 × 1000 users) = 50 per second.
- Total volume of data on the network (excluding protocol overhead) is $[(100 \times 40) + 1000 + 400] \times 1000$ bytes per minute = 5400×1000 = 5.4 MB per minute.
- Bandwidth required is determined by the need to retrieve 4000 bytes of customer data in 10 seconds. Using the same overhead assumptions as in the previous example, then the bandwidth required is $(4000 \times 10/8)$ bits per second = 5000 bits per second.

In this example, we see that the bandwidth and data volume both increase—bandwidth from 3000 to 5000, volume from 3.5 to 5 MB/min. The transaction rate, however, has dropped from 117 to 50 per second.

Since mainframe load is often some function of transaction rate, then this conclusion would appear to point to a reduction in mainframe capacity requirements. We will pick this up again shortly (in Sec. 14.3.1).

In general, then, there will be pressures to reduce response times for larger amounts of data to match the almost instantaneous response times of the PC. Careful design will be needed to optimize use of the PC and yet not place overwhelming requirements on to the network.

14.2.2 Number of sessions

By 'session' is meant a reliable connection between a client PC and a server system. While this may take several forms, in this section we assume, for illustrative purposes, that the sessions are SNA LU6.2 sessions. The overall considerations presented here will be similar regardless of the network being used; however, the terminology and some of the detail level concepts will be different.

There are probably two main concerns about the number of sessions in a network:

- People and resources to manage them
- Time taken to start them

Today's PCs are capable of running a large number of LU6.2 sessions concurrently. Suppose each PC starts up 15 sessions with a single mainframe system. If the network is small (say 200 PCs), then this may or may not be a problem—we would have 3000 sessions—and there are many organizations who run more than this. However, if there are (or are planned to be) say 8000 PCs, then we would be outlooking 120 000 sessions. This number may give severe management and/or start-up problems.

Now, the design of PC applications—unless controlled from the start with the idea of limiting the number of sessions used—can sometimes tend to lead to the use of a separate session for each different type of server request. (Before you start laughing at this statement, go and check who is designing this end of your client/server system.) Clearly the use of multiple sessions must be controlled from the start. However, it is also fairly evident that each PC will have more than one concurrent session (perhaps one to each server system, plus those sessions which may be used by proprietary software or packages).

So, from the point of view of IT planning, the network management department will be faced with a growing demand for session volume. The implications of this will vary from one organization to another. With some protocols, the technical volume will not matter, but the systems management of them will. Whatever the case, this factor certainly needs to be considered and planned for.

14.3 Systems management

'Systems management' can be defined as the tools, techniques and procedures for managing the planning and delivery of IT services to all users. In this section, I limit myself to the specific areas of:

- Capacity planning
- Software and data distribution
- Version control

Each of these areas is impacted by client/server systems and applications.

14.3.1 Capacity planning

There is sometimes expressed the notion that the use of PCs will off-load processing from the mainframe, and hence reduce the capacity requirement of that mainframe. This, of course, is known as *down-sizing*. However, it would appear that client/server designs—optimized to support the user—will need to provide more complex database access, and also access more data (even with simple searches) than would otherwise be the case. On the other hand, it would also seem that the transaction rate will be less (per unit of work).

Whether this means that the mainframe 'server' capacity demand will increase or decrease in the future is as yet unclear. What is certain, however, is that the potential for an application to put a sudden increased load (database access) on the system is increased. And some observers think that client/server processing will substantially increase the demand for mainframe power. (*Business Week*, 29 May 1989, quoted a Mr Martin of Pru-Bache as saying, '. . . if cooperative processing works, use of mainframe MIPS could go through the roof'.)

This means that effective capacity monitoring and planning become more—perhaps much more—important than before. Indeed, the concept of *right-sizing* seems particularly appropriate.

14.3.2 *Software and data distribution*

Use of 'remote intelligence' (in the form of PCs) in a system leads to a need to distribute both software and data to that remote intelligence. In particular, the growth of client/server systems means that this will become a normal part of operational or 'line-of-business' systems. While many IT organizations have experience of managing software delivery for essentially stand-alone PCs, the notion of software and data distribution as a regular part of day-to-day operational systems is perhaps new.

We can define three different aspects of this topic, as follows:

- *Operational software*—which includes operating system software, plus line-of-business application code (which performs required business processes). New versions of this code must be pushed down to the PC (by PC here I mean either the PC or a file server) and activated at times predetermined by IT.
- *Discretionary software*—the software tools that individuals choose to use to support them in their jobs. One example of such a tool is a spreadsheet. Widespread use of PCs in an organization tends to lead to the development of a significant repository of such tools, some bought-in, others developed in-house. A major driver for this approach is the cost reduction achieved by bulk ordering. This software is pulled down to the PC (or file server) at the behest of the user. Updates are automatically sent if the user has requested them.
- *Business or technology copies of data*—see Sec. 9.2. These will be sent to the PC (or more typically to a LAN server) at times predetermined by IT.

There is a need for both 'push' and 'pull' techniques (shown in Fig. 14.2). By 'push' I mean a mechanism driven by IT, where IT builds the sets of software and/or data to be sent, maintains a directory of recipients, and manages the

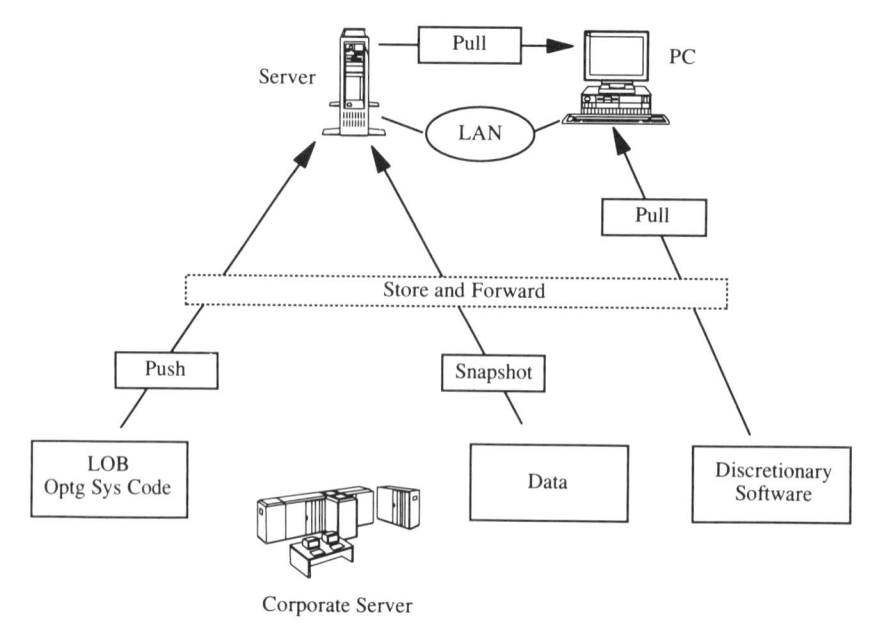

Figure 14.2. Software and data distribution.

automatic distribution and activation of that software/data. In other words, software is pushed out to the PC from the centre. An example of this might be upgrading an operating system component for a large number of PS/2s, or installing a new version of a line-of-business application.

By 'pull' I mean a mechanism whereby the PC pulls the software from a repository somewhere in the network. In this case, the repository is passive, and the PC selects what it needs. This can either be done overtly by the user (typically for discretionary software) or automatically by the PC when it detects that a new version of some software is available.

The rationale for a 'push' mechanism is fairly obvious—you need some way of keeping software and some data current at the PC without putting this systems management burden on to the user.

But why a 'pull' technique? Well, for discretionary software, there will probably be as many software profiles (a profile here is the set of tools used by any given individual user) as there are users. Suppose there are 1000 users. Then if the only mechanism was a 'push' mechanism, IT would have to maintain 1000 different profiles. This might be manageable by packaging—having the users opt for one of perhaps 20 predefined sets. But how do you manage the change requests from all these people? What about people who are comfortable with the version they have, and do not want to be updated?

Again, a 'pull' technique is important where you push to a small number of server machines, then allow the PCs to pull from there. Although for core business applications there will be a smaller set of profiles than for discretionary, the number of groups of users who have different profiles may be large. In that case, a push/pull technique is useful.

I implied a push mechanism for operational software and data, and a pull mechanism for discretionary software. However, a combination of both may well be the best approach for all categories. Operational software and data could be pushed to a server machine and automatically pulled to the PC only as and when required. If the latter were done automatically, then this could be a way to check version levels and update if necessary, on a demand basis, thereby spreading the software update load over a greater period of time. Discretionary software could be pushed to say a location server, then pulled by the user from that server.

Finally, it is worth noting that, while I have discussed an automated process, in some situations a manual procedure may be acceptable. For example, if the initial roll-out of PCs is small, then software could be distributed manually on diskette. I do not suggest that this is a general answer—but it could serve perfectly well for a time if the initial numbers are small.

The point here is not the techniques of distribution, but rather that such distribution must be planned for, and this will be a new area for many IT organizations.

14.3.3 Version management

The problem of version management derives from having many software components in the system, each with an interface to one or more other components. As one component is upgraded to a new version, then not only must all occurrences of that component be upgraded, but testing must be done to ensure that the interfaces have not changed. Managing change in this environment is not easy—and without tight control may become impossible.

Broadly speaking, there are two solutions to this:

- Minimize the number of components
- Minimize the impact of interface change

Minimize the number of components

Client/server systems almost always involve a mixture of middleware components—APIs, communications, operating system facilities, databases, application generators, etc. The interfaces will be either proprietary, or proprietary implementations of open standards. The greater the number of interfaces between these components, the greater is the effort in making them all work in the first place, and keeping them working as individual components are upgraded.

However, if two components are supplied by the same supplier, then that supplier is very likely to ensure version compatibility between them. If the two components are from different suppliers, then the chances of version compatibility inevitably decrease.

Consequently, one way to minimize the number of interfaces is to minimize, if possible, the number of suppliers providing the middleware components.

How about in-house application development? This too provides a versioning problem—and it is all from one 'supplier'! This brings us to the second factor in version management—minimizing the impact of a change in interfaces.

Minimize the impact of interface change

Programming interfaces are often very tightly bound. That is, a given API is very strict about the individual parameters allowed—their types, and their position relative to other parameters.

When there is a change in parameter type or position, or size, this often means that everything that talks to that API must be relinked—or even recompiled. Further, before this can happen, they must be identified—and then they must be found!

Some RPC (remote procedure call) interfaces are of this nature. A program that calls a remote procedure will be tightly bound to that procedure—not geographically, but syntactically. If widely used at the application level, then it may be that a huge maintenance problem develops.

One way to loosen the binding between interfaces, and so reduce the impact of change, is to use the kind of self-defining data mechanism described in Sec. 8.4.2. Of course, there is a trade-off in such a mechanism between performance and flexibility. What I am suggesting here is that it may be well worth assessing that trade-off, given the possible alternatives for version management.

14.3.4 Summary

In this section, I have not attempted to address all of the systems management topics that are impacted by client/server systems (for example, I have not mentioned access authorization). Rather, I have tried to show that there are a number of new system management considerations that IT will become involved with as a result of implementing such systems.

15
People implications

In this chapter, we continue examining some of the implications of client/server systems. Here, we concentrate on the people aspects of the new technology—on skills, on organization and on 'myths and panaceas'. The chapter:

- Discusses what are, in my experience, the three most prevalent myths and panaceas.
- Shows why development projects must include a system architect—a chief designer–who has an 'end-to-end' view of things.
- Presents the likely effect on IT organization of adopting object orientation—especially CBOs. We find that not only are new skills in analysis and design required, but that the organization that is needed to exploit the re-use potential cuts right across current AD organization structures.
- Discusses possible future AD organization structures that support object development for re-use.

15.1 Myths, dreams and panaceas

A major responsibility of IT management is to understand that there are no easy answers.

Too often, client/server systems are seen as essentially the same as terminal-based systems, where the PC is a kind of super-terminal. This is a highly misleading concept. Client/server systems are systems comprising numerous independent computer systems, some of which (the PCs on people's desks) are optimized to serving a single user.

This system shape is quite different to the shape of character-based terminal systems. Handling this new and different shape is not easy (although having accepted the difference, it is surprising how much remains the same . . .).

In this section, we look at three of the dangerous myths and panaceas that have led promising projects astray. They are:

- Client/server systems are all about the selection of a GUI-building tool.

- An expert but quite junior PC programmer can drive all of the development in a project.
- Open standards will solve everything.

15.1.1 Tool selection

A great temptation is to buy a tool on the grounds of its immediate visual appeal—without asking whether or not it will help you build the thing that *you want* to build. This is particularly the case with GUI layout tools.

Seeing is believing. But there are those who, thinking that the only problem in a client/server system is to drive the GUI, see a GUI solution as a complete solution. Here is the short story of one such.

The protagonist, for a long time an expert on mainframe terminal-based systems, one day saw a GUI-building tool demonstrated. He saw interactive window layout; he saw business logic being coded in an English-like interpretative language; he saw a database query being embedded in the application; he saw the application being generated and run. All in half an hour. This was his first experience with PC development tools; previously he had only seen mainframe-based development tools. He confessed to being flabbergasted. Never had he dreamed of—far less seen—such ease of use, such elegance, such raw productivity!

He immediately decided that this was the tool of choice for a client/server application for which he was responsible (the question of why he was responsible for a development that was to use technology of which he had zero experience is a management question).

One year later, he had discovered that the tool did not address application integration, it did not allow other languages to be used, it did not provide for application-to-application connection over a network, and it did not support an object-based user interface. All of these, it turned out, were needed in his project. Had he asked, the tool vendor would happily have informed him that the tool did not address these areas. In short, he started the project without understanding the nature—the shape—of the thing he wanted to build.

This is not an isolated example. After some time implementing their first application, and once they are past the 'first flush of GUI-ness', many IT people then discover that the tool is not a complete solution. The tool then gets most unjustly blamed for not being what it never set out nor claimed to be.

Of course, the problem here is that developers quite often do not really understand what it is that they *want* to build. This is not surprising; it takes a long time, and much experience, to understand all of the implications of a new-technology curve.

The real point here is that IT management should understand that this *is* a new-technology curve, and that new skills and know-how are needed. Furthermore, such skills are only acquired by doing. This points to a much greater emphasis on prototyping, and on treating the first few client/server systems as opportunities for experience-building.

15.1.2 Who drives the development?

Several times, in organizations where management and senior professionals do not realize what it is they do not know, I have seen the choice of build tool be allowed to default to someone whose only qualification is that he or she knows about PCs. This person is often a junior programmer. He or she will be a very able and valuable asset to the company, understanding much about the technology, tools and programming languages on PCs.

Because of his or her knowledge, this junior programmer often has a significant influence on the choice of tools. However, he or she often has no conception of the end-to-end requirements of the client/server system. Thus factors such as data integrity, transaction authorization, systems management, network loadings, batch windows, the development of build methods and processes that will scale up from a prototype, etc., are addressed late in the project—to the obvious detriment of the project.

This all points to the need for IT management to make it possible for senior technical professionals to acquire PC and distributed processing skills. In general, it is much quicker—and better—for an experienced IT technical professional to learn about PCs than to teach a junior PC programmer (no matter how good, or how promising) about the many aspects of real, large-scale, robust systems.

15.1.3 Open standards

First, let me say very firmly that open standards are a good thing. Over time, they tend to coalesce into frameworks for true inter-operability. It is also, of course, very appropriate to ask suppliers what their intentions are as to a specific standard, where adherence to that standard in the future is seen as being materially advantageous to the IT mission. What is *not* good is the way that standards are often hailed as the single solution to client/server, or the way they are specified as prerequisites to development when the specifiers cannot clearly articulate the reasons.

Standards take time to develop. Some fall by the wayside, or are made irrelevant because technology takes a route different to that on which they were posited.

In addition, each standard has to be implemented. Sometimes a standard will provide sets of implementation options. If different implementors choose different sets of options, then their products may not be able to communicate—even though they all conform to the standard.

IT management should ensure, when they define adherence to a standard as a prerequisite for their future developments, that:

- The standard is relevant to them—that they can articulate in detail why the standard is essential.
- The standard is implemented on the systems selected for the development in question.
- The options (if any) chosen for the implementation are not such as to cause problems when another supplier's implementation is installed.

15.2 The 'end-to-end view'

PC and mainframe development departments are often in separate parts of the IT organization—sometimes meeting only at the IT director level. Indeed, sometimes the PC department is not part of IT at all.

Again, it is typically the case today that PC application developers have little knowledge of network and mainframe environments, although they are often highly skilled in user interface design, in connectivity to other PCs, and in the PC operating environment. And the same can be said—in reverse—for mainframe application development people.

Clearly, in developing a client/server system, both PC and mainframe skills are needed, in addition to networking skills. If a single development team is not set up, reporting to the same first or second line manager, then all sorts of unfortunate misunderstandings can arise. Such misunderstandings can severely impact the project.

Two examples may help illustrate this. Both resulted from a single client/server system being developed by two separate sets of people—who seldom talked to each other; and when they did, they did not have a common language.

1 *A session too far* In this example, most of the development was done by the PC team. It was decided that the PC team would define the mainframe 'server' modules required, but would not have any other involvement in their design and development. The mainframe designer did pick up in time that the host database access rate required by the server specifications would have meant a fourfold increase in hardware at the centre; but what was not picked up until much of the code had been written was that the PC designers had really exploited the OS/2 communications capabilities, and had required 15 concurrent LU6.2 sessions from each of a large number of PCs! In a small network this would not have been a problem. But in this case, the volume of sessions threatened to swamp the network management resources. The design had to be revisited, and much code had to be rewritten.

    In this case, clearly the presence of a networking person on the development team would have prevented this from happening. And had someone with mainframe application development experience also been on the team, then the database access problem might never have arisen.

2 *Too much control* The second example was where the mainframe team designed the application, assuming that the PC was merely a rather superior sort of display terminal. Their design included a comprehensive set of flow-of-control modules (as is normal for design of terminal-based applications). The mainframe side was coded and tested, and was then handed over to the PC team, who had meanwhile been working hard on a PC design that made full use of the PC GUI facilities—including a comprehensive set of flow-of-control routines behind the GUI. The result was that the two ends of the design just did not match—and could not match. The mainframe side was function-oriented, the PC side object-oriented. In the end, it was decided to throw away the mainframe code and start again (mainly because the users really liked the GUI design). Had the two teams worked together from the start, much wasted work (about three man-years in this case) could have been avoided.

The lesson here is that client/server development must be seen as a single whole. While the PC and server ends can often be designed and built separately, they must both fit into a single architecture. That architecture must be implemented in a design that takes account of the realities of both ends of the system. This means that such design must be done by a team that has a view of the whole system—from one end to the other, and back! The technical leader of this team must also have this end-to-end view.

Figure 15.1 shows, on the left, how teams separated by an organizational brick wall tend to deliver things that will not fit together. A single team is needed. The right-hand side of the figure illustrates the kind of skill balance required for a small

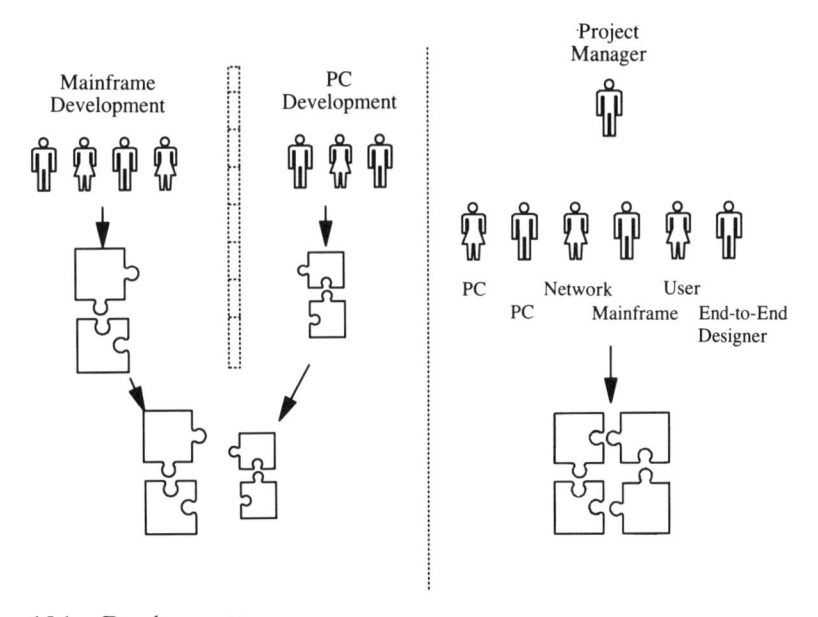

Figure 15.1. Development teams.

initial client/server development. These skills, shown as people with those skills, are:

- An 'end-to-end' designer.
- A PC designer, who understands the principles of PC object-based user interface design, and object design.
- A PC programmer, with programming skills in the tools being used. Some C or C++ skills may also be needed.
- A network person, with understanding of how PC and mainframe systems are connected—from the physical level up to the session level. This person may not be full-time.
- A mainframe person, with skills in mainframe transaction processing application development, in database and in data integrity design. This person should also understand the overall client/server application structure, and the role of the mainframe as a server.
- An end-user representative, with good understanding of both the business process being addressed and the business problem for which the process is a solution. This person will be involved heavily in the initial phase of design, where the user interface is defined and prototyped, and in final testing.

A major benefit from this kind of mixed team is that each team member can learn a great deal from the other members, so increasing the skill and experience levels in the IT organization. Given the source portability of CBOs, in the future we may see less emphasis on PC vs server programming skills, and more on SRD vs UID skills—or even just on CBO skills.

15.3 Object orientation skills

One of the pleasant aspects of CBOs is that they do not force us to learn an object-oriented programming language. It may be that an OOPL is useful in its own right; the point is, that with CBOs, there is a choice.

However, any serious acquisition of object technology will require new skills in design and analysis. As in other aspects of OO, when we look at CBOs, we discover quickly that we need to use OO design. This takes us straight into OO analysis, and eventually to OO business modelling.

Then we learn that OO techniques do not lend themselves to the traditional *process* of AD—first analysis, then design, then code, then test, etc. What is needed is a much more iterative approach. And although there are now techniques for managing such iterative build processes, their introduction and application needs to be managed.

All this means that there is much *understanding* that must be gained before large-scale application of OO techniques can be undertaken without excessive risk. This understanding can be broken down into the following areas:

- User interface design
- Software object design
- Object building and testing
- Analysis
- Business modelling

15.4 Impact on organizational structure

But more than skills are involved. Consider first that many CBOs should be re-usable across several (maybe many) business processes. A given CBO is a single deliverable, and hence its production can be effectively managed by only one person.

Now consider that most IT functions are organized by business process—either departmentally or on a project basis. Development work is typically funded on a process (or application) basis.

These two considerations are at cross-purposes. For if a single customer object (for example) is to be built, then we have to answer the question: Who owns the customer object?

Generally one can answer questions such as who owns the order entry application; or who owns the customer database. But this new question cannot be answered (in general) through the typical current IT organizational structure. Thus it is possible that the greatest inhibitor to building CBOs can be the organization of the IT department (or at least in the AD part of it).

So probably the most important implication of object orientation is that the organization must develop new ways of managing software production. Not only must new techniques and production processes be learned, but new organizations, new funding mechanisms, must also be developed.

This is particularly evident when we look more closely at the issue of CBO re-use. Re-use is a capability offered by object technology; but is does not come free. It must be planned for, funded and designed for. Experience has suggested that we need a new role in IT, that of the object librarian.

The job of object librarian is a heavily technical role. Consider a customer object. In reality, it is unlikely that there will be a single customer class. Rather, there may be a customer superclass, with a number of subclasses. In addition, the customer object may contain several 'role' objects (for example, for when the customer is also a supplier, or an employee, or a Government department as opposed to a private firm). Finally, there may be several IT-supported customer view objects. When a new aspect of customer is required, it will be the object librarian who makes the technical decisions about how this new facet will be implemented. Clearly this calls not only for technical expertise, but also for experience and understanding of the business.

Since the object librarian function is necessarily cross-business (cross-application area), then the question arises as to how it should be funded. One idea is to make it a profit centre. Individual development projects will choose whether to build their own objects, or whether to buy one from the object library. If the library is doing its job then the choice should be obvious. If developments build their own objects, then there is clearly something wrong with IT's re-use strategy.

How do the development projects *know* about the objects in the library? The answer seems obvious if the library is a profit centre; the library is motivated to sell their wares to the development groups.

The CBO librarian may also be responsible for the data dictionary used for labels in self-defining data. This function is normally part of the data side of an IT organization. In future, it is possible that this particular aspect may be moved to the object library. Indeed, since there is a distinct similarity in scope of view between an object library and a data management section, it is possible that both may become part of the same department group within IT.

16
Getting started

A wise old mountaineer was once asked the best way to train for climbing mountains. He replied, 'There's only one way to train for climbing mountains, and that's to climb mountains.'

You cannot learn how to do client/server by talking wisely about it. You have to do it. But you want to move things forward *without* incurring a high risk, and with a small amount of resource.

But there are many different flavours of client/server, and, in getting started, we not only have to have a process to follow, but we must also decide which particular flavour of client/server is the one with which we want to start.

This chapter first presents a process that answers the questions: 'How do we start? What do we do—starting tomorrow morning?' We call this the 'kick-off' process. Secondly, we discuss briefly two kinds of project (further detailed in Appendix 6) that might follow on from the kick-off process. One of the things that the kick-off process must decide is what *kind* of client/server system should be addressed. In the last subsection of this chapter, we present a way of categorizing the spectrum of client/server possibilities. This categorization has proved useful in a number of areas; for example, in comparing build tools.

16.1 The 'kick-off' process

The first client/server project is similar to making a journey. And like any journey, it is useful first to decide where you are now; then decide where you want to get to; thirdly, plan the first step; and then—start.

Here we outline a process that maps to starting a journey. We first define a kick-off process that you can start literally tomorrow morning. This process aims at defining the first client/server project. The project itself will vary depending on many factors. We outline two such projects.

Of course, the process and projects described are not the only way to get started; there are many other routes. However, the road map presented here has worked before, and it is in that light that it is presented—something that has worked before. Here it is:

1 *Authorize a project* Hold a meeting to agree:

(a) *Why*: The business requirements behind the wish to 'move forward'

(b) *What*: The overall project objectives, plus
   (i)   The general area to be addressed by the project
   (ii) The overall benefits expected
   (iii) An estimate of costs involved

   Notes As part of delivering a working system, the project objectives could include:
   - Develop a transition plan
   - Build a 'vision prototype'
   - Build an 'infrastructure prototype'
   - Build a core of expertise to seed subsequent developments, and so spread the skills
   - Gain an understanding of the benefit

   The area to be addressed should not be an application. Rather choose a category of *user*—especially users whose job is expected to widen or change (for example, order entry clerks becoming customer service people, or bank tellers becoming customer advisers). Look at that user's job. Take one of the more important *aspects* of that job. Then look for the *things* needed to do it. Then address another aspect (or some aspect of another user's job). Look at the things needed to do it. Assess how objects defined for the first aspect can be re-used in the second.

(c) *How*: The process to be followed, including
   (i)   Skills and resources
   (ii) Source of resources
   (iii) The management process, together with go/no-go decision points in the process

(d) *Who*: Identify the project sponsor

(e) *When*: The rough timescales (start and finish) for the project

   Document agreements, and then get the project sponsor's authorization to complete this kick-off phase.

   Notes This meeting is not a project kick-off meeting. It is a meeting primarily to clarify *purpose*. Questions to be answered should follow the above structure. For example:
   - If we were to do something, then why, what, how, etc.
   - Shall we go ahead and do it?

2 *Determine immediate action plans* Immediate actions should include:

(a) *Appoint* a project manager

(b) *Schedule* a technical orientation session

(c) *Arrange* for a project definition session

> *Notes* The project manager should be someone who can manage resources, and who is enthusiastic about this new technology. This person is not necessarily a technical leader. The technical orientation session might be a one-day workshop, or could involve a three-week effort in building a GUI prototype.

3 *Set up the project* Factors in setting up the project include:

(a) *Confirm* availability of
  (i) Project members
  (ii) Work location
  (iii) Equipment
  (iv) Assistance from other functions

(b) *Educate* project team members

(c) *Produce* the project plan

> *Notes* The item 'assistance from other functions' is an area often overlooked. The project may well need assistance from people outside the project. For example, assistance in reconfiguring the network controllers (and agreement on when this could be done) might be needed from the operations department.

4 *Start the project*

An important point in the above is that there is no tool selection at this stage. Do not just choose a tool. First find out what it is you want to build. Then choose a tool that will help you build it.

Having said that, it is often the case that, in the initial project, it is essential to use tools to build something, the development of which will add to your experience level, and so help define your ideas about what you *want* to build. In that case, the tool chosen for the initial efforts should be seen as potentially throw-away.

16.2 The project

There are, of course, several different kinds of project that, depending on circumstances, can fit the requirements. Two such projects are what might be called a 'vision project' and a 'pathfinder project'. Here we briefly summarize the project objectives and possible resource requirements and timescales. Each of these projects will normally be presented to senior management for approval. Sample proposals for each kind of project are in Appendix 6. These sample proposals include further detail on the project contents.

16.2.1 The 'vision' project

This is a very short project, requiring minimum investment. It will address a specific area of the business.

- *Objectives and deliverables*
  —Build a prototype of an object-based GUI, so providing a 'vision' of how things could be, with today's software and hardware.
  —Develop initial skills in GUI design and object design.
- *Resources and timescale*
  —The elapsed time is around two to three months.
  —There will be two people full-time on the project.
  —Outside consultants knowledgeable in object-based GUI design will be used (probably about 20 days' worth).

16.2.2 The 'pathfinder' project

This project is an investment in establishing the technical base for serious operational client/server systems. It defines, through doing, standards and skills for most aspects of a client/server system.

- *Objectives and deliverables*
  —Prove the benefit; build a 'vision' prototype.[1]
  —Enable the benefit; implement the client/server system (hardware, operating systems, database software, network and connectivity, communications software).
  —Implement the PC CBO infrastructure.
  —Choose tools (the main criterion is: does the tool produce the thing you want to build?).
  —Identify and develop design methods.
  —Build a migration plan.
  —Identify and make recommendations to AD management about the organization required to support CBO re-use.
- *Resources and timescale*
  —The elapsed time is around nine months to a year.
  —There will be six people full-time on the project.
  —Outside consultants knowledgeable in CBO design and CBO infrastructure software will be used (probably about 120 days' worth).

---

[1] The word 'prototype' can have unfortunate connotations for some. It is used here in the sense of an initial project, which will not only produce a useful deliverable, but will also serve as a vehicle for initial climbing of the learning curve. Other words that are used to express this include 'pilot', 'start-up' and 'research'.

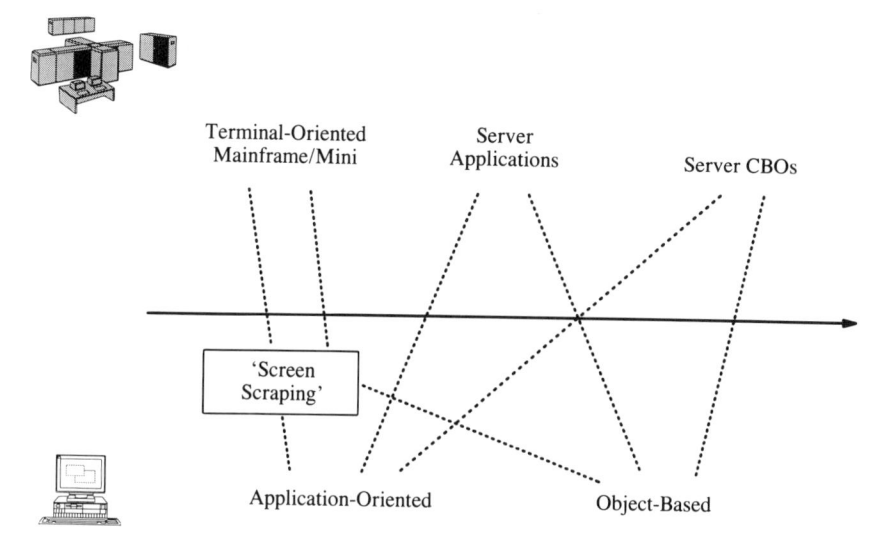

Figure 16.1. Client/server spectrum.

16.3 The client/server spectrum

There are, of course, many different shapes of client/server systems. Figure 16.1 shows a useful categorization based on the type of server, and on the type of PC user interface. According to this categorization, there are three kinds of server:

- Existing terminal-oriented code on a mainframe/minicomputer (with screen-scraping front-end—see below)
- New non-CBO server function
- CBO-based server code

and there are two types of GUI:

- Application-oriented
- Object-based

16.3.1 Types of server

In this book, we have spent some time in discussing the advantages of object-based user interfaces, and of CBO-based server structures. Let us now discuss briefly some of the characteristics of front-ending existing systems that were built to support character-based terminals. Such front-ending is often called 'screen scraping', based on the PC software seeing a terminal screen in an in-memory buffer, and 'scraping' the data off it to present to the user interface.

Screen scraping

A very useful starting point for client/server implementation is to front-end existing terminal-based transaction systems. Although this approach is in general not scalable (see below), it can be an extremely useful first step, enabling a measured migration towards the goal.

The existing transaction code takes the place of the SRD. Data that goes up and down the line must be formatted to satisfy this existing terminal-based code at the server. The infrastructure on the PC must therefore include an adapter to do the screen scraping—that is, to map server requests to and from the correct terminal data formats and protocols.

Now the dialogue between traditional transaction code and a screen is very different from the 'dialogue' between a UID CBO and a server-oriented SRD. The adapter must therefore be able to 'navigate' through the existing screen dialogue as part of its screen-scraping function. It must understand how to get from wherever the dialogue happens to be positioned to the point required to satisfy a given client request. Such navigation code is an important attribute of the screen-scraping adapter.

For example, a model CBO in the UID might send a message to what it sees as (say) the customer database. This will be routed via an adapter to the navigator, which in turn drives the screen-scraping API.

The effect of this is that when certain parts of the SRD are rewritten—or when new SRD code is developed—the PC UID part will not change.

Screen scraping does not scale up

Consider today's mainframe applications that drive character-based terminals. The flow of control is in the mainframe.[2] Design is functionally oriented; that is, we use one of the many methods based on functional decomposition techniques.

Let us suppose that we start by merely putting a pretty front-end on an existing system, so that the essence of the user dialogue remains the same—although it is now in a GUI form. What happens when we enhance this design? We might do this by:

1. Moving application logic to the PC. For example, we start doing things like including some local data (probably read-only, such as rate tables). However, the code driving the business process is in the mainframe. As more application logic of one sort or another gets moved to the PC, there comes a point where we spend a great deal of time keeping the mainframe and the PC

---

[2] By 'flow of control' I mean the code that decides what to do next, particularly as regards the business process or the appearance of the screen. For example, it is the code that says 'Ah-ha! The user has pressed Enter. I must now go and take the data entered, update file X with it, and display panel Y.' Or the code that says, 'Oh yes, this customer record is flagged category A, so we need to calculate a discount.'

application states in sync. At that point, it becomes easier to move the flow of control to the PC. But the only way of doing that is to have the mainframe act as a server.
2   Improving the user interface at the PC by moving towards a more object-based form. For example, we start to use techniques such as multiple secondary windows and direct manipulation. This inevitably leads to thinking of windows as views of objects, and eventually to object-based user interfaces.

However, a move away from the original dialogue implies a move *towards* treating the legacy mainframe code as a set of servers. We then have to put navigation code in front of the terminal dialogues produced by the mainframe. This in turn leads to three undesirable results:
(a) The requests from PC to 'server' can be such as to mess up the commit scopes and/or operation of the legacy code. In this case, we need to have the navigator do many interactions just to satisfy the mainframe code, not to satisfy the user interface. This can prevent the desired user interface enhancement. The only way to overcome this is to rewrite the legacy code.
(b) Having to navigate round a potentially complex menu/panel hierarchy between two consecutive client requests can take time. A lot of time. If response time is important to usability, then the only solution is to rewrite the legacy code.
(c) The navigation code gets extremely complicated, and too much time is spent keeping it in sync with further development of the legacy code. The only solution is to rewrite the legacy code.

All of these undesirable results are to do with scalability. In every screen-scraping situation that I have seen, these undesirable results have surfaced. The good news is that they do not necessarily surface on the first implementation. Thus although screen scraping is in general not scalable (that is, the level of complexity often increases exponentially as more and more legacy applications are front-ended), it can be an extremely useful first step, enabling a measured migration towards the goal. (The position of the elbow on the complexity curve depends on the nature of the existing screen dialogues, the structure of the existing code, and on the approach to out-of-line situations.)

Server applications

By 'server applications' we mean application code written specifically as servers, but not written as CBOs. This will almost certainly require new code.

Existing character-based terminals can still access these servers, but only through separate dialogue code. This dialogue code may be a modification of legacy code, or may be newly written, and is the UID code for the terminal users.

Server CBOs

As already discussed previously in this book, server application code is best designed using an object-based approach. If implemented as CBOs, then additional advantages can be gained, especially through inheritance techniques.

16.3.2 Types of GUI

We have already examined the differences between application-oriented and object-based GUIs in Part One. In general, the object-based GUI gives much better usability characteristics, and makes application integration a realistic goal.

16.3.3 Categories from the spectrum

Breaking down the spectrum of possibilities into two categories at the PC and three at the server end gives a combination of six kinds of client/server designs. This categorization is very useful when assessing what it is you want to build. Then you can assess what tools are needed, and assign project priorities. Here are two examples:

Example 1

We would primarily like an object-based user interface. Secondarily we would like server-oriented SRD code. We do not want to do screen scraping (against existing transaction code). In this case, the following ranking might be made (on a scale of 0 to 5, 5 being the highest):

	GUI	
Servers	Application-oriented	Object-based
Existing	0	0
Server apps	1	4
Server CBOs	2	5

A development tool that gave application-oriented GUIs and application-oriented server code would then score 1. A tool that enabled object-based user interfaces against application servers would score 4.

Example 2

We primarily want to develop CBOs on the server. The user interface can be object-based or application-oriented. In this case, the ranking might be as follows:

	GUI	
Servers	Application-oriented	Object-based
Front-ending	0	0
Server apps	2	2
Server CBOs	5	5

Such ranking can be a useful aid in establishing project objectives. It can also be particularly useful in positioning various development tools. Thus if your goal is an object-based user interface that (at least in the first instance) front-ends legacy code, then the tools chosen must support that style of design. Appropriate questions of tools vendors can then be more tightly focused than they might otherwise be. One of the most important factors in building client/server systems is to choose the tools that will allow you to build the thing you intend to build.

Part Five
The future of CBOs

Many experienced technical professionals across a number of industries have responded to the concept of CBOs with the comment 'This is the right *shape*!' CBOs as the end-product of a development process precisely match the software requirements of distributed and client/server systems. Further, they provide the technical base for realizing the promise of 'out-of-the-box' application integration.

In many ways, CBOs are an evolution. They borrow from many well known software techniques and structures. Indeed, none of the component concepts of CBOs is new. In that sense, they are not a new invention; rather they are an engineering solution, using tried and tested principles, to a new set of problems. Just as the first motor cars were.

In this section, we look to the future. Several previously intractable problems seem to be addressable with CBO technology. We look at some of them.

One problem faced by many companies today is how to support new organizational structures. Increasingly, companies are reorganizing into fluid task- or mission-based groups, and are using an increasing number of contractors. Each group has a defined responsibility, and provides a number of published services to other groups and to the outside world. Corporate prime data is increasingly 'owned' by a specified group.

Does this remind you of anything? It appears as if organizations may be becoming increasingly object-oriented! If this is true, what better software structure to support them than CBOs?

But such speculation is beyond our current scope. We will satisfy ourselves by discussing several aspects of CBOs that are currently being proven, or which may be proven in the near future. These are:

- Customization
- Cross-platform portability
- IT as a facilitator of change
- User programming of core business systems(!)
- 'Out-of-the-box integration'
- A market in objects

17
CBOs today

17.1   Customization

In producing packages, vendors often provide a way for IT departments to tailor the code. This often brings problems when a new version of the package is produced, since new code may cause IT-built modifications to fail.

Again, there are often areas where IT would like to provide modifications, but the package vendor did not foresee this. In this case, IT has to modify the original package code—which brings not only problems when a new version of the package is produced, but significant technical problems in making the modification in the first place.

However, if the package was built from CBOs, then these provide a ready-made structure and mechanism to effect modifications. What IT would do is to subclass the provided CBOs, and modify behaviour in this way. This approach is well known in object-oriented programming; what CBOs offer is the ability to do this across language boundaries, and across executable module boundaries. Thus modification can be done *without touching* the original package code in any way.

Again, modification could in certain conditions be left to the users themselves, using the techniques described above.

17.2   Portability

CBOs have proved to be remarkably portable. Most, and often all, of the code specific to an operating system is hidden by the CBO infrastructure. This means that, given language portability, a simple recompile will often enable a given CBO to run on another platform. (I do not wish to imply 100 per cent portability of source code. However, we have found its percentage portability to be generally in the middle to high 90s, and not infrequently to be 100.)

Further, since inter-CBO messaging is location-independent, then moving a CBO from one platform to another does not affect the function derived from cooperation among CBOs. This level of portability has so far applied both to UID

(PC) CBOs, and also to SRD (server) CBOs. There are two general benefit areas here:

- Testing can be done on one system, then the tested CBO can be recompiled for another system and run there. We have found this particularly useful in building Windows-based CBOs, where the CBO development was done on an OS/2 machine.
- CBOs can be developed for one platform, then, on replacing or expanding platforms, they can simply be recompiled to run on another platform. This is particularly attractive for package developers.

17.3 IT advantages

For IT, there are the advantages to be gained from object orientation *per se*—re-use, limited impact of change, etc. In addition to these, however, additional advantages of CBOs include the following.

Language choice

CBOs are language-neutral. They can be built with either procedural or object-oriented programming languages. They can be built with COBOL. The advantages of object orientation can be gained *without* having to move to an object-oriented programming language.

Base classes and frameworks

A CBO infrastructure product would provide a set of 'base classes'. These would be used by the CBO programmer as superclasses, thus allowing him or her to inherit behaviour that is either complex or repetitive or both. Such base classes could also provide for 'behaviour frameworks'. These are advantageous when particular inter-CBO patterns of behaviour are very common. For example:

- The interactions between a model and its views.
- The interactions between the infrastructure, CBOs and base class CBOs in providing persistence over power-off.
- The interactions between objects when one wishes to be informed about state changes to others.

Platform independence

The reader is referred to Sec. 17.2.

Client/server infrastructure

The CBO infrastructure, in providing location independence, provides an excellent client/server infrastructure. Where the server end is non-CBO, then the infrastructure will provide an entire PC-end facility, from screen to communications line.

18
CBOs tomorrow

18.1 IT as the facilitator of change

It has long been a goal of IT to get off the critical path of business change. It would be rash to claim that CBO technology can do this unaided. However, what CBO technology may prove able to do is to provide a technical base on which such a goal may be reached.

Rapid development

If we can achieve the goals of user programming, of re-use and of rapid development, then certainly business change may be best prototyped through the use of CBO technology. Such prototypes, given appropriate IT rigour, may be developed to production strength.

'Gauge' testing

Experience has shown that a general-purpose 'messaging' CBO can be built for use in testing other CBOs. This sends messages to CBOs, and catches the responses. Together with a message trace tool, work is being done at the moment to develop this into a more general-purpose tool that can be driven from 'scripts' provided by the CBO under test.

This moves us towards the idea of general-purpose 'gauges' that can be used to check that a given CBO works to specification (where the specification is the script).

18.2 User-written function

The major problem in users writing their own (departmental-level) code is that there is no way to allow them access to corporate data resources (other than perhaps limited read-only access). This is because a user department, no matter how capable in writing small BASIC programs on a PC, does not typically have the necessary professional training and development rigour in methodologies to ensure that they do not adversely affect vital corporate IT resources.

How do CBOs make a difference? Well, it is partly CBOs, and partly the model of cooperative processing we have developed that help us to overcome this problem.

There are perhaps two main areas where users would like to do their own thing:

- Tailor their own 'views' of objects (we assume here an object-based user interface, although the argument has wider applicability).
- Build their own departmental procedures or processes that assist them to discharge their corporate mission.

Consider Fig. 18.1, where we show a number of servers (non-CBO), and a number of models and views in a system. Suppose that we allowed users to develop their own view objects—for example, object 'A' in Fig. 18.1—using a suitable layout tool, plus some interpretative language such as REXX. How do we protect the rest of the system from being corrupted?

Well, given our overall system structure, we notice the following:

- The model responds to requests from views.
- It is the model that accesses servers.
- The model will only respond to valid requests from views—and it is the model that determines what 'valid' means.

Thus the very structure of our cooperative model, and of CBOs, provides an environment that can allow user definition of views to be done with much lower risk. Access authorization would be handled by the infrastructure.

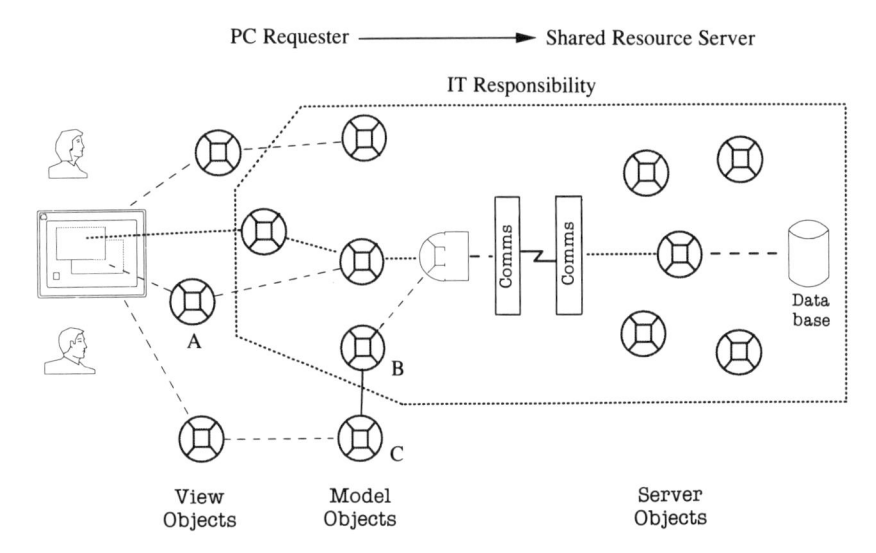

Figure 18.1. CBO re-use—user development.

This introduces an interesting new possible definition of the scope of IT responsibility—to provide the servers and models (and maybe some views) plus tools for users to make their own views. This scope is shown by the area surrounded by the dotted line in Fig. 18.1. Such a definition of IT scope might have some effect on the application backlog.

But in Fig. 18.1 we show a model object ('C') *outside* this scope. What is this?

Consider that business processes are surfaced on an object-based user interface as 'intelligent forms' or 'intelligent folders'. Some current work suggests that both of these can have a large element of workflow management encapsulated within them. But there is much common function between many different processes (for example, most processes include the notion of a given step not being do-able until some previous step(s) has (have) been completed).

Thus if a superclass 'folder' or 'form' were to be built, then through the cross-language inheritance mechanism implicit in CBOs the user (again using a simple language such as REXX) could subclass an IT-provided CBO to produce their own process, inheriting much of the more complex logic from the IT-provided CBO. This is illustrated by CBOs 'B' and 'C' in Fig. 18.1, where 'C' is created by a user, subclassed from the IT-provided 'B'.

There is much more work to be done on this to prove the idea—but if it turns out to be a realistic approach, then the impact on the application backlog (on the 'software crisis') could be significant.

18.3 'Out-of-the-box' integration

Imagine that one development team produces a 'customer' CBO. Its data items include a phone number and a name. A number of users are given this CBO as one of several to use for customer service.

Now suppose that another development team (perhaps working in a different company) produces a 'telephone' object, providing auto-dial facilities to any given number from the PC. This object is also provided to the customer service people.

Would it not be pleasant if the customer service user could call up a customer just by dragging the customer object and dropping it on the telephone object? That is, use it in this way *without* any developers having to modify code, rebuild and then maintain the result.

With CBOs this can be done, and it is a solution to a problem identified several years ago when considering the full implications of object-based user interfaces. It is the problem often referred to as 'application integration'.

Are we really saying that we can take two bits of software—each developed in total isolation of the other—and the user can have them interact in a useful way? Yes, we are saying just that!

Clearly the two alien CBOs have to have *something* in common. What we have developed over the past year or so are the standards to enable this sort of 'out-of-the-box' integration to happen (other than the two CBOs being built to execute on the same infrastructure, of course!). These include:

- All CBOs should use the same self-defining data stream (SDS) for data carried on messages to/from other CBOs. SDS includes metadata—data about data—or data labels. (Readers who are well versed in object-oriented programming may feel that messages should not carry data—they should carry objects. However, while CBOs can indeed send objects with messages, because a target object may be remote—and indeed may not be another CBO, but (for example) may be an old-style transaction program—we require, for talking to alien objects, the lower common denominator of data.)
- All CBOs should support a 'query' method (that is, function invoked when a 'query' message is received), which responds with whatever information—in SDS form—the CBO feels comfortable in imparting to the requesting CBO.

Using these standards, the two alien CBOs operate like this. The user drops a customer onto the phone. What happens (in brief) is this:

1. The infrastructure sends a 'you have been dropped on' message to the phone CBO.
2. The phone CBO send a 'query' message to the source object—that is, the customer CBO (the phone is given the source object ID in the 'you have been dropped on' message).
3. The customer CBO responds with SDS data including the label 'phone' plus an associated phone number.
4. The telephone CBO recognizes the label 'phone', and so gets the associated phone number....
5. ... and dials that phone number.

Clearly there must be a standard for common data labels, or some external configurable synonym arrangement. Such standards and facilities are currently being worked on. For example, there are various industry-specific standardizations of data names under development.

What is also very clear is that exploitation of this facility of CBOs does not *have* to wait until some cross-industry data dictionary is established and accepted. All that has to happen is an agreement across the domain of CBO interaction—which may be easily achieved by specific companies in specific situations.

While there is still a great deal of work to do in this area, the principle has been shown to work.

18.4 A market in objects

In spite of the promise of OO technology, we do not yet have a market in objects. Although some areas are starting to develop (for example, C++ class libraries), they tend to be for developers only—not for users.

CBOs may change this. Their execution-time independence means that CBOs from different producers can be mixed and matched. Even though more work is required in the standards area, the base technology of CBOs and their infrastructure is sufficiently developed to indicate that the technical basis for this level of software freedom is well within grasp. Indeed, there has already been some work done on understanding the administrative and legal aspects of a market in CBOs.

If this potential is realized, then we may not only have open systems, but also open software vending—on a truly mix-and-match basis.

Certainly the development of CBOs within a single company will show significant payback in terms of re-use and integration. And this does not need industry-wide standards.

18.5 Looking forward

Of all the dreams of software engineers, the dream of re-use—of 'plug-and-play' software—has been the most elusive. In this book, we have examined the start of a new approach to delivering business and user function through computer systems. Over the past four years, I have watched this approach grow to industrial strength, and have seen many of our early hopes realized. Perhaps above all, I am encouraged by the many comments I have heard that CBO technology is the 'right shape' for distributed systems of the nineties. I am convinced that CBOs—as the thing that IT should be delivering—will play a large part in turning the dream of real re-use, and of moving IT off the critical path of business charge, into reality.

Appendix 1
Object orientation

A1.1 Introduction

Ask not first what the system does; ask what it does it to!
(Meyer, 1988, p. 50)

The other day, someone said to me something like this: 'Wow, this object-oriented stuff is really mind-blowing. But do you think it's going to be any use in real systems? Is it more than a passing fancy? Do I really need to know about it?'

I replied, 'Yes, yes and yes.'

Why so positive? Well, over the last five years or so it has become obvious that application of OO techniques is the only real way to build and maintain business function that is delivered on a client/server base, and presented through a 'thing-based' GUI. But it is much more than this. OO is not something that we reluctantly have to adopt as merely a user-interface development tool. It is a whole new approach to building systems that promises *huge* increases in AD productivity—in design, in development and in maintenance of application code.

So I believe we *do* need to understand what OO is, and why it promises such programming productivity.

This appendix is intended to be a beginner's guide to OO. It does not attempt to be rigorous, nor to give a detailed technical exposition. Rather, it sets out to help those who want to understand the basics, and who do not have the time to delve deeply into the literature (for those who have, see the References and Bibliography).

Specific aspects of OO are not addressed (e.g. OO database, OO design, OO programming). Rather, a high-level view of software structure is taken, so that the essential concepts can be addressed without descending into specific techniques or implementation details.

As you read through, you may find that few if any of the individual concepts in OO programming are new. What *is* new, however, is the effect of combining these concepts.

A1.2 What is an object?

In the software domain, there is a continual search for better ways to modularize—or encapsulate—software. Really effective encapsulation means not only that the software can be re-used across many projects, but also that the effects of change are minimized.

For years IT has been encapsulating functions and processes, and modularizing code on this basis. The techniques for this are typically variants of 'functional decomposition'. However, this approach has not delivered re-use in any appreciable degree; and we have often failed to localize the scope of changes.

On the data side, IT has understood that data is best managed if there is only one prime copy of any given data entity; and that all programs should access that one piece of data (rather than make copies of it). To support this idea, database management systems of considerable power and flexibility continue to evolve.

Object orientation starts with the merging of these two concepts. Essentially it says, let us centre our encapsulation strategy for code around data.

For example, if one reads customer data from a database, then instead of different programs each reading their own copy into storage, the aim is to have one single piece of code read it. Extending this, it is desirable to:

- Package *all and only* the code that handles this data in one module.
- Place the data (retrieved from a database) in the same module.

The result is an 'object'—data plus function.

A1.2.1 Data plus function

An 'object' is data, together with the code (or function) that acts upon it. (This is not, as you will immediately recognize, a formal definition. I do not attempt a formal definition here.)

For example, consider the customer object shown in Fig. A1.1. The data comprises the things you might find in a customer record or row in a database, such as:

- Customer number
- Customer name
- Customer address
- Balance outstanding

However, an object is something you find in main memory rather than on disk. And it has with it, encapsulated along with the data, the code—the function—that acts upon the data, such as:

- Display the customer
- Print the customer
- Query the customer

Object orientation

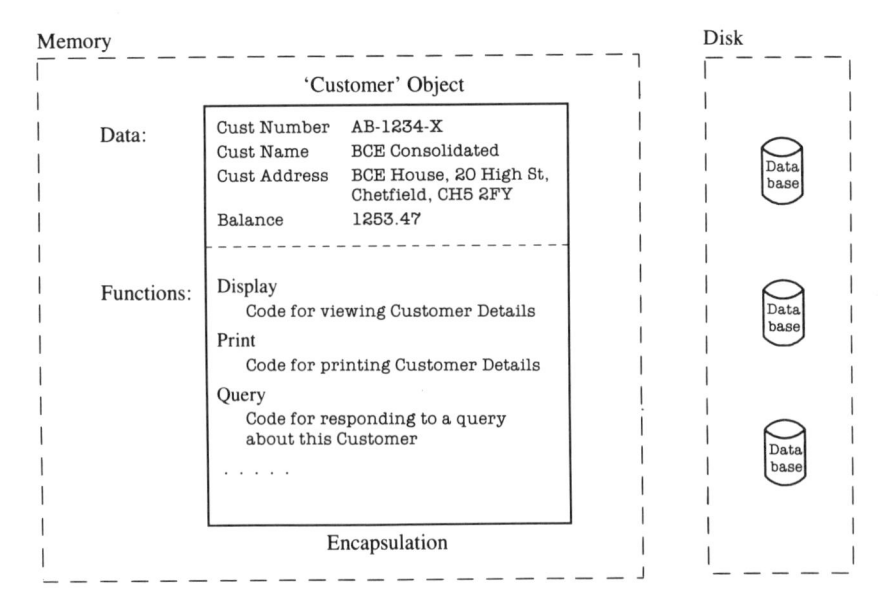

```
Memory                                              Disk
┌─ ─ ─ ─ ─ ─ ─ ─ ─ ─ ─ ─ ─ ─ ─ ─ ─ ─ ─ ─ ─ ┐      ┌─ ─ ─ ─ ┐
│          'Customer' Object                │      │        │
│  Data:  ┌─────────────────────────────┐   │      │   ___  │
│         │ Cust Number  AB-1234-X      │   │      │  (Data)│
│         │ Cust Name    BCE Consolidated│  │      │  (base)│
│         │ Cust Address BCE House, 20 High St,│  │      │        │
│         │              Chetfield, CH5 2FY│  │      │        │
│         │ Balance      1253.47         │   │      │        │
│         │─────────────────────────────│   │      │   ___  │
│  Functions: │ Display                 │   │      │  (Data)│
│         │    Code for viewing Customer Details│ │      │  (base)│
│         │ Print                       │   │      │        │
│         │    Code for printing Customer Details│ │      │        │
│         │ Query                       │   │      │   ___  │
│         │    Code for responding to a query│  │      │  (Data)│
│         │    about this Customer      │   │      │  (base)│
│         │ . . . . .                   │   │      │        │
│         └─────────────────────────────┘   │      │        │
│               Encapsulation                │      │        │
└─ ─ ─ ─ ─ ─ ─ ─ ─ ─ ─ ─ ─ ─ ─ ─ ─ ─ ─ ─ ─ ┘      └─ ─ ─ ─ ┘
```

Figure A1.1. Object orientation—encapsulation.

Notice I say 'the' customer, rather than 'a' customer. This is because the object 'customer' is not any old customer; it is one *specific* customer.

This immediately raises several questions:

- How did it get initiated; that is, how did it get created, and how did it get its data from disk?
- What about other customers?
- What is its relationship to a customer database?
- So what is new? Data and function are in every program ever run.

We will come back to the first question later.

Other customers are handled by other customer objects, so that, if you displayed two customers concurrently on a PC screen, there would be two customer objects in storage concurrently.

The relationship between a customer object and its data on a database is the same as the relationship between a traditional program and database; at some stage, some function in the customer object would have issued a read to the database to retrieve the data. (Does the object *need* to read a database overtly, or is the object already in an object-oriented database? Answering this question would require a discussion of OO databases, which we do not want to do. So for present purposes we assume no OODB; rather we assume that we have a traditional file structure or relational database.)

As to the last question, well, one of the things that is different about OO is this: the data in the customer object is *only* ever accessed through the function *in* the customer object. This is one of the most important aspects of OO—*encapsulation*.

Encapsulation is also known as 'information hiding', and the entity that consists of data-plus-function is sometimes referred to as an 'abstract data type'. (This equivalence of terms is not strictly correct. Information hiding is the process of revealing as little as possible about the internals of an object. Encapsulation is assisted by this process. Data abstraction on the other hand is the principle of defining a data type in terms of the things that can be done to it. However, for present purposes, we can think of them as aspects of attaining a well encapsulated object.)

A1.2.2 Encapsulation

Encapsulation is a vital characteristic of OO. It means more than merely putting data and code together. It means binding them together such that the rest of the system sees neither data nor code; it just sees a 'thing'—an object—that has behaviour.

Clearly if data and function are bound together in this way, then the only way to access the data is through the function in the object.

Let me say this in another way, referring to our example of a customer object: The only way in which the customer data is accessed—whether to look at, to use, to delete, to create, to change, to print, to anything—is through the function in the customer object.

Some implications of this are:

- Since (carrying on our example) there is only one customer object, this means that no other piece of code will have function that accesses that customer data. Thus, for example, we only ever code a 'print customer' routine or a 'change customer' routine *once*. No other part of the system will have function that works directly on the customer.

    Compare this with the traditional approach, where, for example, if we had an order entry application, a marketing application and an accounts receivable application, all produced at different times, by different development groups, each would include its own code for accessing customer record details. If something about 'customer' then changed (whether business rules or data), many more pieces of code would have to be identified, changed and retested.

    In addition, by building objects, you can get started faster. For example, a customer object is useful in its own right—you can do customer locate, and customer maintenance— without waiting till the rest of the system is built.
- The format of the data inside the object is private. No function outside of the object can manipulate the data directly.
- Function inside the object is private. Implementation details are unknown outside the object. This encapsulation of function is celebrated by giving function a new name—a function within an object is called a *method*. And that is the name that we shall use from now on.

Object orientation

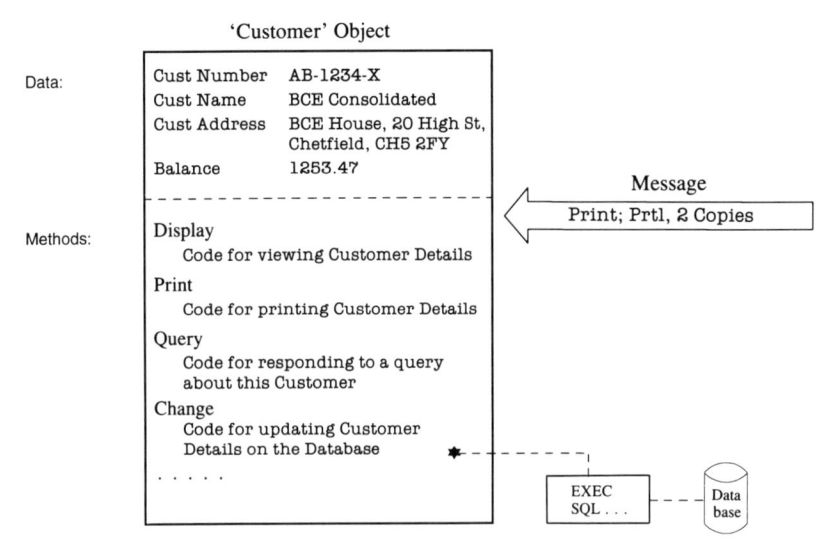

```
                    'Customer' Object
Data:        Cust Number   AB-1234-X
             Cust Name     BCE Consolidated
             Cust Address  BCE House, 20 High St,
                           Chetfield, CH5 2FY
             Balance       1253.47
             ----------------------------------          Message
Methods:     Display                              <=== Print; Prt1, 2 Copies
                Code for viewing Customer Details
             Print
                Code for printing Customer Details
             Query
                Code for responding to a query
                about this Customer
             Change
                Code for updating Customer
                Details on the Database  *------,
             . . . . .                           |
                                              EXEC      Data
                                              SQL . . . base
```

Figure A1.2. Object orientation—messages.

All this means that code outside an object can never branch directly to—or call—a method inside the object, or access directly its data. The only way to get at the data is by invoking a method.

So the next question is: 'How do we execute a method?' Suppose we want to print the customer details. How do we do it? The strict answer is that we do not do it—rather, we cause it to be done, by sending a *message* to the object. The object provides a number of methods that can be invoked by sending it a message.

This implies that there has to be some mechanism for carrying the message, and passing it to the customer record object. Again, this is an important difference between OO and traditional execution environments. In fact, it is so important that we shall discuss messages separately, as follows.

A1.2.3 Messages

Methods in an object are invoked by sending the object a *message*.

For example, and referring to Fig. A1.2, suppose we have a customer object (customer AB-1234-X) and a printer object (Prt1—not shown in Fig. A1.2) on the screen.[1] Now suppose that the user wants to print a couple of copies of the customer details. To do this, he or she might drag the customer (that is, the icon representing the customer) and drop it on the printer icon. Behind the scenes, something like this might happen:

- The printer object receives a message from the system: 'Customer AB-1234-X has been dropped on you.'

---
[1] We refer to the user interface in our argument because it is useful to explain OO in terms that can be visualized. However, it would be quite false to conclude that OO is relevant *only* to the user interface. It applies much more generally than that.

- The printer object displays a dialogue box to get information about the print job (for example, number of copies). The user requests two copies.
- The printer object does *not* do the printing, because it knows nothing about the data in customer, or the required print format. But it does know that the customer object wants to be printed. So it sends a 'Print yourself on me, two copies' message to the customer record object.
- The customer object receives the print message—`Print, Prt1, 2 Copies`. This message evokes the object's corresponding `'print'` method, which then prints the customer details.

The last part of the process is illustrated in Fig. A1.2. (Clearly some additional strategy will be needed to handle different formats of printout.)

Figure A1.2 also illustrates how the data gets into the object from a file or database on disk. Suppose we sent the message `Change` (together with some new values, of course—perhaps a new account balance, for example) to the customer record object. The `Change` method would itself issue an SQL call to update the customer record row on the database—or perhaps send a message to a 'customer table' object (which might be remote) that would itself issue the SQL call. (Part Three includes a discussion of the structural and data integrity considerations for this type of design.)

One of the important implications of this messaging structure is that one piece of code (in an object) is linked, or connects to, another piece of code (in another object) at run-time. This contrasts with the traditional approach of resolving connections between bits of code (e.g. subroutines) at compile time or at link time. In addition, because the 'calling' method (that is, the one that sends a message) need know nothing about the data types of the 'called' object, then the objects that interact with each other are significantly less closely bound than traditional code (even with dynamic linking at run-time).

This loose coupling, with the connection only made at run-time, is called '*dynamic binding*' or 'late binding'. It is one of the things that make for code re-use, and is a fundamental aspect of OO messages.

Let us summarize where we have got to so far. We have introduced two of the essential components of object orientation—encapsulation and messages. But there is more. For example, up to now we have been talking about single objects, and we have been using the example of a customer object. Suppose, however, that we want to work with *two* customer objects concurrently. Can we do that? The answer is yes, and this introduces a vital new piece of the jigsaw—the idea of 'classes', which we now go on to examine.

A1.3 Classes

How do we actually code an object? Well, we do not. We actually code a 'class'. This is a 'template', or 'model', of the object. So we construct a piece of code that:

Object orientation

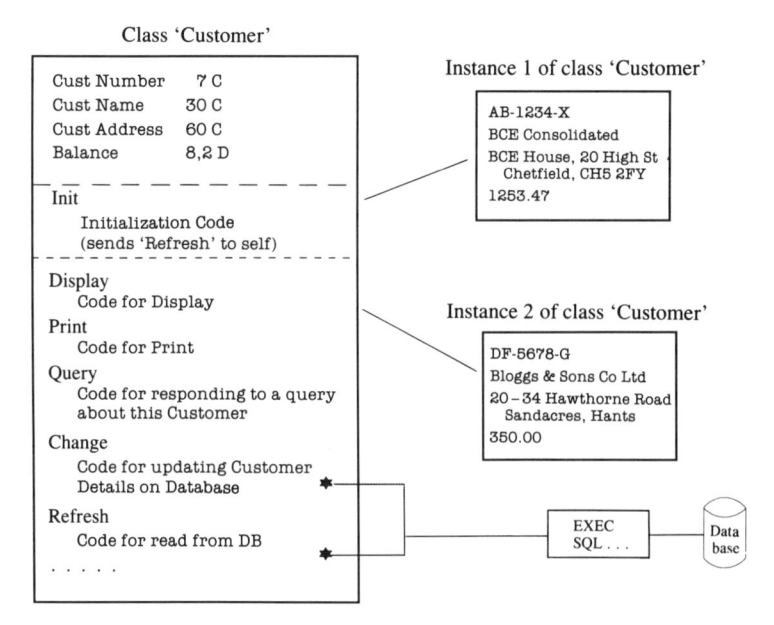

```
Class 'Customer'
┌─────────────────────────────────┐
│ Cust Number    7 C              │
│ Cust Name     30 C              │
│ Cust Address  60 C              │
│ Balance        8,2 D            │
│ ─ ─ ─ ─ ─ ─ ─ ─ ─ ─ ─ ─ ─ ─   │
│ Init                            │
│    Initialization Code          │
│    (sends 'Refresh' to self)    │
│ ─ ─ ─ ─ ─ ─ ─ ─ ─ ─ ─ ─ ─ ─   │
│ Display                         │
│    Code for Display             │
│ Print                           │
│    Code for Print               │
│ Query                           │
│    Code for responding to a query│
│    about this Customer          │
│ Change                          │
│    Code for updating Customer   │
│    Details on Database          │
│ Refresh                         │
│    Code for read from DB        │
│ . . . . .                       │
└─────────────────────────────────┘
```

Instance 1 of class 'Customer'
```
AB-1234-X
BCE Consolidated
BCE House, 20 High St
  Chetfield, CH5 2FY
1253.47
```

Instance 2 of class 'Customer'
```
DF-5678-G
Bloggs & Sons Co Ltd
20-34 Hawthorne Road
  Sandacres, Hants
350.00
```

EXEC SQL... → Database

Figure A1.3. Object orientation—class vs instance.

- Defines the data *formats* to be operated upon.
- Provides the code for the various methods required.

This thing is called a *class*, and is illustrated on the left of Fig. A1.3.

The customer 'object' we have been discussing so far was really an *instance* of the class 'customer'. Let us illustrate this.

In Fig. A1.3, we show (on the left) a 'customer' class, ready to execute, and stored in a program library somewhere. Suppose further that a user has just indicated in some way that he or she wants to look at a particular customer—say customer number AB-1234-X. To create the required customer object (or, in other words, to create an instance of the customer class) something like this might occur:[2]

1. A `'Display'` message is sent to the customer object, asking it to display itself.
2. The system recognizes (in some way) that this object (this instance of class 'customer') does not exist, and so the system creates it as follows:
   (a) If not already loaded into memory, loads the class 'customer'.
   (b) Allocates memory for the data elements defined in the class (shown as the block labelled Instance 1 of class 'Customer' in Fig. A1.3). Only the memory space is allocated—it has no data in it yet.

---

[2] Different systems and languages create objects in different ways. The approach presented here omits some detail, but is in general not atypical, given that instance data is retrieved from some persistent storage such as a database.

(c) Associates the allocated memory with the methods in the customer class; this combination of data (in memory) and code (methods) produces an *instance* of the customer class. The instance may be identified by the customer number—instance AB-1234-X.

(d) Sends an initialization message to the new instance. This message will be predefined by the system—a newly created instance will always receive this message to tell it that it has just been created—or 'instantiated'. Let us assume that this message is `'Init'`

3 When the instance receives the `Init` message, it will drive the `Init` method. This method reads the appropriate customer data from the customer database—either by issuing SQL directly from within the `Init` method, or by having something else do it on its behalf. In Fig. A1.3, the object does this by sending itself a `Refresh` message. This technique of sending a message to yourself is common in object orientation.

4 The `Refresh` method places the data items retrieved from the database into the memory space previously allocated for the instance's data elements. These data elements are collectively called 'instance data'.

5 Finally, the system then passes the `Display` message to the new customer object—which then displays itself.

You can see how, using this approach, a subsequent message sent to another customer object (instance) will result in another instance of the class. Both objects would use the same code (hence the code must be at least serially re-usable). But each object (instance) will have its own area of memory for its data; this is called 'instance data'.

Now, you can see that the message `Init` can be used to initialize any object. Also, thinking back to the `Print` message we discussed, you can see that the same message can be sent to any object that can print itself.

However, `Init` and `Print` can clearly have different results depending on the object class. Compare, for example, the likely result of `Print` on a customer order, a customer, or a part (a product). (Clearly a single 'print' method may be insufficient in real systems. Techniques exist to handle this; they are beyond the current scope.)

This facility of being able to send the same message to different classes of object—and have the objects do different things—is an important attribute of object-oriented programming, and is given a special name: *'polymorphism'*.

A1.4 Polymorphism

An excellent example of polymorphism in operation is this. Suppose there is a library object that handles storing of programs, documents and E-Mail messages. Each of the things stored has a different format, and has different ways of being stored on disk.

Traditionally, code in the library object that handles the 'store' function might look like this:

```
Record the object identification
Startcase 'Type of Object Being Stored'
  Case 'Program':
    ...
    (code to handle writing Program to library)
    ...
  Case 'Document' :
    ...
    (code to store Document and update Search Words index)
    ...
  Case 'E-Mail' :
    ...
    (code to append message to previous messages of same
      subject, or create new subject file)
    ...
Endcase
```

Now suppose that the library needs to be modified to handle image files as well as the other three types. The library code would have to be modified, and retested.

However, if the different things to be stored were themselves objects, then the code in the library that handles storing might look like this:

```
Record the object identification
Send a 'Store' message to the object
```

This is clearly a better approach; *no* changes to the library code are required to handle new types of object. All the objects will handle a 'store' method, and will each be responsible for understanding how it stores itself. The library is responsible for knowing *what* is stored, not how it is stored.

Let us summarize where we have got to so far:

- An object is both data and code, wrapped up together such that no other piece of code can see the internal implementation details of either the data or the function. This is called 'encapsulation'. An individual function within an object, which is 'published' so that the world outside can invoke some function of the object, is called a 'method'.
- Methods are invoked by sending the object a 'message'. Note that a method will often send messages to other objects—or to itself—in order to complete its function.
- What the programmer codes is a 'class'. The class includes a data definition (but no actual data values) and the methods (real code) that access and manipulate

that data.[3] At run-time, 'instances' of that class will be created. Each instance will have different 'instance data', but will have the same set of methods. You can create (or cause to be created) any number of instances of the same class.
- 'Polymorphism' enables you to build things that need know nothing about the internal mechanisms of the objects they manipulate.

The notion of encapsulation and messaging mean that objects that interact to perform some unit of work are very loosely bound; the only links between them are the messages that flow. This provides a major benefit of OO—re-use of code. Imagine that you have built the classes required for order entry, and now you want to address some marketing requirement. Clearly the marketing users will want to access customer information, You find that you can re-use the customer class in this new area. (This assumes that the customer class was well designed in the first place. OO does not guarantee good design. It is just as easy to make a wonderful mess of things with OO as it always was . . . .)

Now let us move on to the next major aspect of OO—'inheritance'. As a vehicle for discussing this, let us assume that a change to the customer class is requested.

The customer class, as shown in Fig. A1.3, does not have methods for delete and add. This may suit one set of users (those not authorized to add or delete customers); but what if we want to use this class for another set of users who *are* allowed to add and delete? (For the purposes of the current discussion, we assume that we can manage the distribution of code without a change/delete capability to one set of users, and code *with* a change/delete capability to another (authorized) set.) Although we might just add those methods in to the existing customer class, that would not only require that we retest the whole class, it would also imply some additional code to check for user authorization. Inheritance provides us with another—and often much better—option.

A1.5 Inheritance

'Inheritance' is the mechanism whereby object orientation delivers the promise of productivity through 'incremental' coding. To illustrate this, let us continue our example of the customer object,[4] and ask the question, how do we enrich the class by adding change and delete methods?

What we do is this: we code a new class ('Customer_R' in Fig. A1.4—the suffix 'R' in the name of the class stands for 'restricted'). But instead of copying the code from the existing customer class (or linking to it, or including it), all we do is say

---

[3] It is worth noting that programmers and designers often use OO terminology rather loosely—they will say, for example, things like '. . . we need to add another method to this object . . .' when they actually mean '. . . we need to add another method to this class . . .'. Indeed, in common usage the term 'object' can refer to either class or instance depending on the context.

[4] Strictly speaking, I should have said 'customer *class*' rather than 'customer object'. However, in OO it is acceptable to use the term 'object' when you strictly mean 'class'—unless you are discussing both instances and classes, when it is clearly necessary to differentiate.

Object orientation

```
Class 'Customer'
┌─────────────────────────────────┐
│ Cust Number    7 C              │
│ Cust Name     30 C              │
│ Cust Address  60 C              │
│ Balance       8,2 D             │
│ - - - - - - - - - - - - - -     │
│ Init                            │
│   Initialization Code           │
│   (sends 'Refresh' to self)     │
│ - - - - - - - - - - - - - -     │
│ Display                         │
│   Code for Display              │
│ Print                           │
│   Code for Print                │
│ Query                           │
│   Code for responding to a query│
│   about this Customer           │
│ Change                          │
│   Code for updating Customer    │
│   Details on Database           │
│ Refresh                         │
│   Code for read from DB         │
│ . . . . .                       │
└─────────────────────────────────┘
```

Class 'Customer_R'

```
┌─────────────────────────────────┐
│ Superclass: Customer            │
│ - - - - - - - - - - - - - -     │
│ Add                             │
│   Code for adding new Customer  │
│   to Database                   │
│ Delete                          │
│   Code for deleting Customer    │
│   Record from Database          │
└─────────────────────────────────┘
```

Inheritance

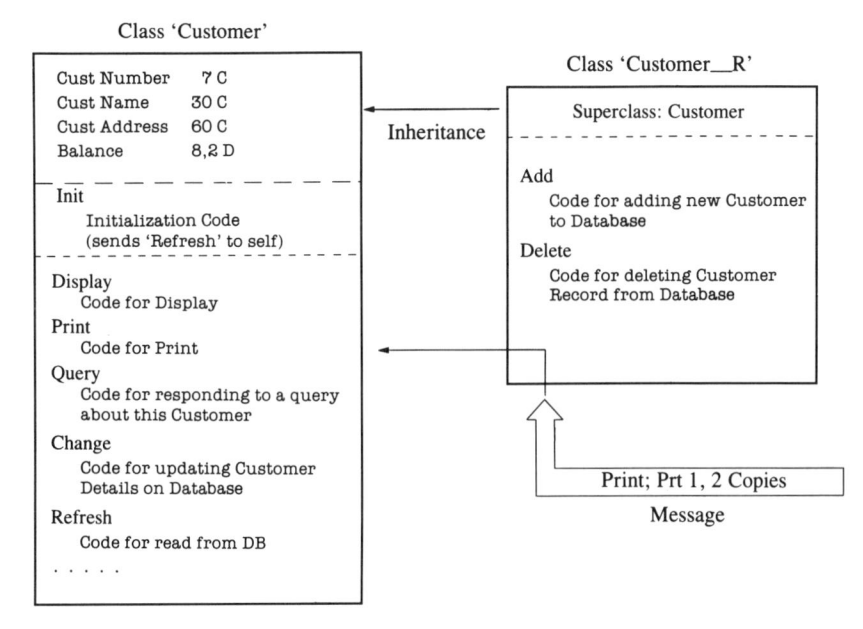

Print; Prt 1, 2 Copies
Message

Figure A1.4. Object orientation—inheritance.

that this new class is to *inherit* all the characteristics of Customer (including the data format). (The precise characteristics and function of inheritance varies from one OO product to another, and the 'best' approach is the subject of much debate. The concept presented here tries to steer a middle course . . . .)

In this new class, we provide *only* the two methods `'Add'` and `'Delete'`.

So, in the class Customer_R, all we have done is:

- Stated that we want to inherit from Customer (by saying that our 'superclass' is Customer).
- Written two methods that provide for change and delete of a customer.

Note that we need know nothing about the customer class other than its name and what its methods are (in other words, what messages it accepts).

Now, the interesting thing is this: when a message whose method we did not write is sent to Customer_R, it is automatically passed on to Customer to deal with.

For example, a `Print` message is unknown to Customer_R, so the system automatically passes it on to Customer, which *does* have a method for print.

Thus inheritance is more than just a method to economize on coding. It not only provides for 'incremental coding' (in Customer_R we only had to code the increments required, given that we had already coded Customer), but it also provides for significant code re-use.

An implementation of inheritance like this is an essential component of an OO system or language. Indeed, this is the essential difference between 'object-based' and 'object-oriented'—the former does not have inheritance mechanisms, the latter does.

Inheritance is also known by some other names, so that, considering the example we have used, you may hear expressions such as:

- Customer_R is a *subclass* of Customer
- Customer was *subclassed* by Customer_R
- Customer is the *superclass* of Customer_R

Now let us put it all together, and see how OO might be used.

A1.6 An example

Here is just one example of how OO techniques might be used. It illustrates code re-use and code isolation (which makes maintenance easier).

Look at Fig. A1.5. The top part of the figure illustrates a completed order form on the screen (as the user might see it). The bottom part shows two objects in memory—an order form object and a customer object. Note that the order form object has no customer data in it (other than the customer number). (Indeed the order form object may not even have that data—it may only have a system-provided reference (or 'handle') to the customer object.) So how was it able to display the order form as shown, since:

- It has no knowledge of the customer data.
- The order form on the screen must include the customer name and address.

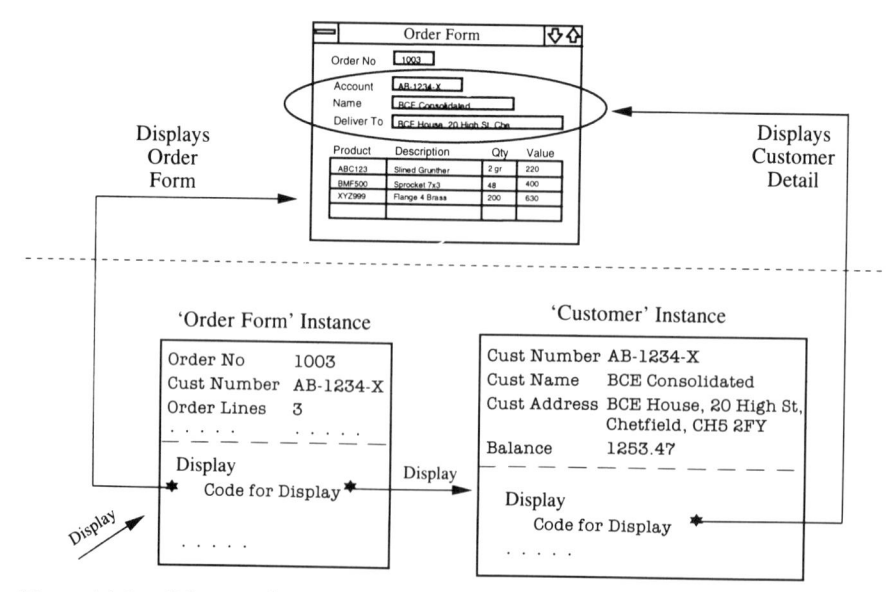

Figure A1.5. OO example.

The customer object, on the other hand, *does* know about customer name and address details. Indeed, OO would say that *only* the customer object should know anything about its own instance data.

So, the way that the order form was fully displayed on the screen might be as follows:

- Something somewhere sent the order form object the message 'Display yourself').
- The 'display' method in the order form object then:
  —Displayed the frame for the order form, together with data peculiar to the order form object (order number, date of order, quantity ordered for each item, etc.), and
  —Sent a message to the customer object saying 'Display yourself (in this area)'.
- The customer object then displayed itself in the area indicated by the order form object.[5]
- In like manner, the order form object sent messages to the parts objects, together with quantities, asking that they display themselves (not shown in Fig. A1.5).

This example illustrates two key aspects of OO:

- *Code isolation* Because all references to customer data are made *only* by the customer object. If something changes (such as the length of an address field, or the data type of the balance field), then only one piece of code has to be revisited—the customer class.
- *Code re-use* Clearly the customer object can be used in other application areas by other objects.

A1.7 Objects, and data on disk

So far, we have not really examined how an object gets its data from a database. In this section, we address this question, and in the process indicate the sort of mapping done in today's systems between objects and relational data.

Figure A1.6 shows the essential characteristics of an object—data plus function.

The bottom part of Fig. A1.6 shows how an object can get data from a database, assuming that access to the database is through a traditional transaction processing system. Here, the object (say on a client PC) merely sends a message to what it sees as a 'database object' but which is actually a composite piece of software (having an object appearance to other objects, but driving a traditional communications API) that front-ends some communication link.

---

[5] At the time of writing, there is little system support for this kind of operation, which is easily accessible to the average application programmer. However, even without such support, the results shown in the example can still be achieved by the careful and knowledgeable programmer.

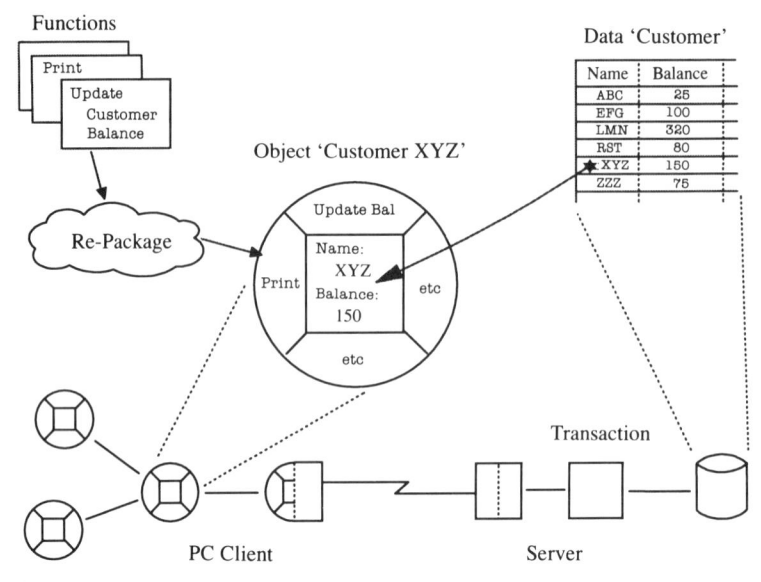

Figure A1.6. Data, functions and objects.

At the other end of the link (say on a LAN server or mainframe), a transaction is started, and the data provided by that transaction is routed back to the original requesting object.

Just as there can be multiple instances of, for example, the customer entity (that is, multiple records or rows) in a database on disk, so there can be multiple instances of the customer object concurrently in the PC memory. Each instance will have its own unique data relating to a specific customer (e.g. the data for customer number A12345, who is located at a specific postal address, and has a unique balance outstanding, and so forth). But each instance will share the same code.

These objects communicate with each other through messages. An object is essentially a piece of code waiting for a message. When it receives one, it processes it, sends a reply, then goes back to wait for the next message.

For applications built using OO languages, all this waiting, routing of messages and management of multiple instances is done by the compiler or language environment. The programmer typically sees none of this. (Note that these messages are not the sort of messages that flow over networks. Although conceptually similar, in implementation they are quite different. For example, in some OO languages, although the programmer thinks and writes code in terms of messages, the compiler can often produce a single machine language branch.) For the independently developed objects called 'CBOs' discussed in the body of this book, we have a separate messaging mechanism provided by CBO infrastructure software.

A1.8 Summary

A1.8.1 *What makes for 'object orientation'?*

To be object-oriented, the following characteristics are generally held to be required (for present purposes, additional characteristics of object orientation such as static binding, multiple inheritance and others are not discussed):

- Encapsulation, provided by some mechanism that provides information hiding.
- Dynamic binding, so that a method is located at run-time, rather than at build time.
- A message mechanism for invoking methods (where the message is sent to an object).
- Ability to define a class, such that multiple instances may be created.
- An inheritance mechanism, so that any given class may inherit behaviour (and perhaps data) from another class. This mechanism enables a hierarchy of classes to be defined.

A1.8.2 *Benefits*

The promise of OO is to revolutionize AD productivity. As always, the realization of benefits depends on good design; use of OO without good design is unlikely to realize the benefits. Some of the major benefits are as follows:

1. *Adaptability*—the ability to react rapidly to change. This comes about through:
   (a) *Code re-use*—the ability to re-use classes already in existence. Owing to dynamic binding, this means that we may not need even to relink a class to which a new class will send messages.
   (b) *Incremental coding*—through subclassing (or inheriting from) existing classes.
   (c) *Integration*—installing a new class can be made simple through dynamic binding. The programmer of the new class need only know about the behaviour of the classes to which he or she needs to send messages. Ease of integration is then a major benefit.
   (d) *Re-use of objects by the user*—given an object-based user interface.
2. *Maintainability* With OO, code and data are much more isolated (within a class) than in traditional approaches. Hence changes tend to have a much smaller impact. This is delivered through encapsulation (and good design!).
   For example, consider the impact of a change to customer name and address format, or balance due data type (say a change from zoned decimal to packed). The only bit of code that knows anything about this is the customer class itself. So such a change would impact *only* that class—or that one piece of code.

Compare this with what would have to be changed in current code structures (be honest).

Hence the ripple effect of changes may be significantly less than in non-OO systems.

3 *Reduction in complexity* OO as an approach to modularization promises a dramatic decrease in the complexity of today's systems. Objects can contain other objects. Hence systems should be able to be built from pretested components, which are bound together at run-time (with smaller components being probably bound at build time). Complexity is hidden within objects, and the complexity of entire systems is reduced through the encapsulation and dynamic binding of the components.

The promise of these benefits is why there is such interest in OO.

Appendix 2
A technical description of CBOs

A2.1 Introduction

The concepts and realization of the CBO as a different form of deliverable from an application software build process has developed over several years of effort. From the beginning, this effort consistently aimed at achieving four specific and linked objectives:

- Delivering *ease of programming* (for both the professional and the casual programmer) in building
- *Object-based user interfaces* for
- Cooperative (*client/server*) systems, which
- Enabled high levels of *application integration*

In the last several years, we have built several 'proof-of-design' sets of code. Some of them were serious blind alleys. But each of them taught us what the next step should be (and what it should *not* be!). One of the first of those which turned out to be a blind alley was a demonstration (known internally within IBM as the 'New World Demo'). Today we have delivered a production-strength system, and are continuing its development, together with our exploration of the new world of CBOs.

Very early in this journey, we were driven towards the concepts of object orientation. Once there, we incorporated these concepts and found them hugely beneficial. Oddly enough, we did not find any of the currently available OO tools particularly helpful. This was because we had realized that the thing we needed to run was not an 'application' (some encapsulation of business or user function) but an object. This meant that:

- The deliverable—the end-product—of the software production process had to be a class.
- Something *outside of that deliverable* and therefore outside the responsibility of the application programmer—*and* of the languages used—had to manage messaging, inheritance, instantiation, etc.

Most OO tools available today deliver applications, not classes. Yes, programmers *use* classes during the build process, and build classes for themselves and other developers; but the thing actually *delivered* to end-users is an application, with the objects all wrapped up—and invisible—inside them. During execution, objects are created and interact with each other; but always within the confines of the application.

Thus we needed to *deliver objects, not applications.*

CBOs, then, are the alternative to applications as a way of encapsulating business function for presentation and use by a human being through a computer.

CBOs cannot exist on today's operating environments. Today, the environments and the development tools are all oriented towards developing and running *applications.* (Even tools such as Smalltalk/V and ENFIN/3 are oriented towards building applications rather than CBOs. And although one may package a 'business object' as a ST/V PM DLL, it will not be a *cooperative* business object—able to talk with other non-Smalltalk CBOs—unless, of course, supported by a CBO infrastructure.) Thus to develop and run CBOs, some form of software 'infrastructure' (or 'layer', plus a set of standard superclasses, etc.) is required.[1]

But what *is* a CBO? That is, what does the designer design, and the programmer program? And what capabilities does the infrastructure have to provide? This appendix presents answers to these questions.

Finally, it is worth noting that, just like batch systems, transactions, or conversational applications, CBOs can be written in either procedural or object-oriented programming languages.

A2.2 The definition of 'CBO'

We define a CBO in terms of its characteristics. This approach to definition is not perhaps totally rigorous, but it is certainly useful for present purposes. In summary, a 'cooperative business object'—or 'CBO'—is *all* of the following:

1 An *object* in the object orientation sense of the word; that is, it exhibits encapsulation, can be part of a class hierarchy (and so can inherit from other CBOs), sends messages to other CBOs, has class and instance data, etc.

2 A *deliverable*—it is the end-product of the software development process; it is the thing delivered to end-users; it is identifiable as an execution unit; a single CBO can be executed by itself (needing only its superclasses).

---

[1] Such an infrastructure was built by the UK software house *Softwright Systems Ltd* in Langley, Bucks, in conjunction with IBM United Kingdom Ltd. Recently, a much-enhanced full product version of this CBO infrastructure has been shipped by Integrated Object Systems Ltd. The product is called 'Newi'. Integrated Objects, located in the UK at Newbury, is an IBM and Softwright joint venture.

3 An *independent* software executable—it can execute by itself, without having to be bound to other CBOs by some build-time process.
4 *Language neutral*—that is, a CBO can be written in any language, whether object-oriented or procedural. (Experience so far suggests that, when using an OOPL, the programmer builds or re-uses language-specific objects *within the confines of a given CBO*. Experience also shows that there is no confusion in the programmer's mind about handling two sorts of objects. In practice, it is immediately obvious which is which.) This means that if something is *called* a CBO, but it cannot interact with other CBOs written in different languages, then it is *not* a CBO.
5 *Easy to program*—a CBO requires no advanced skills of the programmer, such as multi-tasking, system-level GUI API calls, communications programming, event-loop handling, storage management, etc. It also means that casual programmers, using say an interpretative language such as REXX, can produce CBOs.
6 *Easy to integrate*—a CBO can be loaded by a user and used effectively with other CBOs without requiring any recoding, relinking, or any knowledge of data types. This means that binding between CBOs must be done at run-time.
7 *Message-driven* with a high-speed[2] message router external to the CBO, such that both synchronous and asynchronous messages are handled with equal ease of programming.
8 *Location-transparent* to other CBOs—that is, a programmer does not have to know, when he or she sends a message to another CBO, where that other CBO is located. It might be in the same thread; or it might be in another system thousands of miles away.
9 Written in code that is *serially re-usable*, so as to avoid unnecessary blocking of the thread or process in which it runs. However, the programmer does not have to take special steps to achieve this.
10 *Persistent* over power-down and subsequent power-up.
11 Something which, given the constraints of current operating systems, *requires a software infrastructure* to execute. This infrastructure (or 'middleware') handles message routing, CBO loading and initiation, instance creation, superclassing, multi-tasking, storage management, communications, GUI APIs, etc.

We now examine each of these characteristics in greater detail.

A2.2.1 An object

A CBO is an object (or, as the programmer sees it, a class). Thus it:

---

[2] By 'high speed', I mean that messages between CBOs that are in the same task (or thread) should complete in some tens or hundreds of microseconds on the average Intel 386 PC.

1. Encapsulates data (in the programming sense of variables in main storage rather than databases on disk) and the functions (methods) that handle that data into an independently executable piece of code.
2. Can inherit from (be the subclass of) another CBO, and can be the superclass of other CBOs, where those other CBOs may be written in a different language. CBO inheritance has the following characteristics:
   (a) Single rather than multiple inheritance.[3]
   (b) Instance and class data may not be 'inherited'; if not, it is available via messaging (whether inherited or not, access to a superclass's instance/class data must be as loosely bound as message data).
   (c) Multiple class hierarchies must be supported.
   Note Single inheritance with multiple hierarchies does not exclude CBOs written in OO languages that allow only single inheritance within a single hierarchy, or languages that allow for multiple inheritance, since such language hierarchies are local to the CBO (just as they would be local to an 'application' when those languages are used to build one).
3. Sends and receives messages to/from other CBOs. Method resolution is done within the CBO. This adds to the flexibility of CBOs by:
   (a) Allowing for languages such as REXX that do not provide multiple entry points.
   (b) Removing the need for programmers to worry about entry points (ease of programming).
   (c) Not preventing a CBO (or preferably a CBO-building tool) from packaging a class such that (for example) methods can be loaded and invoked independently.
   (d) Allowing a 'wrapper' to be built such that CBOs written in an OOPL can use language facilities to perform method resolution.
4. Is invoked by an incoming message (typically from another CBO). This implies that the event loop is handled *outside* the CBO, and hence outside the programmer's domain.
5. Has multiple instances per class (unless constrained otherwise by the class programmer) but does not have to manage multiplicity mechanisms itself.
6. Has class and instance methods (may have separate entry points for each).
7. Has class and instance data (with system-provided storage management).
8. Can have multiple instances, where creation of new instances (and the associated storage management, etc.) are handled automatically by the CBO infrastructure.

---

[3] The requirement for ease of programming points to a rejection of multiple inheritance. In addition, design techniques and approaches using single inheritance are becoming available for several classes of problem that previously were addressed through multiple inheritance. Thus we feel justified, at least for the present, in defining CBOs as having single inheritance. Certainly were multiple inheritance to be allowed, then for ease of programming reasons it would have to be constrained such that *none* of the CBO classes take part in the decision about which superclass should be invoked.

9   Uses self-defining data for message content. One of the advantages of this is as follows. Suppose a CBO supports method X, and that two of its three superclasses also support X. Data returned from each superclass may need to be accumulated as a message invoking method X is passed up the class hierarchy. This is done automatically through the use of self-defining data as the reply (response) 'blob'.
10 Is able explicitly to call the CBO's superclass at any time.

A point to note is that the class is itself a CBO (an object) as is each instance of that class.

A CBO is typically (but not exclusively) of medium granularity; for example, it is the sort of thing that a user would find useful in performing some business process via an object-based user interface. Examples of CBOs include:

- An order form
- A customer record
- An inventory item
- A Post-It note
- An insurance policy
- A list of suppliers

However, smaller CBOs can be built, such as an *invoice line item*, or a *collection*.

Although functionally one could build an integer CBO, it is unlikely (given current technology) that that would be useful, since various languages already provide that kind of object or type with much higher performance.

A2.2.2 A deliverable

A CBO is a deliverable—the end-product of some development process. Some developers build and deliver applications; others build and deliver CBOs. Thus a CBO is:

1   An independently delivered object that can interact (via messages, or through inheritance) with other CBOs, which:
    (a) Were built and delivered by possible unknown other developers—so *all* binding is done at message time
    (b) Were written in different languages
    (c) May be remote (in a different task, address space, or system)
2   Independently packaged—so that a single CBO could be put on a diskette as one (or more) files and distributed.
3   Executable code delivered to end-users, who can then run it without needing any other classes (other than its superclass(es) if any). If sent to a user, a CBO can be run by that user with no further build-time activity (compile, link, integration, method definition, message definition, etc.) other than a simple administrative assertion that the CBO now exists in the user's environment.

A2.2.3 CBO independence

Independence is an essential characteristic of CBOs. It means three things:

1. Developers need *minimum information* about other CBOs—and should not require header files, IDL definition files, or copy books.
2. CBOs are very, very *loosely bound* (binding with other CBOs happens at message execution time).
3. CBOs can be *packaged independently* from other CBOs. Methods may be packaged independently from other methods (depending on the infrastructure loader implementation).

Minimum information

Different development teams, at different times, will develop various CBOs. The developer of a given CBO should require minimum information about other CBOs, whether those other CBOs are the targets (or sources) of messages, or whether they are superclasses.

Minimum information means that all a developer should *need* to have is a paper description of the other CBOs' public interfaces.

In this way, we can:

- Build CBOs without the *prerequisite* of a corporate object development repository (although obviously such a facility is necessary on a larger scale if only to avoid expensive duplication and overlap).
- Ensure that our CBOs will be designed with eventual coexistence with 'alien' objects (from other organizations).

Thus a CBO that has another CBO as its superclass can be built independently of that superclass CBO. The prerequisite is only knowledge of the public interface of that superclass CBO.

Loose binding

The very loose binding of CBOs requires that:

- When a given CBO is built, then, in order for it to communicate with other CBOs, no header files must be shared. The only thing the programmer needs is an understanding of the protocols provided by other CBOs.
- Where data, as opposed to an object reference, is passed in a message, then the receiver does not have to render the passed data into precisely the same format as the sender. Nor does the receiver have to be aware of the precise data format used by the sender. This implies that data must be passed in a self-describing data stream.

- A given CBO never needs to be either recompiled or relinked to allow it to cooperate with other CBOs. This is essential.

Independent packaging

Independence means that CBOs can be built and distributed in isolation of other CBOs. Hence:

- A CBO is an independently shippable unit of compiled and linked code. It may comprise more than one physical file (example—a view CBO may be shipped together with its layout script file, a help file etc.).
- It must be packaged to require as little operating system overhead as possible in its loading. This means, for example, that on OS/2 or Windows a CBO will probably be a `.DLL` rather than an `.EXE` file. Methods should be able to be loaded independently, depending on the infrastructure loader implementation.
- It can be integrated into a user's environment with no recompilation or relinking process. At most, registration (for use of the new object) requires update of a single line in a flat ASCII (human-readable) file. Preferably, there should be a GUI front-end for this, to avoid spreading `CONFIG.SYS` problems.
- All names (classes, instances, methods) must be codeable by the programmer as names. This means that the programmer does not have to define header files where names are equated with numbers, or any such scheme. Such header files can be a significant source of error, and should be avoided for programmer convenience and ease of development. For performance reasons to do with string handling, implementations should use techniques to minimize the impact of using strings rather than integers (e.g. the Atom Table in OS/2, or better still, some similar facility provided by the CBO infrastructure).

A2.2.4 Language neutral

CBOs can be written in any language, either procedural (such as COBOL) or object-oriented (such as C++). Specifically, this means that CBOs can be written in any language that can in some way communicate with the underlying infrastructure (using, at the end of the day, C function calls). For some higher-level languages such as REXX, this implies that an additional support layer will be needed.

This means that the inheritance mechanism must operate across language boundaries, and must be outside the programming language domain. Thus an object written in a given language, but which cannot send messages to, receive messages from, inherit from or be a superclass of some *other* object written in a different language, is *not* a CBO.

Just as a developer can build an application with either procedural or OO languages, so a CBO can be built with either procedural or OO languages. An

```
Start of CBO   /* (I am 'called' by the system   */
               /* when there's a message for me) */
    Analyse message (passed to me by the Infrastructure)
    IF message is for my Class THEN
        /* Start of Class Methods */
        STARTCASE (message)
          CASE message = 'Xxxx'
             code to handle message Xxxx
             Return

        ENDCASE
        CALL Superclass()
        Return
    ELSE
        /*  Start of Instance Methods  */
        STARTCASE (message)
          CASE message = 'Aaaa'
             code to handle message Aaaa
             Send msg to another CBO
             Return

          CASE message = 'Bbbb'
             code to handle message Bbbb
             CALL Superclass()
             Return

        ENDCASE
        CALL Superclass()
        Return
    ENDIF
End of CBO
```

Figure A2.1. The general structure of a CBO.

implication of language neutrality is that the underlying infrastructure does not care in what language a CBO is written.

The overall structure of a CBO (in pseudocode) is shown in Fig. A2.1. The pseudocode used in this figure is procedural code, and illustrates how the CBO itself does method resolution.

Class and instance data is passed to the CBO (by the infrastructure) on invocation.

A2.2.5 Easy to program

By ease of programming, we imply the following:

1 CBOs can be built by the casual programmer in interpretative languages such as REXX.

2   CBOs are easy to write by the average application programmer, or by the casual programmer ('easy' means what any sensible person would class as easy, given the chosen language; e.g. pointers are hugely difficult in REXX, but easy in C).
3   While the programmer will be conscious of writing a class that may have multiple instances he or she does not have to manage multiplicity mechanisms. This means that the programmer does not have to handle the storage management for class and instance data.
4   The programmer has a choice of languages, and is not constrained by having to match the language used for other CBOs with which his or her CBOs may have to cooperate.
5   The programmer does not need to understand such things as:
    (a) Multi-tasking
    (b) Presentation programming (e.g. PM, Windows, X-Windows, etc.)
    (c) Communications programming
    (d) Managing asynchronous messaging (with their attendant post/wait mechanisms)
    (e) Operating system calls (other than those natural to the language used— e.g. 'DosBeep' in C)
6   The expert professional programmer must not be locked out from using low-level system functions such as presentation manager, DDE, etc. This means that the infrastructure must provide appropriate openness.

A2.2.6 Easy to integrate

This characteristic is aimed at providing a technical solution to the application integration problem. To achieve this, two things must apply:

1   'Applications' must have a mechanism naturally to talk to each other.
2   Given that 'applications' can exchange data easily and naturally, there must be a common understanding of:
    (a) Data types (character, integer, object IDs, etc.)—what one might call the syntax of interchange
    (b) Data meanings—the semantics of interchange (for example, understanding that '21' means someone's age, not a quantity of stock on hand)

CBOs provide for the first of these by their very structure. They are objects. Objects talk with other objects. Hence CBOs talk to other CBOs (via messaging), finding the target method at run-time.

The second requirement—data exchange—is more difficult.

One way of achieving this is through IDLs (interface definition languages) such as one finds in RPC designs, and in CORBA (common object request broker architecture). However, although they provide a way of publicizing an object's interface, they tend still to define data types and data structures and sequences. In addition, they are currently aimed more at the software engineer that at the application programmer. They also require some form of preprocessing and compilation, and are therefore not suitable for the casual programmer. There is an argument that, by adding yet more 'header' files (and shared header files at that) to the development process, they increase the inherent chance of errors during the whole build process.

IDLs are probably best employed where the highest performance is required, regardless of other considerations (such as ease of programming), or where middleware is being built.

An alternative to IDLs is to provide a very high-performance self-defining data stream, together with sophisticated (and easy-to-program) build and parse support. This is the approach we take for CBO data binding. High performance is required because many CBO messages are messages to one's superclass—which may have been built by someone else, in a different language. Thus the data stream and its building and parsing must be able to handle intra- as well as inter-CBO messaging.

CBOs, then, must have available to them a high-performance self-defining data stream, which is easy to build and parse, and which carries sufficient semantic information (data about data) to enable correct meanings to be extracted. For example, the data stream would carry the value '21', together with a label stating that the value is a person's age, not an account balance.

To support this, and also to allow for national language differences and intra-language synonyms, a data dictionary facility is required. CBOs must have access to this.

Thus, for ease-of-programming reasons, CBOs trade performance (which might be provided by IDLs) for run-time type evaluation (provided by self-defining data).

With these capabilities, we can say, then, that a CBO:

- Requires no recompile or relink when used for the first time with another CBO. If sent to a user, the CBO can be run by that user with no further build-time activity (compile, link, integration, method definition, message definition, etc.) other than a simple definition that the CBO now exists in the user's environment.
- Can handle data binding dynamically at run-time (via the self-defining data facilities provided by the infrastructure).
- Can interpret data syntax and semantics dynamically at run-time (the developers of CBOs that interact are not *forced* to share definition files (header files, copy books, IDLs, etc.)).
- Enjoys run-time dynamic binding for:
  —Method resolution
  —Data exchange syntax and semantics
- At run-time, exhibits no indication as to the language used for its building.

A2.2.7 Message-driven

CBOs are message- (or event-) driven. Like OOPL objects, CBOs use messages to communicate with other CBOs. Thus a CBO:

1. Is invoked by an incoming message, where that message originates and is routed outside itself.
2. Sees no difference at all between local and remote CBOs—the programmer does not *have* to know the location of the target CBO.
3. Provides identical programmer semantics for both synchronous and asynchronous messaging *regardless* of the location of the target object, and *regardless* of the communications mechanism used to reach remote CBOs.
4. Can send messages to itself.
5. Can pass messages to its superclass.
6. Has a language-independent way of sending CBO messages.
7. Has *all* events (GUI, client/server requests, etc.) transformed into a single common message form by the CBO infrastructure. Similarly, messages issued by a CBO are transformed by the CBO infrastructure into the appropriate system-level form.

All this implies a defined inter-CBO messaging architecture, implemented by the infrastructure. Using a self-defining data stream function to pack the message data, the pseudocode for sending a CBO message might look something like this:

```
Data = SdsPack ('Name', person_name, 'Age', how_old)
rc = Send (ObjectId, 'DoIt', Data, Reply)
if rc = 'OK' then ...
     /* Response is in the variable ''Reply'' */
```

Several points are of interest here:

- The data sent with the message (variable `Data` is set up before the message is sent in self-defining format (shown by the `SdsPack` function).
- Since we are dealing with interaction between separately developed software deliverables, which may not be on the same machine, then two things must be returned by the message:
  —The response data
  —A return code to indicate the success or otherwise of the message
  The return code is returned by the `Send` function: the response from the target will be in the variable `Reply`.
- For efficiency reasons, the programmer will probably need to know a target CBO's object ID (an internal handle or pointer of some sort) in order to send a message to it. However (and quite contrary to the situation within an OOPL application):

—Often the programmer will not have the object ID, but will know the external name of the CBO. For example, the programmer may know that he or she wants to send a message to an object whose class is 'customer' and whose instance name is 'A1234' (the customer number). But he or she may not know the object's ID (especially if it is remote).
—Consider an incoming message. The programmer may need to find out the class name of the sending object, and perhaps in addition its instance name. But he or she may be given only its ID—which may have been built on another system.

The solution to this is to have the infrastructure arrange things so that:
—A valid object ID can always be unambiguously derived from the external name of a CBO.
—The external name of a given CBO can always be unambiguously derived from its object ID.

What this means is that the name-space design for CBO names must be well thought out, and must be portable over systems. A good solution is to include the external instance and class names in the name space. Thus for communicating with remote CBOs, the infrastructure can translate an object ID into a unique name, which can subsequently be converted back to an object ID at the receiving end—all transparently to the programmer. This scheme also allows an object ID to be sent as data (in its external form) within a message.

The programmer can always find out the class and instance name of the CBO sending the message.

- The programmer sees a difference between asynchronous and synchronous messages. How this is done so as to achieve a consistent model is discussed in Appendix 3.

A2.2.8 Inter-CBO messaging

CBOs communicate (cooperate) with other CBOs by sending and receiving messages. Both the designer and the programmer think in terms of messages. The following characteristics apply:

1 A CBO can issue a message to another CBO no matter where the target CBO is located in a distributed network. To the programmer/designer, a remote CBO can be treated exactly as if it were local. A 'remote' CBO might be another CBO or a non-CBO construct such as a CICS transaction. Any non-CBO remote construct is *always* seen by the CBO programmer as just another CBO.

The remote CBO will respond by returning some response. Note that data might be returned on the return of control (from the remote CBO to the remote system); in addition, the remote CBO might send one or more messages back to the requester.

Facilities are available in the message for carrying on a simple conversation (for example, in the case of sending multiple messages back, to indicate a sequence number, plus a 'last one' flag).

2. Messages can be sent to a receiver CBO by name. That is, the internal reference or handle of the receiver does not *have* to be known by the sender (trivially, the sender would use system facilities to derive an object ID from the external name). CBO names include the instance name and the class name.

3. A CBO, in issuing a message to another CBO, does not have to concern itself as to whether or not the target CBO is instantiated.

The last two items can be exemplified as follows. Suppose a user double clicks on an item in a customer list. Further assume that the customer list object holds only the key (customer number) of the names in it—the relevant customer objects are not instantiated, and hence the customer list object does not have any internal object references to customer CBOs. The customer list object should be able to issue the following message[4] in order to cause the relevant customer object to display itself:

```
Send target=('Cust', 'AB123') message='Show' data=NULL
```

where `Cust` is the class name of the customer CBO; `AB123` is the customer reference (unique key) of the customer instance; `Show` is the customer CBO method for displaying a view of itself; and `NULL` is the data sent with the message (that is, in this example, none).

4. Individual methods in a CBO may be loaded on demand or not, depending on the implementation of the underlying infrastructure. Classes will be loaded on demand.

5. A CBO can (of course) send messages to itself. Some implementations may provide for sending a message directly to a CBO's superclass.

6. Messages not handled by the CBO (i.e. a particular class) are passed to the CBO's superclass—even when the superclass was developed totally separately. This implies that the class structure must be built by the system at run-time.

7. The return code from sending a message may be provided by the system or by the receiving CBO. The programmer can thus find out if the message routed OK, and, if so, if the CBO rejected it for some reason.

A2.2.9 *Location-transparent*

CBOs are location-transparent. This means that a programmer, in sending a message to another CBO (the 'target'), need not know whether the target is local

---

[4] The syntax shown here is representational. However, whatever the syntax in a given implementation, the programmer should understand that he or she is sending a message. Thus the implementation should *not* present itself as, for example, manipulating a queue (of messages).

(in the same thread) or remote (in another thread, process or system). Specifically, the target may be written in another language, running on another operating system, at the other side of a wide-area network (WAN).

This means that the infrastructure must provide a communications subsystem, handling multi-tasking, storage management, queues, routing of messages to the target CBO, routing of the response back to the requesting CBO, and the comms code itself. It should also provide a framework where additional communications protocols can very easily be integrated.

In addition, the programmer does not have to be concerned with loading the target CBO. Thus:

1 If its code is not already in memory, it will be loaded automatically.
2 If the class is loaded but the instance is not active, then it will be activated automatically.
3 If the instance is not instantiated, then it will be instantiated automatically (and the appropriate instantiation message(s) sent to it).

The point here is that all of the function required to do the above—other than sending the message—is handled outside the programmer's domain, by the infrastructure.

A2.2.10 Serially re-usable

Let us consider first a situation such as that shown in Fig. A2.2. Here, object A invokes object B's method B1, which in turn invokes A's method A2 before returning. This scenario is not at all uncommon, and leads us to the conclusion that a CBO must be able to be invoked recursively.

Again, it might seem desirable for a given CBO method to be blocked while it is being invoked. This would mean that methods need not be coded as being re-entrant; they would be serially re-usable.

However, what if method B1 in object B needs to invoke object A's A1 method before returning? Well, you might say that this is unlikely. OK, but what if method

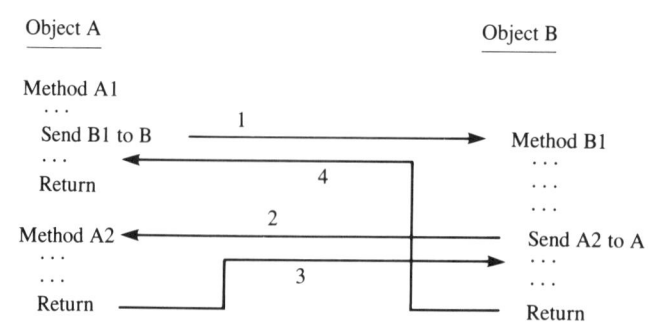

Figure A2.2. Recursive invocation.

B1 were to invoke object C, and then object C invoked method A1 in objectA? This kind of recursion might be unlikely within a single (object-oriented) application, where a single programmer has a solution-wide view. With CBOs, however, this situation becomes much more likely, particularly where CBOs communicate across process and system boundaries in many parallel interactions.

For example, suppose that object B in Fig. A2.2 is remote. While the CBO infrastructure is handling the communications to object B, a message for A's A1 method might well be received.

If we were to block invocation by both local and remote objects, then we would have a design that was particularly susceptible to deadly embrace—to say nothing of performance. In addition, since method resolution is done within a CBO, and the infrastructure does not know which method is being invoked, it is difficult to see how such blocking could be effected. (Blocking the whole CBO is out of the question—this just plain does not work. As to methods, the infrastructure could be built to understand all methods provided by all CBOs, and to disallow recursive invocations by queuing them. However, this would not only open the door to deadly embrace, but could also seriously block up an entire network. In addition, the overhead of understanding and tracking method invocations would be likely seriously to impact the infrastructure's performance.)

Thus blocking a method during its invocation is undesirable in a world of distributed CBOs, which must be able to communicate synchronously (as well as asynchronously).

It looks as if we need to write CBOs using wholly re-entrant code. Clearly this cannot be done with anything like ease of programming. The solution is to have the infrastructure present a small and predictable set of recursive call circumstances to the programmer. One way to do this is to ensure that such recursive invocation is only possible when the programmer 'opens the door' through some specific interaction with the infrastructure—such as sending or posting a message.

A2.2.11 *Persistent*

Until the advent of effective and pervasive OODBs, the system has to provide for CBO persistence, where such persistence is required. This is handled by superclass behaviour (where the superclasses are provided by the system). The CBO designer/programmer can get CBO persistence by default.

When a CBO is first created, it is said to be 'instantiated'. If not destroyed, then is is safe-stored on disk over shutdowns. On start-up, it is not automatically reloaded. Rather, if a message is sent to it, it is automatically 'activated' by the system. Similarly, automatic 'deactivation' can be arranged for classes of CBOs through system facilities.

Finally, automatic 'destruction' can be arranged through a garbage collection mechanism. This does not necessarily remove data from a database from which the CBO may have retrieved its data. Thus:

1   The system provides a 'persistence database' (PDB), and a framework for persistence. When closing, and when restored, CBOs can override superclass behaviour to do their own save/restore if that is what is required. CBOs are persistent unless the programmer overrides the persistence framework (or unless subclassed from a non-persistent class).
2   View objects, in addition to model objects, are persistent (that is, the size and position of the window are remembered by the system). However, they typically would not include business data as part of their instance data. (Consider a 'customer' CBO in the UID. The view instance data would include such things as window size and position; maybe its z-order on the screen, the position of the cursor, etc. The model instance data would include such things as customer number, name, address, etc. When the CBO is instantiated next time, the view object would get the data to be displayed in fields from the model. It would not store that data as part of its own instance data.) The CBO programmer does not have to do anything to make views persistent.
3   CBOs can be destroyed by the system (and so removed from the PDB) after a given time. This is done through a 'garbage collection' mechanism provided by the CBO infrastructure.

A2.2.12 *Requires a software infrastructure*

It should now be quite apparent that, just as batch systems require an infrastructure (the spooling subsystem), and transactions require an infrastructure (the transaction processor), so CBOs require an infrastructure.

The CBO infrastructure is a run-time layer of software, together with several superclasses from which CBOs can inherit common behaviour. Provision of a set of base classes, which include appropriate frameworks, is an inportant ease-of-programming aspect of the infrastructure. In addition, the infrastructure should provide a set of CBO build tools.

The CBO infrastructure is described in Chapter 8.

Appendix 3
Messaging—'send' vs 'send/post'

There are two fundamentally different ways of messaging. The first is what we shall call 'immediate'. An immediate message is akin to a call. The sender says, in effect, 'Hey, you, please do what I ask, and I'm waiting for your response, so please hurry up.' In this form, the receiver (of the message) returns the response with the return of control to the sender.

The second is what we shall call 'deferred'. A deferred message is where the sender says, 'Hey you, please do what I ask, but I can't wait, so send me back a message with your response.' Here, the receiver returns the response in the form of a message that is sent to the sender.

Both types of message are necessary, and since there are situations where the programmer *cannot* afford to wait, then the problem is to provide the programmer with a consistent conceptual model, and a consistent API, that embraces the two modes of messaging. (The alternative, to give the programmer quite different ways of doing each, while retaining a common response view of messages arriving as events, was deemed early on in the development of CBOs to be considerably more difficult for the programmer.)

There are broadly two approaches to this problem:

- Provide a single API (say 'send')
- Provide two APIs (say 'send' for the immediate message, and 'post' for the deferred message)

In the first approach, the decision as to whether to issue an immediate or deferred message could be made by the infrastructure, dependent on, for example, availability of communications resources. In the second approach, the programmer decides on the message type by using one or the other of the two APIs.

In both cases, for a deferred message, the sender must be able to provide the receiver with the name of the message to send back. Without this, in the world of independently developed CBOs, things can get rather awkward. For example, a CBO might be coded to send back the message 'ResponseData' in response to some given message. In that case, if the sender sends a deferred message to this

CBO, then the sender must provide a 'ResponseData' method to deal with the response received.

But what if the sender does not have a 'ResponseData' method? Sending the name of the reply message required in the original request message overcomes this problem. It ensures that the sender can process response messages in the most appropriate way. This may be to have one method for all response messages, or one method for every CBO to which a deferred message is sent, or something in between.

But let us now look at the options of single and dual APIs.

A3.1 Single API

The single 'send' API might look something like this:

```
rc = Send (TargetCBO, 'Query', Data, Response, 'ReplyMsg')
```

In this example, the programmer sends a `'Query'` message to the target CBO (the receiver), together with message data in the variable `'Data'`. A variable `'Response'` is provided in case the infrastructure treats the message as immediate, and also provides the name of a message—`'ReplyMsg'`—in case the infrastructure decides to treat the message as deferred, and send a message back.

Now, because the infrastructure determines the behaviour of the interaction, then the sender has to code defensively for both situations, both in the send itself and in checking for a response message. The programmer must always check for a response, since, if the message was sent immediately, the response will be available at the next statement. If the message was deferred, then the processing of the response must be done in the method invoked by the reply message when it is received.

Let us now turn to the receiver of a message. How does the receiving CBO know whether the message is immediate or deferred? It would be possible for the infrastructure to provide this information, and for the receiver to handle its reply accordingly. But coding at the receiving end will be made much easier if we arrange things in the CBO infrastructure such that the receiver *always* treats a message as if it were immediate. The infrastructure could then decide, when it gets the receiver's response, to return it to the sender on the return of control, or send a message back.

That would certainly make things easier at the receiving CBO. However, the sender would still have to code for both eventualities. After all, the communication mechanism might, at some future time, be enhanced such that messages previously sent deferred by the infrastructure are now sent as immediate. In effect, that would make the behaviour of the sending CBO code dependent on an underlying connection mechanism. This is not goodness!

It seems that, whatever, we do, having a single API for both immediate and deferred messages puts significant strain on the sender. The sender is not in control of what happens.

Let us look at the alternative.

A3.2 Two APIs

A 'send or post' API might look something like this:

```
Immediate:
    rc = Send ( TargetCBO, 'Query', Data, Response )
Deferred:
    rc = Send ( TargetCBO, 'Query', Data, 'ReplyMsg' )
```

In these examples, the programmer indicates whether the message is immediate or deferred by providing either a response variable or a reply message respectively. The programmer's model is that specifying one means immediate, while specifying the other means deferred. In fact, this is bad API design, since the same API is being used for two different things, with the difference being reflected in the type of the parameters used. Again, something 'under the covers' has to work out—if possible(!)—whether the programmer provided a response space or a reply message name.

For these reasons, it is much preferable to provide different APIs, with identical parameters for identical behaviour, like this:

```
Immediate:
    rc = Send ( TargetCBO, 'Query', Data, Response )
Deferred:
    rc = Post ( TargetCBO, 'Query', Data, 'Reply' )
```

Here, the sender is in control. However, the implication is that the receiver is *required* to honour the message mode—immediate or deferred. That is, the receiver must return a response on the return of control in the case of an immediate message received, and send a reply message back in the case of a deferred message received. Otherwise the sender would be confused(!). This adds complexity to the receiver's code, and is hence error-prone.

However, if we could arrange things (as above) such that the receiver *always* treats a message as immediate, then the problem is solved. In this case, the CBO infrastructure has to 'catch' the receiver's response, and if the sender had used 'post', then it must turn the response into a message to be sent back to the sender.

Here we have perhaps the best of all worlds, ensuring consistent behaviour and simple programming for both the sender and the receiver. The implications of this approach are:

- The receiver *always* returns a response (rather than sends a response back on a different message).
- Whether the target is local or remote, a 'post' tells the CBO infrastructure to return control to the sender *before* routing the message to the target.
- 'Send' will always be synchronous with respect to the sending CBO (regardless of the underlying connection), and 'post' will always be asynchronous with respect to the sending CBO (even when the target is in the same address space).

Thus the 'two API' approach leaves the programmer in no doubt, and provides transparency of location, as well as transparency of the underlying connection type (synchronous or asynchronous). Indeed, experience points to the 'send and post' approach being much the better, even though the first approach on first sight (and ignoring the real detail problems faced by the programmer) may appear more elegant. In fact, is is not.

Appendix 4
Model vs local model

In the course of this book, I have defined five types of CBO—view, (local) model, focus, entity and resource. This terminology is not really new, and some of the terms have been used by various writers on object orientation—but in subtly different ways. For example, some writers see the model object as being the thing itself (this is the equivalent of our entity object—my use of the term 'entity' follows Jacobson *et al.* (1992)). Others see a 'model' object as being the equivalent of our focus, entity and resource objects all rolled into one—so that the SRD would be said to contain just one type of object—a model.

We have found, however, that a single model object in the SRD is insufficient in distributed systems. This appendix shows why another kind of model—in the UID—is required. We call this second model object the 'local model'.

A4.1   A single model object?

Both intuitively and from the point of view of good object design, it is arguable that there should only be one model object.

Consider a system where the resource manager domain extends over all operating systems in the network. Let us also suppose that reading and writing data can be done in a millisecond or so, and that there is no network delay. Finally, assume that only one view of some object ('customer' for example) is required.

In this case, we need only build one object, 'Customer', as shown in Fig. A4.1(a). Note that our single object not only handles view and data access, but also handles the icon (e.g. application logic, which might be required for 'templateness', icon copy, display name, etc.). Note also that this object handles, within itself, three different things:[1]

- View and icon logic

---

[1] These things are all IT-specific, and nothing much to do with the essence of 'customer'. Thus in implementing a set of useful classes, we might generalize the IT-specific behaviour (user interface, database, transaction awareness) into superclasses, and have a single 'customer' class that knows nothing about such IT specifics. This makes no difference to the argument presented in this appendix, however.

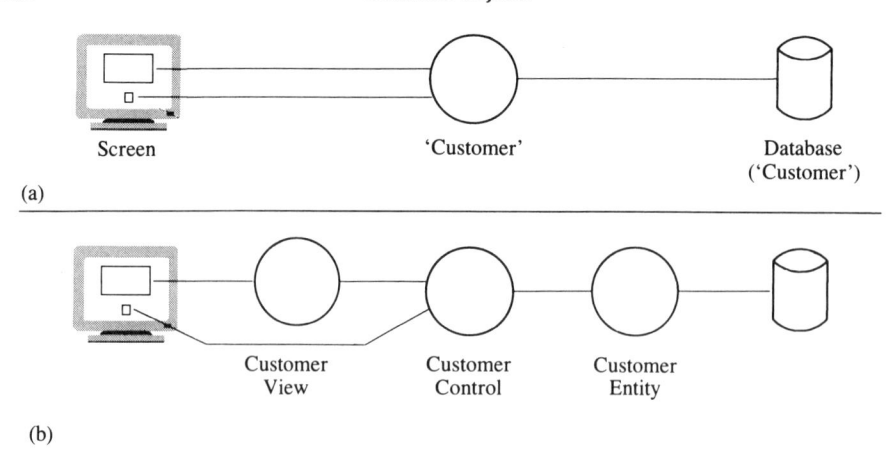

Figure A4.1. Model and local model (1).

- Commit scope logic
- Data access logic

This agglomeration of function does not make for particularly good modularization. We could make a very strong case for splitting things on responsibility lines into 'view' and 'model' objects. Perhaps better is to split into 'view' on the one hand, and, instead of model, into 'entity' and 'control' (following Jacobson) on the other. This is shown in Fig. A4.1(b).

A4.1.1 View, control and entity

Splitting 'model' into 'control' and 'entity' makes more sense if you think of an order form, where the model has to coordinate changing several entities (item, order, customer). In this case, the control object is either an encapsulation of some business process (e.g. order form), or a general-purpose transaction object.

An important aspect of this split is that, since at any given time there may be an icon on the user interface but no view in existence, then the control object has to handle icon-related logic.

'Icon logic' is that business logic which may be required to handle the various attributes of an icon on an object-based user interface. These responsibilities include:

- Validating that a DisplayName, which has been changed by the user, conforms to business rules (example—business rules may say that the display name for a given customer can be changed to anything as long as the customer name is retained).
- Deciding whether a 'copy' operation is valid.
- Determining whether a template can be made, and, if so, with what data to populate it.

- Providing icon-related information to the user (e.g. some form of animation, perhaps, or, more likely, some indication of state—over credit limit, for example).
- Handling drag/drop.

However, we can imagine an infrastructure that handled all this user interface stuff for us, and requested all the information required, perhaps based on some configuration information, from the control. This is especially so if we abstract the above into the following, which can be seen as valid 'control' responsibilities:

- External name for DisplayName
- Copy request
- Standard copy source for template
- State information
- Introduction protocol

We can also imagine that any persistence required would be handled automatically by the infrastructure. This means that the control object would not have to remember which user has which DisplayName (for example). In other words, the persistence of data of scope 'personal' (such as a display name set by an individual user) is not handled by the control or entity objects, but is handled by the infrastructure.

Now let us introduce technology—let us enter the implementation domain (or, as Jacobson has it, the 'design'—as opposed to analysis—domain).

A4.1.2 The problem

There are two major problem areas for us in the above analytical model. Both are to do with implementation (which is why Jacobson introduces a fourth leg in the design phase—the environment). These two problem areas are related, and they are:

- Commit scopes
- Performance

A4.1.3 Commit scopes

One of the imperatives of any IT system is data integrity. This presents particular challenges in the distributed and client/server environments.

A major responsibility of the control object is to handle commit/rollback. This means that it must run in the shared resource domain (SRD). For present purposes, we can classify SRDs into three types:

1 Distributed database, with commit control available to distributed data APIs.

2   Distributed database, with commit control available to non-distributed APIs (all API calls within a given UOW must be issued from the same thread of control).
3   Non-distributed database.

Let us assume that the database is on the server.

A type 1 SRD will allow the control and entity to be run together anywhere (PC or server), or separately (one on the PC, one on the server).

Type 2 allows *both* the control and entity to run in a single thread of control *either* on the PC (all other things being equal) *or* on the server.

Type 3 requires that the control and entity run on the server, not on the PC.

A4.1.4 Performance

By 'performance', I mean all aspects of performance that imply delays—network, data access, path lengths, size of database, etc.

Now, another of the imperatives of client/server systems is to preserve the responsiveness of the GUI. This means that there must be no long waits (say longer than 50–100 milliseconds) in the task that is driving the GUI. By 'task', I mean a thread of control that can be pre-empted by the operating system.

This means that a view object must respond within times of this order. Note that a view object could operate entirely asynchronously with respect to the GUI—but that would not only make response-time considerations in the code much more critical, it would also make the code much more complex. In addition, it would not remove the need for the view to respond to any event within the same time—else the user interface will get quite out of step with the business logic in the view.

This means that long-running blocking calls must be avoided in the view.

However, it can never be assumed that *all* the entity and control objects will be able to provide a response time of 50–100 milliseconds. Indeed, today one can safely assume that most of them will not. Indeed, some may not respond within half a minute.

Thus if a given call against some shared resource (typically data) takes an order of magnitude longer than the required view response time, then those calls *must* be issued in a thread of control other than that of the view.

A4.1.5 Placement options

We then have the following possibilities:

Control in same thread as view, entity in a different thread

This option requires a type 1 SRD, and is illustrated in Fig. A4.2(a), where the thread boundary is shown by a dotted line. Note that, today, type 1 SRDs are extremely rare (if they exist at all . . .).

(a)

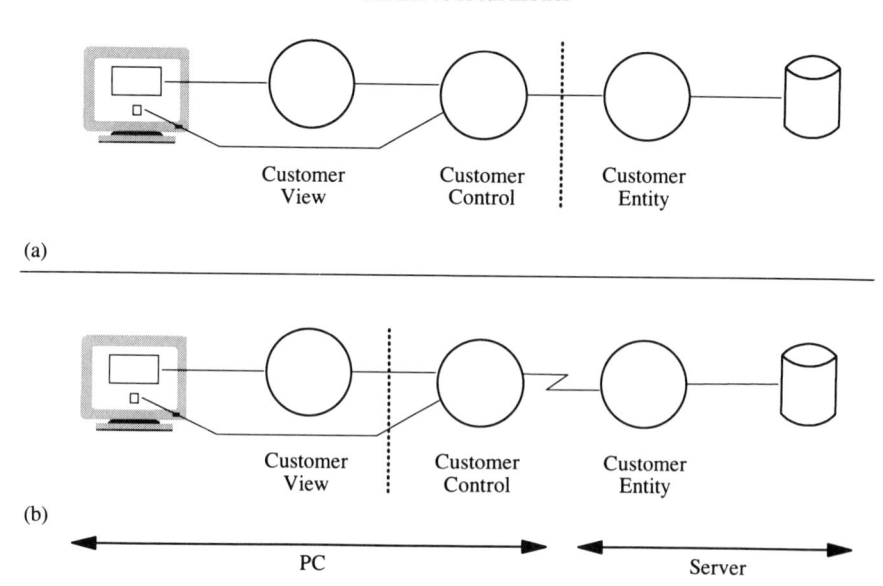

Customer View — Customer Control | Customer Entity

(b)

Customer View — Customer Control | Customer Entity

PC ←——→ Server ←——→

Figure A4.2. Model and local model (2).

Control and entity in a different thread of control from view

This capability is fairly common today, with the control and entity being placed either on the server or (less commonly) on the PC. On the PC, this looks like Fig. A4.2(b), where not only are they in a different thread of control from the view, but the control object is on the PC while the entity is on the server.

If placed on the server, it looks like Fig. A4.3(a).

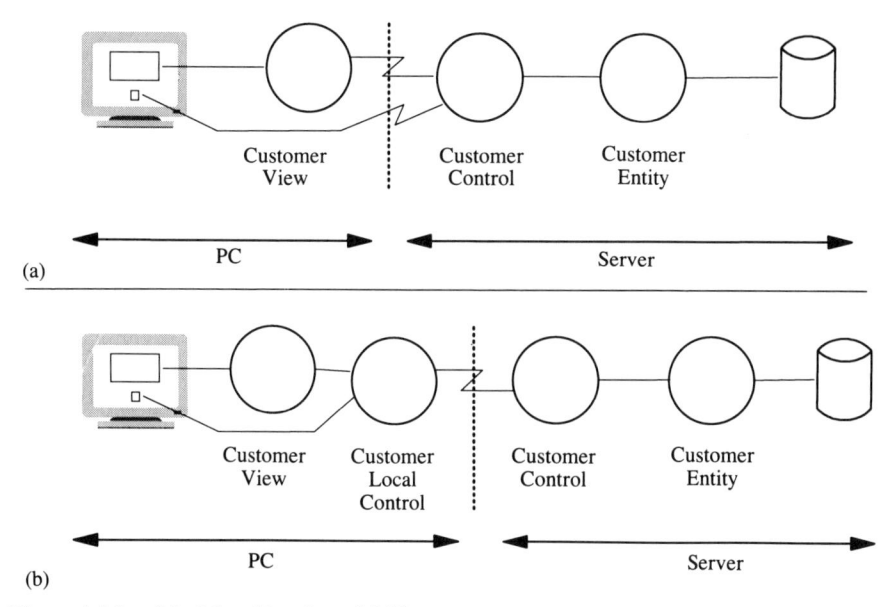

(a)

Customer View | Customer Control — Customer Entity

PC ←——→ Server ←——————→

(b)

Customer View — Customer Local Control | Customer Control — Customer Entity

PC ←——→ Server ←——→

Figure A4.3. Model and local model (3).

There is not much difference between the two—the lightning flash (the communications link) is in a different place, that is all. A major advantage is the ability to move the control object from one system to another without changing the code. However, these two designs introduce two major problems:

- The view is far away in time (in fact or potentially) from the control object. This means that business logic (such as cross-field validation, trivial queries, etc.) cannot be sent to the control. So, such code must be placed either in the view, or somewhere else—*on the PC*. Good design—as well as the possibility of having several view objects for the same model—suggests strongly that it ought to be outside the view object. But where?
- The 'icon logic' is now remote from the view thread; and icon-related interactions are among those which do require a very fast response time. Sticky pointers on drag/drop are one thing; frozen pointers (for say 10 seconds) are another! Logic to handle icon-related things cannot be placed in the view object, since the view object may not always be there when the icon is there (detail design tends to favour discarding the view object when the window on the GUI is closed).

A4.2   The need for a local model

These considerations point strongly to the need for another object on the PC—a local representative of the control/entity (or model), as shown in Fig. A4.3(b). The responsibilities of such an object would be a subset of those of the model. They would not include commit/rollback (and associated shared access conflict detection). They would include:

- Icon-related function
- Trivial view–model interactions (which do not imply a commit)
- Requesting function of the (real) model
- Providing local support to other local PC-based objects on behalf of the model

We shall call this object the 'local model'. When we are clear that the context is the PC, and the real model (whatever combinations of control, entity and resource objects that might mean) is not on the PC, then we may refer to the local model as just the model.

A4.3   Conclusion

There are a large number of situations today (and tomorrow) where the exigencies of the technology dictate that local models are necessary in the PC (or more precisely, in the UID). The inter-object behaviours provided by this analysis are:

- The view talks to what it sees as the model. This may sometimes (or often) be the local model.

- The local model talks to the model, and to other local models (just as the model talks to other models).
- A local model instance can be omitted, and the view can talk directly to the model as long as fast-response requests (e.g. drag/drop) are filtered out. This implies that drag/drop may not be able to be supported. Proper support of this and other trivial but important (to the user) interactions will often dictate the presence of a local model.

A4.4 Advantages

This separation of local model and model is not merely a technology-driven inconvenience. It has several advantages:

- Implementations can separate the SRD from the UID very effectively. This means that they can be built separately.
- In particular, if an SRD set of models exists, then adding function through adding views and local models—which cannot affect data integrity—is a positive benefit.
- In particular, it opens the route to allowing the 'ambitious end-user' to write code without jeopardizing the integrity of corporate IT resources.
- This must be a major part of getting IT on the critical path of business change.
- It is also a major part of bringing together personal computing and corporate computing.

Appendix 5
A UID prototyping technique

The essence of UID design is to identify the objects that a given user (or class of user) would best *like* to use to perform the required processes and tasks.

This chapter presents a set of techniques, and a process, for defining UID objects in a prototyping environment. These techniques, and the design process, were developed as a tool for rapid prototyping, and do not pretend to be anything else. Using the process, it is possible to define within a single day a useful set of objects that are relevant and buildable as a prototype.

Since it is essentially a 'bottom-up' (screen-in, outside-in) process, it cannot be used to identify all and only the objects required for any given type of user. And it certainly cannot be used, for example, to develop an entity model!

A5.1 Some initial considerations

Here are some predesign hints and tips:

Understand the benefit

Understand the proposed or hoped-for business benefits to be gained from this prototype. Agree them, and document them.

Understand the requirements

Understand (and document) the business requirements in the area to be addressed. Often these requirements will be about enabling people (users) to address a wider area than hitherto.

Choose something relevant

Choose a business process area that is relevant. For example, if customer service is an important aspect of current business objectives, then choosing to prototype an internal stationery stores ordering process will probably be a waste of time.

Do not *choose an application*

In designing object-based user interfaces, it is important to focus not on some application, but rather on the user—and the set of *things* the user needs to perform some set of business processes.

So the first thing to identify is *not* which application to address, but which *users* to address.

Then identify two or more business processes that are performed by one of these users, and that probably have objects in common between them. This will help focus on the fundamental advantages of an object-based user interface, and on its 'application integration' potential. If the processes themselves are too rich to prototype fully, then take slices through them—slices that provide valid user scenarios.

User input may mislead

Users provide necessary input to the process. However, often users have no experience of object-based user interfaces. Again, users will try to help you by expressing their wants and requirements in terms of older-style computer systems—in the mistaken belief that they are helping you!

Before starting, introduce to the users the concepts of an object-based user interface. Demonstrate one. Ensure that they understand its capabilities.

For example, make sure that they understand that they can have what I call 'magic machines'—shredders that can de-shred, forms that can tell them if they have entered something wrongly, folders that can never be filled up, Post-It Notes that never lose their stickiness, never drop off and never obscure the thing to which they are stuck; etc.

Prototype what users would like

Ensure that users understand that what you are looking for are the things they would *like* to have to do their jobs. Encourage them to use their imagination on this one. Emphasize that they can have whatever things they would like. Keep stressing 'things'.

No 'classes' on the user interface

Do not propose to surface a class on the screen. The idea of an object-based user interface is to represent the real world. No one has ever seen a class. Yes, everyone can handle the concept of a class 'table', but actually seeing and touching the class table (as opposed to a specific table—an instance of the class) would be an experience unmatched in the long history of humanity. (In object orientation, a system that has no inheritance mechanisms, but which does support encapsulation of objects, is said to be 'object-based' rather than 'object-oriented'. The absence of classes from the user interface, and the consequential absence of visible inheritance hierarchies, is what makes the user interface 'object-based' rather than 'object-oriented'.)

The user interface should consist of objects that encourage categorization ('I see that this invoice object is a kind of form'), as long as such classification as is done by the user is supported by the behaviour of the underlying CBOs.

Making new objects at the user interface should be done through the use of templates (themselves instances of a class, not a class) or through copying or some other mechanism that deals with instances, such as picking an item from a list (of instances).

Focus on benefit

For a prototype, focus on business areas that suit an object-based user interface, but which are difficult with application-oriented interfaces. Examples include:

- Re-use of a given object across business processes
- Folders and containers
- Creating new things by copying, or through the use of templates
- Drag/drop interactions

Likewise, include things that an application-oriented interface finds easy. Examples of this are:

- Enforcement of business rules
- Following a required sequence of operations

A5.2 Overview

Here is a summary of the design process, given that the business requirements and the overall application area have been identified.

1 Describe the overall business area.

For each of three or four of the major business processes in that area:

2 Describe a desired user scenario—what the user would *like* to be able to do. Do not merely record what happens currently. If there is an application-oriented computer system installed currently, then what happens currently is unlikely to be a good base for an object design.
3 List the things (objects) that will be seen by the end-user—that is, the things that the user would *like* to have with which to do their work.

Note If this is your first ever try-out of this process, then at this point you might like to do a bit of step 6, just to see what an object definition looks like.

4 Make a 'window flow sketch' for each scenario by running through it, drawing rough sketches of the user interface as you go, noting probable message flow, and ensuring that you can see roughly that it will work.
5 Use the results of the previous step to refine the list of objects. Some may be added, some may drop out.
6 Define what major data attributes are required for each object identified.
7 Make a rough sketch of views of objects. Note that the technique proposed is a sketching technique, not a documentation technique.
8 Walk through the scenario, ensuring that it will work as far as data availability is concerned, and that any necessary forms/folder objects are identified.
9 Repeat steps 2 through 8 for each of the other major business processes identified.

If there are (say) four user scenarios to be addressed, it is not uncommon to discover that while the first takes quite a time to go through, the second will take less, and the third and fourth even less. This is because you find you will re-use objects defined in previous scenarios.

A5.3 The design process

We now look at this design process in some detail, and discuss what goes on in each step. We also define the deliverable from each step in terms of a notional section in a design document. Finally, I mention some rough timings for each step. These times do not include documentation.

A5.3.1 Describe the business area

This is a one- to three-page description of the business and application area, and should include:

- Business benefits to be gained from the new system
- Business requirements
- Type or types of user (note that a user may have more than one role—for example, a person may be both a receptionist and a stock clerk; in this case, identify the roles)
- The number of users
- The number of locations
- The user's relationship to other parts of the organization

If there are existing applications then these should be mentioned. The current or proposed use of office and/or decision support functions should also be noted. This section should be written primarily in terms of what users *do*, but should be technology-free. Some guidelines and examples are:

1. In discussing the general application area, several proposed applications (in the traditional sense) will probably be mentioned. If only one is mentioned, then this is a signal that you are probably not addressing the user. It is important to focus on users rather than on applications. You should not be prototyping an application—you should be prototyping the *things* that a user needs to perform one or more business processes. For example, do not talk about an order entry application, talk about customer service representatives.
2. Do not say things like: '... A tape containing input from another department is received every morning and is loaded onto the existing departmental machine. A batch process checks for errors, and users are presented with a list of errors that they then correct....' This is much too oriented towards current practice, and is nothing to do with what we are trying to get at in this design step. Rather, say: '... A supervisor allocates correction work to users at the start of each day ... the users make corrections based on their own experience and knowledge....'[1]
3. Try to avoid describing the application area in terms of applications. For example, do not say 'The users run the general ledger input verification application.' Rather, say 'The users verify that general ledger input is accurate.'
4. Sometimes, timescales and committed dates will mean that development will be phased. Do *not* restrict this step to phase one only. If you do, you may miss important aspects of the system.

This step might take around two–three hours.
Deliverable—'Business area'.

A5.3.2 Describe user scenarios

By 'scenario' I mean a description of what a real user (in a specific role) might actually do in performing a specific business process. This is not a design step, it is a description step. The idea is to describe some of the *desired* scenarios from the more important business processes. What you are trying to do here is to tell a story—'half an hour in the life of'—that is, half an hour (or 10 minutes or whatever) in the life of this person doing that business process in this specific case. A simple example from an order processing application area is shown in Fig. A5.1.

Here are some pointers to the sorts of things to consider in doing this step:

1. Many business processes include decision points for the user (example—if an item is out of stock in order entry then the user does something different than if the item is in stock). Do *not* describe the options in the scenario. Either leave

---

[1] This example is a real one, and introduced the question of why data was not corrected prior to getting to these users. This sort of question should be vigorously pursued, since the answer may well point to an area that the proposed system development *should* be addressing but is not. In the real case, it was not being addressed because the analysts concerned had been told to address one department only, and therefore assumed that anything outside that user department was outside their brief!

> *Scenario 1—Joe Bloggs creates a simple customer order*
>
> Joe Bloggs, a relatively new employee, enters the office at 9 o'clock. The phone rings. It is George Smith from BCE Consolidated, wanting to order some parts. Joe looks up his administrative procedures manual to find out how to take an order (he cannot remember all the steps for sure, and he would like to create a good impression by doing things right). He finds the right place, and looks at the procedure.
>
> The first step is to get an order form, which he does. George says he is in a hurry, and all he wants is three cases of part X.
>
> Joe skips the next step (entering the customer details) because he reckons he can come back to that after George is off the phone, and looks up part X in the parts list. He enters part X on the order fom.
>
> 'That should be OK,' says Joe.
>
> George replies, 'Please mark it to be left with Security if it is delivered after hours. Thanks. Bye.'
>
> 'Bye', says Joe, entering the delivery instructions onto the order.
>
> Joe then opens the customer list to find BCE Consolidated. He finds it, and enters the details on the order form.
>
> Finally, Joe commits the order, and is told that all is well.

Figure A5.1.   Sample business process scenario.

   the options till later (step 4) or, if an option is particularly important (such as 'new customer'), then describe the 'subprocess' as a separate (small) scenario.

   So, in this step, describe just one of the possible many paths a user might take. For example, the scenario should say something like: '... Three items are ordered. One of them (the second one) is out of stock. The user looks for an alternative ....' rather than: '... Three items are ordered. If one or more are out of stock, then the user should ... otherwise the user does ....' The scenario is really a story—'ten minutes in the life of a user'—not a general description of a process.

   If two or more paths are really important, then describe them each as a separate scenario.

2 Often you will find that various automatic (or 'batch-like') things take place between processes. One example in entering a customer order is that, when the order is committed, a picking slip may be produced automatically in the warehouse (unknown to the user who entered the order). In this case, append those automatic things to the *end* of a scenario, rather than to the beginning. It is useful to define these automatic things passively at this stage; for example, say '... The picking list is then produced in the warehouse' rather than '... the system then schedules a background task ...'.

3 It will probably be useful to describe an 'out-of-line situation resolution' scenario. This will tend to focus on the objects needed, and will also highlight potential added business value.

Clearly there will almost certainly not be an administrative procedure for such a scenario. The main thing later on in design will be to ask how easy it is for a user to resolve the situation described. Is the required information easily and intuitively available? One solution is to provide a help facility that allows the user to 'launch' or find objects from it.

4 Start off by picking two or three of the major (or most representative) business processes. Do these first, going through the whole process. Then reiterate for the others.
5 Use technology-free language. That is, avoid reference to any system—manual or computer. For example, say 'User looks up customer details' rather than 'User accesses customer database'. However, *do* consider the business objectives, so describe the *desired* scenarios rather then merely reiterate what is currently done. Allow free rein to your imagination here.

This step might take around one hour per scenario.

Deliverable—'User scenarios'—a prose description of each scenario, not only describing the business process scenario, but also illustrating how the business objectives can be achieved. Each scenario should be about one half to one page.

A5.3.3 List objects

This is a kind of 'brainstorm' activity. Its purpose is to make a first-cut identification of the objects that will eventually appear on the object-oriented user interface. While this step may take some time, you should concentrate on making it a 'first pass'. Later we come back and refine this list. A typical time might be one hour; perhaps as little as 15 minutes. Do not spend more than one day on this.

One approach that works well is to pick out all of the nouns in the scenario description. Do not qualify them at this stage; just list the lot.

What are the *things* that—if this were a manual system—the user would use? Some examples are forms, files, books, containers of various sorts (e.g. in tray, cupboard).

Consider the application area. Ignore technology. Now list the objects a user would deal with—or would like to deal with—in performing the business process.

Here are some guidelines as to what is and is not an 'object':

1 The name of an object consists of a *noun*, with no verbs or gerunds. For example, neither 'order processing' nor 'process order' is an object. However, 'order' could be, as could 'order form'.
2 An object is something that a person can *touch*, throw out of the window, see, feel, etc. You cannot feel/touch/etc. a 'calculate tax'. You can feel/touch/etc. a 'tax calculator'.
3 Objects are things that exist in the *real world* (or could in principle exist). It is useful to think about pre-computer times to get at these things. Thus we allow ourselves things like forms, manuals, printers, folders, records,

calculators, etc. But in addition, we allow ourselves 'magic' or futuristic things, such as a 'grapher' (a device into which we feed some numbers, plus perhaps some instructions such as 'calculate moving average', and it produces a graph or chart), or a 'shredder', which not only shreds things of any thickness, but also de-shreds (unshreds?) the last thing shredded if we say the magic word 'undo'.

4   Avoid a *too-rigorous* 'data' view. For example, it might be said that 'customer order' is not an object because it depends on customer and product. Wrong. As far as the user is concerned, *order* most certainly *is* an object. You can point at a completed order form and say 'That order is . . .'.

Note that how data is held in the system is not the question here.

Note also that the 'object' we are talking about here is not necessarily the same as a data analysis object or entity. However, do use any such definitions of objects or entities. They can, and should, help greatly. It is just that you should not be *bound rigidly* by them. If the data analysis has been done properly, then you should find a large number of matches between the things the user deals with in the application area and the things defined as being of key interest to the enterprise. Examples of things not identified by data analysis are folders, cupboards, magic machine, etc.

5   Remember that there are, broadly, *three types of object* in an object-based user interface: a container, a data object and a device object. A data object is just an ordinary object, such as a customer, or an order. A container object is an object that contains other objects, such as a customer list (or file), or a cupboard. A device object is what it sounds like—examples are a printer, a calculator. These are not rigid categories, but are characteristics along a spectrum. A given object will sometimes have all three characteristics. It is useful to make a preliminary note of the major characteristic.

For example, an object such as a 'customer order' might at first glance be seen as a data object. However, depending on various things, you might like to think of it as a container object (it contains picking list, order lines, delivery history, comments from various people, etc.).

6   You will find that you define '*batch*' or 'background' or 'non-visible' objects. For example, if a picking list is automatically produced, then you will probably define that as an object. It is probably a good idea to separate out the visible objects (that is, visible to the user on the screen) from the non-visible objects.

This step should take around two hours. Do not spend more than one day on it!

Deliverable—'User objects'—a list of objects that the user needs to use or refer to while performing a business process, together with any brief one-line descriptions of some of the objects. About one page.

An example of such a list is shown in Fig. A5.2. Note that obvious file or list container objects are not shown separately—rather they are indicated by a 'Y' under

Object	Type	File/List
Customer	Data	Y
Part	Data	Y
Printer	Device	
Order	Container	
Order Form	Data	
Order History	Data	
Delivery Schedule	Data	
...	...	

Figure A5.2. Sample list of objects.

the heading 'File'. Thus in Fig A5.2 *Customer* is a data object, and there is also a container object for customers (which will probably be called 'customer file' or 'customer list').

A5.3.4 Identify administrative procedures

Sometimes the formal administrative procedures that are within the scenario are obvious—especially if the scenario describes all of and only a single such procedure. Sometimes, however, the scenario includes several such procedures. The objectives of the step are:

- Help to identify objects (including forms or folders)
- Identify any required business rules—including any *sequence* of operations that the business requires to be enforced (for example, a customer order cannot be submitted without a customer number being identified and placed on the order)
- Identify the completion criteria for each such set of business rules
- Identify likely sources of requests to a server to make changes to prime data (through, for example, a focus object in the SRD)

Some rules of thumb are:

1. Show each step in the procedure as a verb and (grammatical) object, where the object is a noun, and is also one of the objects listed in the previous step. For example, 'get order form', or 'identify customer record', or 'calculate average price of invoice'.
2. If you need to define a new object, then do so, and add it to the list.
3. Do not include all possible permutations of procedure, but do include some samples of logic (if present) in the procedure.
4. Include the definition of completion criteria.
5. Where part of the business justification for the proposed system is some form of proaction, then do not include that proactive step in the procedure.

   For example, consider a user in a financial institution who is doing, say, a shares transaction for a customer. There will be an administrative procedure for this. Also assume that the user is encouraged to ask the customer about, say, insurance (while said customer is sitting on other side of desk from said user). What this rule of thumb means is, do not include a step 'ask customer about insurance' in the middle of steps to do with selling or buying shares. Or, in other words, do not put cross-sell steps into a procedure covering other processes.

This is because cross-selling is best done through separate objects (perhaps prompted by the completion of some step in a procedure). That way, the cross-selling logic is separated from the procedure, and so can more easily be changed.

In the course of this step you may have identified some new objects. In any case, revisit the object list, and amend if necessary. Certainly in the last iteration of this process, delete from the list any objects that it is now clear will not be used.

Deliverable—'Administrative procedures'—about one to two pages per procedure.

A5.3.5 *Make window flow sketches*

The idea of a 'window flow sketch' is to provide something simple and useful for getting an initial handle on how the objects will interact on the screen, how the flow of work will appear to the user and what the 'shape' of the system will be.

Note   The window flow sketch is *not* intended to be a form of documentation. It is a design technique only.

The process is as follows:

- Get a piece of flip-chart paper and divide it into six areas.
- Pick a business scenario. For example, in an order processing application area, you might have described a scenario as shown in Fig. A5.1.
- Write the scenario name at the top of the flip.
- On the first square at the top left, show (as icons) the few objects that are needed to kick the scenario off. Also at this stage you should define how the user will initiate other objects. This may produce one or more further container objects, such as a cupboard or a store—which will probably be visible.
- Now go through the scenario, sketching the flow.

A sample window flow sketch for the scenario shown in Fig. A5.1 is shown in Fig. A5.3. The symbols used are described in Fig. A5.4. Some notes on the window flow sketch in Fig. A5.3 are given below:

- Sketch 2—The order number is generated automatically (example: O/No 123).
- Customer numbers and part numbers can be entered directly on the order form; however, this scenario implies that Joe knows neither. Two ways of bringing up the lists are shown—the parts list is initiated from the order procedure object, the customer list directly from the customer list icon.

314 **Business objects**

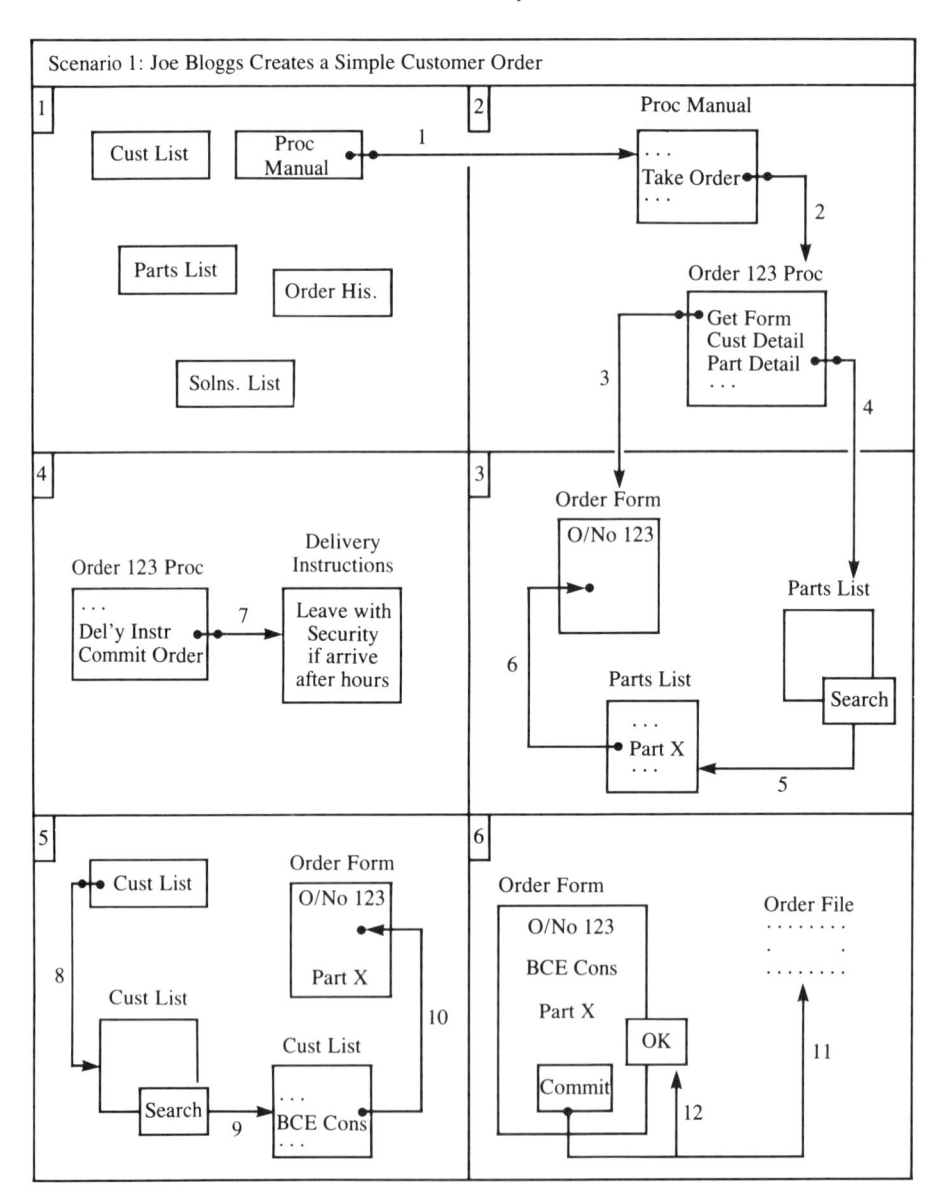

Scenario 1: Joe Bloggs Creates a Simple Customer Order

[Sketch 1] Cust List, Proc Manual, Parts List, Order His., Solns. List

[Sketch 2] Proc Manual: Take Order → Order 123 Proc: Get Form, Cust Detail, Part Detail

[Sketch 3] Order Form O/No 123; Parts List: Part X; Parts List: Search

[Sketch 4] Order 123 Proc: Del'y Instr, Commit Order → Delivery Instructions: Leave with Security if arrive after hours

[Sketch 5] Cust List; Order Form O/No 123, Part X; Cust List: Search; Cust List: BCE Cons

[Sketch 6] Order Form: O/No 123, BCE Cons, Part X, Commit, OK → Order File

Figure A5.3. Sample window flow sketch.

- Both parts and customer lists come up with a 'search' dialogue box. This is because it is first thing after IPL, and both lists are empty on their first invocation. The next invocation will bring up the list with the same data, and without a search box. If another search is required, then it will be user-initiated from within the list window.
- Sketch 6—The orders file is updated and committed before the 'OK' dialogue box is displayed. We may need to display a 'wait' symbol first.

A UID prototyping technique

Figure A5.4. Notation for window flow sketch.

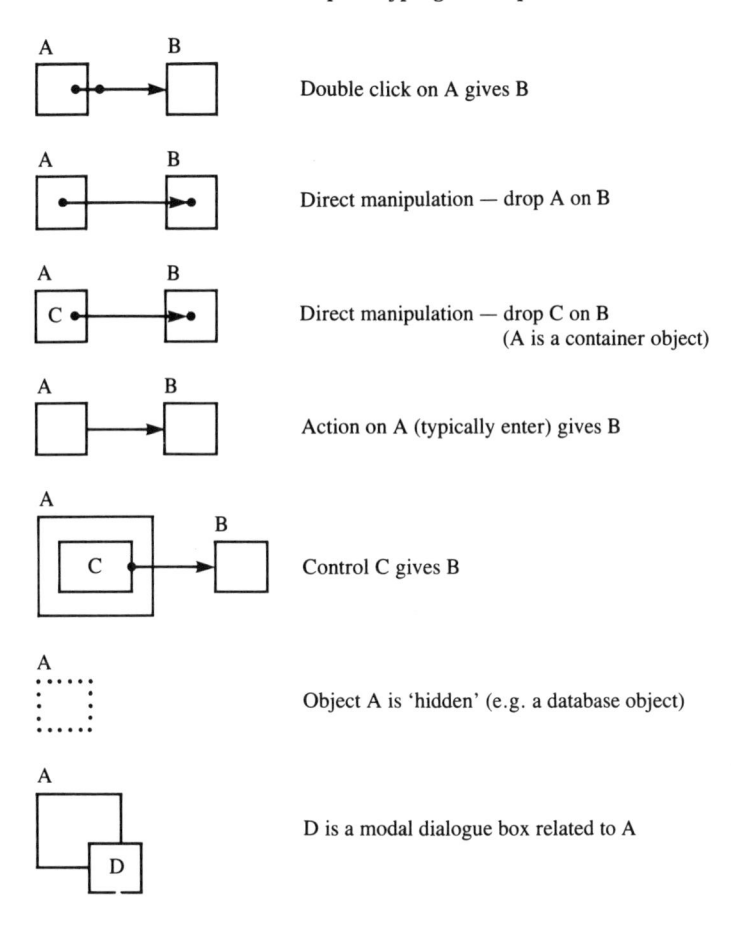

- Double click on A gives B
- Direct manipulation — drop A on B
- Direct manipulation — drop C on B (A is a container object)
- Action on A (typically enter) gives B
- Control C gives B
- Object A is 'hidden' (e.g. a database object)
- D is a modal dialogue box related to A

Numbers on the action lines show the sequence of user action (action lines are the lines with the arrows)

Here are some guidelines for using this technique:

1. Do one flow for each of the user scenarios described.
2. In the first area, show around three objects. Describe how other objects will be displayed by the user (either through a menu bar or by having a general 'store' or 'cupboard' container object).
3. In the second area, show what happens when the user kicks off the scenario from the objects shown in the first area. This will typically be 'opening' some container object.
4. Do not repeat all objects in all areas—the idea is not so much to draw what a real screen might look like, but to show how the user manipulates specific objects to execute the scenario.
5. Do show how the user gets to information, and how the business process flows.

In summary, the idea of this step is to run through each scenario, making sketches of objects and views of objects as you go. Do not try to show the state of the screen at each stage; rather show the specific objects you are using.

Try to test the independence of objects by checking whether they would work unchanged if moved to an entirely new application area.

Deliverable—'Window flow sketches'—an indeterminate number of these, certainly one for each scenario.

A5.3.6 *Make initial specification of the objects used*

Here we document the data that is owned by each object class. In addition, if any specific methods have been identified as useful, then document them. Methods to do with drag/drop, and exchange of information, should probably not be documented, as these tend to be standard methods anyway in UID CBOs.

Define the overall format of views of objects (that is, window layouts). You might use a layout tool to do this. In particular, record menu bar items, push buttons and any other controls used to initiate actions in the window flow sketch.

Deliverable—'Initial UID object definitions'—a collection of initial design specifications for each UID object.

A5.3.7 *Walk through each scenario*

Walk through each scenario, checking that the potential message flow between objects does in fact provide for the accomplishment of the business process, and that, as far as you (the IS professional) can see, it will all work technically. Reiterate if necessary.

In this step, make a note of all messages going to SRD objects, and UID objects that are not visible, and also any messages coming from those objects.

Ensure that any one database update does not extend over more than one message out to an SRD object. This is to retain the commit scope and hence to retain update integrity.

Finally, check that the design allows for the user to get out of any SRD transaction rejections as easily and naturally as possible.

Deliverable—'SRD object message flow'—a list of the SRD server objects to which messages are sent and from which messages are received.

A5.3.8 *Reiterate*

Now reiterate for the next scenario, from the 'list objects' step. You should not build more than 10 scenarios at most. More likely between three and seven will be appropriate to illustrate the essential parts and some of the byways of the business area.

Note that, as you go through each business scenario and process, you should find yourself re-using objects significantly. The first process will take a long time to do. The last several should be very easy and quick.

A5.4 Build the prototype

In practice, I have found it better to start building the prototype *after* a day of design, rather than during the design. This allows for consideration as to what (of possibly several objects) to build first. It also allows for discussion on what might be left out of the prototype....

Again, if the tool used is the same as that planned for production systems, the code built in prototyping may be found to be useful in production. 'Prototyping to production' is sometimes held to be a useful approach to building the UID.

Appendix 6
Sample project proposals

> Hear and forget;
> See and remember;
> Do and understand.

The initial client/server project will almost certainly require approval by senior IT management. Approval often requires the presentation of a proposal. This appendix contains two such sample proposals for:

1 A 'pathfinder' project that aims to equip an IT department with the skills and software infrastructure required to build operational client/server systems. This project would take around six man-years, and would have a duration (elapsed time) of around 12 months.
2 A 'vision prototype' project whose deliverables are:
   (a) Demonstration code that shows how things might (and could) be
   (b) Skills acquisition
   This project would take around 6–8 man-months, and would have a duration (elapsed time) of around 2–3 months.

Both proposals are assumed to have been prepared by a group in an IT organization for presentation to the management of that same IT organization. Variables are in square brackets. For example, instead of saying 'The project will start in June 1994,' we say 'The project will start in [month and year].'

A6.1 The 'pathfinder' project

A6.1.1 Management summary

This is a time of major changes in information technology. In response to the organization's need for change—particularly in the range of functions that users are being asked to use—not only is the structure of systems changing—moving towards distributed client/server networks with powerful PCs on users' desks—but the scale and rate of change is also increasing. However, something that is sometimes overlooked is this: Getting the full potential from these new system structures requires new and innovative approaches to building client/server infrastructures and to application development.

In essence, we are at the beginning of a new system technology curve. A major challenge to IT organizations at such a time is to gain an *understanding* of potential business benefits, on the one hand, and technical innovations and their required set of new skills, on the other.

Gaining such understanding can be a slow process of osmosis over several years—or it can be made into an organized and structured process.

Without such a process, each development project team can find themselves reinventing the wheel—building their own 'middleware' for connecting PCs to mainframe and other systems. And since this effort is not 'more of the same', significant design effort—not originally budgeted for—can be used up. To avoid this, a standard *client/server infrastructure* should be implemented.

Furthermore, deriving the greatest possible business benefit from the resulting client/server system base requires *new approaches to application development*—especially at the user interface. The process should address these areas as the second major area.

This document proposes consultancy services from [your favourite CBO-capable consultancy firm] to assist you in a rapid acquisition of skills and understanding in these major new areas. The process is structured through the vehicle of what we call a 'pathfinder project'. This project has these major deliverables [modify as appropriate]:

- A migration plan, based on knowledge, for establishing our core business systems on a sound client/server base that exploits the new user interface capabilities to deliver greater business benefit.
- A client/server infrastructure, together with a workstation user interface platform for delivering the usability potential of client/server systems.
- Acquisition of required new design skills. With the assistance of experienced consultants, the staff who participate in the project will climb the new learning curve through designing and building real software. Essentially, they will learn by doing—which is the only effective route to real understanding. At the end of the project, there will be a core of people who will provide the technical knowledge on tools, on techniques and on design approaches so as to seed further projects of this kind.

The project should commence in [month and year] and run through to [month and year]. A project team of [n] people should be established for this project. This document proposes [n] days of consultancy to the project over its lifetime at a cost of [cost].

A6.1.2 Introduction

Many organizations today see a need for application integration, for satisfying users' increasing demands for access to a wider range of business function, for faster reaction to change and for gaining the full potential from human resources.

An important part of satisfying these needs is the full exploitation of client/server (cooperative) systems that deliver business benefit through PCs rather than through character-based terminals. Systems are needed that lead to a new world, not only of potential business benefit, but also of opportunities for IT to reduce build cycles and re-use one of their key assests—design.

This is a time of major changes in information systems. Not only has the structure of systems changed, moving towards distributed client/server networks with powerful PCs on users' desks, but the scale and rate of change has increased.

However, something that is often overlooked is this: Getting the full potential from these new system structures requires new and innovative approaches to client/server infrastructures and to application development.

A *client/server infrastructure* must be designed and implemented to connect programs on PCs with programs on other systems. And *new approaches to application development* are needed to realize the full potential of the resulting system base. The two go hand-in-hand. Future systems must deliver both of these requirements.

The information technology industry is at the beginning of a new-technology curve that can offer significant benefit. Figure A [refer to Fig. I1.1 in this book] illustrates how each technology curve experiences initial slow growth while the impact of the new technology on user interfaces, application design and system design are understood, and while tool support for the new development methods and processes emerge.

Exploiting client/server systems

A major reason to exploit the PC is to exploit its graphical user interface capability. Graphical user interfaces for core commercial applications are a new phenomenon, and standards and guidelines for their exploitation are still emerging. However, a number of factors are becoming clear:

1   Usability of computer systems is significantly enhanced by consistent graphical user interfaces, but a more significant breakthrough in usability comes from a single system image which supports a user's tasks in a manner that closely approximates to the real-world environment in which the user operates. Figure B [refer to Fig. 1.2 in this book] is based on research work that was done originally at Xerox Parc, though not formally published. It indicates that 60 per cent of system usability derives from successfully mapping to the user's

conceptual model of the real world as against 40 per cent for look-and-feel characteristics.
2. A key characteristic of these emerging user interfaces is that they are oriented around 'objects' rather than applications. They are object-oriented user interfaces.
3. Building object-oriented user interfaces requires a dramatically different approach to encapsulating business function in software. Rather than building 'applications', it is necessary to build what we call 'cooperative business objects'.
4. Environments, development tools and methods, and standards to support industrial-strength implementations of these advanced user interfaces are beginning to be available.
5. These advanced user interfaces will significantly influence systems architecture, design methods and development processes. For example, it is possible to design mainframe transaction processing applications such that 'server' transactions can be used by both character-based terminals (where the client is a mainframe-based dialogue application) and by PCs.

The client/server platform

A client/server system is one that fully exploits the potential of PCs in a distributed system environment. The reasons information systems are moving towards a client/server structure are:

- To exploit fully the potential of PCs
- To provide those PCs with access to the extensive investment in data and function inherent in mainframe systems

The design of client/server systems presents a number of important questions to the developer:

1. Information technology (IT) systems can only deliver *potential* benefit to the business. If IT delivers systems that the users cannot use, then no benefit is realized. It is users, through their *use* of IT, that turn potential into reality.
   So how do we exploit the PC to allow users to realize the potential inherent in our IT systems? Is there a significantly better way of delivering the potential benefit? Can we provide our users with the real key to *realizing* the potential?
2. How do we design and implement these new user interfaces? Are new development techniques and approaches required? Are new application software structures required? If so, how do we gain proficiency in the new skills required?
3. Do these new approaches and techniques require a change in our approach to the server end of the system? Can we build server application software that will be common to both the new PCs and also to our large existing base of

character-based terminals? Do we need to take new approaches to the design of mainframe application software?

4   Can we provide our application programmers with a client/server infrastructure that they can use effectively with minimum effort? How do we ensure maintenance of commit scopes and data integrity in this new environment?

5   Who will be the technical architect to ensure that all the required pieces fit together, and that APIs do not merely export complexity to the application programmers? Who will provide a tested design framework for increasing rather than decreasing system availability?

Clearly there are a number of learning curves to climb. This can be done as a process of osmosis, over several or many projects, and over several years. A much better way is to address the necessary skills acquisition as a structured process.

The next subsection presents our proposal for a 'pathfinder project' that can provide the vehicle not only for fast and directed skills acquisition but also for developing a migration plan for taking the organization into production client/server systems.

A6.1.3 Project proposal

We propose a project to develop a validated migration plan to a coherent client/server platform for all future systems. Validation of this plan would be provided by technical skills acquisition during the course of the project, plus the building and/or acquisition of any prototype infrastructure code which may be required to 'glue' different pieces of the client/server platform together. The project, together with the resource requirements anticipated, is fully described in the next subsection.

The proposed project, which we call the 'pathfinder project', would be primarily staffed by ourselves, with consultants from [XYZ Consulting] providing design assistance. There is significant know-how in [XYZ] about the technical nature both of client/server platforms or infrastructures, and also of the advanced user interfaces required to exploit them fully.

A key aim of the project is to develop an understanding of the implications of client/server systems with advanced user interfaces. Acquisition of such skills would move us quickly and smoothly onto the steep and beneficial part of the technology curve.

This pathfinder project will address the provision of client/server software components, where a PC provides a high-value front-end through innovative cooperative applications. In proposing this project, we make the following assumptions:

1   The long-term aim is to reap the business benefits of graphical user interfaces on PCs in a distributed systems environment.
2   The short-term objectives are:
    (a) To gain understanding of new techniques.

(b) To feed back into imminent and current development projects to enable a better positioning for future migration to full exploitation of client/server systems.
(c) To develop a migration plan for our core systems so that we can exploit the opportunities of advanced client/server systems.
(d) To establish a firm base of required skills within the company.

The project is low-risk, inasmuch as it will not produce operational application systems. However, it is high-value inasmuch as it accelerates our understanding of how to exploit fully the new-technology curve that IT finds itself upon.

A6.1.4 Project description

Objectives

[Delete or amend any of the following as required]

The objectives of the project will be:

1. To gain a thorough understanding of the business potential that advanced client/server systems will offer us, together with the issues involved in implementing them.
2. To ensure that short-term development of a practical front-end to our core systems can be done so as to ease migration to a client/server structure at the appropriate time.
3. To feed other projects as soon as possible with information and design advice for ensuring that eventual migration to a common platform can be done as easily as possible.
4. To develop a migration plan to enable us to implement production client/server systems starting in [timescale—say six months from now].
5. To develop a migration plan towards basing all client/server projects upon a single firm infrastructure base.
6. To establish skills in new (required) areas (e.g. object orientation, client/server system design, server structure, graphical user interface design, etc.).
7. To identify and define any modifications to our current business modelling method that may be seen to be advantageous for designing software objects.

Scope

[Delete or amend any of the following items as appropriate. Consider stating at the end why you are *not* addressing any particular area.]

1. Identify the business benefit that can be derived from advanced object-oriented user interfaces by building 'vision' prototypes of selected elements of our core systems, in conjunction with end-users and development staff.

2 Define and validate an appropriate infrastructure to support an object-oriented user interface, including:
   (a) Understand the software infrastructure needed, both in the PC and in the server systems
   (b) Understand the techniques and tools required
   (c) Support for 'remote object' structure, giving transparent client/server support
3 Design and deliver a set of cooperative business objects that, at a minimum, address two or more specific business processes or functions for a given type of end-user. This includes:
   (a) Selection of business processes to be addressed
   (b) Analysis and design based on objects
   (c) Selection of objects
   (d) Standard methods and self-describing data requirements
   (e) Use of iterative production techniques that involve (a) rapid prototyping to production and (b) inclusion of users as an essential and permanent part of the development team
   (f) Definition of the required process for rolling out skills and organizational changes (if any) needed for building production-strength systems
4 Design and validate mainframe server transactions that can be used by both character-based terminals (where the client is a mainframe-based dialogue application) and by PCs. This will build the skills for moving towards this style of transaction structure for mainframe systems, so that the server code can be re-used or shared by many PC clients.
5 Define the overall shape of a client/server distributed software platform, including the desired application programming model, to ensure that all elements from 'end to end' of the system fit together.
6 Understand the organizational changes, and new development processes, that may be required to enable the realization of effective client/server systems.
7 Monitor the evolution of production-strength tools and methods to determine how best to move towards widespread adoption of client/server technology.
8 Provide inputs to other projects (possibly running concurrently) in order to ensure that appropriate advantage is taken of new methods and standards, both for immediate benefit and to position for future migration. This might include:
   (a) User interface design techniques
   (b) Identifying appropriate additional function
   (c) The impact on technical standards
   (d) The impact on networking standards
9 Develop a migration plan including the scope, cost and timescales of tasks necessary to enable migration of both core and non-core systems to a client/server implementation.

10 Review the methods used in business modelling with a view to defining changes that may be required to support new application software objects.

We do not, in this proposal, include the development of new methods in the business modelling and data/process analysis area. Understanding of current and evolving methods will, however, allow such development of methods to be included in a subsequent migration project.

Prototype environment

[Amend the following as appropriate. Whatever you do suggest, make sure that it is capable of addressing the scope and objectives defined.]

We recommend that the initial prototype is based on [the CBO infrastructure of choice]. This recommendation is not intended to prejudge our choice of PC operating system or CBO environment. The project will enable the functional requirements for future software procurements to be determined.

The project will include understanding the effort to transfer the skills learned on this environment to our eventual chosen products. Clearly we cannot size this effort at this time, and our estimates have assumed that any more than a nominal transfer load will be accommodated within a subsequent migration project.

Deliverables

The deliverables from the project will be:

1 Full understanding of the benefits and costs of client/server technology through having prototyped a subset of our core systems. This prototype will provide a test-bed for determining business opportunity, and developing skills, technical architectures, standards and methods.
2 Recommendations and inputs to other projects.
3 A detailed plan for the migration of our core systems to a client/server architecture starting in [proposed start date].
4 New design skills developed by our IT people.
5 Well designed prototype code that can be enhanced to production strength in a subsequent project.
6 Initial definition of the nature of software objects for input to a review of business modelling methods.

Quality criteria

The understanding gained from the pathfinder project must be able to assist the subsequent projects to adopt technology, standards and methods that deliver robust core systems within the required time, and demonstrate how to migrate those systems to exploit advanced client/server technologies as they become viable, and in a managed and cost-effective way.

Risk

Major new core system projects using new technology typically carry high levels of technical risk. The objective of this pathfinder project is to help reduce that risk, especially the risk of an inability to migrate to exploit client/server technology fully. The pathfinder project itself is a low-risk project in that its deliverable is not an operational application system; rather its deliverable is the *know-how* required to build such systems.

Schedule

The project should commence in [start month/year], and should run for 12 months, ending in [finish month/year]. We believe that by this time the knowledge gained from the project, together with the emergence of appropriate methods and tools, will allow a firm migration plan to be developed. An outline project schedule, showing the major project activities, is illustrated in Fig. A6.1.

Resources

[Modify the following as appropiate.]

A project team of six IT people, including a project manager, should be established for this project. The ideal skill profiles of the team members should be as follows:

1 Project manager—project management skills, knowledge of our core system, skilled in current application development techniques and business models, willing to learn object-orientation analysis and design methods.

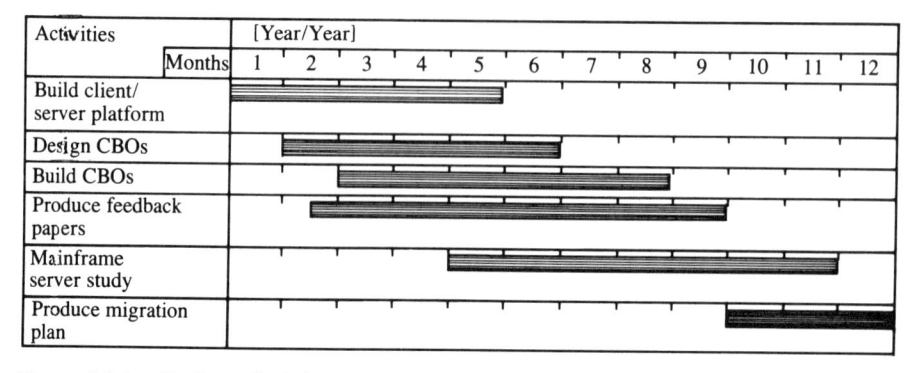

Figure A6.1. Project schedule.

2 User—experience in the use of and requirements for our systems, willing to learn object-orientation analysis and design methods.
3 Analyst/programmer—[language] programming skills; good knowledge of our systems design; willing to learn object-oriented analysis and design techniques.
4 Analyst/programmer—[language] programming skills; graphical user interface programming experience; willing to learn object-oriented design techniques.
5 Analyst/programmer—[language] programming skills; capable of learning how best to exploit the CBO infrastructure; willing to learn object-oriented design techniques.
6 System designer—broad communications and transaction processing skills.

In addition there would be a need for networking and communications support, for occasional mainframe systems programming support, and access to end-users and end-user managers for detailed feedback on the prototype.

All these skills may not exist in people available to us at the start of the project. They will be gained over the life of the project as part of the learning process. The important thing is that people with the capability of building such skills, and the desire to do so, are assigned to the project.

We propose that [Consultancy Firm XYZ] provide 125 man-days of consultancy to the project over its lifetime. This would be made up as follows:

1 Project consultant—80 days. This represents a continuous involvement in the project of two days per week (excluding holidays).
2 Specific specialist resource—25 days. We believe that it is important to provide the best and latest experience from within [Consultancy Firm XYZ] across the entire scope of the project. This is best achieved by using the consultant's professionals most experienced in the specific areas. The most productive way to introduce this knowledge will be through workshops. It would be the responsibility of the project consultant to introduce the appropriate specialists into the project at the appropriate time.
3 Project reviewer—20 days. His or her role would be, as the project develops, to:
   (a) Ensure appropriate technical coordination with and feedback to other concurrent projects as appropriate
   (b) Provide technical reviews of designs, systems and recommendations developed by the project
   (c) Assist the project team in ensuring overall technical coherence while meeting the aims of the project

A6.2 The 'vision prototype' project

A6.2.1 Introduction

We are currently at an early stage in decision making about our adoption of client/server and object technologies. A major area of concern is the level of business benefit to be gained from these technologies.

This proposal presents an evaluation process that addresses this concern by delivering much greater understanding of potential business benefit and of the technical risk element. The vehicle to be used for gaining this greater understanding is the development of a 'vision' prototype. Our suggested process optimizes the scoping and development of this prototype so as to maximize its business value, and minimize the 'throw-away' aspects.

Since we are short of skills in this new area, our proposal includes use of outside consultants. The prototype building process will be a valuable skills acquisition exercise in its own right. We therefore propose a two-stage approach to the evaluation:

- A brief initial *planning stage* that should set the terms of reference for the evaluation, including exact method, scope of study and evaluation criteria.
- An eight-week *evaluation project* that will use the development of a prototype to demonstrate actual performance versus the criteria.

This project will deliver an evaluation report, and will assist significantly in building our skills in this new area of technology.

A6.2.2 Planning stage

This will consist of the following elements:

- Initial meetings to set up a planning workshop
- One-day planning workshop
- Documentation of the planning workshop

At this stage, we will also produce a formal document to management proposing the subsequent evaluation.

The planning workshop would be run by an outside consultant for six of our people. Suggested attendees would include the project sponsor, a designated project leader, two people representing application development and two people representing user interests.

The agenda would include the following:

- The sponsor's objectives for the project
- Definition of evaluation criteria
- Choice of application area
- Scope of prototype
- Scope of post-prototype evaluation activity and analysis needed to complete the evaluation report
- Resource requirements for the project

This planning workshop should be run as soon as diaries permit. Both the workshop report and a proposal for the follow-up work could be prepared within two weeks.

A6.2.3 Evaluation project

For your information, this section describes the kind of evaluation project that might emerge from the planning workshop. Our description is based on a range of assumptions that would need to be modified in subsequent discussions and during the workshop.

A major assumption, at this stage, is that the planning workshop will establish major potential benefits that warrant the scale of the subsequent evaluation.

The evaluation project would use as its vehicle a real business process to deliver the prototype defined by the planning meeting. It would be done by a team consisting of outside consultants, IT personnel and selected users.

On completion of the prototype, an analysis of its development and lessons learned would be made, and this, together with planned and agreed interviews of participants, would form the basis of the evaluation report. The content of the evaluation report will be defined by the planning meeting, but could include:

- User and business benefits
- IT-related benefits (including capturing metrics, cross-LAN/language messaging, cross-application object integration, etc.)
- Assessment of skill development requirements within IT
- Assessment of the technology applicability

We anticipate that this work could be carried out in eight elapsed weeks, with the bulk of the work being done in an intensive four-week period.

Possible staffing required would include two users for a significant portion of the four weeks, two development staff for the first six weeks, and a part-time project manager. The size of IT involvement could be increased to allow for increased skills transfer requirements.

A6.2.4 External costs

For costing purposes, we have made assumptions about the possible composition of the consultant's team as follows:

- A management consultant
- A software design consultant
- An application designer
- A programmer

Their exact roles and contributions would be defined as part of a proposal from the consultants subsequent to the planning workshop. Based on our assumptions, a budgetary cost for the consultant's participation at this stage would be £50 000.

References and bibliography

Beer, S. (1981). *Brain of the Firm*, 2nd edn, Wiley, New York.
Bingham, J. E. and Davies, G. W. P. (1977). *Planning for Data Communications*, Macmillan, New York.
Booch, G. (1991). *Object Oriented Design*, Benjamin/Cummings, Menlo Park, CA.
Coad, P. and Yourdon, E. *Object Oriented Analysis*, Prentice-Hall (Yourdon Press), Englewood Cliffs, NJ.
Cowlishaw, M. (1990). *The REXX Language*, 2nd edn, Prentice-Hall, Englewood Cliffs, NJ.
Cox, B. J. and Novobilski, A. J. (1991). *Object-Oriented Programming—An Evolutionary Approach*, 2nd edn, Addison Wesley, Reading, MA.
Hofstadter, D. R. (1979). *Godel, Escher, Bach: An Eternal Golden Braid*, Harvester Wheatsheaf, Brighton.
IBM (1991a). *IBM CUA-91 Manual: Common User Access—Guide to User Interface Design* (IBM form SC34-4289).
IBM (1991b). *IBM CUA-91 Manual: Common User Access—Advance Interface Design Reference* (IBM form SC34-4290).
IBM (1992a). *Business System Development Method—Introducing BSDM* (IBM form GE19-5387).
IBM (1992b). *Business System Development Method—Designing Business Systems* (IBM form SC19-5313).
IBM (1992c). *Business System Development Method—Establishing Business Requirements* (IBM form SC19-5312).
IBM (1992d). *Business System Development Method—Business Mapping, Part 1: Entities* IBM form SC19-5310).
IBM (1992e). *Business System Development—Business Mapping, Part 2: Processes* (IBM form SC19-5309).
IBM (undated). *Systems Application Architecture Overview* (IBM form GA26-4341).
IBM (undated). *Systems Application Architecture, Common Programming Interface, Communications Reference* (IBM form SC26-4399).
Jacobson, I., et al. (1992). *Object-Oriented Software Engineering*, Addison Wesley, Reading, MA.
Liddle, D. F. (undated). *What Makes a Desktop Different*, Metaphor Computer Systems, Mountain View, CA.
Meyer, B. (1998). *Object-Oriented Software Construction*, Prentice-Hall, Englewood Cliffs, NJ.
Norman, D. A. (1988). *The Psychology of Everyday Things*, Basic Books, New York.
Norman, D. A. (1990). *The Design of Everyday Things*, Doubleday, New York.

Orfali, R. and Harkey, D. (1992). *Client/Server Programming With OS/2 2.0*, 2nd edn, Van Nostrand Reinhold, New York.

Rumbaugh, J., *et al.* (1991). *Object Oriented Modelling and Design*, Prentice-Hall, Englewood Cliffs, NJ.

Schofield, D. (undated). *Distributed Data—Placement and Design Considerations* (internal IBM paper).

Taylor, D. A. (1990). *Object-Oriented Technology—A Manager's Guide*, Servio Corporation, USA.

Tibbets, J. and Bernstein, B. (1992). *Building Cooperative Applications Using SAA*, Wiley, New York.

Tognazzini, B. (1992). *TOG on Interface*, Addison Wesley, Reading, MA.

Wills, G., *et al.* (1972). *Technological Forecasting*, Penguin, Harmondsworth.

Wirfs-Brock, R., Wilkerson, B. and Weiner, L. (1990). *Designing Object-Oriented Software*, Prentice-Hall, Englewood Cliffs, NJ.

Yourdon, E. and Constantine, L. L. (1979). *Structured Design*, Prentice-Hall, Englewood Cliffs, NJ.

Glossary

ACID (Atomicity, Consistency, Isolation, Durability)
These are the key attributes that have come to define what a 'transaction' is. For example, one might say, 'A "transaction" must possess the ACID properties.' By saying this, the speaker is also defining the attributes that a transaction processor must provide to writers of transaction programs.

While I have not found (yet) a formal definition of ACID, the components of the acronym are usually used in the following way:

- *Atomicity* means that a transaction, once begun, is either completed (and all changes committed), or is terminated in such a way that the before state and after state of the system are identical. It does everything it is supposed to do, or does nothing at all.
- *Consistency* means first that the state change caused by a transaction should always be the same for each invocation of the transaction. Secondly, it means that data must be left in a consistent state; that nothing outside the transaction should be allowed to interfere in such a way that the transaction may be 'fooled' into leaving things in an inconsistent state.
- *Isolation* indicates that a transaction will not impact other transactions running concurrently (and vice versa).
- *Durability* means that changes to state must be permanent.

AD (Application Development)
For example, 'the AD organization' is that part of the IT organization which is primarily concerned with the design and production of application programs.

Address space
On a multi-programming (or multi-tasking) system, each program runs in a section of the computer's memory that is protected from other programs that are running concurrently. If the program crashes, it does not affect

other programs. The operating system provides this protection by assigning a specific range of memory addresses to the program, and thereafter ensuring that no other program can access within that range, and vice versa. This is sometimes done entirely by the operating system, but usually with assistance from the hardware. Of course, the average application programs never see this. They just get run. The operating system runs the program in one of its 'address spaces'. Often, when the precise differences are not relevant, the terms 'address space' and 'process' are used as synonyms, as are the terms 'multi-programming' and 'multi-tasking'.

Amodality
Lack of modality, modelessness, non-modal. The author invented this word to avoid the negative connotations of 'non-modal' and the clumsiness of 'modelessness'. Strictly speaking, in English the prefix 'a-' does not necessarily imply the negative; but it does generally imply a lack.

API (Application Programming Interface)
The programming interface presented to application programmers by other pieces of software (often middleware). Often the real problem with APIs is not their programming complexity; rather it is the complexity of the underlying model of what it is the programmer is doing when using one of the APIs.

APPC (Advanced Program-to-Program Communications)
An API definition for the LU6.2 communications protocol. Implementations of the APPC API definition vary from system to system. However, although the precise APIs may differ, they all perform the same functions—due to them all implementing the APPC API definition. See also CPI-C.

ASCII (American Standard Code for Information Interchange)
Originally a standard for representing graphic characters in seven-bit units, it has become extended to handle additional characters, and now generally defines characters for all values of an octet (that is, it uses eight-bit units). ASCII is generally used on PCs of all types, on many minicomputers, on UNIX systems and on some mainframes.

Atomicity   See ACID.

Bandwidth
Originally a telecommunications term, 'bandwidth' is often used today to indicate the amount of information that can be sent through a given channel. Hence a 'bandwidth constraint' is a constraint caused by the

Glossary

inability of something to handle the amount of information you would like. A more precise definition is offered by Bingham and Davies (1977), as follows: 'The range of frequencies available for data transmission within a given channel. In general, the greater the bandwidth the higher is the possible rate of transmission.'

Batch window

On-line databases may have to be taken off-line in order to run batch jobs against them. The longer a database is on-line the greater the service provided to the users. Thus there are significant pressures to keep them on-line as long as possible. The period of time they can be taken off-line is called the 'batch window'.

Character-based terminal

A video display terminal that cannot be programmed at the application level, and which is completely dependent on programming in some other system for its function. An example of a character-based terminal is almost any member of the IBM 3270 Display family.

Hence the phrase 'a character-based terminal system' denotes a system where character-based terminals are connected to one or more mainframes or minicomputers. The system will probably be doing transaction processing.

CICS (Customer Information Control System)

An IBM transaction processor and resource manager that runs on most IBM operating systems. It is often found on IBM System/370 architecture mainframes, from small to large. The acronym reflects its ancestry, rather than its current usage.

Client/server

The term 'client/server' has three separate meanings that are in general use:

- *Distributed systems* where users have powerful PCs with graphical user interfaces on their desks. The PCs are connected to one or more machines containing shared resources such as data. This is the meaning generally used in this book.
- *A specific design technique* for connecting independent software units (whether or not on the same machine). Hence one piece of software acts as a 'client' in requesting some function from another piece of software—the 'server'. When the server has processed the request and sent a response, the unit of work is ended. This use of the term makes no assumptions about the mechanism for communication. Thus code that

uses system-level communications protocols may be said to be built following a client/server design.
- *A layer of middleware software* (typically in a LAN environment) such that a call from a program for a standard service (e.g. file I/O, or printing, or an SQL database access) is redirected to a server, where the actual service is performed. The key characteristic of this is that the programmer does not see this redirection, and so treats remote services *exactly as if they were local*. In general usage, this form of the term 'client/server' often refers to clients and servers hidden in the supplied operating system software (as, for example, with file access across a LAN using LAN management software). Such software often uses an RPC mechanism to provide the connection.

Commit processing
When a given unit of work (such as 'create a customer order') has to be written to a database, then it is usually required that all of the tables or files that have to be updated to reflect the completion of that unit of work should be updated successfully—or, if there is any failure, then all the tables or files should be left as they were before the unit of work was started. The unit of work is either 'committed' or 'rolled back'. This ensures that the database is always in a consistent state after the completion of the unit of work, regardless of whether the unit of work failed or succeeded.

The 'commit scope' is the solution space—the lines of code—between (and including) the start and the end of the commit process.

Commit scope See 'Commit processing'.

Cooperative processing
A cooperative processing application consists of two or more separate but cooperative pieces of application code, where the pieces may be in different systems. In particular cooperative processing is a form of distributed processing where application code in a PC cooperates with application code in one or more other systems (often, but not necessarily, one or more mainframes running transaction processing software) to perform some business process. The software design approach adopted by the application code is frequently 'client/server', where the PC code is usually the client, and the other system's code acts as a server. The connection between these two pieces of code must be able to be asynchronous.

CORBA (Common Object Request Broker Architecture)
A standard developed by the Object Management Group (OMG) that defines an IDL by which objects written in different languages, and running on different systems, may inter-work.

Glossary

CPI-C (Common Programming Interface, Communications)
CPI-C was designed by IBM to be a *common* APPC API for LU6.2. It is currently provided on most if not all IBM systems, as well as on others. With CPI-C, the programmer has to learn only one API to use LU6.2. See 'Systems Application Architecture, Common Programming Interface, Communications Reference', IBM form SC26-4399.

CRUD (Create, Read, Update, Delete)
A term used in E/R (entity/relationship) modelling, where processes are mapped to entities in a CRUD matrix.

DBMS (Database Management System)
A DBMS not only manages the database, it also provides for protection against multiple concurrent updates, makes an API (such as SQL) available, provides administration services, etc.

DDE Dynamic Data Exchange

DLL (Dynamic Link Library)
A member of a DLL is typically a function that can be called by other code, but where linking is done at call time (during execution) rather than at link time (prior to execution). Conventionally, such a function is often called 'a DLL' (rather than 'a member of a DLL') because often on PC environments a DLL has only one member in it—and that member has only a single function.

EBCDIC
(Extended Binary Coded Decimal Interchange Code) A standard for representing graphic characters in eight-bit units (bytes, or octets). EBCDIC is widely used on mainframes and minicomputers, both IBM and other.

EDI Electronic Data Interchange

GUI (Graphical User Interface)
A general term applied to modern PC user interfaces, where sizable windows, icons, scroll bars, etc., are implemented. By contrast, traditional character-based terminals are (generally) only capable of 'CUIs' (character user interfaces) where any graphical attributes are generally produced by an arrangement of characters. Note that many PC/DOS applications are more CUI than GUI.

GUIs can be either application-oriented or object-based.

IDL (Interface Definition Language)
A way of defining the calling interface to a module of code through an external file that describes the parameters and structure in a language-neutral way. This approach is often used for RPC implementations. It is also used for object-to-object interaction by the CORBA specification. CORBA is defined by the Object Management Group.

IMS Information Management System

IS (Information Systems)
A general term applied to all of a company's computing and associated communications systems; often a synonym for 'IT'.

IT (Information Technology)
A term given to computing and networking in general. Hence 'IT director', or 'CEO for IT'. Also, you might refer generally to a company's 'IT department' or 'IT organization' as another way of referring to its 'DP department', 'System development department' or 'Computer department'.

LAN (Local Area Network)
A high-speed network suitable for connecting computers within a limited area.

LOB (Line of Business)
LOB systems are those which drive a customer's core day-to-day business; for example, order entry, or accounting.

LU6.2 (Logical Unit type 6.2)
One of the SNA-defined LUs (logical units), LU6.2 is the LU designed specifically for program-to-program (as opposed to program-to-terminal) communications.

Line of business
Operational, transaction processing, core business applications.

Middleware
Software that lies between the system software and the application code, and which provides some service to the application that is not provided by the system software. Ideally this middleware code would be part of the system software. However, in times of rapid change, the system software cannot change quickly enough (and maintain compatibility!). Hence the appearance of middleware.

Examples of middleware (some of which started out as middleware but are now seen as system software) include database managers, encryption services, object managers, transaction processors, RPC mechanisms, etc.

OBUI (Object-Based User Interface)
A user interface that allows the user to manipulate objects (things) rather than applications (functions). It is called 'object-based' rather than 'object-oriented' because the user does not overtly see and deal with classes and inheritance.

OODB (Object-Oriented Database)
A database management system where the items stored and managed are objects (instances).

OOPL (Object-Oriented Programming Language)
A language such as C++, Objective C, SmallTalk.

OS/2 IBM's Operating System/2
A multitasking operating system for PCs.

PC (Personal Computer)
A desk-top programmable workstation capable of running application-level programming, equipped with a high-resolution colour graphics screen, and able to run an operating system capable of supporting multi-tasking and/or multi-processing, in addition to communications links.

PM See 'Presentation Manager'.

Post code Zip code.

Presentation Manager
The component of OS/2 that manages the screen, the windows and the controls (such as push buttons) on the windows. It provides a fully windowable and graphics environment, together with an API (application programming interface) for application program use.

Process See 'Address space'.

Resource manager domain See RMD.

REXX

REXX is a fully fledged programming language with extremely friendly characteristics. It is an interpretative language, and there is therefore no compile or link requirement for REXX development (although some implementations provide a compiler in addition to an interpreter). For a full description of REXX, see Cowlishaw (1990).

RMD (Resource Manager Domain)

That part of a computing system which is responsible for the integrity, management, back-up, recovery and maintenance of shared resources. The most typical shared resource is data. The RMD must also provide for controlled access to resources. An RMD equates to the scope of the commit capability of a distributed database system.

RPC (Remote Procedure Call)

A layer of middleware that gives to the programmer an API such that remote software can be 'called' transparently in the same way that the programmer might call a local procedure or subroutine. The RPC mechanism must also provide the programmer with error information (such as 'link to remote site is down'), which the programmer would not normally be concerned with for truly local calls.

SAA (Systems Application Architecture)

A collection of selected software interfaces, conventions and protocols that are published in various IBM documents. SAA was announced on 17 March 1987 as the framework for development of consistent applications across future offerings of the major IBM computing environments—System/370, System/3X and Personal Computer. Since then, SAA has grown to address client/server computing, distributed relational database and many other aspects of the overall computing environment. SAA is described in *Systems Application Architecture Overview* (IBM form GA26-4341).

Shared resource domain See SRD.

SQL (Structured Query Language)

A platform- and language-independent programming API for accessing relational databases. Introduced by IBM, SQL is now an industry standard and is widely implemented by DBMS suppliers. SQL is not just a query language, as its name might imply; it provides for a very wide and rich range of RDB (relational database) functions, including update, addition, deletion, joins, etc.

SRD (Shared Resource Domain)
> That extent of a computing system which can provide commit/rollback support for a given unit of work as seen by the programmer of a single transaction. An SRD will always be some subset of an RMD.

System software
> The operating system software, plus that software provided by an operating system supplier which effectively provides an integrated extension to the operating system. An example of such an extension is IBM's DB2 Data Base system, which runs on the MVS operating system.

Systems Application Architecture   See 'SAA'.

Task
> The basic unit of program concurrency, a task represents a thread of control through some code that is separated from other threads of control in such a way that the threads can run concurrently. Task management is often an operating system function. Tasks typically run within an address space, and are usually not protected in the same way that address spaces are. The term 'thread' is often used as a synonym for task, especially when any detailed differences between the two terms is irrelevant.

Technology curve
> A graphed line illustrating the life cycle of a successful technology. The vertical axis is effectiveness, or 'factor of merit' of this as opposed to other (competing) technologies. The horizontal axis is time. The curve has an 'S' shape. When new, the technology starts off slowly as some few companies pioneer; then, if it shows promise, more investment (in both the technology itself *and* the know-how in applying it) is put into it. At some point it takes off into rapid growth and wide acceptance. Finally, it reaches its full potential, and no matter how much further investment is made, it delivers very little additional benefit. Typically, a given technology will be overtaken by a new technology at some time. A good exposition of technology curves can be found in Wills *et al.* (1972). An excellent discussion of their importance to management is found in Beer (1981, chap. 1).

Terminal   See 'Character-based terminal'.

Thread   See 'Task'.

Transaction
> A single recoverable unit of work. See also 'ACID'.

Two-phase commit
When a resource manager such as a distributed database management system does a coordinated commit across several systems, in order to ensure that resources are either committed or not changed at all, the commit process is done in two phases. Briefly, and at a certain level of abstraction, the two phases are as follows:

- Each system is asked to lock the resources that will be changed. When all systems have responded affirmatively, then that is the end of this phase. If any responds negatively, then the resource manager informs the other systems to release their locks, and roll back any changes made.
- The resource manager instructs all involved systems to commit the changes. Each system then commits, removes locks and tells the resource manager that they have completed.

The key to two-phase commit is what happens if there is a failure in the second phase. Essentially, the affirmative response from a given system at the end of the first phase is a guarantee to the controlling resource manager that the change *will* be made. The controlling resource manager must keep a note of who has not responded affirmatively to the second phase. Until all systems involved have so responded, the two-phase commit is not complete.

UID (User Interface Domain)
That part of a computing system which is responsible for servicing a single user. There will be one UID per user. Often, all the UIDs will be identical.

UOW Unit of work.

WAN (Wide Area Network)
A network capable of connecting computers across a large area (for example, world-wide). Because of cost constraints, WANs are generally much lower speed than LANs.

WYSIWYG (What You See Is What You Get)
An acronym originally applied to word processors, it means that what you see on the screen of the word processor is what you will get printed out on paper. WYSIWYG is now used for all kinds of layout tools, including screen definition tools.

Index

Abstract data type, 264
Adapter object, 86
Address space, 147, 333
Advanced Program-to-Program
    Communication (APPC), 334
Ageing, 137
Alerts, 127
Alien objects, 147
Amodality, 14, 334
Application:
  an artifice, 9, 189
  iconic, 23, 24
  interaction with CBOs, 147
  problem, 5
  structures, 41
Application Programming Interface (API),
    334
Application Development (AD), 331
Astonishment:
  least, principle of, 23
Asynchronous:
  messaging, 124
    insufficient by itself, 63–66
  the need for, 46
Atomicity, Consistency, Isolation,
    Durability (ACID), 333
Authority:
  owned by a CBO, 196
Automatic generation of CBOs, 132
Availability, 161, 216

Bandwidth, 224, 334
Batch window, 335
Behaviour of a CBO, 199
Binding, 138
  dynamic, 266
  loose, (of CBOs), 282
  the problem, 139
Blind alley, 183

Business copy data, 160
Business logic, 47
  in the UID, 170
  location of, 200
  on the PC, 77
Business needs, *xvii*, 4
Business processes, 17, 189–201
  on an object-based user interface, 17, 190
Business rules:
  and objects, 189
  on an object-based user interface, 190
  on the PC, 77

Capacity planning, 228
Case tools for CBOs, 132
Change management, 127
Character conversion, 144
Character-based terminal, 335
CICS, 335
Class, 266–268
  bad idea at the user interface, 305
  name, vs code, 126
Classical server approach, 169, 170
Client/server, 335
  as a design approach, 51
  programming models, 52–55
  spectrum, 245
Code pages, 144
Commit processing, 336
Commit scope, 336
  nested, 177
  start and end, 176
Common Object Request Broker
    Architecture (CORBA), 285, 336
Common Programming Interface for
    Communications (CPI-C), 87, 337
Common User Access (CUA), 15
Communication models:
  conversation, 55

Communications models (*continued*)
  messaging, 55
  remote procedure call, 54
Communications:
  data conversion, 144
Components:
  of the end-to-end model, 110
  of the SRD, 96–99
Concurrency:
  in the user interface, 14
Concurrent update control, 173
Connection:
  kinds of, 50
  to the server, 85
Content:
  of messages, 128
Context:
  of a CBO, 199
Control:
  the user in, 207
Conversation, 55
Conversational server approach, 172
Cooperative Business Object (CBO), 27, 123, 277
  ageing, 137
  automatic generation of, 132
  business rules 189
  behaviour of, 199
  Case tool, 132
  customization, 253
  definition, 278–292
  different types:
    entity, 98
    focus, 97
    local model, 102, 297
    model, 80
    resource, 99
    view, 80
  infrastructure, 114–149
    operating system implications, 147
  librarian, 239
  Model, UID vs SRD, 102
  Models and views, 78–82
  persistence, 133, 211
  portability, 253
  re-use (by the user), 24
  in the SRD, 99–108
  transactions, 103
    single vs multiple instances, 104
  wrapper, 147
Cooperative processing, 42, 336
Coupling, 138
Create, Read, Update, Delete (CRUD), 94
Currency:
  of data, 167, 209
Customization, 127, 253

Data:
  access logic, 46
  as work-in-progress, 167
  business copy, 160
  conversion, 144
  currency, 167, 209
  integrity, 152, 166
    the classical server approach, 169, 170
    the conversational server approach, 169, 172
    the journal entry approach, 169, 171
    units of work, 169
  local data and availability, 161
  locking, 173–176
  on the PC, 209
  operational copy, 161
  persistence, 167
  placement, 155
  prime, (or master), 158
  scope, 155
  typing, 143
  UID (in the), 167
  update:
    incremental vs replacement, 163
Database Management System (DBMS), 337
Delete (an object), 138
Design:
  client/server, 51
  data on the PC, 209
  direct manipulation, 212–214
  guidelines:
    droppability, 192
  master/slave, 50
  peer-to-peer, 51
  SRD, 93
  the user in control, 207
  single system image, 211
  timeliness of data in the UID, 209
  UID, 206
  UID vs SRD, 202
  units of work, 208
  what goes where, 214
Development tools, 234
Dinosaur, (not the mainframe), 75
Direct manipulation, 14, 212–214
  droppability guideline, 192
  framework, 132
  megadata, 188
  transaction, 213
Discard, 138
Distributed object manager, 123
Distribution of software and data, 229
Down-sizing, 229
Drag and drop (*see* Direct manipulation)
Droppability, 192

Dynamic binding, 266
Dynamic Link Library (DLL), 337

Encapsulation, 31, 264
End-to-end:
  model, 110
  view, 236
Entity CBO, 98
Event loop programming, 59
Event notification (*see* Interest registration)
Events, (GUI), 68
Extended Binary Coded Decimal
      Interchange Code (EBCDIC), 337

Flurry, (of messages), 104, 148
Focus CBO, 97
Frameworks, 131
  direct manipulation, 132
  GUI independence, 135
  interest registration, 134
  model/view, 134
  object persistence, 133
Front-end, 96
Front-ending legacy systems, 246

Garbage collection, 136
Generation of CBOs automatically, 132
Ghost objects, 128, 187
Graphic character conversion, 144
Graphical user interface (GUI) (*see also*
      User interface), 337
  code, 49, 59
  events, 68
  principles, 13
Grouping of objects on the user interface, 25

Hourglass problem, 30

Iceberg, 8
Iconic applications, 23, 24
Implications:
  capacity planning, 228
  client/server infrastructure, 223
  network loading, 225
  number of sessions, 227
  software and data distribution, 229
  systems management, 228
  technical, 223
  version management, 231
Incremental update, 163
Information hiding, 264

Information Systems (IS), 338
Information Technology (IT), 338
Infrastructure, 114–149
Inheritance, 270–272
Instance, 267
  data, 268
Instantiation, 268
  single vs multiple, 104
Integration:
  CBOs, 38
  CBOs and 'alien' objects, 147
  'out-of-the-box', 258
  problem, 27, 285
Integrity:
  data, 152, 166
Interaction:
  UID and SRD, 70–72
Interest registration, 134
Interface definition language (IDL), 285, 338
  and semantic data, 142

Journal entry approach to units of work, 171

Language neutrality, 127, 283
Late binding, 266
  of view CBO and layout, 84
Layout script, 83, 135
Least astonishment:
  principle of, 23
Legacy systems:
  do not scale up, 246
  front-ending, 246
Librarian, (object), 239
Line of business (LOB), 338
Local area network (LAN), 338
Local data and availability, 161
Local model, 102, 297–303
Location of business logic, 200, 214
Location transparency, 289
Locking of data, 173–176
LU6.2, 338
  number of sessions, 227

Mainframe culture, 75
Master data, 158
Master/slave design, 50
Megadata, 180–188
  and drag/drop, 188
  approaches to solutions, 183
  ghost objects, 187
  the problem, 180

Merge on the fly, 163
Message:
    content, 128
    flurry, 104, 148
    send/post transparency at receiver, 130
Messages:
    in OO, 265
Messaging:
    for inter-program communication, 58
    need for both synchronous and asynchronous, 63–66
    recursive, 67
    'send' vs 'post', 293–296
Messy desk, 16
Method, 264
Methodologies, 216–219
    UID prototyping technique, 304–316
Middleware, 338
Modal user interfaces, 12
Model:
    of application structure, 43
Model CBO, 80
    ageing, 137
    and view, 78–82
    model vs local model, 102, 297–303
    UID vs SRD, 102
Model/view:
    controller, 79
    framework, 134
Models:
    for communication (see Communication models)
    programming, for client/server, 52–55
Multiple instantiation, 105
Multiplicity, on the user interface, 14
Multi-tasking, 30

Name, class, vs code, 126
Name space, 125
Names, object, 125
Nested commit scope, 177
Network loading, 224–227
Newi, 278

Object (see also Cooperative Business Object):
    ageing, 137
    librarian, 239
    names, 125
    persistence, 133, 211
    re-use, by the user, 24
    what is an object?, 262
    wrapper, 147

Object-based:
    user interface (OBUI), 11, 24
        list objects, 185
        object re-use, 24
        principles, 24
        user-defined grouping, 25
        vs iconic applications, 24
    vs object-oriented, 272
Object Management Group (OMG), xii
Object orientation, 31, 261
    encapsulation, 31, 264
    skills, 238
Object-oriented database (OODB), 339
Object-oriented programming language (OOPL), 32, 339
One-shot interactions, 93
On-line transaction processing (OLTP), 93
Operational copy data, 161
Optimistic data locking, 175
Organizational structure, 239
OS/2, 339
Out-of-date data, 167, 209

Paradigm, 152
PC, 339
    not simply a souped-up terminal, xiii
Peer-to-peer design, 51
Persistence:
    data on the PC, 167
    object/CBO, 133, 211, 291
Placement of data, 155
Polymorphism, 268–269
Portability, cross-platform, 253
Presentation Manager (PM), 339
Principle:
    of least astonishment, 23
    object re-use (on the user interface), 24
    user-defined grouping (on the user interface), 25
Principles of a Graphical User Interface, 13
Problem:
    application, 5
    binding, 139
    hourglass, 30
    integration, 27
    megadata, 180–188
    two-account, 191, 205
    workbench, 21
Process, 339
Processes:
    business, 17, 189–201
Programming:
    event-loop, 59
Programming models:
    for client/server, 52–55

Prototypes, 219
Prototyping the UID, 304–316

Recovery, 214–216
Recursion, (messaging), 67
Registration, interest, 134
Remote procedure call (RPC), 54, 340
Remove, (object), 138
Replacement update, 163
Resource manager, 91
Resource manager domain (RMD), 91, 340
   compared with SRD, 92
Resource CBO, 99
Responsibility:
   of a CBO, 196
Re-use:
   of object, by the user, 24
Re-usable tools, 39
REXX, 178, 340
Right-sizing, 160, 229
Router, 119

Scope:
   of data, 155
Screen-scraping, 246
Screen size, 17
Scrolling:
   large data volumes, 182
Selection:
   development tool, 234
Semantic Datastream (SDS), 140
   advantages, 143
   performance, 142
Self-defining data (*see* Semantic datastream)
Separation:
   of class from code, 126
   of UID and SRD design, 218
Serial re-usability, 290
Server:
   data integrity:
      classical server approach, 170
      conversational server approach, 172
      journal entry approach, 171
Session manager, 119
Sessions:
   number of, 227
Shared resource domain (SRD), 89, 341
   access to other SRD, 179
   CBO advantages, 100
   CBOs, 99–108
   compared with RMD, 92
   components, 96–99
   design points, 93
   entity CBO, 98
   focus CBO, 97
   illustrative example, 92
   in stand-alone application, 166
   interaction with UID, 70–72
   multiple CBO instantiation, 105
   single CBO instantiation, 107
   unit of work, 204
Single instantiation, 107
Single system image, 211
Skills:
   object orientation, 238
Spectrum:
   of client/server, 245
Structure:
   organizational, 239
Structures:
   application, 41
   model of, 43
Subclass, 272
Surface area:
   of software, 139
Superclass, 272
Synchronous:
   connections, 63
   messaging:
      need for both synchronous and asynchronous, 63–66
   referring to the programmer's view, 124
System software, 341
Systems Application Architecture (SAA), 340
Systems management, 127, 228

Task, 341
Technical implications, 223
Techniques:
   design, 216
Technology curve, *xix*, 341
Terminal:
   character-based, 341
Thread, 341
Timeliness:
   of data, 209
Tool objects, 19
Tools:
   development, 234
   re-usable, 39
Transaction, 341
   and direct manipulation, 212
   CBO mapping, 103
      single vs multiple instances, 104
   object design, 122
   unit of work, 204
Transparency:
   of location, 289

Two-account problem, 191, 205
Two-phase commit, 342
Typing:
 of data, 143

Unit of work (UOW), 168
 and processes, 193–195
 encapsulated, 194
 interaction with SRD, 70–72
 UID vs SRD, 208
 user, 169
Untrusted environment, 201
Update:
 increment, 163
 replacement, 163
Usability, 3, 7
 iceberg, 8
User in control, 207
User interface:
 business rules and processes, 189
 class—do not show one, 305
 GUI, 337
 modal, 12
 new technology, *xxi*
 Object-based, 11, 24
  list objects, 185
  object re-use, 24
  principles, 24
  user-defined grouping, 25
  vs iconic applications, 24
 Principles, 13
  amodality, 14
  concurrency, 14
  direct manipulation, 14
  least astonishment, 23
  multiplicity, 14
  object re-use, 24
  user-defined grouping, 25
User interface domain (UID), 74, 342
 prototyping technique, 304–316
User logic, 45, 76
User unit of work, 169
User-defined grouping, 25
Users:
 exporting problems to, 6

Varying behaviour of CBO, 199
Version management, 231
 and loose vs tight binding, 141
View CBO, 80
 ageing, 137
 and model, 78–82
 layout, 83
Views:
 in user logic, 78

Wide Area Network (WAN), 342
Workbench, 15
 problem, 21
Workflow management, 195–197
Wrapper:
 object, 147
What you see is what you get
  (WYSIWYG), 342

Further Titles in the IBM McGraw-Hill Series

OS/2 Presentation Manager Programming Hints and Tips	Bryan Goodyer
PC User's Guide Simple Steps to Powerful Personal Computing	Peter Turner
The IBM RISC System/6000	Clive Harris
The IBM RISC System/6000 User Guide	Mike Leaver Hardev Sanghera
MVS Systems Programming	Dave Elder-Vass
CICS Concepts and Uses A Management Guide	Jim Geraghty
Dynamic Factory Automation	Alastair Ross